Teaching U.S. History through Sports

TEACHING
U.S. HISTORY
through SPORTS

Edited by

Brad Austin
Pamela Grundy

The University of Wisconsin Press

The University of Wisconsin Press
1930 Monroe Street, 3rd Floor
Madison, Wisconsin 53711-2059
uwpress.wisc.edu

Gray's Inn House, 127 Clerkenwell Road
London EC1R 5DB, United Kingdom
eurospanbookstore.com

Printed in the United States of America

This book may be available in a digital edition.

Library of Congress Cataloging-in-Publication Data
Names: Austin, Brad, 1972– editor. | Grundy, Pamela, editor.
Title: Teaching U.S. history through sports / edited by Brad Austin and
    Pamela Grundy.
Description: Madison, Wisconsin: The University of Wisconsin Press,
    [2019] | Includes bibliographical references and index.
Identifiers: LCCN 2018046044 | ISBN 9780299321208 (cloth: alk. paper)
Subjects: LCSH: Sports—History—Study and teaching—United States.
    | Sports—United States—History. | United States—History—Study
    and teaching.
Classification: LCC GV583 .T43 2019 | DDC 973.071—dc23
LC record available at https://lccn.loc.gov/2018046044

To all teachers and students

Contents

Contents

Illustrations

Illustrations

Acknowledgments

The study of sports has been at the center of my academic life since my junior year in college, when I turned to the Lyon College archives after discovering that I couldn't find the resources needed to write what surely would have been a riveting study of the cultural effects of a new lock and dam system on Arkansas's White River. I wrote, instead, a history of college football at my alma mater, and with the guidance of George Lankford, Terrell Tebbetts, Helen Robbins, Jane Fagg, and John Dahlquist, I began a career of considering the ways that sports have both reflected and shaped the American experience.

In graduate school, I was fortunate to have mentors who were willing to support work in what was still a somewhat new field, and I consider myself incredibly lucky to have had John Finger, James Cobb, K. Austin Kerr, Susan Hartmann, and Mel Adelman guiding me through my studies. At Salem State University in Salem, Massachusetts, I found friends who have mentored and inspired me, who have made me sharpen my thinking in our countless meandering lunchtime conversations, and who have helped this southern boy make a home in New England. I've always appreciated the way my colleagues in the history and education departments care about teaching while pursuing ambitious scholarly goals. In many ways, this book's dual focus on scholarship and pedagogy is the natural product of the type of department we try to be.

As this book has neared completion, I have thought often about a conversation I had one afternoon on Ohio State's Oval with Susan Hartmann. We were discussing what I would need to do to turn my dissertation into a manuscript, and I was telling her about this amazing new book about sports and education, *Learning to Win* by Pamela Grundy. I could easily imagine that day that I would borrow heavily from Pamela as I authored a book, but I didn't dare imagine that I would enjoy trading emails with her as we finished another one together. Working with Pamela has been a true education and a pleasure. I'm glad my initial email didn't end up in her spam filter and that I got a chance to know and work with her.

I've had a chance to work with the editorial and production team at the University of Wisconsin Press on a variety of projects over the past decade, and I can't praise enough the work of their team, especially Adam Mehring, Anna Muenchrath, and Gwen Walker. Over the years, I've learned that Gwen is a thoughtful editor, a dedicated advocate, and a kind, generous person. I will miss working with her.

I have already thanked many of these people in the front matter of previous books, but there is a group of folks who I have yet to acknowledge in print. I know that because they have pointed it out to me. Repeatedly. (Who knew they read books?!?) It is appropriate to honor their influence here because although we have spent more time together on courts and fields than in classrooms, reviewing beer lists instead of books, they have made my life immeasurably better by helping me balance work and play. I hope that Lance, Sallee, Stan, Otis, Thuong, Dorton, Andy, Derrick, Masur, Fronda, Bill, Nate, Jelani, Malcolm, Frank, Alex, Graham, Joe, Chuck, Steve, Chase, Meagan, Jess, Courtney, Laura, Mattias, Jordan, Kerry, Lisa, Liz, Danette, Dean, Andy, Legend, Quin, Tom, Katie, Dennis, Julie, Danette, Bailey, Jay, Jonathan, Tam, Dean, Chief, Stader, and Steigerwald know how much I've treasured our time together. I also hope that each of them buys this book.

I want to thank my mom, who made sure our new house had a basketball hoop, and my dad, who would drive two hours on random Tuesday nights to see me in pretty bad recreation league games. Your unquestioning and uninterrupted support of all my endeavors has meant the world to me. The same goes for Andy, Dianne, Shelly, Jason, Lorrie, Chad, Mallory, Matthew, Hunter, Peyton, Larry, and Virginia, all of whom have helped me to focus on what is important along the way. Thanks, gang.

Finally, I must thank LaGina, for being the best partner (tennis, life, Scrabble, etc.) I could ever hope to have, and Stella and Phoebe for making life more fun and interesting than I imagined it could be. Y'all are the best.

Brad Austin

Back in 2016, when a guy named Brad Austin sent me an e-mail with the subject line "Possible new sports history book project?," it didn't take me long to respond. It sounded like fun. And it was—primarily because of all the great people we were able to work with along the way. Special thanks to Rita Liberti and Daniel Nathan, who helped us conceptualize the work early on, and to Gwen Walker and Anna Muenchrath at the University of Wisconsin Press, who have kept the process moving. Katherine Mooney and an anonymous reader provided us with ideal manuscript reviews—supportive and enthusiastic as well as full of helpful suggestions. We couldn't have asked for a better group of contributors. We only wish we'd had the time and space to ask more folks to share their work.

Most important, we could not have written this book without the many dedicated scholars of sports history who have built this once-marginalized field of study into an especially rich resource for understanding American history and culture. We're delighted to have the chance to share their insights with new generations of teachers and students.

Pamela Grundy

Teaching U.S. History through Sports

Introduction

Using Sports History to Teach American History

Brad Austin and Pamela Grundy

In August 2016, at a preseason game between the San Francisco 49ers and the Green Bay Packers, the 49ers starting quarterback, Colin Kaepernick, sat quietly on the team bench while the national anthem played. Deeply troubled by recent deaths of African Americans at the hands of police, Kaepernick had decided to use his prominent position to make a statement. "I am not going to stand up to show pride in a flag for a country that oppresses black people and people of color," he told a reporter. "To me, this is bigger than football and it would be selfish on my part to look the other way. There are bodies in the street and people getting paid leave and getting away with murder."[1] Kaepernick's decision to sit, and then to kneel, during the pregame anthems that had become a standard component of NFL games produced strong reactions. Some 49er fans burned Kaepernick jerseys. A group of military veterans penned a letter supporting Kaepernick's right to free speech. President Barack Obama responded to a question by saying that Kaepernick was "exercising his constitutional right to make a statement."[2] Donald Trump, who would soon be elected to succeed Obama, suggested that Kaepernick "find a country that works better for him."[3]

The 49ers management initially expressed support for their quarterback. "In respecting such American principles as freedom of religion

3

and freedom of expression, we recognize the right of an individual to choose and participate, or not, in our celebration of the national anthem," they announced. But NFL investors were clearly uneasy. At the end of the season Kaepernick opted out of his 49ers contract. No other team offered him a job. Kaepernick—who had led the 49ers to the 2013 Super Bowl—filed a grievance that charged owners with colluding to keep him off the field. The 2017 season opened to further turmoil, as several players continued to kneel or sit in protest during the anthem. In September, President Trump sharply criticized the NFL, describing the protests as disrespectful to the flag and to the country and urging fans to boycott teams who allowed the gesture. Players pushed back. Every NFL game played that following Sunday saw some form of protest, as players knelt, sat, locked arms, or stayed in the locker room during the anthem.

The furor over the NFL protests underscores the significance that competitive sports holds in American politics and culture, highlighting the way that sporting events can dramatically embody both national ideals and national divisions. This book showcases some of the many insights that historians of sport have drawn from this multifaceted subject. We seek to encourage teachers to undertake the challenging but rewarding task of teaching American sports history. We also want to offer American history teachers ways they can use the power and drama of athletic competition to explore key issues in more traditional American history courses, including the surveys. Incorporating stories of sports and athletes into history classes can heighten student interest. It can also help students and instructors delve more deeply into historical issues, especially those involving community and identity. Because sports are so all-encompassing—engaging body, mind, and spirit—they offer an especially wide field for exploration.

This is a book of strategies as well as ideas. The history of sports includes an abundance of subjects—fascinating teams, coaches, individuals, and communities, as well as countless dramatic moments. These can be explored not only through written sources but through drawings, paintings, photographs, census data, and both documentary and feature films—see, for example, Ron Briley's insightful essay on teaching sports through film and the way Brad Austin uses the shifting footprint of professional sports to help students explore demographic change. Our essayists highlight significant themes and moments, and then explain the materials and techniques they use to engage students in exploring their subjects. Starting in the colonial era and continuing to the globalizing present, they offer insights into multiple facets of the American historical experience.

As Marc Horger details in the opening essay, sports became an integral component of the American society that took shape in the late nineteenth century—a society molded by industrial consolidation and racial reconfiguration. Like other emerging institutions, organized sports became a powerful, public endorsement not only of organized competition but of white male supremacy, relegating women, African Americans, and members of other less-favored groups to separate and unequal arenas. Essays that document that process include Sarah Fields's exploration of the close relationship between sports and concepts of gender and sexuality, Pamela Grundy's description of sports and Jim Crow segregation, Andrew Frank's assessment of the proliferation of Native American team mascots, and Leslie Heaphy's account of the origins of baseball.

At the same time, however, sports also became a part of the way that those excluded from arenas of power worked to expand their social roles. Vibrant sports communities developed in historically black colleges and universities, women's colleges, ethnic enclaves, and other areas: arenas explored in essays such as Derek White's reconceptualization of sports in African American institutions, Jorge Iber's wide-ranging compilation of athletic activities among people of Latin American descent, Daniel Pierce's account of the genesis of NASCAR in working-class southern communities, and Pamela Grundy and Rita Liberti's exploration of several decades of black women's sports. The ways that communities and individuals used sports to build confidence, strengthen community bonds, and prepare young people for the mental, physical, and emotional challenges they would face in a wider world offer multiple insights into the obstacles that so many Americans have faced and the creative ways they have worked to overcome them.

Those occasions when marginalized individuals broke into national or international prominence offer particularly promising opportunities for illuminating both the structures of American society and the strategies that various individuals employed to challenge them. Such efforts are detailed in essays that include Rita Liberti's insights into the ways that African American athletes were used to promote American democracy during the Cold War, Susan Cayleff's account of Babe Didrikson's life, Lauren Morimoto's consideration of Muhammad Ali

5

and the Olympic Project for Human Rights, and Bobbie Knapp's account of the work required to make the equality promised in Title IX a reality.

Sports also offer an especially valuable way to examine conflicts in American society. Chris Elzey's chapter explores how sports scandals reveal social rifts. Matt Alexander's masterful piece on Jack Johnson demonstrates some of the ways that sporting events encompass conflicts that play out within individual communities and on a national stage. Sports also helps detail the multiple cultural and political currents that flow between the United States and a wider world, such as those connections explored in Lars Dzikus and Adam Love's dissection of globalization, and Derek Catsam's account of Olympic politics.

We have divided the essays into four groups: Modernization and Globalization, which addresses some of the ways that sports have been linked to significant structural shifts in American society; Gender and Sexuality, which focuses primarily on the sporting experiences of women; Race and Ethnicity, which explores the long and tangled relationship between sports and race; and Case Studies, which offers an assortment of other questions, topics, and tools. But the all-encompassing nature of athletic competition means that such divisions are largely artificial. As all of these chapters demonstrate, an academic exploration of almost any sporting event naturally touches on multiple issues, and many of the same themes run throughout all four sections. Within the sections, we have arranged the essays in roughly chronological order, but each has been written to stand on its own. We do not expect that everyone will read the volume from cover to cover. Instead, we assume that teachers will start with the chapters and sections that most interest them and which will best help them enrich their classes.

A single collection of essays, of course, cannot cover the full range of insights that sports history has to offer. Nor can it include all of the innovative ways that teachers use sports-related stories and sources to engage their students. Sports history has been a vibrant, innovative field for decades. There is a rich literature on the history of many individual sports, and a little research will turn up plenty of useful material (we highlight a few additional subjects in the "Resources and Suggestions" section at the end of the book). Our goal was to create a resource that would introduce readers to some of the field's top scholars and teachers and allow these educators to share their knowledge and classroom strategies with instructors who share their passion for helping students explore the rich complexity of the American past. We hope you get as much pleasure out of reading these essays as we have found in bringing them together.

Notes

1. *New York Times*, August 27, 2016.
2. *Los Angeles Times*, September 5, 2016.
3. *Washington Post*, August 29, 2016.

Part One

Modernization and Globalization

Organized, Team, Sport

Teaching a Powerful American Idea

Marc Horger

In December 1907, a New York City Public Schools administrator named Luther Halsey Gulick addressed
the second annual convention of the Intercollegiate Athletic Association
(ICAA). The ICAA had been formed the previous year as part of an effort to save college football from a crisis caused by, among other things,
the violence inherent in the game itself. Eight people had died, and
more than a hundred people had been seriously injured playing college
football during the previous three seasons. Only a series of elaborate
machinations, including the creation of the ICAA and the introduction
of the forward pass, had spared the game from widespread damage.
Even as Gulick spoke, football had been suspended at major institutions
such as Columbia, Cal, and Stanford. Nor had the crisis yet passed, as
another sixteen players were to die on the gridiron over the next two
seasons.[1]

Gulick's topic was "Amateurism," but his speech presented a wide-
ranging defense of the legitimacy and moral necessity of team sport—
including the willingness to accept a few casualties. "This game in
particular—and intercollegiate sports in general—cannot stand or fall
because of the number of knees sprained or the number of hearts di-
lated or even the number of lives lost—because lives are lost in a far
larger way and with far more direful results through social and moral
demoralization than through the physical injury of a comparatively

11

few persons," he said. "The question must turn upon the effects of this playing upon the moral character of the general student body."[2]

Many students interested in studying American history through the lens of sport will have directly experienced the idea that sport, when engaged in for the right reasons and under the right circumstances, can be beneficial. How many coaches believe they teach social values along with skills and techniques? How many young athletes believe they develop resilience, perseverance, and determination along with the ability to shoot with their off hand?

Team sport as an analogue of a just, hardworking, and harmonious society has long been a powerful idea in American culture. Explaining the origins of that idea does much more than explain the resilience of American football in the face of multiple controversies and obvious physical dangers—it unlocks entire sectors of American culture in the late nineteenth and early twentieth century. It illuminates the era's deep skepticism about the industrial city; its fear that a modern industrial society might lack the social conditions necessary for self-government; the ubiquity of racialized thinking shaped by a prevalent yet misunderstood Darwinism; and the widespread belief that properly trained educators and social scientists—people like Luther Halsey Gulick, standing before bodies like the ICAA—could solve these problems, and more, by the application of their professional expertise. This worldview shaped public education, built playgrounds and stadiums, spread interscholastic and intercollegiate sport, created the game of basketball, and hypothesized that a healthy democratic society might be understood as a team, and vice versa.

Fear of the Modern City

As of this writing, "the city"—or at least the idea of urban living as undertaken by young educated professionals in gentrified zones of tasteful consumption—is hip. Teaching about the emergence of the American industrial city in the late nineteenth and early twentieth centuries is, among other things, an exercise in explaining the origins of just about everything that makes "the city" an attractive and entertaining place to live. This is so even if we limit ourselves to the world of sport. Explaining, say, the basic structure of Major League Baseball in 1903 involves turn-of-the-century innovations in mass communication and transportation, consumer recreation, urban infrastructure, middle-class leisure, and the geography of the walking city. Much of the basic infrastructure of urban sport-entertainment emerged in this period. Cities filled with ballparks, armories, and municipal auditoriums; high schools and college campuses sprouted football stadiums and field houses. Show students any of the photographs of the 1903 World Series, ask them to squint hard enough, and they should be able to see the basic outline of what we still mean when we talk about a "major league" city.[3]

It is nevertheless also the case that teaching about the emergence of the American industrial city in the late nineteenth and early twentieth century requires emphasizing that many Americans at the time viewed its emergence with horror and believed it might pose an existential threat to democracy. This was especially true of Americans who believed themselves by birth and education to be in a position to explain American democracy to others. Protestant clergymen like Josiah Strong, muckrakers like Lincoln Steffens, and social workers like Jane Addams each in their own way viewed the city as the location of the nation's most pressing social, political, and economic problems.[4]

Much of this concern was rooted in fear of the social and cultural consequences of recent immigration patterns, as a spike in labor migration to the United States from southern and eastern Europe began to turn some cities, and some public school systems, into majority-immigrant environments. Some of it was also falsified nostalgia for an allegedly ideal New England small-town democracy, which never really existed. Luther Halsey Gulick and many of the other people most responsible for establishing the idea of organized sport as a tool of national betterment nevertheless believed deeply in the dangers of the increasingly polyglot, decreasingly Protestant modern city and the need for people such as themselves to help engineer solutions. Explaining who they wanted to target, what they wanted to build, and how they thought it would work permits a deep dive into the worldview of American social reform and the tension in American culture between the city as the alleged location of social pathology and as the alleged location of advanced modern civilization.[5]

Darwin Misunderstood

Another core contradiction in American culture at the turn of the twentieth century is that, on the one hand, influential American educators and social thinkers were increasingly committed to applying scientific expertise to public policy questions; on the other hand, their science was lousy. That is, what they viewed as cutting-edge social-scientific discourse on issues like education, intelligence, race, ethnicity, and political science was contaminated by chromatographic layers of racism. The science underlying Gulick's theory of team sports offers a particularly clear example of this, and examining it in some depth with students will demonstrate how widely Darwinian analogies of evolutionary development had spread, and how badly they had been misunderstood.

Gulick began his professional career as a physical educator in the 1890s at the International YMCA Training School in Springfield, Massachusetts, where he reorganized the YMCA's program of physical work around team sports and games. Gulick and other physical educators of his generation were deeply influenced by G. Stanley Hall, an American psychologist and educator best known for his contribution to child study and the idea of adolescence. Hall believed, sensibly, that a system of education should bear some relationship to the developmental needs of the student. He also believed, less sensibly but understandably given the scientific era in which he worked, that the developing individual recapitulated, in a literal sense, the stages of social evolution allegedly passed through by world civilizations, a process that culminated in the presumed sociological genius of the adult male Anglo-Saxon. Adolescents, for instance, were naturally "tribal" in their behaviors and instincts. The child passed from savage to civilized as he—and it was always he—grew and developed. His program of education thus needed to aid him in his progress.[6]

To Hall and Gulick, this upward recapitulation toward Anglo-Saxonism was not an analogy. It was how Hall believed "race progress" took place and how Gulick believed organized team sport, properly designed and deployed, contributed in a literal sense to the quality of the nation. Gulick expressed this idea bluntly, frequently, in phrasing that pops at the contemporary reader. "By team-play, I mean the play of individuals in such a way as to advance the interests of the team as contrasted with the interests of the individual," he wrote in 1901. "Games demanding team-play are played by the Anglo-Saxon peoples, and by these peoples alone, and may thus be said to be a differentiating characteristic of the Anglo-Saxon adolescent male."[7] At the time, American political citizenship was still male by definition, the term "Anglo-Saxon" was increasingly treated by historians and political scientists as synonymous with the capacity for self-government, and American cities were in the process of becoming less and less Anglo-Saxon. Men like Gulick and Hall therefore believed quite sincerely that they were hunting for big game. A particular sort of American male was necessary to the health of society, a sort of male under threat by modern industrial urbanism. How to create a civilized culture of masculinity without creating an effeminate one? How to create a competitive culture of masculinity without creating a greedy one? How to replicate the imagined perfection of New England boy life in a multiethnic New York City?[8]

Organized team sport offered a potential solution—a solution that seemed scientific. It offered physical competition and achievement tempered by fair play; individual performance in the service of team; natural expression of instincts deflected to positive social outcomes; aggressive masculinity constrained by the rules of the game. Each word in the phrase was important: organized, team, sport.

Here is a social philosophy tailor-made to demonstrate to contemporary students the odd shapes into which a racialized Darwinism was pounded and the strange places it turned up at the turn of the twentieth century. Furthermore, it was at least partially responsible for underpinning large chunks of the infrastructure of American sport.[9]

The Clean Sheet of Paper

Basketball was the sport most obviously generated by this worldview. It was designed from scratch, literally on a clean sheet of paper, as a challenge from Luther Halsey Gulick to create an ideal team game. Presenting the game of basketball to students—as originally conceived, not as subsequently developed—offers an exceptionally clean case study of "organized, team, sport" in practice.

Gulick had challenged James Naismith, one of his students at the YMCA Training School, to invent an indoor game that would hold the interest of a wide variety of athletes, provide the physical and social benefits they believed resided in team games, and do so without destroying an 1892-sized gymnasium. After a series of failed experiments with modified existing games—football, soccer, lacrosse, all proved disasters—Naismith began thinking about games in the abstract, in order to construct a new one from first principles: What kinds of behavior do I want to encourage or avoid, and what elements of play will provide or eliminate them? This would be an interesting exercise for

Basket Ball.

The ball to be an ordinary Association foot ball.

1. The ball may be thrown in any direction with one or both hands.

2. The ball may be batted in any direction with one or both hands (never with the fist).

3. A player cannot run with the ball, the player must throw it from the spot on which he catches it, allowance to be made for a man who catches the ball when running at a good speed.

4. The ball must be held in or between the hands, the arms or body must not be used for holding it.

5. No shouldering, holding, pushing, tripping or striking, in any way the person of an opponent shall be allowed. The first infringement of this rule by any person shall count as a foul, the second shall disqualify him until the next goal is made, or if there was evident intent to injure the person, for the whole of the game, no substitute allowed.

6. A foul is striking at the ball with the fist, violation of rules 3 and 4, and such as described in rule 5.

7. If either side makes three consecutive fouls it shall count a goal for the opponents (consecutive means without the opponents in the meantime making a foul).

8. A goal shall be made when the ball is thrown or batted into the basket from the grounds and stays there, providing those defending the goal do not touch or disturb the goal. If the ball rests on the edge and the opponent moves the basket it shall count as a

The original rules of basketball (*continued right*), as written and annotated by James Naismith, 1891. (Courtesy of Kenneth Spencer Research Library, University of Kansas Libraries)

teachers: give their students the same assignment and see what they create and how they explain the reasoning behind their decisions.

After deciding that all worthwhile team games used a ball of some kind, Naismith decided that a large ball would be easier to handle than a small one, that games requiring use of some other tool to handle the ball—like lacrosse, his favorite outdoor sport—were too difficult for novices, that prohibiting running with the ball would reduce violence and force teamwork, and that a goal placed high and horizontal rather than on the ground would prevent the sort of high-velocity shooting that might do damage indoors. "Basketball was thus made in the office," Naismith wrote in 1894, "and was a direct adaptation of certain means to accomplish certain ends."[10]

#2.

goal.

0. When the ball goes out of bounds it shall be thrown into the field, and played by the person first touching it. In case of a dispute the umpire shall throw it straight into the field. The thrower in is allowed five seconds, if he holds it longer it shall go to the opponent. If any side presists in delaying the game, the umpire shall call a foul on them.

10. The umpire shall be judge of the men, and shall note the fouls, and notify the referee when three consecutive fouls have been made. He shall have power to disqualify men according to Rule 5.

11. The referee shall be judge of the ball and shall decide when the ball is in play, in bounds, and to which side it belongs, and shall keep the time. He shall decide when a goal has been made, and keep account of the goals with any other duties that are usually performed by a referee.

12. The time shall be two fifteen minutes halves, with five minutes rest between.

13. The side making the most goals in that time shall be declared the winners. In case of a draw the game may, by agreement of the captains, be continued until another goal is made.

First draft of Basket Ball rules. Hung in the gym that the boys might learn the rules – Dec. 1891 James Naismith 6-28-31.

Naismith turned these principles into thirteen rules, typed them up, and posted them. In its original conception, the emphasis on teamwork was extreme. Players could not run with the ball or cradle it like a football; the ball, not the player, moved down the floor toward the goal; no "shouldering, holding, pushing, tripping, or striking in any way the person of an opponent" was allowed. Especially in the early years, players might well occupy the entirety of the floor space (Naismith initially assumed any reasonable number of players per team could participate); forwards and guards were conceptualized as offensive and defensive players, respectively, and guarded each other rather than one of their own number. The *teaminess* of it, for lack of a better phrase, was very much the point.[11]

This emphasis gradually changed as the result of a number of factors, including the development of the dribble and the growing popularity of the game after 1900 as a collegiate and commercial spectacle. In fact, the version of the game that represented its original philosophy the longest, and which best presents that idea to the modern observer, is the version played by women. Naismith's original rules pamphlet featured a diagram showing six-player teams divided into three zones on the floor. This was meant to be suggestive. Spread your players out; divide them into forwards, centers, and guards. Senda Berenson, director of physical education at Smith and a firsthand observer of early basketball games at Springfield, decided to mark the divisions on the gym floor and prohibit players from crossing them, creating the "line game." It fit not just the team vision of the game but also the idea that sport and play for girls needed to be circumscribed for their own good. Berenson's version was eventually endorsed by physical educators at a conference in 1899 and published by Spalding Sporting Goods as the "official" women's version of the game.[12]

This represented the beginning of a long debate, however, rather than a permanent settlement of the question, and the debate is itself deeply revealing not just of American culture at the turn of the century but also of perennial debates about the relationship between competitive sports for women as compared to men. Contemporary students will be well aware of them, or at least recognize them easily when presented: softball rather than baseball, to take an obvious example, or the significant differences between men's and women's lacrosse, or the degree to which intercollegiate competition for women was long frowned upon by physical educators. In fact, a number of different versions of "modified" basketball rules for women proliferated early in the twentieth century, as did arguments about intramural versus varsity competition. A women's basketball rulebook wasn't just a rulebook; it was a contested zone of the culture (for more on the early development of women's sport, see Grundy, "The Shaping of 'Women's Sport.'")[13]

Early Spalding women's guides offer especially concentrated doses of the organized team sport philosophy, which make them ideal for classroom use. The 1903 version, for example, contains the Berenson "line" rules, along with her editorial endorsement; an essay from Gulick on "The Psychological Effects of Basket Ball For Women," expressing his customary obsession with team loyalty; essays and editorials emphasizing the physical perils of women's sport, particularly in terms of

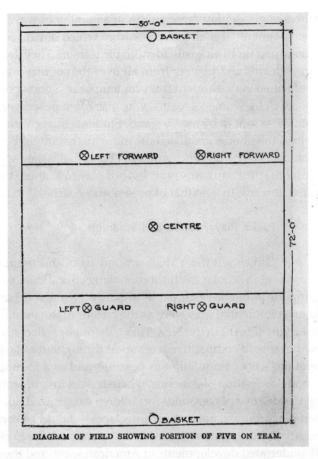

DIAGRAM OF FIELD SHOWING POSITION OF FIVE ON TEAM.

Diagram of three-division women's court, reproduced from
Spalding's Official Basketball Guide for Women, 1913.

reproduction; a direct comparison of the men's and women's rules; practical coaching and training suggestions; and pictures of women's teams from around the country. Furthermore, even when editorializing about the necessity of organized team sport for women, the preoccupation with modern masculinity constantly pokes forth, especially in Gulick's essay.[14] Although physical copies of these rulebooks and guides can be a bit difficult to search for, they now live inside Google Books, archive.org, and other databases and make excellent primary source reading material for students.

Teachers might deploy these guides in a number of ways. They almost always contain at least one essay from which dated sociological assumptions pop up in an easily identifiable fashion. They are also full of pictures—teams and players from all over the country—and those pictures are often very different from contemporary sports portraiture. Pictures sent in by women's teams were also often posed very differently from those sent in by men's teams. Students might want to think through how the photos are different, and why that might be. Finally, they are all rulebooks, and the games of "basketball" they specify are much closer in spirit, structure, and style of play to Luther Halsey Gulick's moral universe than to that of present-day coaches.

Parks, Playgrounds, and Stadiums

Gulick left the YMCA around 1900, and the rest of his career was spent in secular institutions making educational policy and advocating for public investment in organized team sport and play. His two most influential gigs were as the creator of the Public Schools Athletic League (PSAL) in the New York City public schools, where he attempted to spread competitive team sport throughout as large a percentage of the school population as possible, and as a founder of the Playground Association of America, where he was instrumental in developing the idea that playgrounds for children—organized, supervised, equipped playgrounds, not just vacant spaces—should be considered baseline urban infrastructure provided at public expense. These are severely underrated developments in American sport, and they permit the opportunity to discuss the degree to which the theories of organized team sport under discussion here were increasingly built into the permanent infrastructure of the modern city and the modern public school. Gulick's PSAL wasn't limited to "physical education" in the contemporary sense, although it contained elements thereof. It was closer to an expansion of the AAU down into the largest school district in the country. Not every city or school system developed as comprehensive a program as New York City, but by the 1910s Americans began to take for granted a built environment in which cities contained play spaces and schools contained gymnasiums and athletic fields.[15]

The combination of organized play ideology and physical infrastructure in promoting and sustaining highly competitive, heavily capitalized intercollegiate athletics has also been underappreciated. If we return now to Gulick's remarks in front of the ICAA, we recall that the game of football was widely believed to be in serious trouble in the first decade of the twentieth century. Gulick was far from alone, however, in his intellectualized support for elite competitive sport, up to and including the point of physical danger. Even many critics of football as then played nevertheless accepted the basic logic of competitive sport as a legitimate component of elite education at a modern college or university.[16] When Cal and Stanford stopped playing football after the 1905 crisis, they didn't stop playing a "big game" against one another. They just switched to rugby for a while. Even schools that dropped football altogether, such as Columbia, maintained the remainder of their intercollegiate athletic programs, which, for better or worse, were already standard equipment at American colleges. Stanford had begun playing football more or less immediately upon its opening in 1891, as had the University of Chicago, where the very first faculty hire was Amos Alonzo Stagg, tenured professor of physical education and coach of the football and baseball teams. The first-ever week of classes at Chicago, Stagg called a mass meeting of students to determine what their "'varsity yell" should be.[17]

Furthermore, in 1903 Harvard built the first permanent football stadium in the nation. It cost more than $300,000, predated the first steel-reinforced baseball stadium (Philadelphia's Shibe Park, 1909), and was, for a while, the largest steel-reinforced concrete structure in the world. Other colleges followed: Syracuse in 1907, Yale and Princeton in 1914, and a raft of schools after World War I. Even before the war, many other schools had substantial wood-frame facilities that held thousands of spectators. Basketball, too, was partly a story of recently built infrastructure. Gulick and Naismith wanted an "inside" team sport. Basketball spread so rapidly in part because a vast national (and international) system of "inside" spaces—gymnasia, National Guard armories, municipal auditoriums, YMCAs, dance halls—had recently come into being. Few of the gyms of this generation were designed with basketball in mind, but this would change in the generation of field houses built after World War I.[18]

Sport and Preparedness

One final set of ideas that powerfully demonstrates the centrality of organized team sport to American culture involves the use of organized sport by the American Expeditionary Force and affiliated organizations during World War I. When U.S. leaders self-consciously attempted to mobilize the entirety of a modern industrial society to fight a war, they made sure that soldiers had access to football, baseball, boxing, and other sports. Like the rest of the AEF's efforts at morale promotion and social service for soldiers, sport was organized and provided by the YMCA and conducted, at least in part, on the theory that it would keep soldiers out of unwholesome trouble. But sport as a key component of "preparedness" was also actively supported by many of the same people responsible for sport's growing role in domestic culture, which resulted in a significant expenditure of men and material. In fact, AEF sport culminated in the Inter-Allied Games of 1919, wherein American troops staged a series of championship tournaments to determine who would go on to contest teams and athletes from an invited selection of Allied nations. In order to hold the games, the U.S. built the multipurpose Stade Pershing in Paris: a gift of infrastructure from Uncle Sam.[19]

The "Amateur Sport" Professional

I will close with a word about amateurism, the topic of Gulick's 1907 speech to the ICAA. Everyone in that room took the amateur ideal for granted, even as Gulick discussed what they all knew were powerful countervailing forces—high school athletes seeking alumni aid for tuition, college baseball players making money in the summer under assumed names, and so on. Athletic competition for its own sake, rather than for profit, was a fundamental assumption among those who believed sport could serve larger social purposes. Yet, in another sense, Gulick and his audience were themselves "professionals." They had built lives around professionalized modern values: the acquisition of a narrow but deep body of specialized knowledge, deployed over the course of a lifetime, not just "as a career" but also in the belief that it represented a positive contribution to their chosen fields. Gulick was such a professional. So was Amos Alonzo Stagg, who pointedly declined to play major league baseball after his career at Yale was over, yet coached college football for more than sixty years. So was James E. Sullivan of the AAU, and Walter Camp at Yale, and Glenn Warner, Fielding Yost, and a host of others around the country.[20] This too was infrastructure under construction at the turn of the twentieth century:

the world of the "amateur sport" professional. We are professionals; you are not. This too survives.

A final teachable topic, then, presents itself: Should the amateur ideal have survived? Should it continue? Should college athletes be compensated more fully, or more openly? Should they remain "amateurs" at all? Were other outcomes possible, or preferable?[21]

Notes

1. See, for example, John Sayle Watterson, *College Football: History, Spectacle, Controversy* (Baltimore, MD: Johns Hopkins University Press, 2000), 80–120; statistics on casualties taken from 401.

2. Luther H. Gulick, "Amateurism," *American Physical Education Review* 13 (February 1908): 98–104.

3. For more see Steven A. Riess, *City Games: The Evolution of American Urban Society and the Rise of Sports* (Urbana: University of Illinois Press, 1989), and *Touching Base: Professional Baseball and American Culture in the Progressive Era* (Urbana: University of Illinois Press, 1999).

4. See, for example, Josiah Strong, *Our Country: Its Possible Future and Its Present Crisis* (New York: American Home Missionary Society, 1885); Lincoln Steffens, *The Shame of the Cities* (New York: McClure, Phillips and Co., 1904); Jane Addams, *Twenty Years at Hull House* (New York: Macmillan, 1910).

5. See Mark Dyreson, *Making the American Team: Sport, Culture, and the Olympic Experience* (Urbana: University of Illinois Press, 1998) for a good discussion of organized sport as a social tool and its relationship to many of these factors.

6. A brief but good sample is Strickland and Burgess, eds., *Health, Growth, and Heredity: G. Stanley Hall on Natural Education* (New York: Teachers College Press, 1965). For the brave, there is also G. Stanley Hall, *Adolescence: Its Psychology and Its Relations to Physiology, Anthropology, Sex, Crime, Religion, and Education*, 2 vols. (New York: D. Appleton and Company, 1904).

7. Luther Gulick, "The Psychological Effects of Basket Ball for Women," *Line Basket-Ball, or Basket Ball for Women* (New York: American Sports Publishing Co., 1901), 12. See also Luther Gulick, *Philosophy of Play* (New York: Scribner's, 1920).

8. On New England "boy life," see G. Stanley Hall, "Boy Life in a Massachusetts Country Town Thirty Years Ago," *Proceedings of the American Antiquarian Society* 7 (October 1890): 107–28. See also "New Departures in Education," *North American Review* 140 (February 1885): 144–52, and "The Contents of Children's Minds," *Princeton Review* 11 (May 1883): 249–72. Biographies include G. Stanley Hall, *Life and Confessions of a Psychologist* (New York: D. Appleton

and Company, 1923), and Dorothy Ross, *G. Stanley Hall: The Psychologist as Prophet* (Chicago: University of Chicago Press, 1972).

9. Although Gulick's ideas might easily be referred to as "Social Darwinism," I tend not to use this formulation in my own teaching. Gulick was less interested in Spencerian "survival of the fittest" and more interested in how individual instinct could be funneled toward collectively beneficial sociological outcomes. Furthermore, Hall and Gulick seldom figure prominently in the secondary literature of Social Darwinism. For more, see Mike Hawkins, *Social Darwinism in European and American Thought, 1860–1945* (Cambridge: Cambridge University Press, 1997); Carl N. Degler, *In Search of Human Nature: The Decline and Revival of Darwinism in American Social Thought* (New York: Oxford University Press, 1991); Hamilton Cravens, *The Triumph of Evolution: American Scientists and the Heredity-Environment Controversy, 1900–1941* (Philadelphia: University of Pennsylvania Press, 1978).

10. James Naismith, *Basketball: Its Origin and Development* (New York: Association Press, 1941), 32–38; C. Howard Hopkins, *History of the YMCA in North America* (New York: Association Press, 1951), 261.

11. James Naismith, *Rules for Basket Ball* (Springfield, MA: Springfield Printing and Binding Company, 1892).

12. Naismith, *Rules for Basket Ball*; *Line Basket-Ball, or Basket Ball for Women* (1899).

13. Robin Bell Marks, "Bloomer Basketball and Its Suspender Suppression: Women's Intercollegiate Competition at Ohio State, 1904–1907," *Journal of Sport History* 27 (Spring 2000): 31–49; Elma L. Warner, "Inter-School Athletics," *American Physical Education Review* 11 (March 1906): 182–86; Elizabeth Burchenal, "Basket Ball Under the Auspices of the Girls' Branch P.S.A.L. of New York City," *Spalding's Official Basket Ball Guide for Women 1912–1913* (New York: American Sports Publishing Company, 1912), 69–77.

14. Senda Berenson, ed., *Basket Ball for Women* (New York: American Sports Publishing Company, 1903).

15. For more on Gulick and playgrounds, see Dominick Cavallo, *Muscles and Morals: Organized Playgrounds and Urban Reform, 1880, 1920* (Philadelphia: University of Pennsylvania Press, 1981).

16. See especially Brian M. Ingrassia, *The Rise of Gridiron University: Higher Education's Uneasy Alliance with Big-Time Football* (Lawrence: University Press of Kansas, 2012).

17. Robin Lester, *Stagg's University: The Rise, Decline, and Fall of Big-Time Football at Chicago* (Urbana: University of Illinois Press, 1999); *Chicago Tribune*, October 2, 1892, 8. On Cal, Stanford, and rugby, see Roberta J. Park, "From Football to Rugby—and Back, 1906–1919: The University of California-Stanford University Response to the 'Football Crisis of 1905,'" *Journal of Sport History* 11 (Winter 1984): 5–40.

18. On Harvard Stadium, see Ronald A. Smith, "Commercialized Intercollegiate Athletics and the 1903 Harvard Stadium," *New England Quarterly* 78 (March 2005): 26-48. More broadly, see Ingrassia, *Rise of Gridiron University*, 139-70.

19. See especially Thierry Terret, "The Military 'Olympics' of 1919: Sport Diplomacy and Sport Politics in the Aftermath of World War One," *Journal of Olympic History* 14 (August 2006): 22-31; S. W. Pope, *Patriotic Games: Sporting Traditions in the American Imagination, 1876-1926* (New York: Oxford University Press, 1997), 121-56; George Wythe and J. M. Hanson, *The Inter-Allied Games, Paris, 22nd June to 6th July, 1919* (Paris: The Games Committee, 1919).

20. Ingrassia, *Rise of Gridiron University*, 115-38; Ronald A. Smith, *Sports and Freedom: The Rise of Big-Time College Athletics* (New York: Oxford University Press, 1988).

21. For more on the amateur ideal in American sport, including its relationship to ideas about social class, see Dyreson, *Making the American Team*; Michael Oriard, *Reading Football: How the Popular Press Created an American Spectacle* (Chapel Hill: University of North Carolina Press, 1998); Julie Des Jardins, *Walter Camp: Football and the Modern Man* (New York: Oxford University Press, 2015.

Teaching Sports Scandals

Chris Elzey

Most students, when they hear the words "sports scandals," think of something provocative: sex, cheating, drugs, conspiracy, payoffs, gambling, crime, or violence. It is often said that America's national obsession is sport. Throw in scandal, and, well, you have something much bigger: the 1919 "Black Sox" game-rigging scandal or the Penn State child sex-abuse scandal or, even, the O. J. Simpson murder trial.[1] Instructors who use sports scandals in their courses will have no problem holding the interest of students.

But what is the educational value of studying sports scandals? And how might instructors teach them? Because the list of sports scandals is long, and because that list contains a wide variety of wrongdoings committed in nearly every sport, the notion that there is a single best approach is ludicrous. Still, in my experience of teaching sports scandals, I have come to learn that what seems to be a shortcoming is actually a strength: the thematic and historical range of sports scandals is so expansive that instructors should have no trouble identifying a scandal that fits their instructional needs.

The essay that follows is not intended to be a comprehensive review of sports scandals but rather a guide for educators interested in using sports scandals in the classroom. I have selected three types of scandals—amateur eligibility, doping, and gambling—to illustrate my points, but I could have just as easily picked other categories: violence, gender, race, cheating, sexual misconduct, quest for fame, or abuse of power. The historical processes and forces evident in the scandals examined in this chapter were also present in many scandals from the other groups. Similarly, the suggestions I offer regarding methods, approaches, assignments, and points of emphasis can, with a little tweaking, be applied to many of these other scandals.

What Is a Scandal?

At the beginning of my course on sports scandals, I ask students to define the term "scandal." We discuss the definition in class, but some instructors may want to have students answer the question in a writing assignment. Even for courses that do not focus exclusively on sports scandals, instructors will find it beneficial to devote a brief amount of class time to discussing what a scandal is. Not only will it provide interpretative access to the material about to be explored, but students will also be better equipped to understand the process by which sports scandals bring history into sharper focus.

So, what *is* a scandal? In his preface to *The New Encyclopedia of American Scandal*, George Childs Kohn defines a scandal as "a grave loss of or injury to reputation resulting from actual or apparent breach or violation of morality, ethics, propriety, or law."[2] Kohn's definition identifies the basic elements of a scandal. One element is the rules and norms that govern society. Another is the transgression of those standards. And a third is the humiliation suffered by the wrongdoer. It is important that students understand that most scandals consist of these elements. Why? Because such knowledge opens up important paths of inquiry.

One of these paths explores the norms themselves. To whom did they belong? How did they come to be? What was their purpose? Asking such questions can lead to fascinating insights. Consider the controversy surrounding the African American boxer Jack Johnson, world heavyweight champion from 1908 to 1915. Much of white America despised Johnson—not just because of his successes and his haughty style but also because of his public courtship of white women (he married three). To black Americans, though, the controversial fighter was a hero, in part because he challenged the codes—racial as well as sexual—that privileged whites over African Americans.

Another path examines the ways in which norms were upheld. Sometimes, the legal system enforced these codes—Jack Johnson's career was destroyed when he was prosecuted in federal court for violating the Mann Act, which, as Johnson's biographer Randy Roberts has written, "forbade the transportation of women in interstate or foreign commerce 'for the purpose of prostitution or debauchery, or for any other immoral purpose.'"[3] Sports organizations and leagues also worked hard to enforce rules that reflected widespread social norms. In the highly commercialized era of modern sport, sponsors and advertisers played roles as well, often severing ties with athletes who were seen to violate social conventions. One reason sports scandals prompted such widespread action was that fans and journalists alike tended to idealize sports figures. Scandalous behavior breached social norms; it also betrayed faith in what sport seemed to represent. Caretakers of "national values," as well as organizations wishing to maintain public good will, aspired to ensure that the games with which they were associated remained socially acceptable.

Amateur Eligibility Scandals: Class and Privilege

The amateur eligibility scandals that were a common feature of sports during the late 1800s and early 1900s are excellent tools for exploring issues of class privilege, social exclusion, and national identity, as well as emphasizing the extent to which a particular kind of scandal is tied to a set of values prevailing at a particular time.

I start by making sure my students understand the roots of amateurism. Most are surprised to learn that the concept originated in Victorian England as a means to prevent workingmen from competing against members of the elite classes in sport. Early amateurism restrictions in Britain prohibited athletes from being paid and forbade would-be competitors who toiled as workmen, invoking the so-called "mechanics clause."[4] Implicit were assumptions about social status, wealth, and sportsmanship: only elite gentlemen could be honest athletes, and it was only these gentlemen athletes who played sports purely for pleasure. By the early 1880s, the mechanics clause had been stricken from most British rulebooks.[5] But the elitism remained. The amateur code adopted in the United States largely embodied this ideal, while emphasizing a vision of "clean" and orderly democratic sport (see Horger, "Organized, Team, Sports").[6]

By far the best amateur eligibility scandal to use in class is the Jim Thorpe scandal, which erupted in early 1913. A Native American with white ancestry, Thorpe had been an All-American football player and track star at the Carlisle Indian Industrial School in Pennsylvania. At the 1912 Stockholm Olympics, he captured gold medals in the pentathlon

28

Jim Thorpe being greeted by New York City officials on his return from the 1912 Olympics. (New York World-Telegram and Sun Newspaper Photograph Collection, Library of Congress, Prints & Photographs Division)

and the decathlon. Americans cheered as the twenty-five-year-old Thorpe returned home to enormous fanfare. Steering the Carlisle football team to a 12-1-1 record that fall, the star athlete had the world at his feet.[7]

Then trouble intervened. In late January 1913, Americans learned that Thorpe had spent part of 1909 and 1910 playing minor league baseball in North Carolina.[8] That meant he had competed as a professional at the Stockholm Games—a clear violation of Olympic amateur rules.

The AAU's secretary, James E. Sullivan, a relentless protector of the amateur ideal but also a man fiercely driven by his own self-interests, worked to contain the growing scandal. Declaring that the AAU would adjudicate the matter, he accepted a written statement from Thorpe in which the Olympic star shouldered all the blame. On January 27, the letter, which had likely been penned by Thorpe's coach and mentor at Carlisle, Glenn S. "Pop" Warner, was released to the press.[9] "I never realized until now what a big mistake I made by keeping it a secret about my ball playing and I am sorry I did so," the letter ran. "I hope I will be partly excused by the fact that I was simply an Indian schoolboy and did not know all about such things."[10] His plea for understanding went unheard. The next day, a page-one headline in the *New York Tribune* announced: OLYMPIC HERO TO BE STRIPPED OF HIS HONORS.[11] Overnight, Thorpe had gone from being a superstar to an outcast. In May, the International Olympic Committee (IOC) voided his Olympic victories.

One aspect of the Thorpe scandal I focus on in class is the role played by such amateur sports gatekeepers as Sullivan. Why, I ask students, did officials act so quickly? Here, instructors should note that similar questions were raised after Thorpe had confessed. Some critics argued that given Thorpe's popularity, and also that he did not use an alias as a ballplayer, there was no way the AAU and Warner *could not* have been aware of his semiprofessional status. Having Thorpe confess, of course, absolved officials of guilt.[12] Other critics questioned the AAU's dictatorial control over amateur sport that, in essence, only athletes who fit the organization's definition of "gentlemanly" standards of amateurism were worthy of representing the United States.[13] Still others bemoaned the harshness of Thorpe's punishment. One journalist wrote that Thorpe "has been more sinned against than sinning."[14]

In a nine-page article published in *Baseball Magazine* in April 1913, F. C. Lane berated amateurism in general and the AAU more specifically.

Calling Thorpe "a pawn in the game," Lane blasted the amateur ideal as being "moth eaten and age worn," and lambasted the AAU for enforcing a code that failed to discriminate Thorpe's semiprofessional ballplaying from his amateur participation in track and field. The idea that amateurism was sport's only guiding principle vexed Lane. "Professionalism," he wrote, "is not the foe of sport; it is . . . the strongest of the many strong factors which have been responsible for the wonderful growth of athletic culture."[15] To help students understand the amateur-professional polemic that existed during the early 1900s, instructors could compare Lane's article to *A Sporting Pilgrimage* by Caspar Whitney. Published in 1895, the book is an unabashed paean to elitist sport.[16] Instructors could even pair Lane's piece with more recent articles critical of amateur athletics, such as Taylor Branch's provocative 2011 essay in the *Atlantic Monthly* titled "The Shame of College Sports."[17]

There were many, though, who believed Thorpe's ouster was warranted. The reasoning was straightforward: Not only did the future of amateurism and all that it represented seem at stake; so, too, did American prestige. The scandal, *Outlook* warned, "will afford an opportunity to those unfriendly to [the United States] to declare again their opinion that ideals of the gentleman are beyond comprehension of American athletes, and that American sport is thoroughly commercialized."[18] To the *Cleveland Plain Dealer*, the AAU's swift yet stern handling of the matter was "sufficient proof that in no other country do amateur athletics stand on a firmer and purer basis."[19]

Not surprisingly, the issue of race also came into play. In a formal statement released the same day as Thorpe's confession, the AAU explained that the disgraced Olympian had violated the rules of amateurism, in part, because "Mr. Thorpe is an Indian of limited experience and education in the ways of other than his own people."[20] The statement (and Thorpe's confession) could be used in class to start a broader exploration of Native Americans, sport, and cultural assimilation during the first decades of the twentieth century.[21]

Doping Scandals: A Long Time Coming

By the 1960s, tellingly, scandals were less likely to involve the fading amateur ideal and far more likely to center on performance-enhancing drugs. For much of the twentieth century, doping scandals were rare. Not that athletes eschewed drugs. During the late 1800s and early 1900s competitors consumed a wide variety of performance-boosting substances, including strychnine, caffeine, alcohol, coca, and kola. By the 1950s, the drugs *du jour* were amphetamines and steroids. That some athletes took drugs did not bother most fans. Few sports organizations and leagues banned doping.[22]

Things began to change in the 1960s. Even though the IOC had suspected for years that athletes doped, it would not be until 1968 that Olympic competitors were officially tested for drugs.[23] What helped prompt the IOC's decision was the shocking death of Knud Enemark Jensen at the 1960 Olympics in Rome. A member of the Danish Olympic cycling team, Jensen toppled over during a race on a scorching hot day, smacked his head, and, shortly thereafter, died. While officials announced that he had succumbed to heatstroke-induced cranial bleeding, information challenging that conclusion soon emerged. The press reported that Roniacol—a pharmaceutical that boosts blood flow but can also produce faintness, especially when one overheats—had been part of Jensen's pre-race regimen. A trainer had supplied the stimulant. The athletic world was stunned. Afterward, it was alleged that Jensen had also used amphetamines.[24]

The tragic story of Knud Enemark Jensen is a good scandal to use in class because it acts as a temporal bridge, connecting an era that evinced few qualms about doping to one that drew a hard line against performance-improving drugs. The shift in perception laid the groundwork for a less tragic but far more shocking scandal.

In late summer 1988, Ben Johnson seemed poised for superstardom. The previous year, at the World Track and Field Championships in Rome, the Canadian sprinter by way of Jamaica had shattered the 100-meter world mark. In his adopted Canada, he was beloved. Victory at the 1988 Seoul Olympics promised to spread that glory. In Seoul, Johnson rocketed down his lane, edging out his rival, the American Carl Lewis. Incredibly, his time was 9.79 seconds, four-hundredths of a second faster than his record-setting time in Rome. Already revered, Johnson became sporting royalty. To the *Montreal Gazette*, he was "Canada's Hero."[25]

But then, with six days left in the Games, IOC officials delivered earth-shattering news: Johnson had failed a drug test administered after the 100-meter finals. The drug he was accused of taking was stanozolol, an anabolic steroid also formulated for veterinary applications. As the media storm broke, a bewildered Johnson was hustled out of Seoul. The IOC, meanwhile, vacated his win.[26]

At first, Johnson repudiated allegations that he had willfully doped. By denying the accusations, however, Johnson inadvertently deflected blame onto his longtime coach, Charlie Francis, an erstwhile Canadian sprint star who had once run in the Olympics.[27] In October, authorities began investigating the charges as part of a wider probe into the prevalence of doping in Canadian amateur sport. Hearings opened the following year.

The probe, popularly called the Dubin Inquiry, aired on Canadian TV. Viewers were riveted as the web of deception unraveled. Both Francis and Jaime Astaphan, a physician who had treated Johnson, admitted to administering steroids and other drugs. In June, a teary-eyed Johnson took the stand and confessed. He also divulged that he had started taking performance-boosting pharmaceuticals in the early 1980s. "I lied and I was ashamed for my family and friends [and for kids] who look up to me as a Canadian athlete," the one-time national hero stated.[28] The penalty handed down earlier by Canadian officials was harsh: Never again was Johnson to sprint for Canada. (The punishment was withdrawn in 1990.)

It is difficult to overstate the importance of the Ben Johnson scandal. Not only did it alter how the public perceived doping, it also intensified efforts to address the widespread use of performance-boosting drugs—efforts that eventually led to the founding of the World Anti-Doping Agency (WADA) in 1999.[29] One could also argue that the Dubin Inquiry presaged the congressional hearings on steroids and baseball in 2005. Having students compare the two investigations could be a topic for a research paper or an exam question. Good sources on both probes exist, including government documents from the baseball hearings, which are available online through the website of the Society of American Baseball Research (SABR); and the Dubin Report, which can be accessed via the Government of Canada Publications web page.[30] The Canadian Broadcasting Corporation Digital Archives contains a compelling five-minute "audio montage of the voices behind Canada's steroid fiasco."[31] "9.79*," an ESPN *30 for 30* documentary episode that takes a hard look at the Johnson scandal, also explores the idea that doping was so rampant that many athletes believed the only way they could compete at a high level was to take the drugs—even if it harmed their health.

To help students understand the evolution of popular attitudes toward doping, instructors might want to contrast the Ben Johnson scandal with a controversy from the 1904 St. Louis Olympics, or with a two-page ad that appeared in *Outing* magazine in 1896. Interestingly, the scandal in St. Louis arose not because the eventual winner of the marathon, Thomas Hicks, had downed brandy and strychnine during the race, but because the first-place finisher, Frederick Lorz, had hitched a ride in a car. Officials soon uncovered Lorz's ruse, and Hicks was declared the victor. But no fuss was made over Hicks's drinks.[32]

Likewise, no fuss was made over the product promoted in *Outing*. The product, a wonder beverage called Vino-Kolafra, contained kola, a stimulant. In the ad, which was titled "A New Factor in Athletics. The Banishment of Fatigue," one prominent coach was quoted as saying: "I used Vino-Kolafra freely myself before giving it to my men. It acts at once on the nervous system, and in this way braces up the muscles. More, it keeps them braced, and . . . improves the general health. . . . It certainly is a remarkable drug."[33]

Ninety-two years later, *Sports Illustrated* ran an article on Ben Johnson's positive drug test in Seoul. The cover of the issue containing a "Special Report" titled "The Loser," shows Johnson, sprinting. Superimposed over the image is one word: "BUSTED!"[34] Instructors might ask students in a writing assignment to explain why the *Outing* ad and the *Sports Illustrated* coverage differed so much. The numerous doping incidents involving Olympians after the Ben Johnson scandal—particularly the doping program in Russia (allegedly run by state officials) that resulted in the ousting of the nation's Olympic squad from the 2018 Winter Games in PyeongChang, South Korea—shows the degree to which athletes and government leaders continue to stress winning.[35]

Gambling Scandals: Show Me the Money

Gambling, of course, has provided a regular source of sports scandals. At the heart of virtually every gambling scandal is one thing: money. Most students know that. But chances are they have not thought much about how gambling scandals can shed light on historical issues and themes—or why that is even possible. Sports and gambling have had a long, complicated history. In many ways, the rise of modern sports fueled the rise of modern gambling. Conversely, as gambling became more prevalent in society, sports were forced to adjust.

In my class, I suggest that three factors helped create the conditions for gambling scandals. The first is greed, or at least a sense that a player who shaves points or fixes games is underpaid. Another factor is the creation of the point-spread system in the 1930s or 1940s, which increased gambling—particularly in basketball—by reconfiguring how bets were wagered (the new system also made game fixing more palatable, since point-shaving players could get paid while still winning games). The third factor is the commercialization of intercollegiate athletics after World War II. As college basketball and football became increasingly profit-oriented, some players felt, as amateurs, that the system was rigged against them. Point shaving seemed an easy—and equitable—way to enjoy some of the profits.

The gambling scandal I examine first is the 1877 Louisville Grays game-rigging scandal in baseball. Since it was the first major gambling scandal in American sports history, the Grays scandal serves as a point of reference for the other gambling scandals we explore in the course.

As with most other game-fixing scandals, what first raised suspicions with the 1877 Grays was uncharacteristically sloppy play. Those suspicions only increased after the Grays, who had been a strong pennant contender, finished the year in second place. Earlier, Grays executives had been made privy to several telegrams linking Louisville players to gamblers. Confronted with the evidence at the end of the season, three players, including ace pitcher Jim Devlin, confessed to rigging games. It was soon determined that a fourth player, shortstop Bill Craver, also fixed games. All four were banned from playing again for the Grays. The National League barred them for life.[36]

In class, I underscore the significance of the lifetime ban, which reflected efforts to clean up baseball's sullied image. For years, gambling and baseball had mixed openly, sparking significant criticism. But in the late nineteenth century, as an insurgent group of moral reformers sought to "clean up" urban life, many argued that baseball gambling attracted unruly crowds and undermined the sport's "moral" purpose. "Gambling is growing to be the dominant evil of our day, and base-ball matches are mainly responsible for it," one reformist publication lamented in 1870.[37] The founding of the National League in 1876 involved the promise that it would redeem the national pastime. As the new league's constitution put it, the aim was: "To make Base Ball playing *respectable* and *honorable* [italics original]."[38] Unsurprisingly, league rules worked to advance this agenda, including barring both gambling and drinking from ballparks.[39]

When discussing the Grays scandal, I try to help students understand that the indignation heaped on the four Louisville fixers— "Disgraceful Exposures of Rascality Among Ball-Players," ran a subhead in the *Chicago Daily Tribune*—did not just result from a failure to follow league rules.[40] It also resulted from a belief that the players had broken social norms. Having students analyze the press coverage of the scandal—particularly in relation to the cultural and social milieus in which the scandal broke—is a good way to help them grasp the latter point. Newspapers nationwide covered the scandal, so there are plenty of primary and secondary sources. The *Louisville Courier-Journal*'s coverage was particularly good.[41]

The 1919 "Black Sox" World Series scandal also warrants attention. An important and especially well-documented chapter in the history of sport, the scandal provides students with opportunities to explore broader historical themes. Arguments that the players may have opted to fix games because of their relatively meager salaries might lead to larger questions about unfair labor practices at the time. The intense disappointment caused by the scandal suggests post–World War I disillusionment. The unilateral decision to ban the players made by Commissioner Kennesaw Mountain Landis could even be used to open a discussion of the concept of authority and how it was wielded during the late 1910s and early 1920s (the Palmer Raids come to mind).[42]

Instructors can also choose from an abundance of other scandals, many of which explore additional themes. The 1981 "outing" of the tennis star Billie Jean King highlights key themes regarding shifting cultural norms around gender, sports, and sexuality. The 1994 Olympic ice skating scandal involving Tonya Harding and Nancy Kerrigan raises issues that include the obsession with fame and success, class bias, gender ideals, and—following the 2017 release of the movie *I, Tonya*—psychological and domestic abuse. The 2002 Salt Lake City Olympics bid scandal exposed the presence of graft and corruption in not only government-backed organizations but also such venerable bodies as the IOC. The concussion scandal in the National Football League (NFL) demonstrated a lack of concern for workers' well-being—

in the name of profit.[43] Because they garner considerable attention and evoke such strong feelings, sports scandals are an ideal instrument to explore history and to cast light on cultural spaces that otherwise remain obscure. Students, no doubt, will be intrigued.

Notes

1. Sports scandals as a group have drawn recent attention from scholars. Books on the topic include: Peter Finley, Laura Finley, and Jeffrey Finley, *Sports Scandals* (Westport, CT: Greenwood Press, 2008); Edward J. Lordan, *Sports and Scandals: How Leagues Protect the Integrity of Their Games* (Santa Barbara, CA: Praeger, 2014); and Shaun R. Harper and Jamel K. Donnor, *Scandals in College Sports* (New York: Routledge, 2017).

2. George Childs Kohn, ed., *The New Encyclopedia of American Scandal* (New York: Facts on File, 2001), vii.

3. Randy Roberts, *Papa Jack: Jack Johnson and the Era of White Hopes* (New York: Free Press, 1983), 144. Roberts's book is a superb biography of Johnson.

4. For more on early amateurism, see Richard Holt, *Sport and the British: A Modern History* (Oxford: Oxford University Press, 1989), 98–117; John Lowerson, *Sport and the English Middle Classes, 1870-1914* (Manchester: Manchester University Press, 1993), 154–90; Peter Bailey, *Leisure and Class in Victorian England: Rational Recreation and the Contest for Control, 1830-1885* (New York: Methuen, 1987; 1978), 139–44; and David C. Young, *The Olympic Myth of Greek Amateur Athletics* (Chicago: Ares Publishers, 1984), 15–28. Young also discusses amateurism in the context of the 1896 Athens Olympics. See Young, *The Modern Olympics: A Struggle for Revival* (Baltimore, MD: Johns Hopkins Press, 1996).

5. Holt, *Sport and the British*, 109.

6. The issue is examined in S. W. Pope, "Amateurism and American Sports Culture: The Invention of an Athletic Tradition in the United States, 1870-1900," *International Journal of the History of Sport* 13 (December 1996): 290–309.

7. Kate C. Buford's *Native American Son: The Life and Sporting Legend of Jim Thorpe* (New York: Alfred Knopf, 2010) is one of the better biographies of Thorpe. See also David Wallace Adams, "More Than a Game: The Carlisle Indians Take to the Gridiron, 1893-1917," *Western Historical Quarterly* 32 (Spring 2001): 25–53.

8. Bill Crawford, *All American: The Rise and Fall of Jim Thorpe* (Hoboken, NJ: John Wiley, 2005), 198.

9. For Warner's writing of the letter, see Buford, *Native American Son*, 161–62, and Sally Jenkins, *The Real All Americans: The Team That Changed a Game, a People, a Nation* (New York: Broadway Books, 2007), 288. Among the newspapers that announced the confession were the *Washington Post*, January 27, 1913; *New York Tribune*, January 28, 1913; and *Los Angeles Times*, January 28, 1913.

10. Quoted in *Revue Olympique*, March 1913, 36–37.

11. *New York Tribune*, January 28, 1913. The *Cleveland Plain Dealer* declared: "Thorpe has brought humiliation to athletic America to take the place of the pride which has been felt for his achievement." See *Cleveland Plain Dealer*, January 29, 1913.

12. For examples of such claims, see *Sporting News*, February 6, 1913; *New York Times*, January 29, 1913; and *St. Louis Post Dispatch*, January 28, 1913. The *Dispatch*'s headline and subheads read: "Wanted: One Goat to Bear; Blame in Jim Thorpe Case; A.A.U. Seeking a Victim." In addition, the popular *Reach Official American League Base Ball Guide* for 1910 and 1911 listed Thorpe's statistics. For the 1910 edition, see pages 435, 437; for 1911, see pages 469, 473. There were also claims that Pop Warner and Moses Friedman, the superintendent of Carlisle, were aware of Thorpe's baseball career. See Jenkins, *Real All Americans*, 290, 338.

13. This theme is explored in John Lucas, "The Hegemonic Rule of the Amateur Athletic Union 1888–1914: James Edward Sullivan as Prime Mover," *International Journal of the History of Sport* 11 (December 1994): 355–71.

14. Quoted in *Literary Digest*, February 8, 1913, 302.

15. F. C. Lane, "Amateur Athletics Arraigned," *Baseball Magazine*, April 1913, 26, 30, 31.

16. Caspar Whitney, *A Sporting Pilgrimage* (New York: Harper and Brothers, 1895). To say the least, elitism is a prominent theme in the book. Consider the following passage: "The laboring class are all right in their way; let them . . . have their athletics in whatsoever manner best suits their inclinations. There is no reason . . . why they should play under our rules, or why we should open our rules to admit of their more liberal understandings of an amateur" (167).

17. Taylor Branch, "The Shame of College Sports," *Atlantic Monthly*, October 2011, 80–110.

18. *Outlook*, February 8, 1913, 293.

19. *Cleveland Plain Dealer*, January 29, 1913. Reactions to the scandal also discussed in Buford, *Native Son*, and Crawford, *All American*.

20. Quoted in *Revue Olympique*, March 1913, 39.

21. Other Native American athletes included the Philadelphia Athletics star pitcher Charles Albert Bender, whose sobriquet was "Chief," and Tom Longboat, a marathoner from Canada who had also been accused of professionalism.

22. A good source on the subject is Paul Dimeo, *A History of Drug Use in Sport 1876–1976: Beyond Good and Evil* (New York: Routledge, 2007). Instructors interested in issues related to doping should also consult John M. Hoberman's work.

23. Some sports groups—the IOC included—enacted regulations against doping years before the test. See John Gleaves and Matthew Llewellyn, "Sports, Drugs and Amateurism: Tracing the Real Cultural Origins of Anti-Doping Rules in International Sport," *International Journal of the History of Sport* 31 (2014): 839–53. Instructors may want to point out to students that the first sport

to institute a drug policy was horseracing. See John Gleaves, "Enhancing the Odds: Horse Racing, Gambling, and the First Anti-Doping Movement in Sport, 1889–1911," *Sport in History* 32 (2012): 26–52.

24. Additional information about Jensen and the IOC's drug policy in Verner Møller, "Knud Enemark Jensen's Death during the 1960 Rome Olympics: A Search for Truth?," *Sport in History* 25 (2005): 452–71, and Thomas M. Hunt, *The International Olympic Committee and the Politics of Doping, 1960–2008* (Austin: University of Texas Press, 2011). The *Sport and History* issue that contains Møller's article is devoted to the topic of doping in sport.

25. *Montreal Gazette*, September 25, 1988.

26. For more on the race and ensuing scandal, see Richard Moore, *The Dirtiest Race in History: Ben Johnson, Carl Lewis and the 1988 Olympic 100m Final* (London: Bloomsbury, 2012). The Vanderbilt Television News Archive database provides access to newscasts covering the scandal.

27. Daniel Gordon, dir., "9.79*," ESPN Films, 2012.

28. Quoted in *Washington Post*, June 14, 1989.

29. The Festina pro cycling team doping scandal of 1998 is usually cited as the event that triggered the establishment of the WADA.

30. The SABR website is http://research.sabr.org/business/resources/documents/; the Government of Canada Publications website is http://publications.gc.ca/site/eng/home.html (both accessed December 4, 2017).

31. See http://www.cbc.ca/archives/categories/sports/drugs-in-sports/ (accessed December 5, 2017).

32. Bill Mallon, *The 1904 Olympic Games: Results from All Competitors in All Events, with Commentary* (Jefferson, NC: McFarland, 1999), 56–58. Despite the incident, Lorz continued to race. In 1905, he won the Boston Marathon.

33. "A New Factor in Athletics. The Banishment of Fatigue," *Outing*, June 1896, xxv–xxvi, of that month's advertisement section. For more on the ad and drink, see Dimeo, *A History of Drug Use in Sport*, 24–25. Vino-Kolafra was also touted in newspaper articles. See *New York Times*, October 6, 1895, and *Boston Globe*, January 12, 1896.

34. *Sports Illustrated*, October 3, 1988. The "Special Report" is on pages 21–28.

35. Russian athletes who proved they had not doped were able to compete in PyeongChang as members of the nonaffiliated Olympic Athletes from Russia (OAR) team.

36. For more on the scandal, see William A. Cook, *The Louisville Grays Scandal of 1877: The Taint of Gambling at the Dawn of the National League* (Jefferson, NC: McFarland, 2005), and John Thorn, *Baseball in the Garden of Eden: The Secret History of the Early Game* (New York: Simon and Schuster, 2011), 165–69.

37. *Episcopal Register* of Philadelphia, quoted in *Christian Union*, July 30, 1870, 52.

38. Quoted in Albert Goodwill Spalding, *America's National Game: Historic Facts Concerning the Beginning, Evolution, Development and Popularity of Baseball* (New York: American Sports Publishing Company, 1911), 211.

39. Numerous baseball scholars have examined the development of baseball and the role of gambling, as well as the formation of the National League. Two good books that discuss gambling and baseball are Charles C. Alexander, *Our Game: An American Baseball History* (New York: Henry Holt, 1991), and Harold Seymour, *Baseball: The Early Years* (New York: Oxford University Press, 1960).

40. *Chicago Daily Tribune*, November 3, 1877.

41. In addition to the *Louisville Courier-Journal*, other newspapers carrying the story included the *New York Times*, *Chicago Daily Tribune*, *Boston Daily Globe*, *Atlanta Constitution*, and *St. Louis Dispatch*. The *Courier-Journal* reporter who played a major role in helping expose the scandal was John Haldeman, son of Walter N. Haldeman, the Grays president, who also held a substantial stake in the paper.

42. Daniel A. Nathan's *Saying It's So: A Cultural History of the Black Sox Scandal* (Urbana: University of Illinois Press, 2002) provides a good discussion of the scandal and explores its lasting significance.

43. Among the sources detailing the aforementioned scandals are Susan Ware, *Game, Set, Match: Billie Jean King and the Revolution in Women's Sports* (Chapel Hill: University of North Carolina Press, 2011); Nanette Burstein, dir., *The Price of Gold*, ESPN Films, 2014 (which details the Tonya Harding–Nancy Kerrigan scandal); Stephen Wenn, Robert Barney, and Scott Martyn, *Tarnished Rings: The International Olympic Committee and the Salt Lake City Bid Scandal* (Syracuse, NY: Syracuse University Press, 2011); and Mark Fainaru-Wada and Steve Fainaru, *League of Denial: The NFL, Concussions, and the Battle for Truth* (New York: Crown Archetype, 2013). Newspapers and popular serials extensively covered all four scandals.

"Ambassadors in Short Pants"

Sport and the Cold Warriors

Rita Liberti

Throughout the 1950s, in the face of a rising Soviet Union, the United States expanded its arsenal to include sport as a weapon in a broad propaganda campaign to assert its political and moral supremacy among nations. Propagandizing popular culture became an important avenue for the United States in its overall strategy to win the "hearts and minds" of people around the globe, especially in light of the volatile risks involved in military engagement with the Soviets. American sport and international athletic competitions became highly visible and important aspects of U.S. strategy. Athletes, in turn, became key symbols of this expansive cultural "Cold War." Whether they liked it or not, *Newsweek* noted in the run-up to the 1960 Rome Olympics, athletes were "pawn[s] in a hot athletic war that is a phase of this country's cold political war."[1]

Far more than merely athletes and athletic contests, the games, especially those on an international stage, were thought to represent something of greater significance. For some, achievement and success in the athletic arena symbolized a set of values, a way of being and as such became "the most immediate, confrontational and viscerally resonant points of nationalist engagement."[2] American athletic victories on the worldwide stage represented the strength and omnipotence of political and economic systems, namely democracy and capitalism respectively.

41

Sport's place as a tool used by the United States as part of a larger scale cultural Cold War plan is a fascinating one to share and explore with students for a variety of reasons. Such discussions reinforce broader critical understandings of the ways in which popular culture has long been politicized. There is certainly plenty of culture at work in sport, and the Cold War era affords us any number of angles to explore how national identity was constructed in and through sport. For those teaching American history courses, the topic of sport makes an excellent addition to units on "Cold War Culture," illuminating the extent to which the specter of the "Soviet Menace" affected all aspects of everyday life.

Equally compelling and worthy of classroom attention are the historically significant intersections of the Cold War and racial politics of the period. The experiences of African American athletes who represented the United States abroad provide illuminating angles on sport and government propaganda. Of course, historical narratives on particular topics never occur in isolation, and sport in that mid-twentieth-century moment shines a bright light on this reality. Discussions, for example, about Cold War politics internationally and racial injustice domestically can be incredibly valuable sites for students to engage history's complexity and its richness.

Football in the Cold War

In my classes we begin by examining some of the domestic components of sport and the Cold War. For many in the United States no specific sport epitomized American uniqueness, strength, and values more than the game of football. College football, more precisely, was an important site through which Cold War politics were put on display. As critics charged that America (and Americans) had grown "soft" and that this vulnerability risked our supremacy among nations, football provided a strong, very public counter to those arguments. Saturday afternoon autumn football spectacles were shared by tens of thousands in stadiums around the country and millions more via the relatively new medium of television. Not only did the game foster a particular kind of masculine expression, it also symbolized American technological superiority and economic prosperity.[3]

I find it instructive to have students use primary source material to explore the role that football played in helping a nation construct a Cold War identity. Fortunately, there is no shortage of material for students to review and analyze. The Cold War was "fought" at the level of culture, and any number of examples from mainstream news reports and periodicals attest to this reality. Here, I offer a few of the narrative excerpts I have used in class. I generally lead with a few prompts for students to consider prior to engaging with peers. Included among my guiding questions: How were notions of masculinity defined by the authors? How would you articulate the connections among men, masculinity, football, and nation as described by the authors? I find students' observations often lead to robust discussions about nationhood, sport, and gender.

A sampling of the prompts I use includes:

Football is the most competitive of sports. Its teamwork, its ruggedness, its Spartan spirit, a throwback to our pioneering ancestry, all have tremendous appeal to our basic American characteristics. (UCLA Professor Joseph Kaplan, 1956)[4]

In football, in business, in politics, in the trades, professions and the arts, the normal urge to excel provides one of the most hopeful assurances that our kind of society will continue to advance and prosper. (President Dwight D. Eisenhower, 1958)[5]

[Football is a] vital force in the life of the nation, developing the rugged virtues and tough leadership qualities indispensable for the survival of a free world menaced by a ruthless and conspiratorial tyranny. (*New York Times* reporter Allison Danzig, 1958)[6]

Except for war, there is nothing in American life which trains a boy better for life than football. There can be no substitute for football. (Attorney General Robert Kennedy, 1961)[7]

Beyond these narratives slices I find it useful for students to look at materials that situate football more broadly within a particular primary source. The magazine *Sports Illustrated* provides one such collection at their *SI Vault* site, an archive of every issue of their weekly publication from its beginning in mid-1954.[8] The site is easy to navigate, as are the thousands of individual issues in the collection. It is an excellent source for any number of classroom topics from the mid-twentieth century on, including the Cold War.

As Jeffrey Montez de Oca argues, the place of *Sports Illustrated* in helping to construct a seamless narrative between football and national identity is an important one, especially during the early Cold War. Aided by technological and transportation advances in the post–World War II era, sports in the United States moved in emphasis from local and regional affiliation/concentration to a national athletic scene. *Sports Illustrated* worked to encourage the many sports fans across the country to see their local team loyalties as part of a national athletic landscape. This turn toward sport as a national brand blended well with, and underscored, Cold War rhetoric around nationhood and unity.

There are several *Sports Illustrated* publications between 1954 and 1956 that I ask students to analyze.[9] In each, *Sports Illustrated* details the various athletic conferences by region, and uses figures and illustrations to map these athletic regions onto an outline of the United States, thus fortifying football's relationship to the country as a whole. I ask students to consider the overt militaristic overtones present in the narratives as well as the ways in which football is romanticized in each publication. There is so much material to share that you may want to be a bit selective, depending on class time constraints.

The September 24, 1956, issue, which contains more than forty pages of text about that year's college football season, offers an especially rich example. Under the heading "The Autumn Battleground," and with an illustration that includes warring cowboys and Native Americans, the main article begins with a literal bang: "Like the opening shot at Fort Sumter, the arrival of the autumnal equinox . . . brings violent fraternal strife. The nation divides into its hostile enclaves—empires turbulent with internecine warfare but which frequently unite against the enemy across the border." Still, the author is quick to note that despite regional differences and other tensions (commercialism, for example) the essence of the sport transcends distinctions. "But, north, south, east, and west, the first crash of band music, the first sustained roar from the packed stadiums will herald again a wonderful time of the year." Football, the magazine reminds us, "is a symbol of romance to Americans [who] cannot sit in stadiums . . . without a reaction, somewhere in their souls, to its legends . . . the storied halfbacks who won the game and the girl and lived happily ever after."[10]

Sports Illustrated's efforts to use football in helping to create a national sport market were, arguably, about selling more magazines. But it is important that we aid students in understanding that far more was involved. The magazine's hyperbolic entries on football present an idealized, romantic notion of the game, one in which the idea of what it was to be an American was tightly bound to the sport itself. Athletics, then, did not simply reflect the patterns of the broader society. Rather, sports helped create and reinforce Cold War values and ways of seeing the nation and the world. This certainly is not unique to the Cold War moment, but that reality is vividly on display in the decade or two after World War II.

At some point during our discussions of the Cold War and American football, I start a general conversation about militaristic imagery and rhetoric in the game. I have found these exchanges very helpful in assisting students to better make sense of the deep relationship between football and war during the Cold War era and beyond. Military metaphors abound in football—and have long been a part of the game's history—providing another entry point for a larger discussion about sport and Cold War politics. Football terminology such as "throwing a bomb," "fighting in the trenches," "blitzes," and "enemy territory," are but a few illustrations of the game's connections to militarization, and by extension, particular understandings of masculinity and nation.

Sport and National Identity

Of course, it is athletic competition at the international level that provides some of the most explicit and powerful examples of sport's place within the cultural Cold War, especially in the first two decades following World War II. A nation's superiority, it seemed to supporters, could be confirmed with every victory on the various courts and athletic fields of competition. Sport served an important role for the United States in creating an image of itself and how it wished to be seen by other nations around the globe.

Interestingly, national identity and what it meant to be an American was constructed in opposition to what we believed we were not. Sport and international competition was a primary site in which Russia and its athletic endeavors were created and represented as evil by U.S. strategists and supporters. Often constructed as a strict binary, Russian evil was cast against all that was good, with American sports a prominent example in making the larger case to the world. Again, primary source material from the mainstream periodical press is voluminous on the topic, but perhaps my favorite in spurring student interest is a *U.S.*

News & World Report article from 1954. The three-page article, "Reds Hope to Rule Sports Too," offers up possible explanations for Russian dominance in international sporting competition.[11] Ironically, the piece becomes the very propaganda it claims is so centrally characteristic of the Russians, a point that students are eager to make.

The five excerpts that follow highlight the points around which our discussion of the article flows.

Soviet Russia is pushing a worldwide sports offensive with a calculated goal: Victory over everybody—but most of all over the United States—in the 1956 Olympic games at Melbourne.

In Russia, sports is a big, grim, production-line business, run from grade school to Olympic track by the supercoach, the state.

Russians can't relax anywhere. Even in their continuous round of "friendly" competition within the satellite states, they have to win.

This practice of phony, full-pay jobs for full-time athletes raises the question of the amateur status of Soviet competitors in Olympic contests.

Outside Russia, touring Red teams have been kept under close wraps. Coaches, trainers, physicians, political supervisors, and plain guards, with obvious pistol bulges under their coats, watch their every movement.

Students are asked to consider how these clips and the article more generally described the Russians, their athletes, and supposed approach to sport. Understandings of Russian sport as professional, overly competitive, and noncreative or enjoyable blend seamlessly within larger constructions of the country and its people (not just athletes) as voiceless automatons.

The Cold War and African American Athletes

As I mentioned near the top of this chapter, American racial politics and prejudices in the early years of the Cold War provide some of the most exciting conversations with students about propagandizing culture. African American athletes' participation and success in sport, especially on an international stage, served an important function as part of the larger U.S. Cold War strategy. For the United States, eager to define itself to the world as open and democratic, African American athletes were important characters in telling not just any story but a particular story about the racial progress and equality that supposedly became possible within a democracy.

By midcentury, African American athletes excelled in a variety of sports. Given the many ideological and structural forms of racism that existed, much of what African Americans accomplished in their rise to the most elite levels of sport was achieved within segregated institutions and spaces. By the 1950s long-established sporting opportunities across Historically Black Colleges and Universities (HBCUs), community leagues, and other associations in basketball, tennis, and track fostered some of the best athletic talent in the nation and the world. Some of these African American stars were used as cultural Cold Warriors whose successes were used to prop up mythical narratives about democracy and equality for all.

A 1955 article in the *American Mercury* offers one example of the propagandistic use of African American athletic success. Here, the magazine sang the praises of the all-black basketball team, the Harlem Globetrotters, as they took their athletic and comedic skills abroad. "The Communists," the periodical noted, "have chirped that America persecutes minorities, Negroes actually aren't free, and U.S. athletes are boorish national heroes. But the Globetrotters are gentlemanly, well-dressed, obviously happy and prosperous, and coached by a member of another minority group [Jewish], 54-year-old Abe Saperstein." They were, the writer concluded, "diplomats deluxe—our Ambassadors in Short Pants."

In 1953 the Eisenhower administration's creation of the United States Information Agency (USIA) reflected a significant increase in efforts to shape international opinion of the United States. The agency exported U.S. culture abroad through film, cultural exchange programs, radio reports, books, and other artifacts. African American athletes soon became part of the USIA's arsenal. In the late 1950s and early 1960s, for example, the USIA produced three films that featured African American athletes, each film a slight variation on a similar theme of the achievement and success made possible by American democracy. The films *Althea Gibson: Tennis Champion* (1957), *Wilma Rudolph: Olympic Champion* (1961), and *The Rafer Johnson Story* (1961) were created by the

Tennis great Althea Gibson in 1956. (New York World-Telegram and Sun photo by Fred Palumbo, Library of Congress, Prints & Photographs Division)

agency to be shown only to audiences beyond the United States. Copies are available through the National Archives.[12]

Given their content and length (Gibson and Rudolph's films are approximately ten minutes each; Johnson's is thirty minutes) any or all of the three films are excellent for classroom use. Each of the documentaries rests on a set of shared tropes. The success stories of Gibson, Rudolph, and Johnson, all born into humble beginnings, perpetuated the propaganda that athletic talent nurtured within a free society afforded opportunity for all. While the United States did not necessarily deny the existence of racial oppression, these film reels reinforce the government's position that progress on racial inequality was a forward-moving force. Nonetheless, they completely avoid the harsh realities of ongoing injustice. The images of the three athletes were especially significant in the Cold War context because of the contrast they provided to stories and images of the growing civil rights movement in which

African Americans were disenfranchised and dramatically brutalized. Discussing these more general patterns as they relate to the films is important ground to cover before guiding students to a more critical close reading of film specifics.

I teach *Wilma Rudolph: Olympic Champion* within a larger discussion about Cold War sport and the politics of race within the United States. My approach is to have the class first view the film with simply a general question or two as guide prompts. For example: What is the main message you think the U.S. government wished to promote to international audiences? Said slightly differently: What lessons or ideas are viewers encouraged to take away after watching this film? Follow-up discussions are usually lively, with students eager to share their observations about these general questions as well as make more specific comments about the film. We then watch the short film again. Beforehand, I assign a specific prompt to each of several small groups. Here are two possible directions:

(1) Have students take note of the specific scenes in which white people appear in the film. From what they can tell, who are these people and what are their relationships to Rudolph? In discussion, students should be encouraged to think about race, power, and the implicit messages in the many scenes in which whites pay homage to the African American track star: fans/spectators by the thousands greet Rudolph; she meets with President John F. Kennedy; and her hometown officials welcome her. How do these storylines reinforce the larger narrative that government officials wished to communicate to audiences worldwide, not just about Rudolph but the status of race relations in the United States?

(2) Ask other students to pay attention to the structures (buildings, arenas, etc.) they see in the film. Admittedly, this sounds a bit odd at first. But you can remind students of the American desire to be seen as an advanced society in terms of technology and material wealth. During the short film, viewers are introduced to Rudolph, as well as her life at Tennessee State (a historically black college), and in the United States more generally. Shots of the campus show multiple images of large, brick structures whose grounds are manicured and neatly kept. The sleek, modern lines of the student union, gymnasium, dormitories, president's residence, and various other academic buildings convey an affluence free of struggle and austerity. Other

visual images include Nashville skyscrapers and enormous athletic arenas from around the country.

What remains out of focus, of course, is the reality of a system of white supremacy that gave rise to a separate and unequal existence for African Americans across the nation, including at Tennessee State. You can ask students to consider how the structures depicted in the film underscore American claims of superiority while whitewashing racial inequality and injustice.[13]

Students need to understand that these discourses were far from monolithic. It is crucial that we expose them to a range of voices and perspectives, some of which did not share this dominant view of African American athletes as Cold Warriors. Athletes often resisted becoming part of the standard narrative. The star high jumper Rose Robinson turned down offers to join State Department trips, and also refused to stand for the national anthem at the 1959 Pan Am Games. Other athletes, including Wilma Rudolph, used other strategies to undercut State Department narratives (see Grundy and Liberti, "Black Women Face Obstacles and Opportunities").[14]

Looking at coverage in the nation's robust black press is one of the best ways to examine this resistance. African American publications such as the *Chicago Tribune, New York Age, Pittsburgh Courier, Baltimore Afro-American, Philadelphia Tribune*, and *Atlanta Daily World* certainly spoke with pride about the athletic success of African American athletes. But journalists in the black press also used the opportunity to address racial injustice. These narratives deepen our students' understanding of power and resistance and should find their way into our classrooms.

In the days just after the 1960 Rome Olympics, for example, the *Atlanta Daily World* noted that the American team's performance would have been stronger if it "had a few more Rafer Johnsons and Wilma Rudolphs, Negro Americans." The writer went on to argue that the Soviets were athletically superior to the American athletes because competitors were recruited from the nation's entire population, not simply a fraction of its youth, as was the case in the United States. Limiting African American opportunities ultimately limited U.S. strength. "Just as [the U.S.] gave Russia the advantage at Rome, she is giving Russia the advantage all along the line. How late do the Negro-phobes think it is? Russia is currently too strong to be outdone by our country's nine-tenths."[15]

At the level of culture, sport was, in essence, an important piece of the larger U.S. Cold War strategy to promote democracy and the American way of life. Despite the widely held belief that sport is apolitical and divorced from broader tensions, this has never been the case. While there are many valuable lessons to be learned from studying sport and the Cold War, these discussions also help students understand the deeply politicized spaces that sport continues to occupy in more contemporary moments. The value of that realization cannot be understated, especially given its prominent place across our country and around the world.[16]

Notes

1. "Men–Medals–Marxism," *Newsweek*, August 9, 1960, 79. See also Al Balk, "Ambassadors in Short Pants," *American Mercury*, December 1955, 66–68.

2. Stephen Wagg and David L. Andrews, "Introduction: War Minus the Shooting?" in *East Plays West: Sport and the Cold War*, ed. Stephen Wagg and David L. Andrews (London: Routledge, 2007), 3.

3. Kurt Edward Kemper, *College Football and American Culture in the Cold War Era* (Urbana: University of Illinois Press, 2009), 21.

4. Joseph Kaplan, "The Case for Big-Time Football," *Look*, December 12, 1956, 111.

5. "Eisenhower Receives Award," *New York Times*, October 29, 1958, 40.

6. Allison Danzig, "Sports of the Times: Men with Missions," *New York Times*, February 28, 1958, 24.

7. Kennedy quoted in Kemper, *College Football and American Culture*, 25.

8. The *Sports Illustrated* vault can be found at https://www.si.com/vault.

9. The idea for this classroom exercise originated with Jeffrey Montez de Oca's work *Discipline and Indulgence: College Football, Media, and the American Way of Life during the Cold War* (New Brunswick, NJ: Rutgers University Press, 2013), 93–112. For specific issues, see October 4, 1954; November 15, 1954; and September 24, 1956.

10. *Sports Illustrated*, September 24, 1956, 31.

11. "Reds Hope to Rule Sports Too," *U.S. News & World Report*, August 20, 1954, 35–37.

12. All three films are housed in the National Archives at College Park, Maryland. For more information on *Wilma Rudolph: Olympic Champion*, see https://catalog.archives.gov/id/51465. Information on *Althea Gibson* can be found at https://catalog.archives.gov/id/49457. Finally, details on *The Rafer Johnson Story* can be found at https://catalog.archives.gov/id/52435.

13. For more ideas about critical approaches and topics to cover in these

films see Rita Liberti and Maureen M. Smith, *(Re)Presenting Wilma Rudolph* (Syracuse, NY: Syracuse University Press, 2015), 83–87; Melinda M. Schwenk, "'Negro Stars' and the USIA's Portrait of Democracy," *Race, Gender and Class* 4, no. 4 (2001): 116–39.

14. Dave Zirin and Amira Rose Davis, "Uncovering the Hidden Resistance History of Black Women Athletes," *Nation*, May 21, 2018, thenation.com/article/uncovering-the-hidden-resistance-history-of-black-women-athletes/ (accessed September 3, 2018).

15. Dean Gordon B. Hancock, "Between the Lines: Ten-Tenths versus Nine-Tenths," *Atlanta Daily World*, September 30, 1960, 4. Other examples worthy of note include Frances Walters, "Hail Olympic Winners," *Baltimore Afro-American*, September 24, 1960, 4; Marion E. Jackson, "Sports of the World," *Atlanta Daily World*, September 15, 1960, 6.

16. One additional comment on source material is worthy of note. The Wilson Center's collection of nearly three-dozen podcasts of sport and Cold War–related topics and issues is an excellent site of secondary source material. The resource includes a wide range of sport and Cold War topics. See https://www.wilsoncenter.org/article/the-global-history-sport-the-cold-war.

The Shifting Geography of Professional Sports

Brad Austin

The 2016 fall semester was a fascinating time to teach a modern American history survey class, as the drama of unfolding events made conversations about historical trends and themes seem incredibly relevant. I will never forget the class discussion we had in Sullivan Building, Room 109, the November day after the seemingly impossible happened—an outcome no one had foreseen. Given my students' confusion, I decided to take a pedagogical risk and devote an entire class to detailing my personal allegiances and the historical forces that I believed had helped create them. I also challenged my students to think about their own commitments and why they held them—why they felt they were aligned with the "good guys" while their opponents were "evil." At the end of the class, I'm confident that most of my Massachusetts students disagreed with me (a white man, raised in the rural South). But I hope they understood my positions and my passions better.

I write, of course, not about the presidential election but about the day after the Chicago Cubs completed an astonishing comeback from a 1–3 deficit to win the World Series from the Cleveland Indians, and how I tried to explain to explain my Cubs devotion to my Red Sox–loving students.

My veneration of Andre Dawson, my frustration with Leon Durham, and my continued gratitude to Rick Sutcliffe was partially personal and partially structural. As I explained to my class, in 1984 I was living in

53

Martin, Tennessee, and was too young to ride my bike across town by myself. The Cubs were surprisingly good and still playing most of their games during the day. I spent a lot of time in the company of the legendary Cubs announcer Harry Carey, as he narrated games and I waited for a ride to the town pool. After detailing my entry into rabid sports fandom, I turned to an explanation borrowed heavily from Walter LaFeber's argument in *Michael Jordan and the New Global Capitalism*—an explanation focused on the expansion of satellite technology in the 1970s and the creation of "superstations."[1] For me, the most important factors in my Cub fandom were the existence of WGN, the primary broadcaster of Cubs games, and the absence of many regional competitors for my affection.

The conversation also drew on Bruce Schulman's *The Seventies*, a book the students were already reading. In this accessible volume, Schulman discusses the importance of the dramatic demographic shifts that transformed the American landscape in the decades after World War II. He offers an especially provocative and convincing argument about the "Southernization" of American culture, as seen in the influence of the southern and western "Sunbelt" on American politics, culture, and economic development.[2]

While I correctly guessed that my students would be entertained by seeing old pictures of me in my authentic Ryan Sandburg jersey, and that they might be somewhat interested in my recounting of the greatness of the 1984 Cubs and the unfulfilled promise of the 1989 team, it quickly became clear to everyone that this was not just a "fun day" when the students didn't have to learn "real" history. Instead, our conversation ranged from the little-understood importance of technology and media platforms (satellites, WGN, ESPN, streaming, etc.) to the expansion (and sometimes contraction) of professional sports leagues, and to the increasing importance of NASCAR, hockey, and college football as "national" sports. As I later reflected on the class, I realized that I should have planned on having this discussion instead of just stumbling into it.

Demographic data as seen in the footprints of major sports leagues offers an excellent way to teach students about some of the major themes in modern American history. One of my favorite sources for sparking discussion and critical thinking about geographic growth is the U.S. Census Bureau's lists of the most populated American cities. I love to have my students chart the rise of Chicago from being the ninety-second largest American city in 1840 (4,470 residents) to the second largest in 1900 (1,698,575). Drawing on William Cronon's masterful *Nature's Metropolis*, I ask students to connect the "Second City's" rise to specific aspects of the American railroad system, to Chicago's emergence as the center of a vast regional network of commodities and commerce, and to a variety of other factors.[3]

To help my students understand the scale and impact of Chicago's explosive growth, I ask them what it would mean if our university expanded from approximately 7,000 undergraduates to 500,000 over the next forty years. We consider what would cause such an expansion and then speculate on its implications. They almost immediately make jokes about parking (not usually a laughing matter on our campus). They also discuss the challenge of keeping up with infrastructure demands, the ramifications for social life, and the effects on the surrounding areas, including the environment. We brainstorm about what the university might need to do in order to establish a sense of community and common purpose, to bind a rapidly expanding and largely anonymous student population together. Inevitably, the students propose sports teams as a potential source of unity.

Demography and Geography

In the 1920s and 1930s, millions of Americans left their home regions for opportunities around the country—a process that accelerated with the mobilization for World War II. Most migrants left rural areas in the nation's interior for industrial centers on the East Coast, in the upper Midwest, and on the West Coast. Some Gulf Coast areas also saw rapid growth. These patterns continued after the war, as Americans who had traveled across the country and the globe finally settled in new areas. Thanks in part to the advent of air conditioning, the postwar period also saw the emergence of the powerful "Sunbelt" region, which stretched from Southern California, across Arizona and Texas, and the through the old Confederacy. The demographic explosion known as the "Baby Boom" sparked further expansion. In the words of the historians George Donelson Moss and Evan Thomas, "Americans in the 1950s were the richest, healthiest, and most mobile generation ever. By the millions, people poured into the South, the

Southwest, and the West."[4] Studying the connections between these transformative changes and the sporting landscape can help students visualize trends that were vital to American life but which can be difficult to render interesting in the classroom.

Overall, the American population numbered about 150 million in 1950. Only fifty years later, the nation's population had doubled. As the earlier example of Chicago illustrates, such rapid growth almost always generates profound shifts in how a society functions. Americans living in the postwar era would soon discover that sports teams could relocate just as easily as individuals, and they would live to see a "franchise boom" that mirrored the general population expansion. Helping students explore franchise relocations and the expansion of the number of "major league" cities can reveal a great deal about American life in this period in a lively and engaging manner.

Big League Towns

Our students have grown up in a world where Nashville can compete for a Stanley Cup and where Oklahoma City now hosts the basketball team that used to be the Seattle Supersonics. But it wasn't always this way. For most of the twentieth century, professional sports were isolated in the Northeast and the industrial Midwest. This made perfect sense. After disabusing students of the myth that Abner Doubleday invented baseball in Cooperstown, New York (see Heaphy, "Baseball and American Exceptionalism"), teachers might consider asking students to map the locations of the clubs that made up the National and American Leagues in the early 1900s. They'll soon find that the National League (formed in 1876) had teams located in Brooklyn (an independent city until 1898), Chicago, Philadelphia, Cincinnati, Boston, New York, Cleveland, St. Louis, and Pittsburgh. When the American League assumed its status as a "Major League" in the early 1900s, it had teams in Chicago, Boston, Detroit, Philadelphia, Baltimore, Washington, Cleveland, and Milwaukee. By 1903, these leagues' champions were facing off in an annual "World Series." Given the geographic concentration of their teams, however, it was an American regional championship at best.

Examining the 1900 census records will reveal that of the ten largest cities in the United States, eight were represented by baseball clubs (New York, Chicago, Philadelphia, St. Louis, Boston, Baltimore, Cincinnati, and Cleveland). Several of these cities had multiple teams. Only Buffalo (eighth largest) and San Francisco (ninth largest) lacked teams. While our students might have questions about why Buffalo was excluded (a conversation that should lead them to recognize the fading importance of water transportation and the Erie Canal), they will quickly surmise that San Francisco was without a Major League team for logistical reasons. By the 1950s, however, a West Coast population boom, combined with technological and transportation advances, would provide ample incentives to overcome those challenges.

Go West, Young [Boys of Summer]

By 1950, the geographic scope of Major League Baseball had expanded only a little. New York had three teams (Yankees, Giants, and Dodgers); Chicago had two teams (Cubs and White Sox); Boston had two (Red Sox and Braves); Philadelphia had two (A's and Phillies); St. Louis had two (Cardinals and Browns). Cincinnati and Cleveland had one each, as did Detroit and Pittsburgh. Only Washington, DC, had broken into the "Big League" city club with the addition of the Senators. Professional baseball was still dominated by northeastern and, to a lesser extent, midwestern clubs.

Over the next couple of decades, however, the "national game" would finally establish a national footprint. A great way to illustrate the growing power and importance of California as an economic and population center is to explore how and why New York (including the Dodgers' Brooklyn), with a 1950 population of 7.8 million and three highly successful teams, would in one year lose two of those teams to the West Coast cities of Los Angeles and San Francisco, with populations of 1.97 million and 775,000, respectively.

The Dodgers and the Giants weren't the first teams to move. Earlier in the decade two struggling teams had relocated, fleeing the shadows of more successful intracity rivals and seeking new markets. In 1953, the St. Louis Browns moved to Baltimore and the Boston Braves relocated to Milwaukee. The next year, the Philadelphia Athletics moved to Kansas City. While all of these moves upset local fan bases, none of them dramatically transformed the competitive landscape or substantially expanded the geographic footprint of the major leagues.

The 1957 moves of the Dodgers to Los Angeles and the Giants to San Francisco were a different matter altogether. Most people grudgingly understood why the Giants' owner, Horace Stoneham, would take advantage of improvements in air transportation, which had reduced the trip from California to the East Coast to less than six hours, in order to vacate the antiquated Polo Grounds for a brand-new, publicly financed stadium in San Francisco's Candlestick Park. Fewer were willing to excuse Walter O'Malley's decision to uproot Brooklyn's beloved Dodgers and move them to Los Angeles. New York City leaders had refused to accede to O'Malley's demand for a taxpayer-funded stadium with 12,000 parking spaces (the Dodgers' aging Ebbets Field had only 700, a dramatically inadequate number in an era when Americans relied increasingly on cars for transportation). O'Malley then turned to Los Angeles, whose officials were more than willing to facilitate the move and to finance a new stadium. After a couple of years playing in the LA Coliseum, in which they won the 1955 World Series in front of average home crowds of 90,000, the Dodgers moved to their new home in Chavez Ravine, complete with stunning views, 52,000 seats, and 24,000 parking spots. It was the quintessential architectural embodiment of the new American sporting landscape.[5]

While there are plenty of textual primary sources available that can help students understand the arguments for and against these franchise moves (the *New York Times* archive, available online, is especially useful), this is one of those stories where video gives teachers a variety of pedagogical options. Ken Burns's groundbreaking *Baseball* documentary devotes almost an entire episode to the Dodgers' and Giants' moves. The episode uses abundant contemporary footage and is effective for classroom use. The website associated with the documentary also has a Teachers' Resource page with additional ideas about for a "mapping baseball" lesson.

Creating timelines and maps to chart baseball's expansion and relocation throughout a U.S. history course is an interesting exercise. If you do not want to commit to such an involved and time-consuming process, however, the blogger Andrew Clem has created a fantastic resource that provides essential background information and a series of maps that document the locations of teams across eight eras of baseball history.[6] Teachers can use this resource to help students visualize the expanding spectrum of "major league cities" and invite them to speculate about the relationships between the relocations and expansions and broader developments in American history.

While the relocation of the Brooklyn Dodgers is probably the most famous, and the most consistently lamented, franchise move, it is certainly not the only important one. Throughout the 1950s and 1960s, other "second" teams in cities relocated, looking to be the number one draw in new cities and to take advantage of underserved population centers. As mentioned earlier, the Boston Braves saw an opportunity to stop sharing a city with the Red Sox and moved to Milwaukee in 1953. In 1966, the franchise again uprooted in search of new markets, and the Braves went to Georgia, settling in Atlanta. The team's recent move from downtown Atlanta to a nearby suburb might also be worth considering, especially as part of an exploration of the financial incentives and complicated racial politics of "white flight" in the modern South.

By the mid-1980s, the Atlanta version of the Braves challenged the St. Louis Cardinals as the most popular team in the South. The Cardinals had spent decades as Major League Baseball's southernmost team, with games carried by radio stations across the region. But Ted Turner owned both the Braves and the Turner Broadcasting Network, a new, satellite-supported cable television "superstation" that needed programming to fill its airwaves for much of the summer. The resulting omnipresence of the Braves in the southern popular culture of the 1980s and 1990s was captured in 1995 when the country singer Tim McGraw (son of star pitcher Tug McGraw) had the protagonist of "I Like It, I Love it" document his devotion to his girlfriend by pointing out that he "ain't seen the Braves play a game all year." As a seemingly reflexive contrarian in my formative years, I became a fan of the "other" super-station-supported team, the Cubs.

Other Leagues

While baseball remains a regionally popular sport, with sky-high local ratings for television broadcasts, it is not the most popular national sport these days. Consequently, teachers may prefer to use other leagues to spark discussions of economic, technological, cultural, and population shifts. The growth and expansion of the National Football League (NFL) and the National Hockey League (NHL) both offer ample evidence for classes to consider.

Once again, I advise teachers to use U.S. census data to prep their students for this discussion. Probably the best tool for this stage of the conversation is a chart titled "Distribution of the 10, 25, 50, and 100 Largest Urban Places, by Section and Subsection of the United States: 1790-1990."[7] (If students can't get excited about something with that title, then what hope do we have, right?) While the title seems unnecessarily bureaucratic even for a government document, the numbers are pretty revealing, and it's useful to have them all in one place. I have my students chart the relative rise and decline of different regions from 1940 to 1990, using the "50 largest cities" chart. Doing this draws their attention to the fact that the North had 27 of the 50 largest cities in 1940 (11 in the Northeast and 16 in the North Central), but only 17 of the largest 50 by the 1990s (five in the Northeast, and 12 in the North Central).

If the North lost ten spots in the top fifty, then other regions much have gained. By exploring the table, my students learn that the West gained eight of those slots and that the South claimed the other two. Students who take a close look at the census data from each decade between 1950 and 2000 will witness the transformation of cities such as Dallas, Houston, Atlanta, Phoenix, San Diego, Denver, and other relatively minor outposts into major population centers. You can choose to do this with your students before or after a discussion of national demographic shifts, league expansion, and franchise relocation; it works equally well as a preview or a review exercise.

The NFL is the most popular and powerful sports league in the United States. The day of its championship game, Super Bowl Sunday, functions as a secular national holiday, and television coverage of its draft can generate higher ratings than playoff games for many other sports. The league, however, was not always such a powerhouse.

The NFL began in 1921 in the small industrial cities of the Ohio Valley and the greater Midwest. With franchises in Portsmouth, Marion, and Canton, Ohio, as well as in such hot spots as Decatur, Illinois, and Green Bay, Wisconsin, it was not certain that the fledging league would survive the Great Depression, much less become a national juggernaut. By the early 1940s, though, owners had established franchises in New York, Chicago (relocated from Decatur), Philadelphia, Detroit, Pittsburgh, and Washington, DC, and the league was well positioned for the prosperous years and new media environment that would emerge in the 1950s and 1960s. After fighting off a challenge from the rival All-American Football Conference, moving increasingly toward positional specialization and opening up the rule book to encourage more open, pass-friendly offenses, the NFL put itself in a great position to take advantage of the growing power that television wielded over American life.[8]

A challenge from another upstart league, the American Football League (AFL), expanded professional football's reach. The twenty-seven-year-old Lamar Hunt, whose family had grown wealthy in the Texas oil industry, led the push for the new league after NFL owners rejected his attempt to move an NFL franchise to Dallas. The AFL attracted investors from other non-NFL cities (Denver, Houston, and Minneapolis) and sought its own television deal with ABC. In response to the AFL threat, the NFL created new franchises in Dallas and Minnesota and appointed a new commissioner, Pete Rozelle, who would become the most successful sports commissioner in American history. Rozelle moved the league headquarters to New York's Park Avenue, just a few blocks from the advertising and broadcasting centers of the world, and paved the way for the NFL's lucrative and long-standing partnerships with television networks.[9]

In 1964, after the AFL established its legitimacy and its ability to threaten the NFL with its own lucrative television deal, the two leagues began merger talks. When the details of the agreement emerged, it was clear that the NFL would finally be truly "national." The ten AFL teams became part of the NFL, which also added a New Orleans franchise to encourage Louisiana senators and congressmen to vote for a desired antitrust exemption. The expanded league, whose twenty-six teams included franchises in western and southern markets such as Oakland, San Diego, Houston, Miami, and Denver, decided to schedule a championship game between the representatives of the rival leagues (called "conferences" after 1970), and the Super Bowl was born.

This (abbreviated) history of the emergence of the NFL can be used to highlight a variety of topics in twentieth-century American history, ranging from the significance of midwestern industrial cities in the 1910s and 1920s to the power of television to create new cultural touchstones in the 1960s and beyond. It also reflects the larger demographic shifts highlighted earlier.[10] Discussing the league's expansion west and south, along with the importance of oil men and marketing experts, is a great way to connect the cultural importance of the emerging car culture and the rise of television to other developments in modern American history.

The National Hockey League

The National Hockey League (NHL) provides a similar narrative. The league began in Montreal, Canada, in 1917, and all of its original teams were Canadian. In 1924, the Boston Bruins became the first American NHL team; within two years, six of the league's ten teams resided in the United States. By 1942, after a decade of Depression and the onset of World War II, only six cities remained in the league: Boston, Montreal, Toronto, Chicago, Detroit, and New York. These so-called "original six" constituted the entire league from 1942 to 1967. At that point, the "National" Hockey League (which was both international and restricted to the northeastern region of North America) had an especially misleading name, simultaneously too broad and too narrow.

This changed dramatically over the next three decades. In 1967, the NHL added six U.S. teams: Oakland, Los Angeles, Minnesota, Philadelphia, Pittsburgh, and St. Louis. Teams in Buffalo, Vancouver, Atlanta, Kansas City, and Washington, DC followed shortly thereafter. After a 1979 merger with the World Hockey Association, the league added teams in Winnipeg, Edmonton, Quebec, and Hartford. In 1980, the Atlanta team moved to Calgary. In 1997, following a period of calm, the Hartford Whalers left Connecticut for North Carolina, and the Quebec Nordiques relocated to Denver. New franchises in Tampa Bay, Anaheim, Miami, San Jose, Phoenix, Nashville, Minnesota, Columbus, Atlanta, and, most recently, Las Vegas, highlight the league's shift to the United States, and to the nation's new economic and cultural centers (places where many northerners with hockey roots had already transplanted).[11]

For classroom history teachers, it can be easy to get caught up in the personal narratives of history's protagonists and antagonists, to emphasize the eloquent words and displays of heroism or villainy that helped shape history. While there is definitely a place for those conversations, we also need to put individual decisions in the context of broad cultural and demographic shifts, and to challenge our students to look at different types of evidence as they consider questions of causation.

The patterns of professional leagues' expansion and franchise relocation offer numerous opportunities for teachers to engage their students in the necessary "big picture" conversations while also opening the doors to a wide variety of classroom activities (timelines, mapping exercises, document analysis, discussion of team nicknames, etc.). I blindly stumbled on the value of these conversations in the euphoric days after the Cubs' 2016 World Series triumph. I hope this chapter will give colleagues the resources and information they need to plan for their own productive classroom discussions of demographics, technology, league expansion, and franchise relocations.

Notes

1. Walter LaFeber, *Michael Jordan and the New Global Capitalism* (New York: W. W. Norton, 1999).

2. Bruce J. Schulman, *The Seventies: The Great Shift in American Culture, Society, and Politics* (New York: Free Press, 2001).

3. William Cronon, *Nature's Metropolis: Chicago and the Great West* (New York: W. W. Norton, 1991).

4. George Donelson Moss and Evan P. Thomas, *Moving On: The American People Since 1945*, 6th ed. (Upper Saddle River, NJ: Prentice Hall, 2008), 325.

5. See Richard O. Davies, *Sports in American Life: A History* (Malden: Blackwell Publishing, 2007), 289–92, for a larger discussion of baseball franchise relocation.

6. http://www.andrewclem.com/Baseball/MLB_Franchises.html (accessed September 3, 2018).

7. https://www.census.gov/population/www/documentation/twps0027/tab25.txt (accessed September 3, 2018).

8. Davies, *Sports in American Life*, 235–38.

9. Ibid., 238–40.

10. This conversation could be extended to look at more recent franchise moves. I'm reminded of the confusion Tom Hanks's marooned character in *Castaway* (2000) felt on his return to the United States when he discovered that the Houston Oilers had become the Tennessee Titans. Those who follow professional sports can empathize with his disbelief.

11. All of the information for the NHL's franchise locations and moves came from the Canadian Encyclopedia's entry on the National Hockey League. See http://www.thecanadianencyclopedia.ca/en/article/national-hockey-league/ (accessed September 3, 2018) for a fuller discussion of these moves and their context.

The Globalization
of American Sport

Lars Dzikus and Adam Love

Sport can be an attractive and productive tool to get students interested in seemingly more abstract ideas. This includes key aspects of globalization, among them the increasing interconnectedness of people and places and a "heightened awareness of the world as a 'single place.'"[1] As one of the most globalized forms of popular culture, sport makes an exceptional vehicle for examining this complex phenomenon.

Sport in North America has been both a recipient and donor in this two-way road of cultural exchanges. Native Americans had rich sporting traditions. The arrival of Europeans and Africans led to new games and new traditions that creolized (mixed) local, regional, national, and international influences. Since the second half of the nineteenth century, American sports like basketball, volleyball, and football have become increasingly international, joined recently by alternative sports like skateboarding and BMX racing. The American sporting landscape has also been shaped by an ongoing influx of international activities such as soccer, yoga, and martial arts.

Whether they realize or not, our students are impacted by globalization on a daily basis. Helping students to realize this can be a productive starting point. A common way to facilitate this process is to have students check the labels of their clothing and other products to check where they were produced. They can then discuss what the labels say about power relations and the way products, investments, and people cross borders. When they are initially asked to reflect on how globalization has influenced their own sport experience, undergraduate and graduate students often are able to note that they follow international sporting events, and are fans of international athletes or teams. Some might even have international students on their varsity or club teams.

To bring our students up to speed on a conceptual level, we assign chapters one and eight of Ritzer and Dean's *Globalization: A Basic Text*. The first chapter provides an introduction of selected theoretical frameworks and basic concepts, as well as providing important illustrations that include sports. The second chapter on global culture and cultural flows goes into more depth with a discussion of baseball and soccer (association football). Next, we assign sport-specific readings and discuss how Ritzer and Dean's concepts can be applied to further explain the history of these sports.[2]

Sport and Concepts of Globalization

As a first step, we break down the components of Ritzer and Dean's somewhat intimidating definition of globalization: "a transplanetary process or set of processes involving increasing liquidity and the growing multidirectional flows of people, objects, places and information as well as the structures they encounter and create that are barriers to, or expedite, those flows."[3] We discuss how "transplanetary process or set of processes" that constitute globalization can be political, economic, cultural, or something else. These processes can be characterized by their extensiveness (the area they cover), intensity (the strength of their influence), and velocity (the speed with which they move). "Increasing liquidity and the growing multidirectional flows" conveys the idea is that in an increasingly interconnected world, people, objects, and even places tend to become more mobile. This, of course, is truer for some than others. People around the world, for example, do not have equal access to images and information on the internet, a phenomenon often referred to as the "digital divide." Nevertheless, it can be argued that many people, things, and ideas are less rooted in a single place than they once were. In other words, they are less solid and more liquid, less heavy and more weightless. As Ritzer and Dean point out, this applies particularly to popular culture. "Because much of it exists in the form of ideas, words, images, musical sounds, and so on, culture tends to flow comparatively easily throughout the world," they write. "In fact, that flow is increasingly easy because culture exists increasingly in digitized forms."[4]

In terms of the culture of sport, mediated representations such as streaming video travel far more weightlessly than athletes or teams. In 2015, for example, the New York Jets and Miami Dolphins played a regular season game in London as part of the NFL's annual International Series. American football fans around the world were able to watch the game live, through cable, satellite, or internet. Transporting the teams across the Atlantic, however, took far more energy and money. The teams with their entourages numbered 380 airline passengers who brought nearly 28 tons of equipment and luggage, in addition to separate freight shipments with more field equipment.[5]

This brings us to the next aspect of Ritzer and Dean's definition: "growing multidirectional flows of people, objects, places and information." A point to emphasize here is that globalization is not a one-way road. Although certain countries or regions might temporarily wield more influence over others, such dominance is neither static nor complete. Athletes, coaches, administrators, and fans migrate across national borders and continents in multiple directions. Scholars have used a number of typologies to characterize such migrants. For example, Zygmut Bauman distinguishes between "tourists" and "vagabonds."[6] Here, tourists refers to migrants who move on their own free will, whereas vagabonds move because they have to. Joseph Maguire's typology of sport labor migration identifies five types of migrants: pioneers, settlers, returnees, mercenaries, and nomadic cosmopolitans. Pioneers are motivated by promoting their sport abroad and often have an almost evangelistic zeal. Settlers grow attached to their new surroundings and end up staying, at times beyond their career. Mercenaries look for short-term gains, have little attachment to the host city or country, and are often described as "hired guns." Nomadic cosmopolitans enjoy the experience of living in a new country learning new cultures. All of these types have the potential to turn into returnees, if they eventually chose to return to their country of origin.[7] As an exercise, students could apply these categories to Dominican baseball players hoping for a career in the United States, using sources such as Arturo Marcano Guevara and David Fidler's *Stealing Lives: The Globalization of Baseball and the Tragic Story of Alexis Quiroz*, and the documentary film *Ballplayer: Pelotero*.[8]

Objects also populate the various flows of sport globalization. Students should be able to identify any number of sport-related objects that cross borders. You might encourage them to consider all the gear athletes bring with them for international competitions, such as the Winter Olympics (in 2018, for example, the U.S. skiing star Mikaela Shiffrin arrived in PyeongChang with thirty-five pairs of skis).[9] In more historical terms, the diffusion of sports like tennis, soccer, or baseball was often dependent on migrants (workers, soldiers, or missionaries) bringing along not only their know-how of specific sports but also the necessary equipment, such as balls and racquets.[10] More recently, transnational corporations (TNCs) have become major global distributors of sport-related commodities. In the mid-1990s, for instance, the running shoes that Nike sold around the world were "designed in Oregon and Tennessee; cooperatively developed by technicians in Oregon, Taiwan, and South Korea; then manufactured in South Korea and Indonesia by putting together fifty-two separate components produced in five countries"[11]

The emergence of multinational corporations was not a phenomenon of the late twentieth century; American-based companies like Standard Oil pioneered transnationality a century earlier. Today's TNCs, however, depend on global infrastructures for investments, production, and distribution. Each of these firms has "relatively weaker connections to its 'home' location compared to prior corporate models."[12] By the 1980s and 1990s, for example, American-based multinational corporations produced the majority of their goods abroad and depended on a world market. In 1996, four out of every five bottles of Coca-Cola were sold outside the American market. Thus TNCs gradually transcended and escaped the control of single governments and nations. Furthermore, their success depended not only on the distribution of their goods but on the flow of ideas and information—they "traded in designs, technical knowledge, management techniques, and organizational innovations"[13]

Perhaps more than any other flow, the movement of information in the global age has been characterized by liquidity and weightlessness. This development was already underway when modern sports emerged in the United States. In 1849, for example, several hundred spectators watched the bout between the bareknuckle fighters Tom Hyer and Yankee Sullivan in Maryland. Thousands more followed news about the clash through telegraphed reports read almost in real time at newly established telegraph offices around the United States. Still others read blow-by-blow descriptions in the newspapers.[14] The diffusion of commercialized sport within the United States benefited further from the invention of radio and television. By the 1980s the development of fiber-optic cables, along with direct broadcast satellites and personal computers, catalyzed a revolution in the global telecommunications market. From the 1990s on, greater access to cell phones and the internet made athletes like Michael Jordan and David Beckham into global celebrities and brands with unprecedented reach.

Technology has also transformed sports fandom. Cyberspace has facilitated the emergence of transnational fan clubs or what Giulianotti and Robertson have called "deterritorialized communities" and "self-invented virtual diasporas."[15] The language of these concepts can be intimidating for undergraduate or secondary students, but teachers can help demystify the concepts. After clarifying the meaning of "diaspora," teachers can have students discuss how social media like Facebook have changed traditional meanings of "friends." Today, one might never meet one's "close" friends in person. Similarly, communities of fans are no longer tied to a common place or territory; instead they can be dispersed across the globe from the original "homeland" of their favorite team. In the twenty-first century, United States–based fans of Germany's soccer team Bayern München can socialize online with like-minded enthusiasts in India and Peru. They might never meet in person or even see their team in a stadium, but they can chat and video conference as they follow their team's every move on and off the pitch through blogs, social networks, and live streaming.

The emergence of augmented reality and virtual reality takes this phenomenon one step farther. In 2015, for example, *LiveLike VR*, a startup based in San Francisco, described its efforts to create virtual stadiums in which fans from around the world could cheer on their teams. "Sports is not about being 'on the field' for the whole game, it's about being able to hang with your friends, doing stuff while there's a two-minute timeout, seeing replays, stats, and more," Andre Lorenceau, the company's CEO noted. "We are also focused on infrastructure, with building the capabilities to connect with friends or strangers, multiple 'channels' to watch from, statistical interfaces. There's a whole system that needs to be created before we watch sports in VR, and we're getting close to finalizing that."[16] This example illustrates the notion that even spaces can become less rooted in one place and begin to flow more easily across borders.

Despite these changes, however, barriers such as national borders can continue to impede the flow of people, objects, and ideas, structures that Ritzer and Dean define as "material practices—infrastructure, institutions, regulatory mechanisms, governmental strategies, and so forth—that both produce and preclude movement." Movement is "structured and regulated, such that while certain objects and subjects are permitted to travel, others are not." As a result, they conclude, "Immobility and exclusion are thus as much a part of globalization as movement."[17]

Instructors can help students identify formal structures that regulate the flow of athlete migration, such as leagues, federations, and governments. For example, they might analyze the respective roles of the International Olympic Committee (IOC), national Olympic committees, and national governments had in deciding which, if any, athletes from North Korea and Russia could travel to South Korea to compete in the 2018 Winter Olympics. In U.S. intercollegiate sport, the National Collegiate Athletic Association (NCAA) and its member institutions both enable and restrict the flow of athletes as they determine eligibility criteria for international students to study in the United States and compete in NCAA-sanctioned sports. In addition, the U.S. government controls which athletes come into the country to study by granting or denying student visas.

Social Class and Globalization in the Birth of U.S. Intercollegiate Sport

The origins of intercollegiate sport in the United States provide a useful case for exploring issues of social class in globalization processes. Today, intercollegiate sports in the United States is a widely popular enterprise on which universities collectively spend billions of dollars each year. In American college football, many coaches earn salaries in excess of $1 million annually, and more than 100,000 spectators turn out to attend games on campuses across the nation. Interestingly, a look at the origins of what is today thought to be a quintessentially American phenomenon reveals a practice that was, to a great extent, initially modeled on games from elite educational institutions in England.

Interuniversity sporting competition was initiated in England in the early 1800s, when students at Oxford and Cambridge began organizing rowing crews and football teams.[18] Such activities by aristocratic students in England fostered a growing interest in sports among upper-class collegians in the United States. Enthusiasm among American students for sport continued to grow following the 1857 publication of Thomas Hughes's novel, *Tom Brown's School Days*, a fictional story of a boy at Rugby School in England that included a tale about a soccer game played among the students. The popularity of the novel, which sold more than 225,000 copies in the United States during its first year of publication, helped spread interest in the sport.

The next year, reports from the annual Oxford–Cambridge rowing competition further motivated American students to take action. Writers covering the race praised the English students for their physical prowess while expressing dismay at "the entire disregard for exercise among Americans."[19] In response, student representatives in the United States formed the College Union Regatta Association in 1858. Regattas in 1859 and 1860 drew as many as twenty thousand spectators each. In an early instance of international competition, a crew from Harvard traveled to London in 1869 for a race against Oxford on the Thames River. Overall, the initial development of competitive intercollegiate sport in the United States can be used as an example to explore ways in which social class, particularly aspirations to upper-class social status, may influence globalization processes.

Glocalization and the Development of "American Football"

In addition to highlighting issues of social class, the history of college football in the United States provides a useful case for exploring the ways in which a sport, when introduced in a new geographical setting, may be gradually adapted to fit with local cultural norms and serve particular interests—a process often referred to as glocalization or hybridization. Unlike the concept of homogenization, which emphasizes cultural convergence and uniformity in globalization processes, glocalization highlights the interplay between global and local forces, as the term is literally a conflation between "globalization" and "localization."[20] In other words, when global and local flows collide, a new glocal "hybrid" may emerge as a result.

As previously noted, football became popularized as students at elite institutions in the United States sought to mimic the activities of their counterparts in England. As football gained steam on American campuses in the 1860s, two forms of the sport emerged—one of which roughly resembled modern-day association football (soccer), in which use of the hands was prohibited, and the other of which allowed use of the hands and more closely resembled rugby. In fact, the first intercollegiate football contest between Princeton and Rutgers University in 1869 used "soccer-style" rules, and would have been utterly unrecognizable to fans of American football today. Ultimately, the "rugby-style" version of the game that was popular at Harvard ended up becoming the norm throughout U.S. institutions, in part because of Harvard's esteemed position among the nation's colleges.[21] Over time, this "disorganized" early version of the sport became adapted in a way that university leaders imagined would meet the needs of the emerging American industrial society.[22]

Walter Camp, often regarded as the "father of American football," served a particularly influential role in the process that differentiated American football from its predecessor games in England. Camp, who had played football from 1876 to 1881 at Yale, went on to coach teams at both Yale and Stanford, while also serving as a member of rule-making bodies for the sport. Camp disliked the "unorganized" nature of the sport and was influential in moving the game away from "rugby-style" rules, in which a disorderly scrum formed following a player being tackled. Instead, Camp instituted the practice of "downing" the ball after a tackle and the accompanying "line of scrimmage"—practices that ultimately differentiated American football from English rugby.[23] Such changes were intended to make the game more disciplined, organized, and rational—"just like the rest of American society, and just like the universities in which it was taking root."[24] Overall, the development of American football provides a useful example for exploring glocalization—how a global import (football) becomes adapted in a local context (elite American universities during the early industrial age), and thus produces a new hybrid sport.

International Diffusion of American Football

The way that American football has crossed American borders offers an excellent example of the multidirectional and transnational flow that characterizes globalization. Until globalization accelerated in the 1990s, Americans showed relatively little enthusiasm for

exporting their form of football abroad. Nationally, football was orga-
nizationally confined to institutions of American higher education for
almost a century—professional football did not emerge until the 1920s
and did not rise to national prominence until the age of television in the
1950s and 1960s. Outside the United States, the sport was so exotic and
unfamiliar that its very name expressed its "heavy" state and geographi-
cally limited identity: *American* football. Not until the latter part of the
twentieth century did the sport become more "liquid."

A number of factors contributed to the diffusion of American football beyond its original borders. At the grassroots level, the former West
Germany serves as an example. Today now-unified Germany boasts the
highest number of adult American football players outside the United
States.[25] This development was rooted in the post–World War II era,
when several hundred thousand American soldiers were stationed in
West Germany. The soldiers' presence facilitated the flow of objects
(footballs) and information (know-how).

By the 1970s, advancements in telecommunication made reports
and images of American football far more available. Early local enthusiasts had to literally hijack radio and television signals of the American
Forces Network (AFN) that served American soldiers stationed in Europe.[26] Others relied on expensive video-recording services in the
United States, which sent VHS tapes of college or NFL games but which
might arrive weeks after the actual events. In 1977, German television
featured the first Super Bowl coverage. Although the forty-five-minute
highlight show aired at 11 p.m. three days after the actual game, it was
enough to inspire several Germans to start their own teams. With the
aid of a few pioneers and cosmopolitan nomads, Germans began to
"indigenize" American football within their own amateur structures of
clubs, leagues, and federations.[27] By 2015, there were 475 American
football clubs registered in Germany, with close to 55,000 members.

The growth of American football in Germany has been the result of
push-and-pull factors. In addition to local efforts to popularize the
game (pull), the development was spurred on by American market expansion efforts (push). Attempts to establish the sport in Europe on a
commercial basis date back to the 1930s.[28] In the 1990s and early 2000s,
for example, the NFL operated a professional transcontinental league
in North America and Europe, first known as the World League of
American Football.

Today, German football fans and players are part of a mediated virtual football diaspora, which can celebrate a touchdown with millions around the world as it happens in real time half a world away. Teachers can use the example of football's modifications and development in American universities, along with its spread through technology, political alliances, transnational companies, and human migration, to help students understand the ways that globalization has transformed the nation's and the world's sporting landscapes.

Notes

1. R. Giulianotti and R. Robertson, "The Globalization of Football: A Study in the Glocalization of the 'Serious Life,'" *British Journal of Sociology* 55 (2004): 546.

2. See Lars Dzikus, "Amerika: The Super Bowl and German Imagination," *International Journal of the History of Sport* 34 (2017): 81–100; and W. W. Kelly, "Is Baseball a Global Sport? America's 'National Pastime' as Global Field and International Sport," *Asia-Pacific Journal* 6 (2008): 1–17.

3. G. Ritzer and P. Dean, *Globalization: A Basic Text*, 2nd ed. (Malden, MA: John Wiley, 2015), 2.

4. Ibid., 206.

5. Nigel Thompson, "What Does It Take to Fly an American Football Team to Britain for the NFL International Series?" *Daily Mirror*, October 9, 2015, https://www.mirror.co.uk/lifestyle/travel/usa-long-haul/what-take-fly-american-football-6601503 (accessed September 3, 2018).

6. Zygmut Bauman, *Globalization: The Human Consequences* (New York: Columbia University Press, 1998).

7. Joseph Maguire, "Blade Runners: Canadian Migrants, Ice Hockey, and the Global Sports Process," *Journal of Sport & Social Issues* 20, no. 3 (1996): 335–60. Maguire's typology has been further developed by other researchers, such as J. Magee and J. Sugden, "'The World at Their Feet': Professional Football and International Labor Migration," *Journal of Sport & Social Issues* 26, no. 4 (2002): 421–37.

8. Arturo Marcano Guevara and David Fidler, *Stealing Lives: The Globalization of Baseball and the Tragic Story of Alexis Quiroz* (Bloomington: Indiana University Press, 2002); R. Finkel, J. Paley and T. Martin, *Ballplayer: Pelotero* (Makuhari Media, 2012).

9. *New York Times*, February 21, 2018.

10. S. Szymanski and A. S. Zimbalist, *National Pastime: How Americans Play Baseball and the Rest of the World Plays Soccer* (Washington, DC: Brookings Institution Press, 2005).

11. Walter LaFeber, *Michael Jordan and the New Global Capitalism,* 2nd ed. (New York: W. W. Norton, 2002), 147.

12. Giulianotti and Robertson, "The Globalization of Football," 551.

13. LaFeber, *Michael Jordan,* 55.

14. Pamela Grundy and Benjamin Rader, *American Sports: From the Age of Folk Games to the Age of Televised Sports,* 7th ed. (New York: Pearson, Inc., 2015), 32–33.

15. Giulianotti and Robertson, "The Globalization of Football," 551.

16. *Fortune,* October 19, 2015, http://fortune.com/2015/10/19/livelikevr -vr-sports-stadium/ (accessed September 3, 2018).

17. Ritzer and Dean, *Globalization,*14.

18. B. M. Ingrassia, *The Rise of Gridiron University: Higher Education's Uneasy Alliance with Big-Time College Football* (Lawrence: University of Kansas Press, 2012).

19. Grundy and Rader, *American Sports,* 72.

20. Giulianotti and Robertson, "The Globalization of Football"; Ritzer and Dean, *Globalization.*

21. The best account of the development and popularization of American intercollegiate football is Michael Oriard, *Reading Football: How the Popular Press Created an American Spectacle* (Chapel Hill: University of North Carolina Press, 1993).

22. Ingrassia, *Rise of Gridiron University.*

23. J. S. Watterson, *College Football: History, Spectacle, Controversy* (Baltimore, MD: Johns Hopkins University Press, 2000).

24. Ingrassia, *Rise of Gridiron University,* 36.

25. Dzikus, "Amerika: The Super Bowl and German Imagination."

26. Ibid.

27. Maguire, "Blade Runners."

28. Lars Dzikus, "American Football in Europe," in *Football: An American Obsession,* ed. Gerald Gems and Gertrude Pfister (Great Barrington, MA: Berkshire Publishing, 2018).

Part Two

Gender
and Sexuality

Issues of Sexuality in Sport

Sarah K. Fields

Teaching classes about sexuality and sport have been the most challenging and the most rewarding experiences in my teaching career. The challenges often come at the beginning of the course because most students in sport-oriented classes love sports, and I ask them to critique something about which they are passionate and which is a huge part of their lives and their identities. As a result, some students feel defensive. Early in the term, students have made provocative and sometimes challenging statements, leaving me at a loss as to how to respond. For example, in one class a young heterosexual white male I'll call Marshall announced during the first week that he personally did not care if an athlete was gay, but he did not understand why gay athletes had to announce their sexuality, and if they did, he thought they should have a separate locker room. In another case, a young heterosexual man of color I'll call Robert explained during the first week of class that although he was certainly not homophobic, he saw nothing wrong with motivating male athletes by calling them faggots.[1]

Although these statements have been made in multiple classes, I have almost always been surprised into passivity, reduced to suggesting that the statements were reflections of a complicated topic, which the class would explore in great detail throughout the term. Each time, I worried that I should have handled the situation differently, that I should have risked alienating Marshall and Robert to protect other

77

students in the room. Instead, I have taken the longer road. After a term of using various classroom exercises to work through these and other challenges, the rewards often begin to emerge.

Contextualizing Gender, Sexuality, and Sport

Sport in the United States has long been a bastion of masculinity. Historically, fields of play have been for boys and men, spaces in which men have claimed that they learned to be men, in part because of the absence of women. Women were, in fact, excluded from organized sport for centuries and remain marginalized in many contact and combat sports, in part because their presence and participation threatens to undermine the maleness of sport. Women who have transgressed social boundaries and played sports were long been presumed to be lesbians, and their very gender has often been questioned.

The male-only space of sport has also been a presumptively heterosexual space. As tennis legend and out lesbian Martina Navratilova said in a speech at the 1993 March on Washington for Gay, Lesbian, and Bi Equal Rights and Liberation, people "do not say Joe Montana, the heterosexual football player." No one needs to because the fact that Montana played football implied he was heterosexual. Football is one of the most manly and macho of American sports, and football players have been assumed to be heterosexual because of the stereotypes of toughness, aggression, and strength that go part and parcel with football players, as opposed to stereotypes about gay men.

There are some paradoxes here. Football requires that players spend hours together in close proximity with each other and their male coaches, away from women. The players' equipment and uniforms make them look like supermen, the shoulder pads accentuate broad masculine shoulders; tight pants define muscular legs and well-cupped packages. The quarterback often curves the front of his body around the back of the bent-over center and places his hands between the center's legs, the backs of his hands pressed against his teammate's inner thighs. Players and coaches show affection and emotion in ways not acceptable for men in other areas of American culture: they hug, hold hands, slap butts, wrap their arms around each other, and cry together. But despite the homosocial nature of the game and its culture, football players are presumed to be masculine, heterosexual men. Partly to reaffirm this status, their coaches and leaders traditionally motivated them by

78

comparing them to the absent and presumed inferior women and gay men. Taunts of "playing like a girl" and "faggot" have historically been common in the sporting world in general, and these slurs have only recently begun to receive serious critique.

Gender and sexuality in sport are merged because of assumptions about the way that sexuality connects to the gender of those who participate in sport. Sport has been mostly divided into a gender binary: men and women usually compete separately from each other. Men who compete in sports that highlight stereotypes of idealized heterosexual masculinity, sports which value size, strength, and speed, are presumed to be heterosexual. Women who compete in sports that embody stereotypes of heterosexual femininity, sports that stress grace and flexibility and can be played in a skirt or leotard, have been accepted as heterosexual women. Men and women who have violated social norms and competed in sports that have not historically belonged to their gender have been punished; the men's masculinity mocked, the women often derogatorily described as lesbians or dykes.[2] These suppositions make it difficult to separate sexuality and gender in the still predominantly binary world of organized sport.

Exploring How Sport Is Gendered

One of the first exercises that I do with any class studying issues of gender and sexuality in sport is to ask the students to categorize sports in the United States as historically or predominantly male, female, or neutral. The students begin the exercise without guidance on the definition of any of those words. Although their responses vary some, based on geographical region and age, they are nonetheless fairly consistent. The male sports category is quickly populated with football, baseball, and wrestling. The female sports category is slower to fill but ultimately includes synchronized swimming and rhythmic gymnastics. Over the years, the neutral category has gotten larger, a tribute perhaps to increases in women's sports participation, and usually includes soccer and track. When the lists are more or less complete, I ask the class to consider what the male sports have in common (toughness, size, strength) and what the female sports have in common (grace and flexibility).

Students quickly see that the commonalities are usually based in stereotypes of masculinity and femininity. For example, although both men and women play ice hockey (women in ever-increasing numbers),

79

ice hockey is often placed in the male category both because of the "masculine" attributes of strength and toughness as well as the popularity of the male professional league. Field hockey, however, is often categorized as female in part because teams frequently wear skirts as part of the uniform. The students rationalize their choices for a variety of reasons, including the observed and historical gender of most participants, the style of the game, and the uniforms. The more stereotypically masculine or female the uniform or the attributes of the athletes, the more likely the sport will be described as specifically gendered.

As a class, we then consider how the rules and the basic goals of each sport are, in fact, gender neutral, how a football by itself is genderless, and how we as a society have gendered the sport in a particular way. I ask the students to name sports in which males and females have historically competed by the same rules, with the same equipment, and with the same parameters. That list is short: soccer, rugby, and curling are the few that are usually invoked. This then leads to a discussion about how men and women are often steered into different versions of similar sports; rules, equipment, and uniforms are modified to support the *illusion* that one version of a game is more masculine (or feminine) than another.

Basketball is one such example. Since the beginning of the game men and women have played by different rules; until the late 1980s women and girls in some states played a six-on-six half-court version in which three players played only on the offensive side of the center court line and the other three played only on the defensive side. Early justifications for the rule difference included the concern that running the full length of the basketball court could physically harm females. A series of lawsuits from high-school girls who wanted to play the full-court version of the game helped change the rules so that girls in all states played full-court basketball, but the separation between men's and women's basketball continued. In the late 1980s and early 1990s, U.S. basketball organizations adopted a smaller ball for female players. Other rule changes have continued to differentiate the male and female versions of the game.[3] As a class we discuss how these differences reinforce gender stereotypes (smaller balls suggest weaker, more diminutive female players), what effect the different rules and equipment have on players (varying ball sizes make it difficult for men and women to compete together without one group being disadvantaged), and why those controlling the sports might want to reinforce these differences (masculinity is upheld as long as female athletes are seen as playing by an alternate, i.e., inferior, set of rules).

Similarly, baseball generally falls in the male sport category and softball in the female sport category, despite being very similar conceptually: in both sports, you hit the ball, run the bases, catch and throw, and end the inning with three outs. As a class, we explore the history of Little League Baseball and the rise of Little League Softball after the courts ruled that girls could not be legally excluded from publicly supported youth baseball leagues. We discuss how funneling girls into softball kept baseball a more masculine sport. The goal throughout is to recognize that the baseball/softball divide is a built construction—a way of gendering a sport so as to maintain ideological distinctions between the sexes.

I point out to students that even those seemingly gender-neutral sports we invoked earlier (e.g., soccer and track) have a history of segregation. Advances are tied to specific historical moments and political victories. For example, women ran the Olympic marathon for the first time in 1984, after almost a century of exclusion during which Olympic leadership argued that physical harm would come to females who ran long distances. This 1984 opportunity did not happen in isolation but followed advances in the women's and gay rights' movements in the United States in the 1970s, in addition to the rise of women's participation in marathons and sports more generally.[4]

Soccer provides another instructive example. In the United States, youth soccer became popular in the 1970s as an alternative to the physical riskiness of football and the highly structured nature of Little League baseball. Soccer was touted as a youth sport in which every child got to touch the ball and affect the flow of the play. Perhaps because it was promoted as a kinder, gentler, less stereotypically masculine sport, or perhaps because youth leagues needed participants, girls were encouraged to play.[5] Students respond well to this example because so many have had experience with soccer. This allows us to discuss the historical, social, culture, and geographical aspects of their early participation in sport. I describe my own experiences as the only—and possibly first—girl in my metro area soccer league. When I was about seven years old, an opponent's mother yelled out that I was a dyke. Students respond by discussing their own experiences with derogatory language, and we explore the impact this had on their perceptions of sport as well as the reasons for the slurs. Were they meant to be motivational? To exclude? Our discussions indicate that issues of gender and sexual difference often motivated (and still motivate) our perceptions of those sports, like soccer, that we perceive as gender-neutral.

Exploring the Historical Experiences of Gay Male and Lesbian Athletes

Early in the course, my class considers the historical experiences of athletes with nonnormative gender or sexual identities. We begin by discussing the challenge that the scholar Rita Liberti has so aptly described: How do you identify and discuss gay or trans athletes in eras where the concept of nonnormative gender or sexual identities was not discussed, and when the use of language was so different from the present?[6] The earliest accounts of presumably gay athletes are almost always written by scholars after the fact because the athletes of earlier eras rarely publicly identified themselves as nonheterosexual, and these accounts are now useful tools to discuss Liberti's concerns. Susan Cayleff's biography of the legendary multisport athlete Mildred "Babe" Didrikson Zaharias is an important example (for more details, see Cayleff, "Teaching Sports and Women's History through 'The Babe'").[7] Didrikson, an elite athlete in the 1930s, 1940s, and 1950s, was married to her male manager but had a long-term relationship with a woman whom Cayleff suggests was her romantic partner. After reading this book, we discuss how Babe was perceived as being masculine in the early part of her career, how she changed that perception by changing her hair, her clothes, her sport, and her marital status so as to appear more traditionally feminine. We then consider Cayleff's interpretation of Babe's relationships and the challenges of making that interpretation: Is Cayleff unfairly outing Babe when she herself did not publicly do so? Is Cayleff identifying and honoring Babe's same-sex relationship *after the fact* when Babe could not do so herself because of contemporary cultural constraints? Or is the answer somewhere in the middle?

Beginning in the 1970s, gay athletes began telling their own stories. As a point of reference, and to consider how the status of women and homosexuals in America has changed over time, the class reads at least one autobiography and a news report about a gay male and a lesbian athlete. Ideally, we examine change over time as well as the different experiences of male and female athletes who identify as gay.[8] Historically, more out lesbians have participated in sport than have out gay men. The experiences of gay women participating in softball from the early 1930s through the 1970s have been nicely documented by Susan Cahn and Anne Enke in oral histories; these athletes report searching for and finding in sport a place where they could live their sexual identity more openly than in the nonsport world.[9]

Tennis stars Billie Jean King and Martina Navratilova provide examples of lesbians who faced the costs of coming out under a national spotlight in the late twentieth century. King, who helped found the Women's Tennis Association (WTA), rocketed to superstardom with her 1973 prime-time match against the aging Bobby Riggs; the event was billed the Battle of the Sexes, and the married-to-a-man King's victory was seen as a blow against sexism. Her popularity, however, was diminished when in 1981 she was outed by a former female lover, and she lost a number of endorsements.[10] Navratilova, who had in the 1970s been cast as the foreigner-other in comparison to the all-American girl Chris Evert, came out in the 1980s. Like King, Navratilova faced challenges. Despite her success on the tennis court, she did not receive her first national endorsement contract until after she retired. She also feared the coming out would jeopardize her American citizenship because she had not disclosed her bisexuality in the application. These stories of these gay star players fed assumptions that the WTA was a hotbed of lesbianism.[11] In class, we discuss how American attitudes have and have not changed over time with regard to female tennis players.

Gay men, on the other hand, have found the sporting world less welcoming, perhaps because, unlike the women who played sports, they were not already considered sexually suspect. They have often struggled with the conflicting stereotypes of team sports (where men were expected to be hyper-heterosexually masculine) and the culture of gay men. As a result, most professional gay male athletes in team sports have come out publicly only after or toward the end of their careers. As time has passed, however, and attitudes have changed, there has been an evolution of sorts. Comparing the experiences of Dave Kopay, the first out gay male former NFL player, and Michael Sam, the first out gay male player to be drafted by the NFL, is instructive in this regard. Kopay described hiding his sexuality for fear that he would lose his position on the team in the 1960s and 1970s. Although he tried for years to become a football coach, he suspected that his sexuality kept college and pro teams from hiring him. Sam, on the other hand, came out to his college team before his final season and to the world prior to the NFL draft. Sam was drafted toward the end of the 2014 draft but never made the full roster of an NFL team. He played in one game as the first gay player in the Canadian Football League, but he blamed his failure to make an NFL team on his sexuality. These and other stories offer an opportunity to discuss both change and the lack of change in American sport and American society.

Exploring Transgender Athletes' Experiences

Transgender athletes have complicated and challenged the male-female binary in sport in ways that have yet fully to unfold. The earliest "out" trans athlete was Renée Richards, who successfully sued the United States Tennis Association in 1977 for the right to compete in the women's draw of the U.S. Open. Much was written about Richards at the time of her lawsuit; she herself has written two autobiographies and has been the subject of a documentary film, all of which provide helpful context in discussing the gender binary in sport in the 1970s.[12] Subsequent trans athletes have competed both before and after coming out, some in the category of their biological sex as assigned at birth, and others in the category of their identified gender. Their stories appear frequently in both popular press and academic sources.

In my class, I use a recent story about a trans athlete (every year I try use a different, more contemporary example) to compare that athlete's experience to Richards. Similarly, the class reads the policies that sports organizations at all levels have created to try to maintain the gender binary while still accommodating at least some trans athletes. We compare those policies to their historical predecessors and then evaluate them. If we find a sport or a level that does not have a policy, I ask the students to draft one with an eye toward promoting participation and fairness, however they wish to define these terms. Trans athletes complicate the strict gender binary of sport—perhaps the last dominant binary space after bathrooms in the United States—and my students discuss whether the increasing presence of trans athletes will undermine that binary over time.[13]

Exploring Intersex Athletes' Challenges

If gay and trans athletes confound the gender binary in sport, intersex athletes (those individuals who do not fall into normative biological and/or physiological definitions of male or female even from birth) render that binary thoroughly defunct. Historical assumptions have held that males are bigger, faster, and stronger than females, and thus are inherently better athletes. Conversely, any woman who is successful at sports that reward size, speed, and strength is often suspected of not being a "real" woman. To confirm that successful female athletes in international sport were really women, international sporting organizations—such as the International Olympic Committee—required that they be tested to prove their gender. Early tests were visual and later tests were chromosomal. Testing occurs in the present day if a competitor or official challenges the gender of a female athlete (athletes competing in male events are presumed male and not tested).[14] In the last few years, the cases of intersex track athletes Caster Semenya from South Africa and Dutee Chand from India have raised questions about biological sex and the value (or lack thereof) of the male/female binary in sport. Both women's biological sexes as well as genders were suspect; they were subject to testing, public speculation, and lawsuits before being allowed to compete.

After Challenges Come the Rewards

My classes often begin with challenges from students defending an institution with which they identify and love. Our class discussions of sexuality, sport, history, and society allow the students to identify key presumptions of sport and how those presumptions do and do not reiterate social presumptions about the role of gender and sexuality in this country. In tracing the historical experiences of gay, trans, and intersex athletes, students can see moments where sports and society have been slower to inclusiveness: as of today no out gay man has been on the regular season roster of an NFL team and no out gay man has served in the U.S. Senate. Conversely, multiple out lesbians compete in various professional sports leagues and Tammy Baldwin, an out lesbian, was elected to the U.S. Senate in 2012, thus illuminating how different categories of the LGBTQ community have different experiences even in the present day. Students can also see examples of inclusiveness being embraced: Michael Sam's jersey was the best-selling shirt in the NFL after he was drafted. Looking at the historical documentation of gay, trans, and intersex athletes also allows students to explore questions of how to evaluate representations and interpretations of individuals who lived in a time when they could not safely self-identify.

For me, the rewards of teaching these difficult topics usually come later in the term. My student Marshall, who wanted gay athletes to use separate locker rooms, wrote me a note at the end of his final essay telling me the class had made him rethink his assumptions; he concluded that the experience would make him a better coach and a better parent. My student Robert, who asserted that gay slurs were motivational, was asked near the end of the class if he still believed that, and he said that he no longer did. Many of my students found that learning about and critiquing the history of sexuality in sport would allow them to help make the institution they loved better and stronger.

Notes

1. In this essay I deliberately spell out homophobic slurs when they are direct quotations. All the student names are pseudonyms.

2. See the 1984 *Saturday Night Live* skit about men's synchronized swimming (http://www.holdoutsports.com/2016/08/snl-synchronized-swimming-olympics.html) and the 2010 skit from the same show (http://www.nbc.com/saturday-night-live/video/espn-classic-womens-weightlifting/n12780?snl=1) about the 1986 Women's Weightlifting Championships for satirical representations of gender stereotypes in sport (both accessed September 3, 2018).

3. For a history of women's basketball, see Pamela Grundy and Susan Shackelford, *Shattering the Glass: The Remarkable History of Women's Basketball* (New York: New Press, 2005).

4. For a history of the women's marathon, see Jaime Schultz, "Going the Distance: The Road to the 1984 Olympic Women's Marathon," *International Journal of the History of Sport* 32 (2015): 72–88.

5. For a history of U.S. women's youth soccer, see Sarah K. Fields, "*Hoover v. Meiklejohn*: The Equal Protection Clause, Girls, and Soccer," *Journal of Sport History* 30 (2003): 309–21.

6. Rita Liberti, "Queering Fields and Courts: Considerations in LGBT History," in *The Routledge History of American Sport*, ed. Linda J. Borish, David K. Wiggins, and Gerald R. Gems (New York: Routledge, 2017), 240–51.

7. Susan Cayleff, *Babe: The Life and Legend of Babe Didrikson Zaharias* (Urbana: University of Illinois Press, 1996).

8. Examples include David Kopay and Perry Deane Young, *The David Kopay Story: An Extraordinary Self-Revelation* (Westminster, MD: Arbor House, 1977); Billie Jean King, *Billie Jean* (New York: Viking, 1982); Martina Navratilova, *Martina* (New York: Knopf, 1985); Glenn Burke, *Out at Home: The Glenn Burke Story* (New York: Excel Publishing, 1995); Tom Waddell, *Gay Olympian: The Life and Death of Dr. Tom Waddell* (New York: Knopf, 1996); Billy Bean, *Going the Other Way: Lessons from a Life In and Out of Baseball* (Boston: Da Capo Press, 2003); John Amaechi, *Man in the Middle* (Bristol, CT: ESPN Press, 2007); Robbie Rogers and Eric Marcus, *Coming Out to Play* (New York: Penguin, 2014); and Kate Fagan, *The Reappearing Act: Coming Out as Gay on a College Basketball Team Led by Born-Again Christians* (New York: Skyhorse Publishing, 2014).

9. Susan K. Cahn, *Coming on Strong: Gender and Sexuality in Women's Sport*, 2nd ed. (Urbana: University of Illinois Press, 2015), and Anne Enke, *Finding the Movement: Sexuality, Contested Space, and Feminist Activism* (Durham, NC: Duke University Press, 2007). For stories of gay male athletes, see *Light in the Water*, directed by Lis Bartlett (Logo Documentary Films, 2018), available at http://www.logotv.com/episodes/owv291/logo-documentary-films-light-in-the-water-ep-special, which provides an excellent history of the Gay Games and gay rights as well as the impact of the AIDS epidemic through the stories of members of the West Hollywood Aquatics club.

10. Susan Ware, *Game, Set, Match: Billie Jean King and the Revolution in Women's Sports* (Chapel Hill: University of North Carolina Press, 2011).

11. Nancy E. Spencer, "'America's Sweetheart' and 'Czech-Mate': A Discursive Analysis of the Evert-Navratilova Rivalry," *Journal of Sport and Social Issues* 27 (2003): 18–37.

12. See Renée Richards, *Second Serve: The Renée Richards Story* (New York: Stein and Day, 1983); Renée Richards, *No Way Renée: The Second Half of My Notorious Life* (New York: Simon and Schuster, 2007); *Renée*, directed by Eric Drath (Bristol, CT: ESPN Films, 2011); Susan Birrell and Cheryl L. Cole, "Double Fault: Renée Richards and the Construction and Naturalization of Difference," *Sociology of Sport Journal* 7 (1990): 1–21; and Lindsay Pieper Parks, "Gender Regulation: Renée Richards Revisited," *International Journal of Sport History* 29 (2012): 675–90.

13. For wide-ranging discussions of gay and trans athletes queering sport, see Jennifer Hargreaves and Eric Anderson, eds., *Routledge Handbook of Sport, Gender, and Sexuality* (New York: Routledge, 2014), and Jayne Caudwell, *Sport, Sexualities and Queer/Theory* (New York: Routledge, 2006).

14. For more on sex testing, see Lindsay Parks Pieper, *Sex Testing: Gender Policing in Women's Sports* (Urbana: University of Illinois Press, 2016).

The Shaping
of "Women's Sport"

Pamela Grundy

I love to teach the history of early women's college basketball. The subject has everything a teacher could want: energy, humor, great passages to read, marvelous images to show and discuss. It paints a vivid picture of the assumptions and restrictions that circumscribed many women's activities, much as corsets and long skirts constrained their steps, their reach, their very breath. It showcases the joyous delight young women felt when playing a vigorous, competitive game that allowed them to confront those assumptions and break through some of those restrictions. It also highlights the strategies that women used to cloak an activity that posed a dramatic challenge to social norms.

The development of women's basketball was part of a broader challenge to the nineteenth-century Victorian worldview that cast women as frail and dependent. This worldview did not determine the full experience of all American women—it held its greatest sway among the white urban middle class. But because this group dominated the nation's political, educational, and cultural institutions, Victorian ideas were embodied in every aspect of society, from laws regarding property and political participation to medical pronouncements about the female body to standards of dress and behavior.

As always with sports, this subject makes it possible to address multiple issues. A discussion of the plethora of "medical" arguments about female frailty highlights the ways that "scientific" findings can also be profoundly shaped by social assumptions. Controversy over the outfits women's teams wore, and over whether games should be played in public, both point to issues of sexuality, emotional control, and physical appearance. The development of a distinctive version of "women's basketball" opens an exploration into the ways that social expectations can become embodied in games and rules. These discussions also make it possible to contrast expectations for women in the Victorian era with those of the present day, helping to underscore both the persistence and the fluidity of gender expectations.

I begin by putting together a set of slides. This is an image-rich subject. The lively popular press of the nineteenth century produced countless illustrations that vividly portray assumptions about women and their social roles. Such images also encapsulate reactions to various efforts to expand women's opportunities, from women's suffrage campaigns to female cyclists to the "rational dress" movement that produced the Bloomer Costume that became standard women's sports attire. This approach helps students develop their abilities to interpret images while they explore the relationship between sports and society.[1]

I stress that advocates of women's basketball had to contend with a pair of fundamental assumptions: that men and women were fundamentally different by nature, and that women were the "weaker sex." These ideas had justified male dominance of Western political and economic life for millennia. Middle-class Victorians took them to extremes. For example, the makers of corsets—garments whose physical constraints actually damaged women's internal organs—sometimes argued that women needed a corset's stiff bracing just to be able to stand up. As cities grew, women were endlessly cautioned about the perils that awaited them if they dared to venture onto urban streets alone.

Assumptions about female weakness also permeated the developing field of medical science, which was rife with ideas that claimed to be "scientific" but which were in fact rooted in custom and tradition. I like to spotlight the "vitalist theory," which held that the human body possessed only a finite amount of energy. According to that widely circulated theory, women needed to refrain from vigorous activity in order to conserve their physical energy for the stress of childbearing. As well as discouraging vigorous exercise, this concept of limited energy was also wielded by critics of women's colleges, who charged that the mental effort required by college work would make educated women unfit for motherhood. Although there was no genuinely scientific basis for any of these claims, they were accepted because they fit with deeply held social beliefs. Since present-day students have no trouble seeing the absurdity of this particular set of ideas, they offer an excellent opportunity to make the point about the power of preconceptions to distort how people view the world before them.[2]

In addition to physical weakness, Victorian philosophy also stressed female emotional weakness—harking back to the image of Eve yielding to temptation in the Garden of Eden. From that perspective, any vigorous, emotional activity such as competitive sports threatened to rob young women of the self-control that Victorians prized so highly—a concern laden with sexual implications. These ideas posed a particular challenge for administrators of women's colleges, who had already taken the controversial step of removing young women from the "protection" of their homes, and were thus especially eager to avoid any hint of impropriety.

Image and Reality

The context set, I turn to basketball. I generally start with one of my favorite images, a 1901 picture from what was then North Carolina's State Normal and Industrial College (hence the "Normal" on the women's uniforms) and is now the University of North Carolina, Greensboro. Like many other "normal schools" around the country, the school's main purpose was training teachers.

I ask students what they think the image might say about the qualities of womanhood the players were seeking to convey, the kind of basketball they played, and where the two might clash. There is plenty to talk about. I particularly want students to notice signs of modesty: the high necklines, the skirts that brush the ground, the sleeves that cover the wrists, the way that four of the six women avoid the camera's gaze. I also want them to realize that portrait photographs such as this were often carefully arranged to convey specific ideas.

If the class is small enough, I often skip to the present for a minute and ask about the kind of womanhood that female basketball players seek to convey in the ways they present themselves. This works especially well if there are female athletes in the class—they typically have a lot to say on this subject. That discussion helps to underscore the point that ideas about womanhood change—and have changed over time—but that some things also stay the same.

Basketball team from State Normal College, Greensboro, North Carolina, 1901. (Courtesy of Martha Blakeney Hodges Special Collections and University Archives, University Libraries, the University of North Carolina at Greensboro)

The photo also offers plenty of clues to how turn-of-the-century women played. The uniforms indicate that the game wasn't very fast. The spectacular goal behind them tells a story in itself. There's no backboard, making it harder to score. The net is closed at the bottom—you can see the player on the left holding the string. The basketball is also larger than the modern-day ball. These two details allow me to emphasize that a game's rules can change as society does. Basketball's first set of rules, for example, called for a jump ball after every basket. That practice would not change until 1934, when teams attempted to make basketball more popular by speeding up the game—an effort that involved both eliminating the center jump and reducing the basketball's size.

I then contrast that serene picture with what young women had to say about their play. (The widespread popularity of women's college ball means that almost any college yearbook of the era has great images and descriptions, and I highly recommend seeking out local examples.) Under the picture of the Normal team, for example, was a spirited cheer:

> Hoop-la! Hoop-la! Gold and White!
> The Normal team is out of sight!
> We are the stuff—tough, tough tough!
> We play basketball and never get enough![3]

Similar energy emerges in the newspaper account of the first women's intercollegiate game, played between Stanford and the University of California before seven hundred spectators in April 1896. The score was about as low as it could have been—Stanford triumphed 2–1. But the newspaper description penned by Mable Craft, a University of California graduate, described a vigorous game. The contest, Craft wrote, was "snappy" from the start, with "many calls for time and some disputes. Enthusiastic captains claimed fouls, and some were allowed. . . . Sometimes with a slump and a slide three girls would dive for the ball, and end in an inextricable heap of red, white and blue. In less time than it takes to read it they were all planted firmly on their two feet, flushed, perspiring, intensely in earnest and oblivious of everything except that ball."[4]

Basketball "wasn't invented for girls, and there isn't anything effeminate about it," Craft continued. "It was made for men to play

92

indoors and it is a game that would send the physician who thinks the feminine organization 'so delicate,' into the hysterics he tries so hard to perpetuate."

You can see the potentially revolutionary nature of women's sports in the way that ambitious women such as Craft linked athletics to visions of women who were far stronger and more capable than society presumed. L. I. Mack, a female student at predominantly African American Atlanta University, made similar connections in 1900. "Educated women who seek employment must keep in mind the fact that only by the sweat of the brow is man's bread won," Mack wrote. "They must also remember that if they descend into the arena, they cannot hope for success unless they accept the conditions under which an athlete must strive. They must be prepared for hard work, for persevering work, because the race will be the same for them as for the men. The men will go beside them, struggling for the same prize; and, since men have, in the start, the advantage of the women, they must brace up every energy, and bring into play every faculty, to avoid defeat and ensure victory. Whatsoever they undertake, they must, and will, and do go through with it to the end."[5] (For more about the particular experiences of African American women and sports, see Grundy and Liberti, "Black Women Face Obstacles and Opportunities.")

Gender Tension amid Social Change

The tension between conforming to womanly convention, as seen in this and other photographs, and challenging it, as can be read in the words, is an especially significant theme for women's activities in this era. As the United States became a more competitive, industrial society, young middle-class women actively sought to shake off Victorian restrictions and create new roles for themselves—to get in the game, so to speak. But this was a tricky endeavor. They couldn't challenge gender norms directly. This was particularly true because women began to attend college and to take up sports at a time when the growth of industry, the expansion of corporate bureaucracy, and the changing demographics of American society had already sparked growing anxiety about gender relations.

The later part of the nineteenth century saw what historians call a "crisis of masculinity" among middle- and upper-class white men, brought on by the sedentary routines of office work and concerns about

93

Charlotte News cartoon depicting the stir caused by the first women's intercollegiate basketball game in Charlotte, North Carolina, 1907. (Courtesy of the Robinson-Spangler Carolina Room, Public Library of Charlotte and Mecklenburg County)

competing with the immigrants flooding into to American cities. Many of these men—most prominently President Theodore Roosevelt—sought to avoid "feminization" through vigorous sports. This endeavor firmly stamped the expanding realm of sports as male, and thus limited women to the role of ardent admirers of male athletic prowess. Like other aspects of this subject, it produced a plethora of fascinating images in the popular press. It also meant that female athletes had to walk an especially fine line.[6]

Young women engaged in spirited competition on a basketball court could also become a sexualized sensation—the last thing that college administrators wanted. I like to illustrate this effect with a game that took place in Charlotte, North Carolina, in 1907, when the teams from Elizabeth and Presbyterian colleges played Charlotte's first intercollegiate matchup. The event received enthusiastic coverage in the local newspapers, one of which published a particularly telling illustration.

There's a lot for students to see here. The sketch of the player shows a tight-fitting uniform that offers a dramatic contrast both to the modest picture of the Normal students and to the outfits that the Elizabeth and Presbyterian players actually wore. While young men were officially barred from the game, a number of them climbed on nearby buildings to get glimpses of the action. As the Keystone Kops–style policeman suggests, some were in fact arrested, although the whole episode was treated with lighthearted gaiety in the press—one newspaper account described the scene as "gloriously incoherent and ecstatic."[7] It was not the kind of event that a college administrator would like to see repeated. After the three-game series ended, the two teams never played again.

Creating "Women's Basketball"

To avoid accusations that women were trying to take the place of men, and to stay clear of sexually charged situations, physical educators across the country began to take steps to make basketball an acceptable female activity. In detailing these efforts, I focus on Senda Berenson, the Smith College physical education instructor who became known as the "mother" of women's basketball. There are a number of other women who could be highlighted, including Clelia Mosher at Stanford University and Clara Baer at Sophie Newcomb College in New Orleans. But Berenson was not only influential in physical education circles but also especially eloquent about her views. The Smith College online archives also offer a treasure trove of writings and images, which can enhance lectures or provide material for student research.[8]

Berenson was a deep believer in the value of physical activity for women. She had spent much of her youth plagued by ailments that sharply limited her activities, a situation that was remedied only when she enrolled in a physical education course. By the end of the course, she found it "impossible to tell how my life had altered. I had changed an aching body to a free and strong mechanism, ready and eager for whatever might come." She was soon ready to see her students push farther. "One of the strong arguments in the economic world against giving women as high salaries as men for similar work is that women are more prone to illness than men," she later wrote. "They need, therefore, all the more to develop health and endurance if they desire to become candidates for equal wages."[9] In contrast to accusations that basketball could cause young women to lose their self-control, she focused on the game's capacity to develop abilities that included "alertness, accuracy, coolness and presence of mind under trying circumstances."[10]

Berenson and other female physical educators focused on basketball for a couple of reasons. It was a relatively new game, which meant that female basketball players were not treading on ground that had long been claimed by men (a group of college women had in fact staged the first female contest in December 1891, less than a week after James Naismith unveiled the game's initial rules). Naismith had deliberately designed his game to be far less rough than football, which made it possible to mold it into an activity deemed suitable for women. Football would remain the premier male college sport, and many male collegians initially saw basketball as a "sissy" game.

Berenson and her colleagues also made deliberate efforts to shape a women's version of the game, primarily by introducing additional restrictive rules. They limited movement by dividing up the court and restricting each player to a single section. Berenson split the court into three sections. Clara Baer in New Orleans divided it into nine (court diagrams effectively underscore these physical restrictions, and images are easy to find online). While James Naismith had specifically barred "shouldering, holding, pushing, tripping, or striking," most women's rules banned all physical contact. In the mid-1890s, when the dribble became part of the game, female players were quickly limited to a single dribble per possession.

Physical educators also worked to keep their games in the private sphere. The occasional intercollege matchups of the late nineteenth and early twentieth centuries were soon replaced by intramural contests that matched freshmen against sophomores, juniors against seniors, and so on. Even within the confines of college grounds, modesty was the watchword. "After players put on their 'gym' suits . . . they must put on long black stockings, a top skirt which had a way of hanging down behind, and throw a coat around the shoulders," explained Marion Hood, who attended North Carolina's State Normal College early in the twentieth century. "The rear effect of the whole outfit reminded one of a rooster's tail feathers in wet weather, but we were nothing if not sticklers to the strictest sense of modesty."[11]

Within this carefully designed realm, physical educators labored to give their students the strength and confidence to take on new social roles. They also created powerful professional organizations, which meant that their influence over women's sports would last for nearly three-quarters of a century.

It's important to emphasize that most physical educators weren't trying to completely break down the boundaries between men and women. In fact, they often cast their sporting activities as not only different from but also better than those of men. In this they harnessed another Victorian idea: that by staying out of the rough-and-tumble realms of politics and economics, women could exercise a "civilizing" influence over society. As men's college sports grew, their popularity began to expose the contradictions between athletic success and educational priorities that are so dramatically familiar in today's big-time college sports. Female physical educators kept far more control over their games, and they proudly focused on shaping the character and abilities of individual students, rather than building winning teams. Their efforts also produced some ironic results—young women who sought to break away from the physical education model and play more competitive games were more likely to find support from male coaches than from female physical educators.

I end by reemphasizing that physical educators at women's colleges represented only one cultural component of a large, diverse nation. They were especially important because of the way that the educated middle class dominated national cultural institutions, including the mainstream press. But many other communities had different understandings of women's physical abilities, fewer concerns about women in public, and a more flexible approach to female activities.

An Alternate Approach

In the 1920s, even as physical educators solidified their dominance over college women's play, high schools, factories, and "business colleges" began to sponsor highly competitive women's basketball teams in small towns, rural areas, working-class neighborhoods, and many African American communities. Communities where women performed demanding labor on farms, in homes, or in factories had few concerns about basketball's physical demands. The excitement that accompanied the passage of the Nineteenth Amendment in 1920, along with the growing significance of sexual appeal in popular conceptions of womanhood, created a more favorable cultural context, allowing a new generation of young women to use basketball to claim an expanded role in American society. As one newly formed high school team announced that year: "Man's age has been heretofore, but now woman's age is coming in, not only in politics but in athletics."[12] It's easy to put together a series of slides that depicts a multiplicity of teams and thus conveys the sense of a wide range of eager participation (as with images of women's college teams, this offers a great opportunity to seek out local material). If the schedule permits, this ending can also lead into a class that discusses these facets of women's basketball and American society in more detail.[13]

Notes

1. For an excellent example of how the era's images embodied social expectations, see John Kasson, *Rudeness and Civility: Manners in Nineteenth-Century Urban America* (New York: Hill and Wang, 1990), 117–46. For further description and documentation of turn-of-the-century social expectations and their relationship to sports, see Susan Cahn, *Coming on Strong: Gender and Sexuality in Twentieth-Century Women's Sport* (New York: Free Press, 1994), 7–30. The fascinating story of Amelia Bloomer and the "Bloomer Costume" can be found in D. C. Bloomer, *Life and Writings of Amelia Bloomer* (St. Clair Shores, MI: Scholarly Press, 1976).

2. For a fascinating account of pseudoscientific theories about women's physical abilities, see Patricia A. Vertinsky, *The Eternally Wounded Woman: Women, Doctors, and Exercise in the Late Nineteenth Century* (Urbana: University of Illinois Press, 1994).

3. *North Carolina State Normal and Industrial College Decennial* (1902), 128.

4. *San Francisco Chronicle*, April 5, 1896. More detailed material on teams and games during this period can be found in Pamela Grundy and Susan Shackelford, *Shattering the Glass: The Remarkable History of Women's Basketball* (New York: New Press, 2005), 9–33.

5. Grundy and Shackelford, *Shattering the Glass*, 11.

6. Michael Oriard's discussion of "Football and the New Woman" is an excellent source for images and interpretations and also includes an intriguing account of portrayals of working-class womanhood. See Michael Oriard, *Reading Football: How the Popular Press Created an American Spectacle* (Chapel Hill: University of North Carolina Press, 1993), 247–76.

7. *Charlotte Observer*, April 9, 2017.

8. Berenson's digitized papers are available at clio.fivecolleges.edu/smith /berenson/.

9. Berenson, "Basketball for Women," draft 1 [transcript], 97, Smith College Archives.

10. Grundy and Shackelford, *Shattering the Glass*, 16.

11. Pamela Grundy, *Learning to Win: Sports, Education and Social Change in Twentieth Century North Carolina* (Chapel Hill: University of North Carolina Press, 2001), 62.

12. Pamela Grundy, "From Amazons to Glamazons: The Rise and Fall of North Carolina Women's Basketball, 1920–1960," *Journal of American History* 87 (June 2000): 115–16. One particularly interesting and well-documented story involves the Fort Shaw Government Industrial Indian Boarding School in Montana, which sent its women's basketball team to represent the school at the 1904 St. Louis World's Fair. For an excellent account of the Fort Shaw team, see Linda Peavy and Ursula Smith, *Full Court Press: The Girls of Fort Shaw Indian School, Champions of the World* (Norman: University of Oklahoma Press, 2008).

13. More information on the social context that gave rise to these competitive women's teams can be found in Cahn, *Coming on Strong*, 31–54, and Grundy and Shackelford, *Shattering the Glass*, 37–108. Both works also document the decline of competitive women's basketball in the postwar era, the result of efforts by physical educators to eliminate competitive high school girls' teams and the resultant pressures brought to bear by the gender conservatism of the 1950s. This decline is an excellent caution against the assumption that history always moves in a progressive direction.

Teaching Sports and Women's History through "The Babe"

Susan E. Cayleff

In 1932, Mildred Ella "Babe" Didrikson emerged as the undisputed star of the Los Angeles Olympic Games, with two dramatic gold-medal victories and a close-second silver. For the next three decades, Babe's unmatched skills would make her the most famous female athlete in the nation. But unlike Olympic medalists of today, her feats were criticized as intensely as they were celebrated. Her newfound fame collided with idealized notions of appropriate middle-class white femininity in America, highlighting gender tensions and a profound class divide. While growing numbers of working-class women were playing high school, college, semiprofessional and league sports, class distinctions kept many of these achievements from being widely celebrated. Although 22 percent of all workers were female, middle-class culture envisioned the ideal women as a domestic, nurturing, full-time companion for her husband. Babe was unmarried, androgynous in appearance, rough in demeanor, and the primary means of support for her parents and siblings. In many ways, she was an antihero.[1]

Accounts of Didrikson's appearance and demeanor highlighted the tensions between the qualities that produced athletic achievement and those that defined middle-class white womanhood. One sportswriter described her as a "thin, muscular girl with a body like a Texas cowpuncher, an unfeminine looking, hard-bitten creature with nothing on her mind but setting athletic records."[2] Another questioned whether she should use the men's or the women's bathroom, invoking wide spread assumptions that an "Amazon" who pursued "manly sports" was a member of a "Third Sex," rather than a real woman.[3] For Didrikson to win the acceptance that would allow her to make a living at the athletic pursuits she loved, she would have to learn how to bridge those divides, projecting a conventionally feminine image that differed sharply from the woman that she actually was.

Babe Didrikson's life provides a stellar opportunity to explore multiple tensions in American history, including race relations, ethnic immigration, gendered ideals, political tensions, and homophobia. She was raised in southeast Texas, an area known for its oil refining industries and politically controlled by the Ku Klux Klan.[4] While her Norwegian immigrant family celebrated ethnic holidays, ate traditional foods, and used phrases of their native language (Babe's nickname came from slang Norwegian—"baden" meant baby—not because she could hit the ball like Babe Ruth, as she loved to brag), Didrikson's father constantly asserted his American loyalty through display of the flag, encouraging his children to speak English, and extolling economic self-improvement. For male athletes from immigrant families, sports could prove an ideal way to win approval and acceptance. Female athletes, even supremely talented ones, had a far harder time.

Norwegian culture valued female strength, and family encouragement helped develop Didrikson's stunning athletic talent. After she finished high school, her family defied social norms by allowing her to leave home to work and compete for the Employers Casualty Insurance Company in Dallas, where she was technically employed as a secretary. The growing acceptance of women's sports in working-class communities had created a boom in company-sponsored sports teams across the nation. In Dallas, Employers Casualty was one of several firms, among them Franklin Motor Car, Sunoco Oil, and Piggly Wiggly Groceries, that saw women's teams as a way to win employee and consumer loyalty.

Didrikson first gained national attention as the star player on the firm's basketball team, the Golden Cyclones, which she led to the national Amateur Athletic Union championship in 1930–31. After that victory, "Colonel" Melvin McCombs, who oversaw the company's women's sports teams, suggested that she enter the 1932 AAU Track and Field Championships in Evanston, Illinois. At the event, which doubled as the tryouts for the 1932 U.S. Olympic squad, she competed as a one-woman team, entering multiple events.

Her accomplishments were dazzling. In one afternoon, she won six gold medals (shot put, baseball throw, javelin, 80-meter hurdles, high jump, broad jump) and broke four world records. She earned thirty points and won the national team championship as a one-woman team. The second-place team, Illinois Athletic Club, amassed twenty-two points. These accomplishments, combined with the loyalty and promotional skills of a Beaumont sports writer, Bill "Tiny" Scurlock, rocketed her into the media spotlight. Newspapers across the country exploded with dramatic headlines: "Didrikson, Unaided, Wins National Track Championship" and "Babe Lands Thirty Points to Outclass Nation's Best Feminine Teams."[5]

This stunning performance qualified her for the Olympics, but with a catch—one that allows teachers to bring in deeper historical context. The International Olympic Committee (IOC) had been historically reluctant to allow women to compete. Women's track events were not allowed until 1924, and even then female athletes were allowed to enter only three events. This reluctance reflected the beliefs of many, including medical experts and some physical educators, that competitive sports damaged women's physiology and made them unappealing marriage partners. These beliefs were rooted both in social convention and in nineteenth-century pseudoscientific ideas, particularly the concept that girls and women who overtaxed their bodies would become infertile or bear defective offspring.[6]

While concerns about women's health spoke most clearly to gender issues, they were also heightened by fears about the nation's changing racial and ethnic demographics, which included relatively low birth-rates for native-born white women. In 1917, for example, the former President Theodore Roosevelt wrote in Foes of Our Own Household that every American-born (read: Anglo/desirable/white) woman had the duty to bear at least six children who survived past age one so that their "preferable" population outnumbered the births by the (less preferable) foreign born. Such anxieties were also reflected in immigration laws of the 1920s, which for the first time set immigration quotas based on country of origin, as lawmakers tried to re-create a demographic profile that resembled the United States before the waves of southern and eastern European "New Immigrants" started arriving in the 1880s.[7]

Being limited to three events did not prevent Didrikson from becoming one of the 1932 Olympics' brightest stars. Performing in Los Angeles in front of 105,000 spectators, she won a gold medal in the javelin (world and Olympic record of 143 feet, 4 inches) and another in the 80-meter hurdles (world and Olympic record of 11.7 seconds). She earned a controversial second place finish in the high jump—she tied the gold medalist, but her style was ruled unorthodox, which resulted in the only half-gold/half silver medal ever issued to an Olympian. Newspapers touted her success with enthusiastic headlines that dubbed her "America's Girl Star," "Iron-Woman," "The Amazing Amazon," "The Terrific Tomboy," and the "World-Beating Girl Viking." Dallas feted her with a parade.[8]

Media attention, however, cut both ways. While Babe became famous, with fame came criticism and unkind scrutiny. Some of this was her own doing. Like other "self-made" stars, she learned to be a self-promoter. When she discovered that having a manager jeopardized her AAU amateur standing, she quickly dropped Tiny Scurlock. Although her salary at Employer's Casualty was hefty—she earned seventy-five dollars per week in 1930, a time when the average American household was earning $1,970 annually—she pushed ECC for regular raises, monies for championships won, and other special considerations.[9] These demands opened a rift with her teammates. She was, in fact, a poor teammate, as her goal was self-promotion and individual success, not collective glory and mutual benefit. She was also a skilled practitioner of psychological warfare. In an excellent example of the importance of using multiple sources, this side of Babe's personality comes out most vividly in oral histories, in which Olympic teammates and other sporting peers recount details such as her habit of standing at a locker room's doorway and calling out "What did ya all show up for? See who's gonna finish second?!"[10]

But media accounts focused the lion's share of attention on her gender identity. Members of the nation's corps of prominent male sportswriters suggested that her appearance and abilities made her part of a Third Sex, asked whether she should be addressed as Mr., Miss, or It, debated over which bathroom she should use, called her a lesbian, and a "Muscle Moll." Paul Gallico, the famous author and sportswriting editor at the *New York Daily News*, wrote a vitriolic piece in *Vanity Fair*, titled "Honey," which claimed Babe was a frustrated lesbian who competed in sports because she could not keep a man. Between 1931 and 1938, her sexual and gender identity sparked constant speculation. Writers dissected her physique and features and often presented her as a fascinating not-quite-female creature. One story, for example, assured the reader, "she is not a freakish looking character . . . [but] a normal, healthy, boyish looking girl." Another, in contrast, bluntly stated: "She likes to fight. Her voice is deep, her remarks virulent and pointed. She has few close girl friends and isn't much interested in boys."[11]

The national press obsession with Didrikson's gender and sexuality has created a treasure trove of written and visual material for students to research and examine, asking such questions as how a female athlete's femininity and gender identity were judged and who defined the parameters of normalcy. Teachers can point out the sharp distinctions made between the "beautiful sports" (swimming, horseback riding, golf, skiing, yachting) and the "manly sports" (virtually all team sports, track and field, any sports that required body contact, sweating, and which drew working-class participation).[12] They can use Babe's experience of moving away from the working-class world where she grew up and into the national spotlight to highlight the differing gender expectations in those diverse realms. This latter subject raises especially provocative questions. Didrikson had to relearn what it meant to be feminine, a process that brought with it countless anxieties about achieving that new persona. These anxieties haunted her for her entire life. Questions might involve: "How do girls 'learn' femininity?" and "What price do gender nonconforming athletes pay for their differences?"

Such uneven expectations meant that Olympic success did not bring Didrikson the endorsement success or cinematic stardom of "beautiful sports" athletes such as the swimmer Esther Williams or the three-time Olympic champion ice skater Sonja Henie. Instead, she struck out on her own and earned a living through sensationalized one-on-one competitions in decidedly unusual circumstances for a woman. She pitched pregame batting to major league teams, competed as a bowler and a tennis player, played a version of baseball while straddling the rump of a trained donkey, and donned a fake beard to join a previously all-male bearded barnstorming baseball team called the House of David. She even mock "boxed" with the middleweight champion's *brother*, and was erroneously hailed for knocking out the champion. She also enjoyed a short lucrative stint as a stage entertainer in Chicago.

Still, she yearned to return to serious athletics. To do so, and to make a steady living, she needed a credible sport and a way to shed her controversial image. She consciously undertook a self-feminization process under the tutelage of a Dallas socialite, Bertha Bowen (a wonderful oral history interviewee), who promised to transform Didrikson from an Amazon into a lady.[13] This process included taking up the sport of golf, considered an appropriately ladylike upper-class pursuit. Didrikson saw golf as a way to raise herself above her working-class roots into a sports world with paydays and without rumors of improper femininity. This process of self-feminization also makes for fascinating discussion— a discussion that can be enhanced by examining the many available images of Didrikson in varying outfits and poses. How does being female and feminine vary by social class? To what extent is femininity a conscious performance? A visual performance? What prices are paid by female-identified people who are unable or unwilling to perform conventional femininity?

Babe also boosted her public image in 1938, when she met George Zaharias, a professional wrestler, at a celebrity Pro/Am golfing tournament in Los Angeles. The pair married shortly thereafter, and as one of Didrikson's colleagues recalled, "all of women's golf heaved a collective sigh of relief" because it removed the specter of lesbianism from the sport. Once married, Babe perfected her public displays of femininity. She showed reporters the makeup in her purse, posed with rolling pins in her kitchen, and was photographed in dress and pearls while laying bricks (OK, so not everything was perfectly feminine). She excelled as an amateur golfer and longed for better-paying/more prestigious tournaments for women. She compiled a winning streak of thirteen consecutive tournaments; she later retold this story in hyperbole as seventeen.[14]

This self-conscious, purposeful transformation allows teachers to ask their students to consider Didrikson's life in the context of the changing experiences of ordinary women in the years around World War II. Studying Babe's choices can help students understand some of the debates about "proper" roles for women amid the unemployment and underemployment that marked the Great Depression. It can also shed light on the opportunities available to ordinary women during World War II: high-paying industrial employment, often-autonomous familial decision making; opportunities in the military and civil service that were hailed as patriotic. It can also underscore the dramatic transformation that occurred when the end of the war prompted a return to domesticity and to the nuclear family status quo.[15] In the postwar period, Babe continued to feminize her image to reflect these priorities, creating the public/private spilt so common for exceptional women. She posed as the compliant wife, disappointed that she was childless. In reality, she was the family breadwinner, loved international travel, disliked domestic chores, did not desire children, and tired of George's grueling management of her career, as well as his needs and demands.

In 1948 Babe and several other women formed the Ladies Professional Golf Association (LPGA). Babe promptly dominated the organization. One important sponsor observed, "Babe Zaharias made the women's tour go. She was the color, the gate attraction." It was hard to eke out a living with the modest tournament prize money, so players secured sponsors and worked doggedly to improve the sport's status and following. Babe served as the organization's president from 1953 to 1955. Sheltered by her heteronormative relationship with George, she resumed her boisterous self-promoting ways. She used her fame to help the women's tour when she could—even refusing to finish one tournament in which she had a multistroke lead going into the final round unless the purse money was increased.[16]

She dominated the fairways and the greens. In 1950, she won two-thirds of the LPGA tournaments and earned $14,800, making her that year's leading money winner. In 1951, she won seven of her twelve tournaments. She also played exhibition matches for a hefty $500 each and was the first woman to earn over $100,000 in a year. Ironically, as in most marriages, George controlled the family funds, and she often lacked pocket money. This was kept a secret from the public although her intimates knew.

Students can discuss how, as sports became increasingly commercialized and profitable, the system allowed women like Babe to earn a living. But the costs of this were immense: the national press had, and still has, tremendous power to herald or crush individuals, especially those who do not conform. What examples of this exist currently in our media? Do women have economic equity even now with male athletes? What examples show us that this is not yet the case? For example, the U.S. Women's Soccer Team had to lobby hard for commensurate pay with the men's team, intentionally embarrassing the sport's ruling body to achieve their goal.[17]

In 1950, Babe met Betty Dodd, twenty years her junior and a rising golf star. From then until Babe's death in 1956 they were inseparable. While the details of their relationship were not documented at the time, oral history interviews subsequently revealed their intimate relationship, their cohabitation with George, and their isolation from other women on the tour. In the homophobic McCarthy era of the 1950s they chose to remain closeted. Babe maintained her heterosexual marriage despite increasing friction, and the two women did not interact with any lesbian community.

Teachers can use material about the post–World War II Lavender Scare to help explain why Didrikson and Dodd kept their relationship hidden. It is an excellent opportunity to discuss the ways that cultural norms impact the lives of LGBTQ+ people and their ability to be out. The Lavender Scare proved as virulent as the anticommunist Red Scare, and the charges levied against men and women believed to be "sexual deviants" spelled doom for many. They were (erroneously) thought to be liable to blackmail, deemed unsuitable for military service and government employment, and cast as the antithesis of "good citizens." Why would Babe, who had worked so hard to transform her image from a working-class toughie to a middle-class lady, jeopardize her social capital by outing herself?[18]

Just as Babe Didrikson's athletic accomplishments laid groundwork for the explosion of women's sports that started in the 1970s, the issues she faced around gender identity and homosexuality resonate today as well. Her experiences open the door to an exploration of legal rulings and beliefs about women athletes' sexual and gender identities. Elite female athletes have been hounded by speculation since the 1930s, when some eastern Europeans were accused of taking male hormones for a competitive edge, and when some questioned whether men had been entered in women's events. More recently, IOC mandatory sex testing has included buccal swabs (taken with a Q-tip from inside the cheek), chromosomal testing, and sex certifications provided by gynecologists. The 2008 Beijing Olympics had a "Sex Verification Center" that determined sex via laboratory findings based on external appearance, hormones, and genes, which some female athletes had to pass through before their events.[19] Beyond the Olympics, several notable female athlete's careers were demolished when their chromosomal composition was revealed as hyperandrogenic (a higher than usual level of androgens). This alone has been sufficient to strip women of their titles and honors.[20]

Babe's historical legacy is complex and contradictory. She won the Associated Press's Female Athlete of the Year award six times, was ranked the highest female athlete in ESPN's evaluation of the twentieth-century, and was inducted into several sports Halls of Fame. She was hounded by cruel media speculation but managed her image to create wealth and fame. She felt compelled to remake herself into an acceptable female and live a closeted life. The opportunities and limitations she faced were unique to twentieth-century American women, and her meaning for women athletes cannot be overestimated. Her accomplishments and contentious reception, when coupled with the feminist movement and Title IX, catalyzed radical changes in women's athletic opportunities and attitudes toward female athletes.[21]

Notes

1. See Susan E. Cayleff, *Babe: The Life and Legend of Babe Didrikson Zaharias* (Urbana: University of Illinois Press, 1995); Carroll Smith-Rosenberg, "The New Woman as Androgyne: Social Disorder and Gender Crisis, 1870–1936," in Smith-Rosenberg, *Disorderly Conduct* (New York: Knopf, 1985), 291–92; Glenda Riley, *Inventing the American Woman: A Perspective on Women's History, 1865 to the Present* (Arlington Heights, IL: Harlan Davidson, 1986); Carol Ruth Berkin and Mary Beth Norton, eds., *Women of America: A History* (Boston: Houghton Mifflin, 1979), 109.

2. Cayleff, *Babe*, 43.

3. Donald Mrozek, "The 'Amazon' and the American 'Lady': Sexual Fears of Women in the Industrial and Post-Industrial Eras," in *From "Fair Sex" to Feminism: Sport and the Socialization of Women in the Industrial and Post-Industrial Era*, ed. J. A. Magan and Roberta J. Park (London: Frank Cass, 1978), 59; and Esther Newton, "The Mythic Mannish Lesbian: Radclyffe Hall and the New Woman," *Signs: Journal of Women in Culture and Society* 9 (Summer 1984): 557–75.

4. Judith Walker Lindsley and Ellen Walker Rienstra, *Beaumont: A Chronicle of Promise* (Woodland Hills, CA: Windsor Publications, 1982), 94–95.

5. Cayleff, *Babe*, 50–77. Ellen J. Staurowsky, ed., *Women and Sport: Continuing a Journey of Liberation and Celebration* (Champaign, IL: Human Kinetics, 2016), explores the role of media in contemporary sports. See especially Marie Hardin and Dunja Antunovic, "Women, Media and Sports," 181–93; and Corinne Farneti, "Merchandising and Marketing Women's Sports," 229–46.

6. Susan E. Cayleff, "Prisoners of Their Own Feebleness: Women, Nerves and Western Medicine—A Historical Overview," *Social Science and Medicine* 26 (1988): 1199–208.

7. Theodore Roosevelt, *Foes of Our Own Household* (New York: George H. Doran, 1917); Nancy Ordover, *American Eugenics: Race, Queer Anatomy, and the Science of Nationalism* (Minneapolis: University of Minnesota Press, 2003).

8. Cayleff, *Babe*, 82–88.

9. Lizbeth Cohen, *Making a New Deal: Industrial Workers in Chicago, 1919–1939* (Cambridge: Cambridge University Press, 1990); Michael Denning, *The Cultural Front: The Laboring of American Culture in the Twentieth-Century* (New York: Verso, 1997).

10. Carolyn G. Heilbrun, *Writing a Woman's Life* (New York: Ballantine Books, 1988); Sherna Berger Gluck and Daphne Patai, *Women's Words: The Feminist Practice of Oral History* (Abingdon-on-Thames: Routledge, 1991); Cayleff, *Babe*, 191–96.

11. Cayleff, *Babe*, 82–89; Betty Hicks, "Babe Didrikson Zaharias: 'Stand Back! This Ain't No Kid Hittin,'" *womenSports*, November 1977, 27; Paul Gallico, "Honey," *Vanity Fair*, April 1933.

12. Cayleff, *Babe*, 78–98.

13. Ibid., 113–33.

14. Ibid., 134–78.

15. Susan M. Hartman, *The Home Front and Beyond: American Women in the 1940s* (London: Macmillan, 1983); David Halberstam, *The Fifties* (New York: Ballantine, 1994).

16. Cayleff, *Babe*, as cited in Fred Corcoran, *Unplayable Lies* (New York: Duell, Sloan and Pearce, 1965), 50–77.

17. *New York Times*, July 8, 2016. Also recommended is Jaime Schultz's *Qualifying Times: Points of Change in U.S. Women's Sports* (Urbana: University of Illinois Press, 2014).

18. Excellent sources on this topic are John D'Emilio, *Sexual Politics, Sexual Communities*, 2nd ed. (Chicago: University of Chicago Press, 1998); Byrne Fone, *Homophobia*, 2nd ed. (New York: Picador, 2001); and David K. Johnson, "The Red Scare's Lavender Cousin: The Construction of the Cold War Citizen," in *Understanding and Teaching U.S. Lesbian, Gay, Bisexual, and Transgender History*, ed. Leila J. Rupp and Susan K. Freeman, 2nd ed. (Madison: University of Wisconsin Press, 2017), 186–98.

19. *New York Times*, July 30, 2008.

20. Lindsay Parks Pieper, *Sex Testing, Gender Policing in Women's Sports* (Urbana: University of Illinois Press, 2016).

21. Jean O'Reilly and Susan K. Cahn, eds., *Women and Sports in the United States: A Documentary History* (Boston: Northeastern University Press, 2007).

Black Women Face Obstacles and Opportunities

Pamela Grundy and Rita Liberti

A 1930s photo of the gymnasium at historically black Bennett College in Greensboro, North Carolina, showcases the cramped conditions of the school's basketball court. Wooden walls crowd the sidelines; the basket hangs above an open fireplace; the low ceiling lies in wait for any shot that dares to arch too high. But the young women on the floor have their eyes fixed on the ball, knees bent, arms outstretched, ready to play. Nearly a century after it was taken, the fading image radiates with energetic joy.

The Bennett College photo captures the mix of obstacle and possibility that African American college women faced in a cultural landscape where they stood at the intersection of the powerful hierarchies of white and male supremacy. In a world imbued with damaging racial stereotypes, they had to consider not only the immediate effects of their own actions but also how those actions could be used to challenge or justify those stereotypes. But because of their communities' dire economic straits, and because prominent black men often faced violent reprisal, many black women assumed roles that took them well beyond the limitations of conventional womanhood. The actions and experiences of the era's black female athletes offer ways to help students explore these complex cultural circumstances, as well as learn from the energy and zeal with which these young women worked to improve themselves and their communities.

Bennett College women's basketball team, 1936–37. (Courtesy of the Bennett College Archives at Thomas F. Holgate Library)

Sports can be particularly helpful in illuminating key facets of intersectionality, the analytical strategy that examines the ways that social hierarchies governing arenas such as gender, race, class, and sexuality overlap in varying patterns to create a multiplicity of experience, outlook, and opportunity. Black female athletes were forced to face the double challenge of sexism and racism, which often circumscribed their actions not only in mainstream white society but also in their own African American communities. Still, the meeting of these systems also created some openings.

As the African American philosopher Anna Julia Cooper argued in her classic 1892 work, *A Voice from the South*, black women benefited from an especially "open-eyed" perspective—the ability to see the ways that racism and sexism worked in the world, to understand the damage done by both, and to use that hard-won knowledge to take on new roles and press for greater opportunities for all. During the Jim Crow era, the violence deployed against black men who stepped into the public arena meant that black women, who were perceived as less threatening, often took on prominent community responsibilities that encouraged them to develop expansive concepts of female identity. The variant of sexism that barred white college women from serious athletic competition also meant that black institutions bold enough to challenge those limits were able to shine especially brightly in national and international arenas. As a result, African American communities often fostered particularly vibrant women's sports programs, which in turn nurtured young women's self-assurance.[1]

Two statements from players in the Bennett picture underscore the ways that sports empowered young African American women to move beyond conventional boundaries. Ruth Glover, the crack shooter to the right who reaches out to ball holder Almeda Clavon, saw no contradictions in the way that she and her teammates moved between the demands of high-level competitive sport and those of conventional ladyhood. "We were ladies," she told Rita Liberti in an interview that crackled with happy memories. "We just played basketball like boys." Amaleta Moore, the stalwart defender to the left, recalled in the same interview how the camaraderie and pleasure of sports gave players a confidence that transcended the Jim Crow restrictions that surrounded them. The Bennett team, one of the best in the country, traveled to its matches in the chauffeured Cadillac of David Jones, the Bennett president. "We would be riding along the highway and you'd meet some white fellows thumbing," Moore laughed. "And we'd hang our heads out the window and say: 'Jim Crow car!'"[2]

The balance of opportunity and challenge differed from situation to situation, and accounts of specific teams and individuals reveal different facets of this dilemma, underscoring that black women's experiences were far from monolithic. This essay highlights four stories: Bennett College basketball in the 1930s, Tuskegee women's track in the 1930s and 1940s, and the careers of the tennis player Althea Gibson and the sprinter Wilma Rudolph. All of these stories have been well documented. Each is worth exploring in detail, either in class or through research assignments. Each can stand on its own, as a specific example that helps illustrate a larger point about black women's experiences as a whole. But they work especially well together.[3]

Background

Understanding the challenges black female athletes faced requires examination of the specific racial stereotypes that bolstered white supremacy. While the racist imagery of the early twentieth century can be hard to look at, presenting students with carefully chosen examples—cartoons, advertisements, objects—can help them grasp the powerful effects of these stereotypes. Looking at these images should help students pinpoint two key components: that black women were commonly portrayed as either excessively masculine or as exceedingly sensual.

Examining these images make it possible to introduce a pair of important concepts: double consciousness and the politics of respectability. Double consciousness addresses the ways that African Americans were required to reckon not only with how they saw themselves but also with how their actions would be interpreted by white observers. It includes both a psychological component—W. E. B. DuBois, who originated the term, described it as the "sense of always looking at one's self through the eyes of others"—and the profoundly political awareness that the acts of individual African Americans had repercussions for the race as a whole.[4] That awareness influenced the development of the "politics of respectability," in which educated African Americans stressed the importance of impeccably middle-class behavior, in order to counter the damaging stereotypes that they saw as impeding racial advancement.[5]

Statements about female students from black college catalogs are a great way to underscore these concerns, especially in the case of women. At Shaw University in Raleigh, for example, officials required their female students to be supervised everywhere they went, and devoted part of the annual catalog to discussions of female dress. "Students are expected to dress neatly and modestly," ran one such description. Others forbade the wearing of velvet, satin, expensive jewelry, silk hose, "French heels," thin dresses without slips, and other fashionable garments, going into so much detail that many shifts in women's fashion could be discerned in the changing lists of banned attire. Shaw's catalogs for 1911, 1912, and 1913, available online, are a great way to introduce students to a new kind of historical source and also help emphasize the importance placed on female dress and conduct. The catalogs are illustrated, and the 1911 edition includes pictures of both a women's basketball game and the men's baseball team.[6]

These concepts lay the groundwork for a discussion of the potential advantages and disadvantages that competitive sports held for black women: they offered the possibility of building inner strength and creating school and community spirit, but they could also potentially reinforce stereotypes of excessive masculinity and sexuality. The complexity of the dilemma can be underscored by pointing out that different schools made different decisions. Some black colleges, most notably Howard, Hampton, and Fisk, focused exclusively on noncompetitive physical education. Others, like Bennett and Tuskegee, encouraged competition.[7]

Bennett College Basketball

Bennett College provides an excellent example of the way that one school negotiated these competing demands. Bennett was a small, all-female school that educated about three hundred students in a cluster of brick buildings near the heart of Greensboro, North Carolina. The school prided itself on the ladylike decorum of its graduates who were expected to be paragons of good manners, refined dress, and strict self-control, and to counter negative stereotypes with their every move.[8]

At the same time, Bennett students were being prepared for careers of work and leadership that required an expansive understanding of womanhood, one that focused less on the specific activities a woman undertook and more on whether her actions embodied, in the words of the historian Jennifer Lansbury, "the positive qualities of strength, morality, and family and community commitments that had been forged through difficult circumstances." In oral history interviews, former Bennett players spoke eloquently of how basketball helped them to develop those qualities.[9]

Basketball nurtured individual strengths, helping students to develop discipline, self-control, and confidence, as well as the ability to act decisively under pressure. One night, for example, Bennett was engaged in a heated contest with rival Shaw University, and Shaw forward Frazier Creecy was playing havoc with the Bennett defense. Bennett's coach William Trent told Amaleta Moore to "do something." Moore was ready. "I said: 'I will brace myself and let her come,'" she explained years later. "And I stood there like this and she dribbled straight at me. She hit me, and I didn't move. She fell back on the court—you heard her bones crack when she hit the floor—and they took her off on the stretcher. . . . I didn't hit her or anything. I just stood there, but I braced myself first, because I knew she was going to do it. I said: 'She'll never run over me.'"[10]

The public nature of basketball, and the supportive crowds that cheered the players also helped Bennett students fashion the commitment to community that would fuel their civic endeavors after graduation. "You felt a sense of worth, and a feeling of security," Moore explained. "You learned something about the value of support from your community, from other people. . . . So that you don't have this blown-up idea that you're so important." They also learned that with privilege came responsibility. "You really had the feeling that you were representing the student body," Moore continued. "And you felt that if you didn't win, you were letting them down as well as being disappointed yourself. So I think that sense of responsibility to a larger group was an important aspect. The relationships you develop. You develop these same kinds of relationships with other groups that you work with in the community after you get out of school."

Basketball thus helped students create and practice the kind of flexible identity that would support their work after graduation. It also gave them a self-confidence that allowed them to transcend the psychological restrictions of Jim Crow—as dramatically illustrated by the taunt they issued to white hitchhikers as they sped by in their chauffeured Cadillac.

The value the Bennett players held for their community can be underscored by having students look at coverage of their activities in the black press. For example, many digitized issues of the *Afro American*'s national edition in the 1930s can now be found online. Bennett basketball, as well as other women's basketball activity, can be found on pages throughout the publication's winter months. An assignment could include giving small groups of students one newspaper issue to closely examine. Ask them to record not only how and where the press reports appear in relation to wider sports news but also how the teams and players are presented to readers.[11]

Tuskegee Women's Track

The highly successful women's track team at Alabama's Tuskegee Institute offers an opportunity to explore a different facet of black women's sporting experiences—one whose influence can be seen in the black track stars of the present day. Track and field posed particular challenges for African American women because, like basketball, it was firmly marked as a masculine sport (for more about the coding of "male" and "female" sports, see Fields, "Issues of Sexuality in Sport," and Cayleff, "Teaching Sports and Women's History through 'The Babe'"). Given this context, it is useful to ask students to consider why Tuskegee would have chosen to put so much effort into women's track. There are a number of possible reasons, such as the relatively low cost of track programs, which offer insights into the circumstances of black communities and historically black colleges. But in the end, the most important factor is the makeup of national and international track competition. By the late 1920s, track's highest-profile events—AAU track meets and the Olympic Games—included men's and women's events. And unlike many other high-profile competitions, these contests were integrated, thus offering African Americans valuable opportunities to display their abilities on national and world stages.

The Olympic Games first included women's track and field in 1928, although persisting doubts about women's abilities meant that they would be barred from events longer than the 200-meter dash for several decades.[12] Cleveland Abbott, the legendary Tuskegee athletic director, had already started a men's track team. He added women's competition soon after 1928 and began to look for promising talent around the South.

Tuskegee's female track stars faced many of the same expectations as the Bennett basketball players—they learned the nuances of dress and manners, and carefully guarded their public appearances. But their achievements had wider impact. Since almost no white women's schools sponsored track teams, Tuskegee's women had few rivals. In 1937, led by the speedy Lula Hymes, the Tuskegee Tigerettes captured the national AAU track title. Tuskegee would win the AAU women's championship in ten of the next eleven years before ceding its dominance to another African American team, the Tigerbelles of Tennessee State. The outbreak of World War II meant that no Olympics were held in 1940 or 1944. But in the first postwar Olympics, held in London in 1948, Tuskegee's Alice Coachman took the high jump gold medal. She was the only American woman to win a track-and-field gold that year, and the first woman of African descent to win a medal of any kind.[13]

Did these successes help change the minds of many whites? Probably not. The widespread stigma attached to women's track meant that

116

female track achievements received limited attention in the white press. Even had they been covered, success at a "masculine" sport could in fact reinforce stereotypes that cast black women as overly masculine. The team's successes thus had limited effect on prevailing racial hierarchies.

But one can ask students to think about what else those victories might accomplish. Or, more specifically, who else was watching? In fact, promoters of black athletics were keenly aware that African American athletes performed for dual audiences. Under the right circumstances, black athletic achievement might build respect among whites. But African Americans were watching too. The accomplishments of black athletes—especially in interracial contests—meant a great deal in black communities, whether or not whites acknowledged those successes. Tuskegee women's championships were extensively covered in the black press. At times, these articles displayed the bias familiar to almost any female athlete—they tended to focus more on "proving" the athletes' femininity by describing looks, hobbies, and boyfriends, rather than recounting athletic achievements. But even when white authorities or black reporters failed to fully acknowledge those achievements, the gold medals and national championships spoke for themselves. The runners sparked enormous pride on campus, as well as in African American communities around the country. "Kids on the campus loved you and respected you, and they thought you were the greatest," Leila Perry said. "I think that a whole lot of people looked up to Tuskegee women."[14]

Althea Gibson

In the 1950s, tennis player Althea Gibson became the first black female athlete to attract a significant audience beyond African America. But her path was particularly difficult. As the historian Mary Jo Festle notes, she was "a female in an athletic world that marginalized women, a working-class woman trying to break into an elitist sport, and a black woman in a racist nation, world and sport."[15] She also came to prominence in the 1950s, a period in which particularly conservative views of women dominated both black and white communities.[16] Gibson's experiences dramatically underscore some of the challenges that black women faced both within and outside their own communities.

Much of Gibson's recognition—and some of her challenges—was related to the sport that made her famous: tennis. With its roots in upper-class pastimes and its lack of physical contact, tennis was considered a particularly feminine sport. It also didn't hurt that women played in dresses. For much of the twentieth century, white female tennis champions had been hailed as paragons of both athletic skill and healthy femininity. They had also been held to especially high standards of grace and manners.

It was that prestige that brought Gibson to the game. A tremendously gifted athlete, she grew up playing a wide variety of sports with boys on the streets of New York. Her favorite game was basketball. But the men who spotted her athletic talent steered her into tennis, the game that offered the greatest opportunities for Gibson as an individual and for the race as a whole. The celebration of women's tennis made it the sport where a talented African American woman was most likely to be able to make an impact on the wider world. As the civil rights movement began to gain momentum, African American tennis leaders began to lobby to get black players admitted to major national and international tournaments. To do so effectively, they needed black stars who were capable of playing at the highest levels of the game.

It took years to prepare Gibson for the role of racial pioneer. Unlike basketball or track, tennis was an exclusive, expensive sport, and promising young players such as Gibson needed a wide range of assistance. Two black doctors, Robert Johnson and Hubert Eaton, took on the challenge. Johnson spent summers helping to train Gibson and escorting her to tournaments. Eaton invited her to spend the rest of the year with his family in Wilmington, North Carolina. Gibson, who had dropped out of high school, reenrolled while in Wilmington and began to set her sights on college. While Eaton practiced with her on the family's home court, his wife, Celeste, helped smooth her rough, working-class edges, preparing her for the genteel tennis world. Gibson learned to pay more attention to her dress and hair, to curb her volatile temper, and to be gracious both when she won and when she lost. Step by step, she began to comprehend the duality that the Bennett and Tuskegee athletes had learned to embody. "After a while I began to understand that you could walk out on the court like a lady, all dressed up in immaculate white, be polite to everybody, and still play like a tiger and beat the liver and lights out of the ball," she wrote in her autobiography.[17]

Gibson's talent was unmistakable. By the late 1940s, she was the dominant female player of the all-black American Tennis Association (ATA). In 1950, the United States Lawn Tennis Association (USLTA) bowed to an intensive lobbying effort and invited her to be the first African American to play in the U.S. National Tennis Championship (now the U.S. Open). She would go on to become the greatest female player of her era, with a career that culminated with back-to-back Wimbledon and U.S. championship titles in 1957 and 1958. Some termed her the "female Jackie Robinson," after the pioneering baseball player.

Still, Gibson struggled with the expectations that came with such exalted status. She remained a forceful, independent person who at times stepped beyond the bounds of respectability—bounds that were especially narrow because she was a woman. Despite all her careful training, she still had a strong temper, which sometimes flared and sparked criticism—criticism that took on greater significance once she stepped into the white world. "It was a strain, always trying to say and do the right thing, so that I wouldn't give people the wrong idea of what Negroes were like," she once explained."[18] These difficulties were compounded because unlike the Bennett or Tuskegee athletes she did not have a supportive team surrounding her. She was generally the only African American on the courts or in the women's locker room, and she had trouble making friends with other players.

She also found it hard to live up to the expectations of the black press. As the civil rights movement grew, black writers increasingly looked for outspoken racial champions. This requirement, however, was especially difficult to reconcile with standards of female respectability, especially in an upper-class sport like tennis. In her effort to survive a demanding situation, Gibson chose to focus almost exclusively on playing and winning, rather than on speaking out against racial inequality. This choice created tensions with many black reporters, and in the end she was not accorded the kind of hero status bestowed on Jackie Robinson. After she retired from tennis in 1958, she slipped quickly from the public eye, and struggled for decades just to make a living.

The attention Gibson garnered provides material for a range of student activities. On September 2, 1957, for example, *Sports Illustrated* featured Gibson on their cover. By using the online SI Vault to examine the *Sports Illustrated* covers from 1957 students can formulate questions about whose accomplishments are celebrated, which sports are deemed appropriate for women, and why it was so rare for a black woman to be featured in this way. Students might also look at how a black newspaper, such as the *Chicago Defender*, or a black magazine, such as *Ebony* or *Jet*, covered Gibson. Doing a "close reading" of the covers and the short article that accompanied Gibson's appearance in *Sports Illustrated,* as well as her portrayal in African American publications, can help students put into practice what they've learned about intersectionality, double consciousness, and the politics of respectability. There is also a documentary, *Althea,* that could serve as a jumping-off point for critical discussions about gender and race during this period.[19]

Wilma Rudolph

At the 1960 Rome Olympics, another black woman ran her way to the kind of fame that black athletic promoters dreamed of. The triple-gold-medalist Wilma Rudolph, who had been nurtured by the Tennessee State Tigerbelles, had a classically appealing athletic biography. She contracted polio when she was young and reached stardom only after she and her parents spent endless hours driving to medical clinics and working on often-painful physical therapy. She also fit neatly into female expectations. She was tall and slender, with a dazzling smile and what one admiring writer described "the legs of a showgirl." Her time at Tennessee State had helped her to develop a gracefully sophisticated manner that charmed people wherever she went. In addition, she was competing at an auspicious time—the Cold War competition between the United States and the Soviet Union had spilled over into sports, especially the Olympics, and every Olympic medal won by an American was seen as a blow in favor of what was becoming known as the American Way. When Rudolph won gold medals in the 100- and 200-meter dashes, and in the 4 × 100 relay, she became a worldwide celebrity. The blend of skill and charm displayed by Rudolph and her Tigerbelles teammates began to transform the image of women's track, making it a more acceptable activity for women.

Rudolph, however, faced a new challenge. Both southern and American leaders sought to use her accomplishments to project images of American race relations that differed significantly from reality. When she returned home from her Olympic triumphs, for example, her hometown of Clarksville, Tennessee, mounted an elaborate ceremony. Children were excused from school and thousands of residents lined the streets to watch her parade through the streets in a convertible. That evening, more than one thousand people attended an interracial dinner. The celebration, covered by *Life* magazine and by newspapers around the world, presented a progressive, forward-looking vision of the town.[20]

Shortly afterward, the United States Information Agency (USIA) made a film: *Wilma Rudolph: Olympic Champion*, designed to paint a similar picture about American racial progressivism. This and other such films presented a romanticized picture of race relations in the United States, ignoring evidence of poverty and discrimination and focusing instead on images of prosperity, harmony, and success (for a more detailed discussion of these films, their Cold War context, and how they might be used in class, see Liberti, "'Ambassadors in Short Pants': Sport and the Cold Warriors").

While in Rome, Rudolph had clearly expressed her discontent with American racism, telling the African American *New York Amsterdam News* that "It's going to all but kill me to have to go home and face being denied this, that, and the other, because I'm a Black American."[21] And in fact, her accomplishments had little immediate effect on those underlying realities. After her celebratory homecoming, for example, Clarksville institutions continued to maintain strict racial segregation. Three years later, Rudolph herself would be locked out of a Clarksville restaurant after she joined a protest against segregated institutions.[22]

These materials make great sources for student projects. Students should find it especially revealing to compare descriptions of Rudolph's accomplishments and activities found in both the black and the white press. The many children's books written about Rudolph offer another way to look at which stories from her life do and do not get told, allowing students to assess the specific historical meanings her accomplishments have been given, as well as their larger implications for understanding American society.[23]

As well as detailing the complexities of black women's sporting experience, we believe these stories demonstrate the importance of looking specifically at the experiences of black female athletes, rather than simply including black women in discussions of female athletes or African American athletes as a whole. Only by considering black women on their own is it possible to emphasize the full range of opportunities created by racial circumstances, and the ways black women took advantage of them, while also highlighting the specific challenges they faced—and still face—in confronting the shifting incarnations of patriarchy and white supremacy.[24]

Notes

1. For more detail on Cooper, see Karen A. Johnson, *Uplifting the Women and the Race: The Lives, Educational Philosophies and Social Activism of Anna Julia Cooper and Nannie Helen Burroughs* (New York: Routledge, 2000). For examples of how black women in North Carolina stepped beyond conventional bounds in order to meet community needs, see Glenda Gilmore, *Gender and Jim Crow: Women and the Politics of White Supremacy in North Carolina* (Chapel Hill: University of North Carolina Press, 1996), 165–75.

2. Rita Liberti, "'We Were Ladies, We Just Played Basketball Like Boys:' A Study of Women's Basketball at Historically Black Colleges and Universities in North Carolina, 1925–1945" (PhD diss., University of Iowa, 1998), 167. See also Liberti, "We Were Ladies, We Just Played Like Boys: African-American Womanhood and Competitive Basketball at Bennett College, 1928–1942," in *Sport and the Color Line: Black Athletes and Race Relations in Twentieth-Century America*, ed. Patrick B. Miller and David K. Wiggins (New York: Routledge, 2004), 83–99. All the citations in this article come from Liberti's dissertation.

3. Several historians have examined the lives of Alice Coachman, Althea Gibson, and Wilma Rudolph, and a class could be focused around the life of any one of them. See particularly David K. Wiggins, ed., *Out of the Shadows: A Biographical History of African American Athletes* (Fayetteville: University of Arkansas Press, 2008); Jennifer H. Lansbury, *A Spectacular Leap: Black Women Athletes in Twentieth-Century America* (Fayetteville: University of Arkansas Press, 2014); and Rita Liberti and Maureen M. Smith, *(Re)Presenting Wilma Rudolph* (Syracuse, NY: Syracuse University Press, 2015). Although this article does not deal with Ora Washington, the basketball and tennis star who was the dominant African American female athlete of the early twentieth century, her life provides a fascinating study of sports, the Great Migration, and the making of history. See Pamela Grundy, "Ora Washington: The First Black Female Athletic Star," in Wiggins, *Out of the Shadows*, 79–92.

4. W. E. B. DuBois, *The Souls of Black Folk* (New York: Dover Publications, 1903).

5. The politics of respectability was initially conceptualized by Evelyn Brooks Higginbotham in *Righteous Discontent: The Women's Movement in the Black Baptist Church, 1880–1920* (Cambridge, MA: Harvard University Press, 1994). In the full rendering, middle-class women's respectable behavior was aimed at both directly countering stereotypes and encouraging working-class black women to adopt similar standards. For more recent perspectives on this concept, see the special issue on the subject published by *Souls: A Critical Journal of Black Politics, Culture and Society* 18 (December 2016).

6. Quote from Pamela Grundy, *Learning to Win: Sports, Education and Social Change in Twentieth-Century North Carolina* (Chapel Hill: University of North

Carolina Press, 2001), 63. The online catalogs are at http://library.digitalnc .org/cdm/ref/collection/yearbooks/id/6146.

7. For the development of physical education in African American schools, see Grundy, *Learning to Win*, 234–39.

8. For a comprehensive account of Bennett and how it fit into the broader picture of black female athletics, see Liberti, "'We Were Ladies.'"

9. Jennifer H. Lansbury "'The Tuskegee Flash' and 'the Slender Harlem Stroker': Black Women Athletes on the Margin," *Journal of Sport History* 28 (Summer 2001): 235; see also Liberti, "We Were Ladies'"; Pamela Grundy and Susan Shackelford, *Shattering the Glass: The Remarkable History of Women's Basketball* (New York: New Press, 2005), 69–76.

10. Grundy and Shackelford, *Shattering the Glass*, 74–75.

11. See, for example, www.afro.com/archives/.

12. The ban on longer events followed the supposed collapse of several female competitors in the 1928 800-meter dash, although that story was later shown to be a myth. Women were allowed to run the 400 and the 800 in the 1964 Olympics, the 1,500 in 1972, and finally the marathon in 1984 (see Catsam, "The Political Olympics").

13. For a detailed description of the development of female track teams at black colleges, including the Tuskegee team, see Susan K. Cahn, *Coming on Strong: Gender and Sexuality in Women's Sport*, 2nd ed. (Urbana: University of Illinois Press, 2015), 117–25. See also Lansbury, *Spectacular Leap*, 43–74.

14. Press coverage of the Tuskegee women is worth an exploration in itself. Both Cahn, *Coming on Strong*, 133–39, and Lansbury, *Spectacular Leap*, offer intriguing analyses of those articles.

15. Mary Jo Festle, "'Jackie Robinson Without the Charm': The Challenges of Being Althea Gibson," in Wiggins, *Out of the Shadows*, 189.

16. That growing conservatism meant that many popular black basketball teams, including those at Tuskegee and Bennett, were in fact dismantled between the 1940s and the early 1960s. See Grundy and Shackelford, *Shattering the Glass*, 109–19.

17. Lansbury, *Spectacular Leap*, 86.

18. Festle, "'Jackie Robinson Without the Charm,'" 201.

19. The documentary can be found at www.pbs.org/wnet/americanmasters /althea-gibson-full-film/5387/.

20. Liberti and Smith, *(Re)-presenting Wilma Rudolph*. This work offers an in-depth exploration of the many ways that Rudolph's accomplishments have been portrayed over the years, touching on subjects range from film to children's literature to public monuments.

21. Ibid., 36.

22. Ibid., 87.

23. For a scholarly assessment of these works, see ibid., 155–84.

24. The persistence of racial stereotypes, and players' efforts to combat them, can be emphasized with several more contemporary examples. Students might explore the controversy sparked in 2007 when radio "shock jock" Don Imus referred to the Rutgers's women's basketball team as "nappy headed hos." They might examine Florence Griffith-Joyner's combination of style and power. Or they might look at the ways the remarkable careers of Venus and Serena Williams have been interpreted. Good places to start would be Lansbury, *Spectacular Leap*, 191–245; Nicole Fleetwood, *On Racial Icons* (New Brunswick, NJ: Rutgers University Press), 97–110; and David J. Leonard and C. Richard King, eds., *Commodified and Criminalized: New Racism and African Americans in Contemporary Sports* (Lanham, MD: Rowman and Littlefield, 2011).

Title IX

Contested Terrain

Bobbi A. Knapp

In the decades since its passage, Title IX of the Education Amendments of 1972 has transformed the halls of education and thus our society writ large. Born from the efforts of women frustrated at being shut out of graduate and professional programs, Title IX states: "No person in the United States shall, on the basis of sex, be excluded from participation in, be denied the benefits of, or be subjected to discrimination under any educational program or activity receiving federal financial assistance."[1]

Title IX says nothing about sports. But the effects of Title IX on school athletics has consistently garnered the most attention and controversy. While federal legislators and the general public came to see the value in allowing half the population equal access to higher levels of education, the suggestion that girls and women should have equitable access to and opportunities in school athletics seemed beyond many people's understanding. This presents a conundrum. As the editors of *Equal Play* ask, how is it that legislation that calls for equitable treatment between the sexes has been so controversial in a country where we pride ourselves on equality?[2] I argue that crux of the issue was (and is) the role that sport and its associated physicality plays in the production and reproduction of masculinity in our society. The hegemonic masculinity valued most in sports is also the foundation upon which a patriarchal gender hierarchy is built and maintained. To allow girls and women access to sports, and to value their participation in the same way in which we value male participation, has the potential to disrupt that gender hierarchy.

Teaching about Title IX allows students to examine this hierarchy and the ways that individuals and institutions reinforce it. It also allows them to explore the long, slow process of institutional and cultural change—a process that in the case of Title IX has required not only federal legislation but also constant effort on the part of advocates and allies. The change has been dramatic. Just prior to the enactment of Title IX, 294,015 girls participated in organized sports at the high school level. As of 2015–16, that number had reached 3,324,326, the highest on record at that time. In that same time period, women's participation at the college level has increased 545 percent. But the road was far from easy.[3]

Why Focus on Sport?

Historically sport has often been overlooked by educators as a meaningful site of inquiry and knowledge acquisition. But sporting realms often provide a microcosm of the larger culture of which they are a part—each influencing and being influenced by the other. This symbiotic relationship between sport and culture makes it a valuable focus for examining gender, race, social class, ability, age, nationality, and other points of power. Furthermore, I recommend incorporating sport into your classroom discussions of gender and Title IX because of the way in which gender has been socially constructed in our society. Many Americans have been taught, both formally and informally, that men and women are significantly different—presumptions of difference that are often based on the physical. That is where sports come into play. Taught effectively, lessons on Title IX can connect culture, sport, and legislation not only to history but to the larger gender discussions that are taking place in our students' everyday lives.

Teaching Title IX

Though Title IX has been part of our national landscape for more than forty-five years, I find that most college students have little or no understanding of the legislation. If they have any awareness of it, they often wrongly associate it with a bias toward women and thus a deficit for men. They have a lot to learn.

In my sports history and sports studies classes, I start by teaching students about social construction, critical theory, power, social class, race, and gender. We get to the topic of gender just after midsemester, and by then most students have developed a heightened awareness of power issues. Throughout the course, I encourage my students to ask several key questions: Who benefits from things being arranged this way? How has this been maintained historically, and how does it continue to be maintained? Whose perspective is dominant in our historical understanding of this topic? Especially important: How is this being resisted?

Gender as a social construct is a key concept for students to grasp. After differentiating between sex and gender, I ask students to provide some examples of gendered characteristics we often associate with masculinity—typical responses include aggressive, dominant, and athletic—and with femininity—responses often include nurturing, weak, and soft. To underscore the point that gender is socially constructed through multiple social spheres for the purpose of maintaining the power structure of patriarchy, I ask several follow-up questions. Who benefits the most from these constructions of gender? Which groups are disadvantaged? What are some examples of social spheres that influence our understanding of gender? How does each of these spheres specifically work to impact our understanding of gender? What role does sport play in our understanding of gender?

When discussing the role of sport in our understanding of sex and gender I note that sport is often used as "proof" that all males are physically superior to all females. In fact, sport has been socially constructed to support this very hypothesis. Michael Messner, among others, has noted that after the industrial revolution the narrowing spaces and places in which males could prove their masculinity produced a masculinity "crisis."[4] Sports were used to remediate this crisis and thus became concurrent with our notions of masculinity in this society. Using the same list of gender characteristics the students created before, we then discuss which of those characteristics we tend to associate with being an athlete. Students find that those characteristics we associate with masculinity we also often associate with athleticism. Historical sources such as "Woodrow Wilson Supports Football and its Promotion of Manliness" and "Theodore Roosevelt Examines How Sport Makes Boys into Men" help them strengthen their understanding of the historical nature of this connection.[5]

When we discuss the present day, Mariah Burton Nelson's book, *The Stronger Women Get, the More Men Love Football,* is an excellent source for underscoring that the sports and the types of athleticism we value tend to prioritize characteristics more strongly associated with males and masculinity. As women have gained more opportunities outside of the home sphere, sports such as football have played increasingly prominent roles in justifying the current gender hierarchy.[6]

The Beginning

The footprints of Title IX appeared long before its passage in 1972. Throughout much of the twentieth century, women encountered barriers in their attempts to further their knowledge and professional proficiencies in educational settings. Quotas and other biases meant that women were underrepresented in medical, dental, legal, and many other graduate programs. Before 1972, for example, women made up fewer than 10 percent of medical students in the United States.[7] Women such as Dr. Bernice Sandler—known to many as the grandmother or godmother of Title IX—took a stand against this inequality, and those women became crucial voices in the crusade for gender equality in federally funded educational institutions.

Experiences with discrimination helped inspire Rep. Patsy Mink of Hawaii to pen Title IX. An exemplary student, Mink set her sights on becoming a doctor. After finishing her undergraduate degree in 1942, she applied to twenty different medical schools. Despite her excellent academic record, she was quickly rejected by all of the programs. Based upon some of the comments she received in those rejection letters, she realized her "fault" wasn't her ability but rather her gender. Revising her strategy, and turning her attention to law school, Mink used just her first initials in her law school applications. The strategy worked, and she graduated from the law school at the University of Chicago in 1951. One of very few congressional women, and the first Asian American woman voted into the House of Representatives, Mink saw Title IX as a way to break open some of the barriers she had faced. The significance of her role in the legislation was acknowledged upon her death in 2002, when Title IX was renamed the Patsy T. Mink Equal Opportunity in Education Act.[8]

With a story not unlike Mink's, Rep. Edith Green also became a sponsor and strong advocate for Title IX. A top undergraduate at the

University of Oregon, Green wished to pursue a career in law. However, her family, academic advisors, and cultural norms pushed her toward teaching, a career that was seen as more suitable for women. Green's career as an accomplished teacher influenced her decisions as a politician, and she became known as an expert on educational policy. Green served ten terms in the U.S. House of Representatives, from 1955 to 1975, and played a key role in the development and passage of Title IX. I find that introducing students to women such as Bernice Sandler, Edith Green, and Patsy Mink can help students to understand the impact individuals can have on issues of equality.

Another key figure in the passage and support of Title IX was Sen. Birch Bayh from Indiana. Introducing Bayh into a classroom discussion of Title IX can help to break down the women-versus-men narrative that often emerges in more casual discussions of the topic. Bayh was a strong advocate for Title IX, and his passion and advocacy are believed to be one of the key reasons the legislation passed the Senate. Bayh often referenced the strong women in his life, including his wife and grandmother, as reasons he supported Title IX. Marvella Bayh, the senator's wife, had dreamed of attending the University of Virginia but was denied that opportunity because the university did not accept women at that time. Bayh credited his wife with influencing his stance on Title IX. "She said we can't afford to ignore the development of 53 percent of the brainpower in this country," he later explained. "I had no idea how far that basic idea would go."[9] Bayh would become a tenacious advocate for Title IX, work that including fending off the passage of amendments meant to diminish the scope of the legislation's impact on athletics. His efforts help emphasize the importance of allies in the continued struggle for gender equality.

Post-Passage Pushback

While many people now associate Title IX with interscholastic and intercollegiate athletics, sports were not the motivation for the passage of Title IX and were not originally considered by the author and sponsors. Although the gap in school sports opportunities between men and women was enormous, cultural associations between sports and masculinity were so strong that almost no one noticed—a point well worth discussing. Once Title IX passed, however, regulation-writers for the Department of Health, Education and Welfare (HEW) had to decide what the lofty sentiments expressed in the legislation would mean on the ground (an excellent place to emphasize the complex layers of decision making involved in putting federal legislation into practice). First, they had to determine whether sports would fall under the umbrella of Title IX. Second, they had to decide whether providing equal opportunities for women meant simply allowing women to try out for existing men's teams, or whether schools would be required to create separate women's teams.[10]

In 1974, when the proposed regulations were released, they asserted that sports did fall under Title IX and that providing equality for women required creating women's teams. At that point, a large wave of resistance developed. Much of this resistance was fostered by the National Collegiate Athletic Association (NCAA). When Title IX passed, the NCAA governed most intercollegiate men's athletic programs, which controlled nearly 99 percent of university athletic budgets. Women's programs were overseen by the Association of Intercollegiate Athletics for Women (AIAW). Once the university administrators that governed men's athletics realized the threat that Title IX posed to their control over athletic budgets, they put together what they referred to as the NCAA "war chest"—money to fight Title IX at the national level.[11]

The antagonism against Title IX stemmed from perceptions of loss of control, misplaced beliefs that men's athletics would lose money to women's athletics, and the idea that women weren't interested in sports. Soon after the connections between Title IX and sports were established, members of Congress introduced amendments to end Title IX, to eliminate the need for athletic programs to comply with Title IX, or to remove revenue-producing sports from Title IX requirements. One of the first such amendments was sponsored by John Tower, the Republican senator from Texas. The Tower Amendment of 1974 sought to exempt revenue-generating sports—especially football—from Title IX compliance. Tower also noted that he had heard from university administrators who claimed that female students were not interested in sports. Those in support of Title IX countered that interest cannot be developed in a vacuum and thus one cannot claim that females are not interested in sports if they have never been given opportunities to participate. Hard work by Title IX advocates, along with strong support from HEW and other members of Congress meant that the Tower Amendment and others were rejected. The Title IX regulations were issued in 1975, with compliance required by 1978.

One way to highlight the link between opportunity and interest is by discussing the increased participation rates among girls and women in sport after the passage of Title IX. I often do this with the aid of several projected images that include information gathered from the website of the National Federation of State High School Associations.[12] I start with a graph that highlights the number of girls participating in sports in 1971 and ask students for reasons that might explain the low number of participants. We discuss how the number could be used to argue both for and against the inclusion of athletics under Title IX. I then show the class an image from the 1969–2014 High School Athletics Participation Survey that breaks down boys' and girls' participation rates in various teams in 1971. What often stands out to the students is how few schools offered sports for girls and the limited range of sports provided for girls in addition to the overall lower number of girls participating. I follow up by showing the participation table for 1973, the year after Title IX was passed, and then the table for 1978, the year compliance was required. Both tables show a marked increase in female athletic opportunities. Such a discussion is often fruitful in helping students see how interest can bloom once opportunities are made available.

In response to the regulations, the NCAA developed a new plan of action to help to ensure its domination of control and money in athletic programs. While the AIAW had become the largest governing body in college athletics, the NCAA was by far the most powerful. In the early 1980s, the NCAA used that power to wrest control over women's athletics from the AIAW. Michelle Hosick's 2011 article "Equal Opportunity Knocks" is an informative read that helps students understand some of the AIAW/NCAA dynamics of this time.[13] The takeover of women's athletics by the NCAA allowed men's athletic administrators to control the vast majority of athletic dollars. In almost all instances where women had administrated separate women's athletic programs, those women lost their jobs as the departments merged. The shift had significant consequences, especially in terms of funding. Since the collapse of separate women's athletic departments, for every dollar given to women's athletics, additional money has been given to men's athletics.[14]

How Title IX works

Title IX raises another important issue: How do you measure equality? Title IX's measurement of equality involves three salient points, three requirements, and a three-part test (three prongs). These are known as the "three threes" of Title IX. While this is a lot of material to cover, it shows how difficult it can be to measure equality, and provides plenty of material for students to discuss.

Three Salient Points

The three salient points of Title IX are the three conditions that have to exist in order for Title IX to apply: an educational program, discrimination based on sex, and federal funding. After discussing these salient points, students and I explore what is not specifically stated in Title IX: women and sports. Students are often surprised to learn Title IX is not limited to females. In fact, Title IX wording requires equality for an "underrepresented sex." Historically, and in most current situations, females are the underrepresented sex. But if that were to change, Title IX could be used to benefit males. Indeed, some legal cases have recently been filed by male students, particularly related to sexual assault investigations.[15]

Three Requirements

The three requirements of Title IX involve financial assistance, treatment in program areas, and participation levels.

Regarding financial assistance, it is important to point out that Title IX regulations do not require athletic budgets for men's and women's sports to be equal. This acknowledges that all sports do not cost the same. The safety equipment and uniforms required for a women's volleyball team, for example, are minimal compared to the safety equipment and uniforms required for a men's football team. Additionally, schools are required to provide athletic scholarships substantially proportionate to athletic participation numbers for women and men. Thus, if 56 percent of the athletes are male, male athletes should receive 56 percent of the athletic scholarship dollars.[16]

The treatment in program areas requirement focuses on the quality of experiences, and deals with the benefits, opportunities, and treatment of the underrepresented sex. This is often referred to as the "laundry list" of Title IX and includes items such as practice and competition facilities, equipment, travel, and scheduling of practice and competition schedules. Although Title IX's requirements do not require equal funding, they do require equitable benefits. For example, if a school's Tier 1 men's teams get new uniforms every year, then its Tier 1 women's teams should also get new uniforms every year. This is an area where students have a lot to say. Many of the students in my classes were athletes in high school, and they are often able to provide examples of their own experiences with inequities in benefits, opportunities, and treatment.

Three-Part Test (Three Prongs)

The most significant of the three requirements refers to actual sporting opportunities. Educational institutions can show they are in compliance with this requirement by satisfying at least one part of what is known as the three-part test, which includes three "prongs." As set out in the 1979 Policy Interpretation Manual, the test includes a proportionality prong, a history and continuing practice prong, and an interest and ability prong. Educational institutions need comply with only one of the three prongs to meet this requirement.

Institutions can comply with the proportionality prong by showing that the ratio of male and female athletes is substantially proportionate to the ratio of male and female undergraduate students. This prong is considered the "safe harbor" of Title IX.

They can comply with the second prong by proving they have a history of continuing efforts to add opportunities for the underrepresented sex.

They can comply with the third prong by showing that they have fully and effectively met the interests and abilities of the underrepresented sex.

Foot-dragging

Originally, educational institutions were supposed to comply with Title IX by 1978 or face losing all their federal funding. One might think that with such a devastating punishment on the line educational institutions would be quick to come into compliance. However, as we have seen with other aspects of Title IX, it is not quite so simple. At this point, I remind my students that while Title IX has been federal law for more than forty-five years, no educational program has ever lost federal financing for noncompliance. Not only has this ultimate penalty never been applied, it also has never even been threatened. Combining this lack of penalties with the examples of inequality that students have personally described, and with reports that nearly 80 percent of educational programs remain out of compliance, makes for a fascinating discussion.[17]

If a federal law has been in place for nearly half a century and no educational institution has been threatened with the ultimate penalty, let alone experienced it, how compelled will administrators feel to comply? This question often leads to meaningful discussions about lack of oversight and how it impacts one's perceptions of equity. If few schools have received consequences and none have had their financial funding pulled, it is easy to conclude that interscholastic and intercollegiate athletics have in fact become equitable.

Change over Time

National political changes have had major effects on Title IX enforcement. If the administration in power does not support strong enforcement of Title IX and other civil rights legislation, then the Office of Civil Rights, which is responsible for overseeing Title IX compliance, is often underfunded. Without funding there is no money to do compliance reviews or investigate complaints. If an administration supports the promotion of gender equity, it may take actions to enhance the power of Title IX. Such shifts in enforcement are generally symptomatic of gender struggles and larger social justice issues at a particular time.

Dr. Christine Grant, the former women's athletic director at the University of Iowa and a nationally recognized expert and advocate for Title IX and women's athletics, refers to the 1980s as the "dark ages" of women's athletics. Starting with the election of Ronald Reagan in 1980, there was a concerted effort throughout those years to reduce federal authority over many aspects of American society, rolling back many of the gains made by civil rights and women's rights groups. Title IX became one target. In 1984 the Reagan administration encouraged a lawsuit that led to a key judicial decision: *Grove City v. Bell*. Grove City College, a small, religious school in Pennsylvania, argued that because it was a private school that did not accept direct federal funds, it was not bound by Title IX requirements. Some of its students, however, financed their education with federal grants. In the end, the Supreme Court ruled that Grove City College was required to follow Title IX, but that only those programs receiving direct federal financial assistance— in this case the school's financial aid program—had to comply with the regulations. As athletic programs did not receive "direct" federal funding, they did not have to comply with Title IX. This court decision, which had wide-ranging implications, came just six years after the mandated compliance date for educational institutions.[18]

Grove City v. Bell was one of several lawsuits that threatened to reduce the scope of federal nondiscrimination legislation, including the Civil Rights Act of 1964. In response, Congress passed the Civil Rights Restoration Act of 1987 over President Reagan's veto. The Act stated explicitly that any organization that received any federal funding for any purposes must enforce federal nondiscrimination rules throughout the institution. The philosophies and power struggles that propelled these various actions would make for a meaningful class discussion about the nature of federal legislation and the checks and balances within the federal system.

The impact of politics on Title IX was most debilitating in the first two decades after the legislation's enactment and was experienced at local as well as national levels. Dr. Charlotte West, the former women's athletic director at Southern Illinois University Carbondale and nationally recognized expert and advocate for Title IX and women's athletics, saw this play out in several ways. West found that many college administrators were originally hostile toward those who supported Title IX, withholding key information from them, and, at times, engaging in open threats. At one point, for example, the state of Illinois put together a committee that visited colleges in the state to explore issues around Title IX. When the committee scheduled a visit to Southern Illinois, Dr. West, then the women's athletic director, was not informed of the plans. Only through a call from the wife of a member of the university's Board of Trustees was she made aware of, and thus able to properly prepare for, the upcoming visit. Fortunately, West and others were able to develop a group of allies, including a woman in the school's affirmative action department, a student on the Graduate Student Council, the legal counsel for the AIAW, and fellow members in the AIAW. These dedicated individuals formed a network of support for those on the frontlines of the battle to realize the promise of Title IX.[19]

Allies such as this, even those who did not feel free to openly support Title IX and those fighting for gender equity, had a positive impact on Title IX. Discussing some of these examples with students, or—even better—finding examples from one's own institution, provides an opportunity to discuss the continuing importance of individuals willing to take a stand to support social justice legislation. Over time, these actions (which also included lawsuits brought by courageous individuals) changed institutions and the NCAA, which eventually developed a more equitable stance on issues of gender in college athletics. The NCAA Gender Equity Taskforce has formulated an especially strong declaration regarding equity: "That is to say, an athletic program is gender equitable when the men's sports program would be pleased to accept for its own the overall participation, opportunities and resources currently allocated to the women's program and vice versa."[20] I have found having my students respond to this statement is a good way to end the lecture/discussion on Title IX as it helps to highlight we still have progress to make in this area.

   While Title IX is based on the simple principle of equality, that has proven to be anything but simple in our changing political and ideological landscapes. Title IX is a living history whose story continues to be written. As such, it allows teachers to develop assignments that explore the historical points of Title IX with current-day headlines and court cases. Throughout my courses I try to instill in my students a belief that they have the power to effect change. The foundation for such power is education and awareness. I seek to give my students a basic education about this significant federal legislation and use examples provided in lecture, readings, and discussion to help them become more aware of the gender inequity that still exists in educational programs such as sports, and how this impacts the larger gender hierarchy. It is then up to the students to decide if they will be agents of positive change on this issue. Will they educate others on the topic? Will they interrupt and correct someone who is sharing falsehoods? What will they do when they see gender inequity in their educational institution or another?

Notes

   1. United States Department of Justice, "Overview of Title IX of the Education Amendments of 1972," https://www.justice.gov/crt/overview-title-ix-educationamendments-1972-20-usc-1681-et-seq (accessed July 2017).

2. Nancy Hogshead-Makar and Andrew Zimbalist, *Equal Play: Title IX and Social Change* (Philadelphia: Temple University Press, 2007).

3. "High School Sports Participation Increases for 27th Consecutive Year," www.nfhs.org/articles/high-school-sports-participation-increases-for-27th-consecutive-year/; www.womenssportsfoundation.org/education/title-ix-and-the-rise-of-female-athletes-in-america/; Erin Irick, "Student-Athlete Participation 1981–1982–2015–2016: NCAA Sports Sponsorship and Participation Rates Report" (Indianapolis, IN: NCAA, 2016), http://www.ncaapublications.com/productdownloads/PR1516.pdf (both accessed July 2017).

4. Michael Messner, "Sports and Male Domination: The Female Athlete as Contested Ideological Terrain," *Sociology of Sport Journal* 5 (1988): 197–211.

5. Both articles are reproduced in Richard Ford and Steven A. Riess, eds., *Major Problems in American Sport History* (Boston: Houghton Mifflin College Division, 1997).

6. Mariah Burton Nelson, *The Stronger Women Get, the More Men Love Football: Sexism and the American Culture of Sports* (New York: Harcourt, 1994).

7. United States Department of Justice, "Equal Access to Education: Forty Years of Title IX" (2012), https://www.justice.gov/sites/default/files/crt/legacy/2012/06/20/titleixreport.pdf (accessed July 2017).

8. A good place for students to learn about the important role Mink played with Title IX is Molly Carnes, "What Would Patsy Mink Think?" *Journal of the American Medical Association* 307 (2012): 571–72.

9. Melissa Isaacson, "Birch Bayh: A Senator Who Changed Lives," ESPN, May 3, 2012, http://www.espn.com/espnw/title-ix/article/7883692/birch-bayh-senator-changed-lives (accessed November 2017).

10. Susan Ware, *Title IX: A Brief History with Documents* (Boston: Bedford/St. Martin's, 2007), offers an excellent capsule history of the efforts that produced Title IX, as well as documents that help students explore many of its nuances.

11. Pamela Grundy and Susan Shackelford, *Shattering the Glass: The Remarkable History of Women's Basketball* (New York: New Press, 2005), 148–50.

12. National Federation of High School Associations, "1969–2014 High School Athletics Participation Survey Results," http://www.nfhs.org/ParticipationStatics/PDF/Participation%20Survey%20History%20Book.pdf (accessed November 2017).

13. Michelle Hosick, "Equal Opportunity Knocks: National Girls and Women in Sports Day Celebrates 25th Year," http://www.ncaa.com/news/ncaa/article/2011-02-02/equal-opportunity-knocks (accessed November 2017).

14. Amy Wilson, "45 Years of Title IX: The Status of Women in Intercollegiate Athletics," https://www.ncaa.org/sites/default/files/TitleIX45-295-FINAL_WEB.pdf (accessed November 2017).

15. Brandy Zadronzy, "Student: Notre Dame Expelled Me Because I'm Male," https://www.thedailybeast.com/student-notre-dame-expelled-me-because-im-male (accessed January 2018).

16. For this calculation, athletes are counted only once even if they participate in more than one sport.

17. Wilson, "45 Years of Title IX."

18. See Grundy and Shackelford, *Shattering the Glass*, 200–202.

19. Author conversation with Charlotte West, November 2017.

20. Erianne A. Weight and Robert H. Zullo, eds., *Administration of Intercollegiate Athletics* (Champaign, IL: Human Kinetics, 2015), 90–91.

Part Three

Race
and Ethnicity

Jim Crow at Play

Pamela Grundy

A Black Jockey Revives a Rich Derby Tradition" ran the headline in the *New York Times* on May 5, 2000. Marlon St. Julien would ride Curule in that year's Kentucky Derby, becoming the first black jockey to bring a horse to the starting gate in the nation's most storied race since 1921. As the article noted, that drought stood in sharp contrast to the derby's early years: African American jockeys rode thirteen of the fifteen horses in the inaugural event in 1875, and they won fifteen of the first twenty-eight contests.

Since St. Julien's ride (he finished seventh on the long-shot Curule), media accounts of the nineteenth-century glory days of African American jockeys have cropped up regularly around derby time, a welcome addition to a growing public awareness of the long, distinguished tradition of African American sport.

In recent decades, a sporting history once dominated by the pioneers of integration—figures such as Joe Louis, Jesse Owens, Jackie Robinson, and Althea Gibson—has expanded to include athletes such as pioneering baseball player Fleet Walker, controversial boxer Jack Johnson, college football standout Fritz Pollard, tennis whiz Ora Washington, and the basketball stars of the barnstorming Harlem Renaissance. The Negro Leagues, where African American baseball players displayed their skills for decades, have gained particular stature. Books, films, and articles chronicle teams and players; Negro League jerseys are familiar sights at ballparks and on city streets; and Negro League Days have become a staple feature of minor and major league seasons.

Lithograph of jockey Isaac Murphy spurring his horse to victory in an 1890 match race. Currier and Ives, 1891. (Library of Congress, Prints & Photographs Division)

This expanded story, nurtured by decades of diligent research, is also a boon to teachers of American history. The shifting fortunes of African American athletes offer distinctive insights into a key aspect of this nation's past—the making, unmaking, and remaking of racial hierarchies. In particular, they illuminate the workings of cultural hegemony: the process in which a set of beliefs and assumptions become so thoroughly embodied in the fabric of daily life that they seem "natural," not worth questioning or challenging. Since modern sports are often viewed as a microcosm of society, access to and success in the sporting realm can play especially significant roles in both creating and contesting the idea that a racial status quo is "just the way things are."

This essay focuses on ways to help students glean insights from black athletes' experiences in the years after the Civil War. It was a dramatic time, one in which African Americans seized on the brief window of opportunity that followed the demise of slavery, only to see it slam shut as a reconfigured racial hierarchy once again relegated them to a separate and unequal place in American society. The rising and falling fortunes of black jockeys, baseball players, prizefighters, and cyclists offer multiple insights into the shaping of this new racial hierarchy. The varying strategies with which black athletes confronted the challenges they faced also shed light on the obstacles and opportunities found in the emerging system. This is a complicated story to guide students through, especially as the evidence is somewhat fragmentary. But it is worth the trouble, particularly in the present day, when this country is facing yet another round of racial conflict.

Slavery-Era Sports

To understand the racial realities of the late nineteenth century, it helps to understand the system that came before. The racial dynamics of slavery-era sports, especially horse racing, is worth a lengthy exploration. But if time does not allow, a couple of key points can set the stage.

By the start of the eighteenth century, landowners in the Southern colonies had come to rely on a labor system based on racial slavery. Slaveholders—including several of the nation's Founding Fathers—justified the permanent enslavement of other human beings by contending that Africans and their descendants were innately inferior to Europeans and thus required the guidance and control that slavery provided. The realities of plantation life and the proponents of a growing abolition movement disputed such claims. But portrayals of African Americans as foolish, lazy, and in need of white discipline and control became a fundamental component of American popular culture through newspaper articles, children's books, and the tremendously popular blackface minstrel shows.[1]

Horse racing embodied the assumptions that undergirded this system, as well as their contradictions. Wealthy elites in the South and the North loved horses and horse races. While Northern racing enthusiasts employed white trainers, jockeys, and advisors, Southern stables were run almost exclusively by enslaved African Americans. Generations of black horsemen identified, nurtured, trained, and rode the South's most successful horses, competing regularly against white trainers and jockeys. Stable owners trusted these men's judgment, relied on their advice, and gave them a considerable degree of status and autonomy. But far from being troubled or intimidated by black horsemen's skills, racing enthusiasts took credit for their successes. In their eyes, victory at the racetrack arose from a well-organized society, one that depended

The State Post Stake seems to be everywhere a subject of conversation, and the price of blood stock has risen considerably in consequence of its being certainly a race.

$5,000	have been refused for			Highlander.
4,000	"	"	"	" Berry.
3,000	"	"	"	" Lecomte.
3,700	have been paid for			Compromise.
2,500	"	"	"	" Lexington.
1,500	"	"	"	" Zero.
2,350	"	"	"	" the Jockey Abe.

Chart printed in *Spirit of the Times*, July 23, 1853.

on elites' effective management of the horses and the people that they "owned."[2]

A list published in the *Spirit of the Times* in 1853 offers one way to bring this concept of ownership home. It accompanied an article about the rising value of what the author termed "blood stock." The first six entries addressed the price of horses, recording offers that ranged from $1,500 to $5,000 for Highlander, Berry, Lecomte, Compromise, Lexington, and Zero. The final entry recorded the $2,350 that the Louisiana sugar planter Duncan Kenner had paid for the enslaved Abe Hawkins, termed "the Jockey Abe," whose skills would make him the most celebrated rider of his era.[3]

Post-Emancipation Sports

Then, however, the system that had served slaveowners so well was upended by the cataclysm of the Civil War. The end of slavery gave formerly enslaved Americans the opportunity to pursue their own interests and desires. It was an earthshaking transformation. In 1860, nearly four million Americans of African descent had been enslaved. With the addition of the nation's half million free blacks, African Americans made up close to 15 percent of the total American population. There was no guide for determining the roles that they would play in a post-emancipation society.

The end of slavery was also only one of many changes Americans faced in the years after the Civil War. Rapid industrialization, urban growth, technological advancement, and a new wave of European immigration threw many aspects of American life into question. Americans from all backgrounds scrambled to find places for themselves in a rapidly changing, increasingly competitive social and economic order. In this new situation, sports took on new significance. Prewar sporting spectacles were generally straightforward tests of speed and/or stamina. Riotous, celebratory, and sometimes illegal, they were as likely to stand outside the bounds of the existing social order as to reproduce it. But the spread of industrialization gave rise to new kinds of games: team-focused, rule-bound competitions that were more in keeping with the exacting demands of industrial production and corporate management. Developing sports such as football, baseball, and basketball began to gain in popularity, often promoted as a way to help young people develop qualities that included "self-sacrifice" and "team efficiency" as well as "virility, self-control and daring courage."[4]

African American athletes soon claimed places in these expanding institutions. Black horsemen capitalized on the skills they had gained during slavery and formed a tight-knit group of trainers, jockeys, and racehorse owners that became a significant force in American racing, while nurturing a new generation of stars. African Americans also excelled at the era's new sports. Moses "Fleet" Walker became a catcher for Oberlin College in 1882, and in 1884 became the first African American player in the American Association, the forerunner of the American League. By the mid-1880s, as many as twenty African Americans were playing for the top-flight professional teams. William Henry Lewis played football for Amherst College and for Harvard, becoming the first black All-American in 1892. Black boxing stars included George Dixon, who became the first African American to win a world sporting championship when he captured the world bantamweight title in 1895, and an up-and-coming young Texan named Jack Johnson, who began his professional career in 1897.[5] When advances in bicycle technology sparked a national racing craze, a small, slim, African American from Indianapolis named Marshall "Major" Taylor began to set world speed records.

By the time the century turned, though, most African American athletes had been pushed out of public view. The owners of top baseball teams had cemented an "unwritten agreement" that would keep black players out of the major leagues for nearly half a century. A series of world heavyweight champions had "drawn the color line," refusing to accept challenges from African American fighters. Narrowing opportunities and rough treatment at the hands of white competitors pushed some competitors, most notably the cyclist Major Taylor and the two-time Kentucky Derby winner Jimmy Winkfield, to leave the country and pursue careers in Europe, where their race and their abilities garnered greater respect. Most of the black athletes who remained were limited to all-black teams and institutions on the margins of society.

Pushed to the Sporting Margins

The story of this transformation provides an insightful portrait of an era in which one set of racial norms had been undercut, but a new set had yet to coalesce. Like other such periods, it was marked by uncertainty, by uneven patterns of efforts to move forward and efforts to push back. In the summer of 1887, for example, the directors of baseball's International League officially decided to stop extending contracts to black players. When the move was reported in the sporting press, it drew criticism from both blacks and whites. The directors backed down. In the end, many decisions to exclude African Americans were made privately, without official announcements or concrete documentation. Major League Baseball's famous unwritten agreement was just that: unwritten.

Given the lack of a clearly documented timeline, I find it useful for students to explore this transition through examining a range of statements from the era. This exercise not only encourages them to read historical materials closely, it also gives them a sense of the many different factors that contribute to cultural change. Here, I include a set of statements I find particularly telling. Depending on the situation, students can examine some or all of these statements through an assignment, a small-group activity, or a class discussion. There are plenty of observations to make and questions to ask. I'll touch on a few.

First: there's no hard-and-fast pattern. When white baseball players balked at playing with or against African Americans, for example, some managers yielded to their demands. Others did not. In New Orleans, in 1897, an angry spectator stopped an interracial prizefight. Still, someone had clearly been willing to arrange and promote the contest.

Second: many different groups of people play roles in this process: athletes, managers, spectators, league directors, newspaper editors, and others.

Third: the statements hint at broader issues, such as concern about the fate of the "Caucasian race." They show cultural priorities: the *Toledo*

146

Blade would not print swear words but had no problem with "nigger." They also express some intriguing complications: the editorial in the *Newark Call* criticizes the International League's decision to stop extending contracts to black players but does not wholly reject the idea of drawing the color line.

Key questions include:

- Which different groups of people seem to be involved in the push to exclude black athletes from interracial competitions?
- Who has the power to decide whether African American athletes will be treated fairly? Whether they will be allowed to compete?
- What do the various parties involved have to gain by excluding African Americans?

Statements:

Walker, the colored catcher of the Toledo Club . . . was a source of contention [and Toledo was] informed that there was objection in the Chicago Club to Toledo's playing Walker. Walker has a very sore hand, and it had not been intended to play him in yesterday's game, and this was stated to the bearer of the announcement for the Chicagos. Not content with this, the visitors during their perambulations of the forenoon declared with the swagger for which they are noted, that they would play ball "with no d—d nigger," and when the Club arrived at the grounds Capt. Anson repeated the declaration to the Toledo management. The order was given, then and there, to play Walker, and the beefy bluffer was informed that he could play his team or go, just as he blank pleased. . . . Anson hauled in his horns somewhat, and "consented" to play. (*Toledo Blade*, August 11, 1883)

We the undersigned do hereby warn you not to put up Walker, the negro catcher, the evenings that you play in Richmond, as we could mention the names of 75 determined men who have sworn to mob Walker if he comes on the ground in a suit. We hope you will listen to our words of warning, so that there will be no trouble; but if you do not there certainly will be.[6] (Letter sent from Richmond, Virginia, to the manager of the Toledo Blades, 1884. Walker broke a rib some time before the team traveled to Richmond, which sharply curtailed his playing time. He did not play in Richmond.)

We the undersigned members of the St. Louis Base Ball Club, do not agree to play against negroes tomorrow. We will cheerfully play against white people at any time, and think, by refusing to play, we are only doing what is right, taking everything into consideration.[7] (Letter given by players to the manager of the St. Louis Browns the day before a scheduled game with the all-black Cuban Giants, 1887. The game was cancelled.)

If anywhere in the world the social barriers are broken down it is on the ball field. There many men of low birth and poor breeding are the idols of the rich and cultured; the best man is he who plays best. Even men of churlish disposition . . . are tolerated on the field. In view of these facts the objection to colored men is ridiculous. . . . Better make character and personal habits the test. Weed out the toughs and intemperate men first, and then it may be in order to draw the color line.[8] (*Newark Call* [white-run newspaper] on the International League decision to stop extending contracts to black players, 1887. The league backed down.)

I hereby challenge any and all of the bluffers who have been trying to make capital at my expense to fight me either the first week in August this year or the first week in September. . . . [In] this challenge I include all fighters—first come, first served—who are white. I will not fight a negro. I never have and never shall.[9] (World heavyweight champion John L. Sullivan, 1892. He lost the title in his next fight, to "Gentleman Jim" Corbett. Corbett also drew the color line, denying prime contender Peter Jackson a shot at the title.)

We are in the midst of a growing menace. The black man is rapidly forging to the front in athletics, especially in the field of fisticuffs. We are in the midst of a black rise against white supremacy. . . . How is it that these sable champions spring up all at once? Is it because they are far and away better than their white brethren or is the Caucasian race deteriorating? (Charles Dana, editor, *New York Sun* [white newspaper], 1895)

Why if that darned nigger would beat that white boy the niggers would never stop gloating over it, and, as it is, we have enough trouble with them.[10] (Spectator who broke up a New Orleans prizefight, 1897)

Major Taylor . . . deserves a great amount of credit for the splendid manner in which he has ridden this season, as it has been done under the most discouraging circumstances. All the boys willingly acknowledge him to be the fastest rider on the track and also as a "good fellow" personally, but on account of his color they cannot stand to see him win over them.[11] (Philadelphia newspaper, 1898)

The civilized world holds in high respect the trained and successful athlete. The best of the colleges of the world encourage athletics as a means of strengthening and adding to the health of students and of stimulating their mental powers at the same time. . . . The proud Anglo-Saxon admits that [Lewis's] superior has not appeared on the athletic field. . . . Our race is proud of him because in all his success he stands for us, and the higher he goes in the physical field of athletics or the mental field of law or literature, he must necessarily open the way for others, and lift us all up at the same time.[12] (*A.M.E. Zion Quarterly Review* [black newspaper] on William Henry Lewis, the college football star, 1900)

A [horse] racing establishment partakes somewhat of the features of a family. Its members are thrown closely together. As the two races will not mix in such close quarters, the head of the institution must have one kind or another. Under these circumstances the gradual exclusion of the Negro is inevitable. (*Lexington Leader* [white newspaper], 1902)

Horsemen ascribe the passing of the colored riders to the fact that it is no long considered ignoble to be a jockey, and the money to be made in the profession has drawn boys of good family to essay to learn the art of riding. So the white jockey is now crowding out the colored riders as the pale face is pressing back the red man on the plains.[13] (*Louisville Courier-Journal*, 1905)

One intriguing contradiction likely to result from the students' examination is that while it's fairly easy to chart the benefits that white athletes might derive from eliminating African American competitors, it is harder to pinpoint the advantages for the owners and organizers of major sporting institutions—those people who ultimately controlled which athletes were given opportunities and how they were treated.

White Supremacy and African American Resistance

To understand that dynamic, students need to broaden their scope and look at what's happening in sports as part of an overall cultural shift, one that covers all aspects of American society. While society's elites may have had little to gain simply from excluding African Americans from sports, they had far more at stake in the broader project of white supremacy.

A few examples. In the South, using white supremacy to render African Americans separate and unequal—especially when it came to voting—ensured that working-class whites and blacks would not come together to challenge the political dominance of white elites. White supremacy also became a useful justification for American efforts to gain economic and political sway over overseas territories such as Cuba, Panama, Puerto Rico, the Hawaiian islands, and the Philippines. At home, the concept of white supremacy and a new interest in athletic prowess—"the strenuous life"—bolstered the egos of white elites, whose status was being challenged by the end of slavery, the growth of industrialization, and a massive influx of immigrants from Eastern Europe.

What happened in sports was thus part of a much broader change, one in which white supremacy became embedded in almost every aspect of American life, ranging from the Jim Crow laws of southern states to the informal practices that drove housing segregation in northern and western cities to a new wave of popular culture that romanticized the antebellum South and portrayed free African Americans as hapless buffoons.[14] As sports became an increasingly prominent symbol of a new American society, the exclusion of African Americans reinforced the concept of racial separation and averted unsettling challenges to white supremacist ideology.

If time permits, sports is also an excellent arena for exploring the uneven fabric of white supremacy—which, like most forms of social order, was not monolithic. The ways that white supremacy played out in different sports, along with the energy, creativity, and determination that African Americans devoted to sporting opportunities, offer numerous insights into early twentieth century sports and society.

Boxing, for example, remained a haphazardly organized sport, driven largely by individual fighters and promoters and dependent in large part on working-class ticket-buyers. An African American could get fights if a particular promoter thought that money could be made from them. This fluid situation allowed Jack Johnson to find a way around the color line and rock the world by winning the world heavyweight title in 1908.

Horse racing, in contrast, offered far fewer opportunities. It was a sport controlled by wealthy elites—those who could afford to spend fortunes on prized animals and support the expenses of training and racing them. It was also an insider sport, one that required years of training and connections. Few African Americans prevailed in this arena.

Baseball presented yet another set of circumstances. The tight-knit organization that helped major league baseball become the nation's dominant sport also helped the color line hold firm for nearly half a century. But in this case, African Americans were able to establish parallel structures. Black communities across the country had the interest and the resources to support many different teams, ranging from community teams to professional organizations such as the Kansas City Monarchs. A similar pattern prevailed in college sports. While predominantly white colleges enrolled a few African Americans, most black college athletes played on the thriving teams fielded by historically black schools.

One way for students to explore these differences is to research and compare the different paths that African American athletes took in the early twentieth century. There are plenty of players to choose from. Examples include:

- *Baseball player Sol White*, who played occasionally for integrated teams, but put most of his energy toward playing on and promoting all-black baseball teams. In 1907 he published *History of Colored Baseball*, which made him the first historian of African American baseball.
- *Baseball player Fleet Walker*, who after concluding his career became convinced that African Americans would never thrive in the United States, and who in 1908 published *Our Home Colony*, which urged African Americans to emigrate to Africa.[15]
- *Cyclist Major Taylor* and *jockey Jimmy Winkfield*, both of whom left the United States to pursue careers in Europe, where their sports were well established and racial prejudice was far less entrenched.
- *College football player William Henry Lewis*, the first black All-American, who became a prominent lawyer and politician in Boston.[16]

- *Heavyweight boxer Jack Johnson,* who devoted considerable energy to breaking through the color line, and who gained both the opportunity and the world heavyweight title in 1908.

Jack Johnson's ascension to the heavyweight title, along with the furor that greeted his victory provides a telling example of the role that sports played in the hegemonic complex that reinforced white supremacy. The lack of regular competition between black and white boxers encouraged the rise of a set of assumptions about African American boxers that meshed far more neatly with stereotype than reality. In keeping with popular culture portrayals of African Americans as weak, lazy, and foolish, many boxers and promoters believed that black fighters had weak stomachs, lacked stamina, and were easily demoralized. While six-foot-tall Jack Johnson was an immensely talented and determined fighter and towered over the 5' 7" champion, Tommy Burns, Burns and his backers were confident of victory. That assumption was dashed as soon as the two men stepped into the ring. Burns never had a chance.

Some of the broader significance of that victory, and of Johnson's subsequent pummeling of Jim Jeffries, the "Great White Hope," can be seen in the violent attacks that angry whites launched against blacks following Johnson's defeat of Jeffries, as well as in the federal government's effort to eliminate Johnson from public life by prosecuting him on trumped-up charges. They also show in two especially telling comments on the Johnson–Jeffries contest.

The *Los Angeles Times* responded to Johnson's victory with an editorial titled "A Word to the Black Man." "Do not point your nose too high," editors cautioned. "Do not swell your chest too much. Do not boast too loudly. . . . Remember, you have done nothing at all. You are just the same member of society today you were last week. . . . You are on no higher plane, deserve no new consideration, and will get none. . . . No man will think a bit higher of you because your complexion is the same as that of the victor at Reno."[17]

William Pickens, a Phi Beta Kappa graduate of Yale who taught languages at the historically black Talladega College in Talladega, Alabama, disagreed. "It was a good deal better for Johnson to win and a few negroes be killed in body for it, than for Johnson to have lost and negroes to have been killed in spirit by the preachments of inferiority from the combined white press," the African American professor wrote. "The fact of the fight will outdo a mountain peak of theory about the negro as a physical man—and as a man of self-control and courage."[18]

Notes

1. Ibram X. Kendi, *Stamped from the Beginning: The Definitive History of Racist Ideas in America* (New York: Nation Books, 2016), 169.

2. For a detailed account of the structure of slave-era racing, see Katherine C. Mooney, *Race Horse Men: How Slavery and Freedom Were Made at the Racetrack* (Cambridge, MA: Harvard University Press, 2014).

3. "The Turf and Turfmen," *Spirit of the Times*, July 23, 1853, 271.

4. Pamela Grundy, *Learning to Win: Sports, Education and Social Change in Twentieth-Century North Carolina* (Chapel Hill: University of North Carolina Press, 2001), 24.

5. For an account of early African American fighters, see Louis Moore, *I Fight for a Living: Boxing and the Battle for Black Manhood, 1880–1915* (Urbana: University of Illinois Press, 2017).

6. Robert Peterson, *Only the Ball Was White: A History of Legendary Black Players and All-Black Professional Teams* (New York: Oxford University Press, 1992), 23.

7. Ibid., 31.

8. Ibid., 32.

9. Michael T. Isenburg, *John L. Sullivan and His America* (Urbana: University of Illinois Press, 1994), 301.

10. Andrew Kaye, *The Pussycat of Prizefighting: Tiger Flowers and the Politics of Black Celebrity* (Athens: University of Georgia Press, 2007), 30.

11. Marshall W. "Major" Taylor, *The Fastest Bicycle Rider in the World* (Worcester, MA: Commonwealth Press, 1928), 60.

12. *A.M.E. Zion Quarterly Review* 10 (October–December 1900), 64–65.

13. *Louisville Courier-Journal*, July 24, 1905.

14. This popular culture produced fascinating images that are worth exploring, in class or in student research projects. For example, Currier & Ives and other publishers produced intriguingly contradictory images of African American jockeys during this era: they engraved heroic commemorations of important victories and also comic depictions of chaotic "Darktown" races, underscoring the contrast between reality and ideology as well as the unsettled nature of turn-of-the-century racial systems. See Mooney, *Race Horse Men*, 229–31.

15. See especially David Zang, *Fleet Walker's Divided Heart: The Life of Baseball's First Black Major Leaguer* (Lincoln: University of Nebraska Press, 1995).

16. For portraits of Major Taylor, Jimmy Winkfield, and William Henry Lewis, see David K. Wiggins, ed., *Out of the Shadows: A Biographical History of African American Athletes* (Fayetteville: University of Arkansas Press, 2006).

17. *Los Angeles Times*, July 6, 1910.

18. Chicago *Defender*, July 30, 1910.

Race and Rebellion
in the Progressive Era

Matthew Andrews

The story of the first black heavyweight champion boxer, Jack Johnson, is one of the centerpieces of my Sport and American History course. It is also the one sport history lecture I always give when teaching the second half of the U.S. survey course, The United States since the Civil War. After lectures on Reconstruction and the rise of Jim Crow, I break from the more conventional political narrative and use the story of Johnson as a way of personifying issues of race, reform, and rebellion in Progressive Era America. Specifically, in this lecture students learn about the most significant sporting event in American history, one that illuminates the intense policing of racial boundaries in Progressive Era America, but also highlights the ability of individuals to challenge these boundaries. My students are always interested, often telling me it was their favorite lecture of the semester.

In order to get students immediately and emotionally involved, I begin my account of Jack Johnson with neither a biographical narrative nor an account from one of his fights. Rather, I use a photograph of a lynching. I project the carefully cropped image of a large crowd in Paris, Texas, in 1893, and I ask students to speculate—"What do you suppose these people have gathered to see?" [*Note:* all of the images I use in this lecture can easily be found through a quick internet search using the dates and names I have provided in the text and the specifics provided in the notes.]

Paris, Texas, 1893. (Library of Congress, Prints & Photographs Division)

Aware that we are about to discuss boxing, some students guess it is a crowd at sporting event—probably a prizefight. They point to the top center of the cropped photograph where one can see the base of a platform that might support a boxing ring. Others think these spectators have come to see a traveling circus or maybe they are revelers at a county fair. I then zoom out and display the entire chilling scene. The photograph captures a crowd that has gathered for the ritual murder of Henry Smith, a black teenager accused of murdering the daughter of a white police officer. Smith swore he was innocent. There was no evidence that he had committed the crime, but there was no trial, either. Smith was seized, paraded through town, and then tied to a scaffold erected in the middle of the local fairgrounds. In front of thousands of cheering onlookers, members of the dead girl's family brutally tortured Henry Smith with hot irons, burning his legs, torso, and arms. They stuck the hot metal in his eye sockets and mouth. Then they burned Henry Smith and the scaffold. The grisly event ended with the crowd fighting over the hot ashes to collect Smith's bones and teeth as

Lynching of Henry Smith, Paris, Texas, 1893. (Library of Congress, Prints & Photographs Division)

souvenirs. Attentive students often point out that if you look closely at the photograph, you can see that the word "justice" has been painted on the platform.[1]

I begin with this photograph of the lynching of Henry Smith in order to shock students into the moment and confront them with but one of the spectacles of brutality from the era. As the photograph suggests, lynchings were often more than just mob executions—they were carnivals of racial violence to which many white Americans excitedly flocked, much like sporting events. The radical impact of Jack Johnson is more evident when placed in this context. As students soon learn, some of Jack Johnson's detractors called for him to experience the same violent end. Later I draw parallels between this moment and one that occurred seventeen years later, when Jack Johnson stepped onto a different platform in Reno, Nevada, also surrounded by a sea of angry white faces who had come to see him punished for the way he lived his life and the color of his skin.

The late nineteenth century saw white athletes, promoters, and team owners draw the color line and segregate successful black athletes out of their sports (for more details, see Grundy, "Jim Crow at Play"). The call for exclusion was loudest and most insistent in boxing. In 1893, Charles Dana, the influential editor of the *New York Sun*, warned his white readers: "We are in the midst of a growing menace. The black man is rapidly forging to the front of athletics, especially in the field of fisticuffs. We are in the midst of a black rise against white supremacy. Wake up you pugilists of the white race!"[2]

It's an interesting question. What exactly is Charles Dana suggesting? You can ask students to speculate on what he means by: "Wake up you pugilists of the white race!" But certainly, Dana's clarion call illuminates the immense symbolism of boxing. In an era dominated by Darwinian thought, when the heavyweight champion of the world could plausibly lay claim to being the fittest of them all, it became the solemn racial duty of the white heavyweight champions to deny black men the opportunity to fight for the title and prove their mettle.

Among the fighters dedicated to this idea was Jim Jeffries. Standing 6' 3" and weighing 225 pounds, Jeffries was an immense, muscular fighter who was the heavyweight champion from 1899 to 1905. During that time, he never lost a bout. But like the white champions before him, once he held the heavyweight title, he refused to fight black challengers. Jeffries justified his refusal by saying that black boxers were inferior fighters. Repeating some of the widely accepted stereotypes of the era, Jeffries asserted that black boxers had a weakness in the stomach that made them easy to knock out. He claimed they possessed a yellow streak—they were cowards, and if given the chance to fight for the title they likely would not even show up for the challenge. In 1905, with no one left to fight—or so he said—Jeffries walked away from boxing, undefeated, and retired to his alfalfa farm in California. As I tell my students, he'll be back.

Into this segregated boxing scene came Jack Johnson. Born in 1878 in Galveston, Texas, to parents who had once been slaves, Johnson has to be ranked among the greatest heavyweights of all time. Big and strong with lightning-quick hands, Johnson honed his trademark disciplined and defensive style of fighting through years of itinerant boxing, including participation in "battle royals"—a derisive form of athletic entertainment in which white promoters would put a group of black fighters in a ring, sometimes blindfold them or make them drink alcohol, and have them brawl until only one was left standing.[3]

Johnson became an obvious contender for the heavyweight title, but he ran up against the larger racial restrictions of the era. While interracial fights were sometimes scheduled—generally when there was plenty of money to be made—white fighters were particularly hesitant to give Jack Johnson an opportunity, not only because of his abilities but also because he lived his life in daily defiance of the era's racial status quo. Both inside the boxing ring and out, Jack Johnson's every move was a challenge to the ideology of American white supremacy. Inside the ring, Johnson didn't just beat his white opponents, he mocked and taunted them as if he were trying to publicly extract an ounce of revenge for the nation's long history of racial violence and white supremacy. Outside the ring, he defiantly lived his life as if racism did not exist: he wore expensive suits, drove fancy cars, and unapologetically spoke his mind. Worst of all for his critics, Johnson ridiculed the nation's racial divide by appearing in public with white prostitutes and by marrying a succession of white women. Jack Johnson embodied what many white Americans considered to be a turn-of-the-century epidemic of antagonistic black male sexuality, a social ill that one southern newspaper suggested could be cured only if the transgressive fighter "be given the hemp"—or, in other words, the hangman's rope.[4]

Johnson's narrative and the history of American sports changed dramatically in 1908. Originally denied the opportunity to challenge for the heavyweight title because of the color of his skin, Johnson tirelessly stalked the new, white, heavyweight champion, Tommy Burns, following him around the globe and eventually goading Burns into a fight in Sydney, Australia. On December 26, 1908, Jack Johnson turned the boxing world upside down when he easily defeated the far smaller and less skilled Burns. The sight of a black man as the heavyweight champion prompted the horrified ringside reporter, novelist, and political activist Jack London, to issue his famous declaration: "But one thing now remains. Jim Jeffries must now emerge from his alfalfa farm and remove that golden smile from Jack Johnson's face. Jeff, it's up to you. The white man must be rescued."[5]

Contentedly retired and hopelessly out of shape, Jeffries initially refused to take up the challenge. In his place, a slew of so-called "Great White Hopes" stepped up to try to dethrone the world's first black

heavyweight champion. Johnson defeated them all. One of these challenges deserves special attention for the powerful imagery it produced—
imagery that a simple internet search makes available for classroom
use. In October 1909, Johnson defended his title against Stanley Ketchel
in San Francisco. The two fighters agreed to spar half-heartedly in the
early rounds in order to increase the length of the bout, which would
increase the value of the moving picture (at the time, big fights were
filmed, and the films profitably shown in movie theaters across the
country and sometimes around the world). But in the twelfth round,
Stanley Ketchel strayed from the script. Sensing an opportunity, Ketchel
surprised Johnson with a hard right cross. I show a photograph that
captures that exact moment—Ketchel has delivered the punch and
Johnson is falling to the floor.[6] I linger on this image and give students
the opportunity to comment on the composition of this early twentieth-
century boxing crowd. They mention the overwhelming whiteness of
the spectators, the presence of a few female patrons, the political advertisements on the back wall, the formal attire Americans wore at sporting
events a century ago.

Then I show what this same boxing ring looked like—literally—ten
seconds later.[7] The fighters' positions are reversed, and now it is Johnson
casually standing over the unconscious Ketchel. The juxtaposition between the two photographs always prompts an astonished roar from my
students. Before the referee had even begun his ten-count, the double-
crossed Johnson rose to his feet and floored Ketchel with a punch so
powerful that careful examination of the fight film shows some of the
challenger's front teeth flying across the ring and others imbedded in
Johnson's glove. While it is a remarkable athletic moment, I encourage
students to consider the larger impact of this photograph. Here is an
awesome depiction of black male power and a direct counterpoint to
that lynching photograph from Paris, Texas. Images like this help explain why black Americans reveled in Jack Johnson's accomplishments.
Here was the rare arena where a black man could compete with a white
man on equal terms. Here was a site where a black man was allowed to
strike a white man without fear of murderous retribution. Where else
could one see an image like this?[8]

This moment only heightened white anxieties, and so the pressure grew for Jim Jeffries to return to the ring and defeat Johnson. The
man who finally convinced Jeffries to come out of retirement was Tex
Rickard, a new breed of athletic promoter who believed that boxing

could become a lucrative arena sport. Rickard offered $101,000 to the fighters. The winner would get 75 percent, the loser 25 percent. At a time when the average worker made a dollar a day, this was a staggering sum of money. An organized group of anti-prizefight reformers tried to stop the fight from taking place—and indeed, they did successfully get the governor of California to prohibit the fight in his state. As a result, the bout took place in Reno, Nevada, on the Fourth of July, 1910.

In a sport given to hyperbole, where almost every highly anticipated bout is billed as "the fight of the century," the Johnson–Jeffries fight can justly lay claim to such a title.[9] On the day of the bout, Jeffries received thousands of telegrams from white Americans wishing him luck. One came from the politician and statesman William Jennings Bryan—it read: "God will forgive everything you do to that nigger in this fight. Jeff, God is with you." Even though Jeffries had been out of the ring for nearly five full years, most Americans assumed he would beat Johnson. Jeffries was the heavy betting favorite, and newspapers were filled with expert predictions of his certain victory. Since Jeffries had never lost, many still considered him to be the real champion. As most white Americans saw it, Jeffries was the dominant representative of the dominant race. *How could he lose?*

Here's where I turn to the 2005 Ken Burns documentary about Jack Johnson, *Unforgivable Blackness*.[10] I show the ten-minute section titled, "Independence Day," which uses archival photographs and moving pictures to illuminate the national anticipation for this fight. Millions of Americans gathered at newspaper offices to receive telegraphed updates of the fight. In some cities, including San Francisco, promoters built stages and hired black and white boxers to re-create the fight, round by round, based on these reports. Burns then takes us to Reno where we see thousands of Americans entering the stadium in anticipation for the colossal battle. Voiceovers (including Samuel L. Jackson as Jack Johnson) and interviews with boxing writers and American historians add to the images and convey the immense significance and symbolism of the moment. Finally, Burns shows us the fight itself, edited down to a reasonable five minutes.

Right before showing the video, I remind students of the photograph of Henry Smith, tied to the scaffold and surrounded by thousands of white people who had eagerly come to see witness his torture and murder. I find the parallel with Jack Johnson in the ring in Reno to be striking. What the thousands of white Americans who paid their way

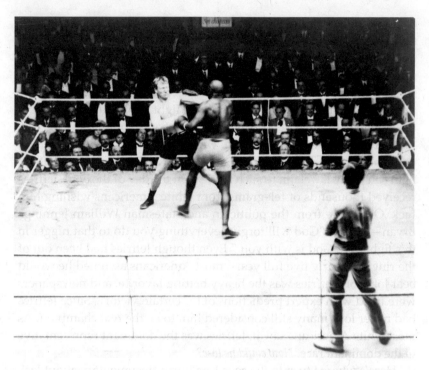

Images of Jack Johnson defeating "Great White Hopes" such as Frank Moran posed a powerful challenge to white supremacy. (New York World-Telegram and Sun Newspaper Photograph Collection, Library of Congress, Prints & Photographs Division)

into the arena and surrounded Jack Johnson hoped to see that day, what they *expected* to see, was a symbolic lynching of Jack Johnson in the ring. Here are a few additional details that Burns does not mention but which one might convey to students: when Jack Johnson climbed into the ring, the overwhelmingly white crowd serenaded him with Ernest Hogan's popular song, "All Coons Look Alike to Me." Johnson had received numerous death threats before the fight. Jim Jeffries felt it necessary to issue a statement imploring his fans not to attack Johnson should the black fighter somehow emerge victorious. This, then, was no ordinary sporting event. As I suggest to my students, the Johnson–Jeffries fight is the most significant sporting event in American history, both for its immense racial symbolism and for the violence that convulsed the nation in its immediate aftermath.

As the documentary depicts, the fight itself was one-sided, and the brutality of boxing is illuminated in this clip. As in earlier fights, Johnson bided his time for the sake of the moving picture. But in the words of ringside reporter Jack London, the "fistic conversation" that all in attendance had expected to see was instead "a monologue delivered to twenty thousand spectators by a smiling negro who was never in doubt and who was never serious for more than a moment at a time."[11] Johnson let Jeffries tire and punch himself out in the intense desert sun before battering him in the later rounds. Jeffries handlers "threw in the towel" and conceded defeat in the fifteenth round.

Johnson's victory ignited racial disturbances across the country. The violence followed a general pattern in which black men boasting of Johnson's victory were chased down, beaten, and murdered by vengeful white mobs. By the next day, at least eighteen black Americans lay dead, victims of what Al-Tony Gilmore calls the first nationwide race riot in American history.[12]

Instead of narrating what happened in the aftermath of the fight, I recommend having students engage in primary source research, write about what they have learned, and discuss their findings in small groups. Having already shown students how to do newspaper research using databases like *ProQuest Historical Newspapers,* I give them the following brief assignment one week before the lecture:

> On July 4, 1910, heavyweight champion Jack Johnson (who was black) fought the recently unretired and undefeated ex-heavyweight champion Jim Jeffries (who was white) in what was perhaps the most significant sporting event in American history.
>
> Explore the July 3–10, 1910, editions of a newspaper(s) of your choice and write a three-page essay that (1) describes the accounts of the Johnson–Jeffries fight and its aftermath and (2) interprets what these events can tell us about early twentieth-century race relations. Some possible questions to consider: How were the individual fighters described? Where did people gather to get the news of the fight? Was the fight described as more than just a sporting event? How did different Americans make sense of the outcome? What happened in the days after the fight?

I tell students that I am giving them the opportunity to be sportswriters by describing what happened inside the boxing ring that day—which they like—but also to be an American historian and make an argument about the larger significance of this event. This is easy and engaging research. The fight and its aftermath were front-page news in American newspapers, and students can choose any number of stories to recount and analyze, including reports of the race riots, the ways white Americans attempted to rationalize Johnson's victory, and the nationwide reform movement that quickly emerged to prohibit showings of the fight film.

Another research possibility is to ask students to compare the reports of the fight and its aftermath in mainstream "white" newspapers with those in black newspapers, such as the *Chicago Defender*. The *African American Newspapers* database provides students with access to the black press between 1827 and 1998. My students are usually surprised by the variety of opinions offered about Johnson in the black press. Some writers describe Johnson as a "messianic figure" and a "godsend to the black race," while others question the strategy of black Americans investing their hopes and emotions in the figure of a prizefighter, particularly one who did not live up to the standards of "respectability" being espoused by black leaders like Booker T. Washington. Dueling interpretations and reports like these provide an opportunity to discuss what Manning Marable calls "symbolic representation"—because black Americans were systematically excluded from the opportunity to demonstrate their worth and abilities as a group, the success of a single black American symbolically empowered all black Americans.[13]

If you don't have time for a primary source research assignment, and instead want to give your students a source to interpret, I recommend the July 5, 1910, *Los Angeles Times* editorial, "A Word to the Black Man." The piece is lengthy, complex, and—it should be noted—was printed in the same newspaper that just days before had confidently predicted a Jeffries victory. The day after the fight, the *Los Angeles Times* editors told their black readers:

> Do not point your nose too high. Do not swell your chest too much. Do not boast too loudly. Do not be puffed up. Let not your ambitions be inordinate or take a wrong direction. Let no treasured resentments rise up and spill over. Remember you have done nothing at all. You are just the same member of society today you were last week. Your place in the world is just what it was. You are on no higher plane, deserve no new consideration, and will get none. You will be treated on your personal

merits in the future as in the past. No man will think a bit higher of you because your complexion is the same as that of the victor at Reno.

Do not dwell too much on matters of race, particularly when it relates to the characteristics in which the dullest of the brute creation is superior to all men of all races and colors. Think rather of your own individuality, of your personal achievements. Be ambitious for something better than the prize ring. Cultivate patience, grow in reasonableness, increase your stock in useful knowledge, try for new things, which distinguish man from the beasts that perish and leave no results of life behind them. Endurance is part of Johnson's good qualities, which stood him in good stead; hopefulness and good nature are others. Try to emulate this member of your race in these qualities. Their possession will do you more good and count for more in behalf of your race than it would if a black man would "knock out" a white man every day for the next ten years.[14]

I also recommend that you set aside time to explore the cost of Jack Johnson's success and defiance. Unable to beat Johnson in the ring, his enemies sought other ways to bring him down. In 1912, the federal government went after Jack Johnson in court, charging him with violating the Mann Act, a new federal law designed to fight prostitution by making it a federal crime to transport a woman across state lines for "immoral purposes." The government brought spurious charges against Johnson, and he was convicted. You might provide students with the following two reactions to the case, the first was printed in the *New York Call*, the second was written by W. E. B. DuBois for the NAACP magazine, *Crisis*:

Johnson is black and has more money than is good for a black man. The Department of Justice must aid the "white hopes" in taking away the superfluous cash of the stupidly brazen Negro pugilist. Anglo-Saxon America is relieved of a most dangerous menace to the preservation of its color.[15]

Boxing has fallen into disfavor. . . . The reason is clear: Jack Johnson . . . has out-sparred an Irishman. He did it with little brutality, the utmost fairness and great good nature. He did not "knock" his opponent senseless. . . . Neither he nor his race invented prize fighting or particularly like it. Why then this thrill of national disgust? Because Johnson is black. Of course some pretend to object to Johnson's character. But we have yet to hear, in the case of White America, that marital troubles have disqualified prize fighters or ball players or even statesmen. It comes down, then, after all to this unforgivable blackness.[16]

Rather than serve his sentence, Johnson fled the country and continued to fight in Europe and Cuba, losing his heavyweight title in Havana in 1915 to Jess Willard, a white fighter. Johnson returned to the United States in 1920, surrendered to authorities, and served one year in Leavenworth Prison. After his prison term, he continued to work as a fighter, entertainer, and celebrity, and died in 1946 in a North Carolina car crash.

I like to end my lecture by bringing Jack Johnson's story into the present. Students are interested to hear that in 2004, Senators John McCain and Edward Kennedy cosponsored a petition asking the president of the United States to posthumously pardon Johnson for his racially charged conviction. Neither George W. Bush nor Barack Obama elected to do so. In 2016, after I gave the Jack Johnson lecture in my Sport and American History course, one of my students was so outraged by the story that she drafted a letter urging President Obama to issue the pardon. Her classmates were given the opportunity to cosign the letter (most did), and together we mailed it to the White House.

Recent events make such a petition unnecessary, as well as providing teachers with another opportunity to use the story of Jack Johnson to explore the story of race in American culture. In 2018, President Donald Trump was informed of Jack Johnson's conviction by the actor Sylvester Stallone, and quickly issued a presidential order posthumously pardoning Johnson. Interestingly, President Trump issued the pardon on the same day he told reporters that NFL players who protested racial injustice by kneeling during the National Anthem should be suspended from the league and suggested they "shouldn't be in the country." Students can wrestle with the contradiction. How might we reconcile having a president who condemns athletes who protest racial injustice, but then pardons a prizefighter who used his fame and athleticism to challenge the harsh racial restrictions of his era?

All of this is to say that the story of Jack Johnson resonates with students. It helps them understand the myriad forces that conspired to limit opportunities for black Americans, illuminates the ways that black Americans challenged these forces, and prompts them to think about issues of race and racial justice both then and now.

Notes

1. For a more complete description of the lynching of Henry Smith, see Philip Dray, *At the Hands of Persons Unknown: The Lynching of Black America* (New York: Random House, 2002), 77–79.

2. *New York Sun*, December 15, 1895.

3. For a depiction of a "battle royal" that can be used to prompt classroom conversation, see chapter 1 in Ralph Ellison, *Invisible Man* (New York: Random House, 1952).

4. The best works on Jack Johnson are Thomas Hietala, *The Fight of the Century: Jack Johnson, Joe Louis, and the Struggle for Racial Equality* (Armonk, NY: M. E. Sharpe, 2002); Randy Roberts, *Papa Jack: Jack Johnson and the Era of White Hopes* (New York: Free Press, 1983); and Geoffrey C. Ward, *Unforgivable Blackness: The Rise and Fall of Jack Johnson* (New York: Knopf, 2004). For a work that places Johnson in global context, see Theresa Runstedtler, *Jack Johnson, Rebel Sojourner: Boxing in the Shadow of the Global Color Line* (Berkeley: University of California Press), 2012.

5. Roberts, *Papa Jack*, 68.

6. This photograph can be found by doing an image search using the keyword terms "Jack Johnson and Stanley Ketchel." A high-quality version of this image can be found at https://theusaboxingnews.com/legendary-fights/. On this site there is also a link to the moving pictures of this fight, but I find the photograph to be better for classroom use.

7. Once again, this photograph can be found by doing an image search using the keyword terms "Jack Johnson and Stanley Ketchel." A high-quality version of this image can be found at http://jaquo.com/all-time-hero-jack -johnson/.

8. Interestingly, moving picture operators appealed to white pride and enticed viewers to see the fight film with the line, "See Ketchel Floor Johnson!"

9. For the intense national buildup to the fight, see Al-Tony Gilmore, *Bad Nigger! The National Impact of Jack Johnson*, National University Publications (Port Washington, NY: Kennikat Press 1975), 32–42; and Roberts, *Papa Jack*, 92–104.

10. Although you can find edited versions of the Johnson–Jeffries fight film online, I recommend using the Burns documentary, which most college libraries will have. In *Unforgivable Blackness*, Burns edits the original silent film to include sounds he has re-created—the roar of the crowd, the punishing smack of Johnson's punches. Alternately, you could show the silent film and re-create for

students what viewing a fight film was like for early cinema audiences. For early boxing films there was often a narrator in the moving picture theater who explained for audiences what was going on in the ring—"And now Johnson comes out of his defensive posture and begins to use his jab to get Jeffries to retreat." For a discussion of the early fight film viewing experience, see Dan Streible, *Fight Pictures: A History of Boxing and Early Cinema* (Berkeley: University of California Press, 2008), especially chapter 2.

11. *San Francisco Chronicle*, July 5, 1910.

12. For accounts of the postfight riots, see Gilmore, *Bad Nigger!*, and Roberts, *Papa Jack*.

13. Manning Marable, *Beyond Black and White: Transforming African-American Politics* (New York: Verso, 1995).

14. *Los Angeles Times*, July 5, 1910.

15. Letter to the *New York Call*, quoted in *Crisis* (August 1913), 177.

16. *Crisis* (August 1914), 181.

Teaching Black College Athletics

Challenges and Opportunities

Derrick E. White

On a Sunday morning in March 1944, two basketball teams filed into the gymnasium at Durham's North Carolina College for Negroes (now North Carolina Central University) and locked the doors behind them. It promised to be an exciting game. One of the teams—the Duke University Medical School squad—could claim to be the best white team in the South, having defeated Duke's Southern Conference–winning varsity squad in a holiday scrimmage. As the reigning champions of the Colored Intercollegiate Athletic Association (CIAA), the North Carolina College Eagles, coached by John McLendon, were without question the best black college team in America. Earlier in the year, players from both squads had met in an interracial Bible study group. When the subject turned to basketball, each claimed to be the superior team. Although the realities of Jim Crow segregation forbade interracial competition, the players decided to settle the issue on the hardwood by arranging a clandestine match.

The game went off without a racial incident, and the Duke players even stayed for on campus for lunch. Still, the historic matchup remained mostly secret for more than a half century (while some blacks in Durham, including a reporter for the local black newspaper, knew about the game, few discussed it openly, and the reporter, fearing a racial backlash, refused to write a story). The courage that the coaches

169

and players showed exemplified the best ideals of sports—competition, equality, and sportsmanship. It also demonstrated that black college teams, like baseball's Negro Leagues, were "no one's sad sister"— McLendon's Eagles ran Duke off of the floor, 88 to 44.[1]

Athletics at historically black colleges and universities (HBCUs) nurtured generations of pioneering athletes that transformed black communities, producing scholars, community and political leaders, as well as athletic pioneers that opened doors for all African Americans. Future HBCU presidents Mordecai Johnson and John W. Davis, for instance, learned leadership lessons on the gridiron at Morehouse College in Atlanta.[2] Earl Lloyd, the first African American in the NBA, described his collegiate years at West Virginia State University as "a friendly port in a storm." He added, "The people at that college gave you such a huge dose of love and nurturing that students cried when they left. . . . It was a magical place."[3] The tennis star Althea Gibson, who attended Florida A&M University, recalled that when she returned to campus after playing in the USTA's National Indoors in 1950: "The whole school marching band was out to play the alma mater when I stepped off the train," leaving her "overwhelmed and very happy."[4]

Unfortunately, however, this history of African American collegiate excellence, much like the "secret game" itself, has largely remained hidden. Returning that history to scholarship and teaching restores a vital component of American sports history. Classroom exploration of the rise, successes, and integration-driven decline of HBCU sports also allows students to formulate and examine key questions about the ways that race and power function institutionally in sports and in American society.

HBCUs and Parallel Institutions

HBCU sports, like the schools that produced them, were a product of the optimism of emancipation and the disappointments of segregation. The vast majority of black colleges were founded in the aftermath of the Civil War, when black and white Christian missionaries from denominations as varied as Baptist, Presbyterian, and African Methodist Episcopal (AME) moved to the South to assist the newly freedmen and women in their transition from slavery to freedom. The schools that these missionaries founded evolved into colleges for African Americans. Private schools like Biddle College (now Johnson C.

Smith University in Charlotte, NC), Atlanta Baptist College (now More-house College), Howard University (Washington, DC), and Wiley College (Marshall, TX) took on the enormous task of educating black Americans in the dawn of freedom.

By the turn of the century, students could also attend state supported HBCUs. Public higher education, generally, received a boost with the 1862 Morrill Act. Sponsored by the Vermont senator Justin S. Morrill, the act focused on making higher education accessible and practical by creating land-grant institutions in the North and West. In 1890, Morrill expanded the act to include southern states; the act would ultimately found seventeen historically black land-grant schools, including, Florida A&M University, Fort Valley State University (Georgia), and North Carolina Agriculture and Technical Institute. The hostile political environment that produced the end of Reconstruction, the "separate but equal" *Plessy v. Ferguson* decision, and the rise of Jim Crow all short-circuited the material resources of black colleges and communities.[5] African Americans, however, built a network of organizations that addressed cultural, economic, political, and social needs. These separate institutions turned segregation into congregation.[6]

Segregation infected the sports world as well, pushing African American athletes out of interracial competition in boxing, baseball, cycling, horse racing, and other sports (for more details, see Grundy, "Jim Crow at Play"). In response, African American athletes mobilized their resources and created separate teams and leagues. These "parallel institutions" provided blacks with amateur and professional athletic opportunities.[7] While Negro League baseball became the most recognizable parallel institution, African Americans founded many others, including the American Tennis Association (ATA), barnstorming basketball teams such as the Harlem Renaissance and the Philadelphia Tribune Newsgirls,[8] and separate associations for recreational sports such as bowling and golf. HBCU sports fit into this tradition. Black colleges started baseball and football teams in the 1890s and, by the 1930s, these institutions had an array of men's and women's sports that included basketball, golf, tennis, swimming, and track.

Race Relations and Sports History

While HBCU athletes were essential to schools and communities, however, they have drawn limited public and scholarly interest. Historical scholarship on African Americans' college sports experiences is overwhelmingly concerned with race relations—the process of African American integration into predominantly white institutions. For the period before World War I, for instance, we know far more about the circumstances of the two dozen black athletes at mostly white institutions than the hundreds of black college athletes who earned their letters at historically black schools during the same period. The exploits of William Henry Lewis at Harvard, Paul Robeson at Rutgers, and Fritz Pollard at Brown have been added to the list of black collegiate sports heroes, as have the young African American men and women who endured ridicule and abuse as they integrated college teams after World War II.[9] The historian Lane Demas summed up this perspective when he described sporting integration as "a movement of people and ideas that exemplifies the true struggle behind the story of the American civil rights in the twentieth century."[10]

While Demas's claim about the importance of pioneering black athletes to the broader cause of civil rights is accurate, it neglects the immense significance of black college sports, most notably the African American community leadership that emerged from black college gridirons, gymnasiums, and courts. One only has to look at Mordecai Wyatt Johnson, the son of formerly enslaved parents and a football and tennis star at Morehouse College from 1907 to 1911. In 1926, Johnson became the first African American president of Howard University. While he de-emphasized football, he assembled an extraordinary group of black scholars that included Charles Hamilton Houston, whose law students led the assault on Jim Crow legislation; Alain Locke, a philosopher and the intellectual leader of the Harlem Renaissance; Howard Thurman, the religious scholar whose works profoundly influenced Martin Luther King Jr; E. Franklin Frazier, a sociologist and pioneer of race and social science, and many others. Including Harvard's W. H. Lewis in the black athletic pantheon while excluding Johnson privileges athletes who crossed racial boundaries over those who focused their leadership on African American institutions.[11]

The emphasis on race relations also saturates primary sources. Given the politics of Jim Crow, it should be no surprise that African American sportswriters used interracial success as a call for broader equality. During the height of Jim Crow segregation, for example, the African American sports media overemphasized African American sports pioneers. E. B. Henderson, the most important journalist and historian of African American athletes in the early twentieth century, cataloged the successes of black athletes in the pages of black newspapers and magazines for more than six decades. Described by scholars as the father of African American sports history, Henderson believed that athletics represented an opportunity for African Americans to lessen racial prejudice and hasten integration, writing in 1911: "The colored college athlete of the past and present bears an enviable reputation. His athletic skill and courage have gained for him the respect and admiration of thousands, and it is impossible to overestimate the effect of his career on the minds of thousands of Americans who have seen him perform or read of his doings."[12] Henderson firmly believed that black athletes and their success in interracial spaces were vital forces moving the country toward integration and equality.

Henderson best exemplified this approach to sports history in his pioneering book *The Negro in Sports*, published in 1939.[13] The wide-ranging narrative covered high school, college, amateur, and professional sports. In his discussion of college football, Henderson framed the importance of black athletes at predominantly white institutions by describing them as "heroes."[14] In his words: "The millions of Americans who have witnessed colored heroes of the gridiron striving to carry their hopes to fruition in victorious contests cannot but grow more tolerant towards a minority element with which their heroes are identified. . . . [These] Negro boys battling on the striped gridirons are rending a social service not to be overlooked as a force of great power in establishing the Negro in the hearts of his brother Americans."[15] *The Negro in Sports* provides valuable insight into how African American sportswriters used sports to further the cause of integration. It also shows how even the staunchest supporters of African American athletes could marginalize black college sports.

A Black Sporting Congregation amid Segregation

Black college sports, like most of black life, was shaped by segregation. In response, coaches, athletes, fans, and sports advocates created a sporting congregation that helped spread interest in college athletics into black communities, north and south. There were several key components of this congregation—players, coaches, communities, and media. Examining each of these components helps illustrate how HBCU sports became an integral part of black life.

Like their white counterparts, black students took the lead in developing athletics as an extracurricular activity. Students at Rutgers and Princeton organized the first collegiate football game in 1869. In 1892, African American students from Biddle and Livingstone colleges arranged the first match between black colleges.[16] Despite these similarities, however, the realities of race in America gave these two events different significance. Segregation, lynching, discrimination, convict labor, scientific racism, and racial stereotypes all endeavored to dehumanize African Americans and especially to strip black men of their manhood. Black college-educated men and women that participated in athletics thus knew they were engaged in more than just games. In the early twentieth century, for example, Mary Mitchell, the director of Physical Education for Women at Prairie View A&M (Texas), noted that "a physical expression of consciousness of the race will go far towards the development, not only of physical manhood/womanhood, but also of mind and character."[17]

In the years before World War I, coaches slowly replaced players in leading and organizing teams. The call for more control over sport swept through the college world. At HBCUs, black educators increasingly replaced whites in the late nineteenth century, setting the stage for the broader development of sports. African American pioneers from predominately white colleges took teaching jobs at HBCUs, bringing with them new training methods, strategies, and energy. No school exemplified this approach better than Morehouse College. The school's first football coach was John Hope, who as an undergraduate had served as a manager for the football team at Brown University. When Hope became president of Morehouse, he hired Matthew W. Bullock, the first black player at Dartmouth College. Bullock was not only a racial pioneer on the field, but was also the first African American head coach at a predominately white college, leading Massachusetts Agricultural College (now the University of Massachusetts) in 1905 while attending Harvard Law School.[18] These coaches and administrators introduced more structure to HBCU sport with the creation of conferences: the Colored (now Central) Intercollegiate Athletic Associate in 1912, the Southern Intercollegiate Athletic Conference (SIAC) in 1913, the Southwestern Athletic Conference (SWAC) in 1920, and the now-defunct Midwest Athletic Conference in 1924. With conferences came the creation of rivalries, conference titles, and ultimately national titles.[19]

As Michael Oriard has noted, the growth of college sports, especially football, was a boon to the burgeoning newspaper industry.[20] HBCU sports were no exception. Although the mainstream press ignored black college athletics, the black media began devoting a significant amount of coverage after 1920, and the black press was essential in narrating the exploits of black college sports and celebrating the stars of the "sepia circuit." The *Chicago Defender* named Frank "Fay" Young the paper's first sports editor in 1915, and other black newspapers followed suit—the *Norfolk Journal and Guide* began its sports column in 1924.[21] The black press also started creating postseason awards. The *Pittsburgh Courier* named Howard University the first national champion in 1920, and its sportswriters named the first all-HBCU All-American team in 1927. A number of HBCUs sponsored competitive women's basketball and track teams, all of which received widespread coverage. When combined with the initial waves of the Great Migration of blacks out of the South, HBCU sports became national news.

The cumulative effect of the sporting congregation was the creation of a sporting community that formulated deep connections to black college athletics and to collective celebration of black athletes' achievements. These connections were heightened by traditional rivalries that played out in annual contests known as "classics."[22] The Howard University–Lincoln University rivalry was as much a competition between the black communities of Washington, DC, and Philadelphia as it was a football game.[23] Florida A&M University created its Orange Blossom Classic in December 1933 as a signal of its commitment to big-time football and also to highlight black tourism in Florida; FAMU's J. R. E. Lee Jr., the school's business manager and the president's son, envisioned "the biggest intersectional contests Florida has ever witnessed."[24] These HBCU sports, which featured black colleges, businesses, and communities, represented black empowerment. The players, coaches, and press had turned the veil of segregation into a sporting congregation.

Desegregation and Institutional Racism

Despite the importance of the sporting congregation created by black college athletics, segregation remained an obstacle. As exemplified by the secret game between North Carolina Central and Duke, black college teams only rarely got to play against white opponents. As in the civil rights movement, HBCU athletic departments had to push to create competitive opportunities.

Although the NCAA stubbornly resisted efforts to promote competition between black and white colleges, black college coaches sought out other possibilities. Eventually, John McLendon and other black college basketball coaches convinced the National Association of Intercollegiate Association (NAIA) to open its ranks to HBCUs. The NAIA added Central State University in Ohio as its first HBCU member in 1951, and invited an HBCU team to its basketball tournament in 1953. By 1955, forty-five of the more than four hundred NAIA member institutions were HBCUs, and McLendon and other leading black college coaches and athletic directors held leadership positions in the association.[25] In 1957, McLendon led Tennessee State University to the NAIA national title.[26]

Sports integration, however, came at the expense of the virtual monopoly that HBCUs had on African American talent, and HBCU athletic departments sought to avoid the fate of the Negro Leagues, which declined and then disappeared as Jackie Robinson and other African American players integrated major league baseball. The titles won by historically black colleges in NAIA play—between 1957 and 1965, for example, historically black colleges won six of the nine NAIA basketball tournaments—make it clear that in football, men's basketball, and women's track and field, HBCU programs were among the best, white or black, in the country.

Despite these successes, however, HBCU athletics faced the laden assumptions of institutional inferiority, assumptions that were ironically enhanced by the NAACP's legal campaign against segregation. When Thurgood Marshall and the NAACP lawyers were preparing their arguments ahead of *Brown v. Board of Education,* they focused on the material inequalities found in segregated schools. But while this perspective reflected the very real inequalities found at black schools and ultimately swayed the Supreme Court, it also obscured the successes of those schools, especially black colleges. As the secret game suggests, for example, the quality of black college athletics upsets the notion that segregated black institutions were necessarily inferior. When one adds in the multifaceted education black students received from coaches like John McLendon, and from skilled black professors, historically black colleges offered many black students excellent preparation for life after graduation. As Florida A&M's legendary football coach Jake Gaither constantly repeated, "If he is a ditch digger, I want him to be the best in the town. If he is a doctor, I want him to be the best in the community. If he is a tackle, I want him to be the best in the conference."[27] White colleges, in contrast, provided opportunity but often far less encouragement.

In fact, athletic integration at the collegiate level can be seen primarily as a resource transfer from black colleges to formerly segregated white colleges. The result has been a loss of power and significance for black colleges, even as college athletics has become a billion-dollar industry with many African Americans on collegiate courts and fields but few in the upper echelons of power.[28] HBCU athletics now suffer from a different kind of institutional racism. While the legal barriers of opportunity no longer remain, assumptions of inferiority combined with ongoing funding disparities have limited black colleges' ability to compete for top athletes and with top teams.

Regrettably, the scholarship on college athletics has tended to equate success with the rise of black athletes at historically white schools—an approach that confuses opportunity with equality. Too often, scholars minimize the nature of exploitation at predominantly white schools or fail to consider the costs of desegregation thoroughly. As a result, the decline of black college athletics in the 1960s and 1970s generally functions only as a footnote to the story of racial integration at predominantly white institutions. By favoring individual narratives of success or failure, this approach ignores institutional and epistemological violence. Jake Gaither pointed out the problem in the early era of collegiate desegregation: "They can take my boys, but I can't take theirs. I know a lot of good white players I would like to have on my team."[29]

At the core of Gaither's comments is a stringent critique of the race relations model of athletic desegregation; a critique that can be applied to scholarship as well. Despite a wealth of new opportunities, integration came at a tremendous cost. In the eleven years after *Brown*, more than 38,000 black teachers and administrators lost their jobs.[30] While schools districts slowly integrated students, black teachers, administrators, and coaches were often left behind. Looking at institutions such as the Negro Leagues and black business districts shows a similar pattern. Although these sites were not panaceas for the social, political, and economic inequalities wrought by segregation, they were sources of pride and represented loci of local power. The narrative of progress too often obscures the costs of losing these institutions.

Teaching black college athletics thus requires the use of narratives that counter dominant assumptions of black institutional inferiority.[31] Critical readings and documentaries can advance this process. Vanessa Siddle Walker and others have explored the ways black teachers and principals worked with students and communities to ensure that young people reached their "highest potential."[32] Walker notes that a considerable amount of the scholarship on segregated black schools "has linked lack of materials and resources—the descriptions most frequently provided—with educational environment and has consigned both to inferiority."[33] The learning environment and human resources have too often been overlooked. Black colleges and universities, while also lacking equitable material resources, had a similar abundance of human resources that helped develop young black men and women, including student-athletes.

Two documentaries—*Tell Them We Are Rising* (2017) and *Black Magic* (2008)—provide valuable counternarratives about black colleges and universities. *Tell Them We Are Rising* covers the 150-year history of these institutions, highlighting the role of education in black communities, and the development, legacy, and pride of black colleges.[34] Including in this documentary are brief discussions of the sports legacy at these schools. More specifically related to sports history, *Black Magic* tells the story of black college basketball. The film highlights the contributions of John McLendon, Clarence "Big House" Gaines, Earl Lloyd, John Chaney, and other black college greats. The documentaries oppose the narratives of black college inferiority and highlight the schools' ability to serve their students beyond the curriculum. The schools were indeed a refuge in a racial storm.

The accomplishments of black college sports on the field and in the arena, and the culture of support for students provide a means to reevaluate the growing white support for desegregation from the mid-1960s through the 1970s. The legal scholar Derrick Bell postulated that "the decision in *Brown* to break with the Court's long-held position on these issues [segregation] cannot be understood without some consideration of the decision's value to whites, not simply those concerned about the immorality of racial inequality, but also those whites in policy-making positions able to see the economic and political advances at home and abroad that would follow abandonment of segregation."[35] Bell argues that the political, social, and economic environment after World War II suggest that "self-interest" and not simply notions of justice undergirded the decision. It still took a popular civil rights movement to break white southerners' massive resistance to desegregation. However, sports were key in helping whites see their self-interest in athletic desegregation.

Self-interest in athletic integrations was made clearly by Buddy Martin, sports editor at *Florida Today*. "There was a time when Earl Warren, the Supreme Court and the Fifth Army couldn't have made some Southern coaches integrate their football teams," Martin wrote. But after disappointing results in the 1968 bowl season, "colleges are recruiting Negroes. Not just because it is in vogue. It's becoming a matter of survival." The University of Florida, which had refused to recruit black players, now needed them. "You can't win without the black athlete," Martin asserted. He identified eighteen black professional football players, including future Hall of Famers Bob Hayes and Deacon Jones, all of whom had attended Florida A&M or other black colleges, and he concluded, "Isn't it about time the state of Florida stopped exporting its commodities?"[36] Martin's promotion of integration, which cast black athletes as "commodities," did not spring from a desire to alleviate inequality or to promote democracy as E. B. Henderson would have suggested. Rather, it was solely for the benefit of Florida's white athletic programs. Once southern white colleges recognized that integration could benefit them athletically and financially, they shifted their position from resistance to selective integration.

Research Assignments

After teachers overturn assumptions about the relative significance of athletic segregation and integration, and establish counternarratives of black college excellence, they can send students on research assignments designed to help them further explore how sports functioned at historically black schools and the challenges that coaches and athletes faced.

The ongoing digitization of primary sources means that students have access to a great deal of valuable material. There has been a substantial effort to digitize black college archival materials through the HBCU Library Alliance.[37] The collective effort has provided a central resource for identifying materials related to black college sports. Available materials include photographs of early teams, student newspapers, and internal memos. Individual schools, such as Florida A&M,

Tennessee State, and Lincoln University, have also begun digitizing some of their materials. These include essential but often overlooked resources: school yearbooks, alumni newsletters, and school newspapers.[38]

African American sports received tremendous coverage in the black press. Companies such as ProQuest have converted black newspapers from microfilm to searchable digital files, thus providing researchers additional avenues for inquiry. Digitized archives of the *Pittsburgh Courier, Chicago Defender, New York Amsterdam News, Atlanta Daily World*, and other black newspapers allow scholars access to the daily and weekly media's sports coverage.[39] Google's massive digitization project, even though it was aborted in 2008 after several lawsuits, includes back issues of the NAACP's *Crisis Magazine, Ebony*, and *Jet Magazine*.[40] After college athletics desegregated in the 1970s, formerly all-white newspapers often assigned beat writers to cover black college sports. Much of this coverage can be located through for-profit digitization projects such as newspapers.com.

Combining this material with secondary sources and with a key documentary reader such as David K. Wiggins and Patrick B. Miller's *The Unlevel Playing Field* allows teachers to craft assignments that encourage students to discover critiques of liberalism, challenge the idea of meritocracy, use counternarratives, and reveal the self-interest of the integration of college athletics.[41] One such assignment might involve asking students to write an athletic biography of a particular black institution. I recommend five themes: (1) the founding of sports at the school, (2) the coach as hero, (3) gender, (4) desegregation, and (5) athletic legacy and future.

In researching the founding of sports programs, student researchers can ask why black colleges began extracurricular athletic programs in the late nineteenth and the early twentieth centuries, given limited financial resources. Who were the individuals that started these sports at a particular school? How had they come to learn about the sports they introduced? Did the efforts to start athletic programs run into any opposition? In the early years of these programs, who did the teams play? Finally, how did black colleges approach the creation of conferences in the 1910s and 1920s?

Research can begin with a school's institutional history—most historically black schools have official accounts in which sports play a vital role.[42] Student research will likely reveal several key themes. First, many of the racial pioneers at predominantly white northern schools in the North had strong relationships to black colleges. Black colleges often were multitiered educational institutions, which included secondary schools, boarding schools, seminaries, colleges, and professional schools. Hence, many black college football players first attended black colleges before traveling to northeastern colleges. Harvard's William Henry Lewis, for example, attended Virginia Normal and Industrial (now Virginia State) College before continuing to Amherst and Harvard.[43] Second, racial pioneers at northern schools founded athletic programs at historically black schools. Finally, the founding narratives of sports at black colleges will uncover commonalities with white schools, such as belief in Muscular Christianity (an English nineteenth-century philosophical movement) or the value of the "strenuous life."

The "Coach as Hero" was and is a common theme in intercollegiate sports, especially during the golden age of college football. Students should be able to identify a school's most legendary coach. What traits made him fabled? What roles did he play in athletics, at the school, and in the community? Newspaper analysis will show how the ways the black press lionized black college coaches.

Regarding gender, black colleges were often ahead of the curve in providing opportunities for female athletes, although some schools were far more progressive than others (see Grundy and Liberti's "Black Women Face Obstacles and Opportunities" for more details). Unlike historically white colleges, which rarely fielded women's varsity teams, some black institutions supported highly competitive women's squads, especially in basketball and track and field. Using student newspapers and the black press for research, students should ask how women's sports were received on a particular campus and in the surrounding community. If there were women's varsity sports, how were they administered? Were there female coaches or athletic directors? What timeline did women's sports programs follow—many schools created women's teams in the 1920s and 1930s and then eliminated them after World War II. What was the effect of Title IX (1972) on black college athletics? Students can add to existing scholarship by looking at schools that have yet to be researched.[44]

Nothing reshaped black college sports more than desegregation. When examining those subject students should consider such questions as: What were the athletic responses to desegregation? What did leading coaches say about the process of integration? How did black college programs work to demonstrate their quality in the face of increasing competition for talented black athletes? Were they able to engage athletically with nearby white institutions? The lens of black college sports, which reveals the struggles of highly talented and successful coaches to maintain and advertise the quality of their teams, allows students to critique the liberal assumptions of integration. Teachers might also have students compare how integration looked from the perspective of both a historically black college and a predominantly white one.

Finally, students need to consider the legacy of black college sports. For what should these athletic programs be remembered? Is there space for them in the current athletic landscape? In what ways has power—financial, cultural, and educational—been lost in the process of integration? One consideration for students would be to evaluate the recently proposed "HBCU League" that seeks to disrupt the power wielded by the NCAA.[45] By seriously engaging the history of black college sports, students will be equipped to reinterpret college sports history—and perhaps American history as a whole.

Notes

1. Scott Ellsworth, *The Secret Game: A Wartime Story of Courage, Change, and Basketball's Lost Triumph* (New York: Little, Brown, 2016); Milton S. Katz, *Breaking Through: John B. McLendon, Basketball Legend and Civil Rights Pioneer* (Little Rock: Arkansas University Press, 2007), 25–57; David Zirin, *A People's History of Sports in the United States: 250 Years of Politics, Protest, People, and Play* (New York: New Press, 2008), 56–59.

2. Richard I. McKinney, *Mordecai, the Man and His Message: The Story of Mordecai Wyatt Johnson* (Washington, DC: Howard University Press, 1997), 20.

3. Earl Lloyd and Sean Kirst, *Moonfixer: The Basketball Journey of Earl Lloyd* (Syracuse, NY: Syracuse University Press, 2010), 50.

4. Althea Gibson, *I Always Wanted to Be Somebody*, ed. Ed Fitzgerald (New York: Harper and Brothers, 1958), 61.

5. Bobby L. Lovett, *America's Historically Black Colleges and Universities: A Narrative History from the Nineteenth Century into the Twenty-First Century* (Macon, GA: Mercer University Press, 2011), 1–97.

6. Earl Lewis, *In Their Own Interests: Race, Class, and Power in Twentieth-Century Norfolk, Virginia* (Berkeley: University of California Press, 1991), 90.

7. David K. Wiggins and Patrick B. Miller, *The Unlevel Playing Field: A Documentary History of the African American Experience in Sport* (Urbana: University of Illinois Press, 2003), 85.

8. Neil Lanctot, *Negro League Baseball: The Rise and Ruin of a Black Institution* (Philadelphia: University of Pennsylvania Press, 2004); Bob Kuska, *Hot Potato: How Washington and New York Gave Birth to Black Basketball and Changed America's Game Forever* (Charlottesville: University of Virginia Press, 2004); J. Thomas Jable, "The Philadelphia Tribune Newsgirls: African American Women's Basketball at Its Best," and Sundiata Djata, "Game, Set, and Separatism: The American Tennis Association, a Tennis Vanguard," in *Separate Games: African American Sport behind the Walls of Segregation*, ed. David K. Wiggins and Ryan A. Swanson (Little Rock: University of Arkansas Press, 2016), 37–60, 165–78.

9. See Lane Demas, *Integrating the Gridiron: Black Civil Rights and American College Football* (New Brunswick, NJ: Rutgers University Press, 2010); Charles H. Martin, *Benching Jim Crow: The Rise and Fall of the Color Line in Southern College Sports, 1890–1980* (Urbana: University of Illinois Press, 2010); John M. Carroll, *Fritz Pollard: Pioneer in Racial Advancement* (Urbana: University of Illinois Press, 1992); Martin Duberman, *Paul Robeson* (New York: New Press, 1989), 19–30; Dawn Knight, *Taliaferro: Breaking Barriers from the NFL Draft to the Ivory Tower* (Bloomington: Indiana University Press, 2007), 20–57; Tom Graham and Rachel Graham Cody, *Getting Open: The Unknown Story of Bill Garrett and the Integration of College Basketball* (Bloomington: Indiana University Press, 2006); Andrew Maraniss, *Strong Inside: Perry Wallace and the Collision of Race and Sports in the South* (Nashville, TN: Vanderbilt University Press, 2014); David Marc, *Leveling the Playing Field: The Story of the Syracuse 8* (Syracuse, NY: Syracuse University Press).

10. Demas, *Integrating the Gridiron*, 26.

11. Raymond Schmidt, *Shaping College Football: The Transformation of an American Sport, 1919–1930* (Syracuse, NY: Syracuse University Press, 2007), 139–41; Zachery R. Williams, *In Search of the Talented Tenth: Howard University Public Intellectuals and the Dilemmas of Race, 1926–1970* (Columbia: University of Missouri Press, 2009), 40–69. McKinney, *Mordecai.*

12. Edwin B. Henderson, "The Colored College Athlete," *Crisis* (July 1911), 115. David K. Wiggins, "Edwin Bancroft Henderson, African American Athletes, and the Writing of Sport History," in *Glory Bound: Black Athletes in a White America*, ed. D. Wiggins (Syracuse, NY: Syracuse University Press, 1997), 222.

13. Edwin B. Henderson, *The Negro in Sports*, 3rd ed. (Washington: ASALH Press, 1939, 2014).

14. Key chapters in *The Negro in Sports* for reference are "Football and Its Heroes of Yore," 97–123; "Later Day Gridiron Heroes,"124–47; "Conference Athletics in Negro Colleges," 277–306.

15. Ibid., 123.

16. *Charlotte Observer*, December 29, 1892.

17. Quoted in Rita Liberti, "Fostering Community Consciousness: The Role of Women's Basketball at Black Colleges and Universities, 1900–1950," in *Race and Sport: The Struggle for Equality on and off the Field*, ed. Charles K. Ross (Jackson: University Press of Mississippi, 2004), 43.

18. Jack W. Berryman and John W. Loy, "Historically Speaking . . . Matthew W. Bullock: First Black Head Coach in College Football," in the University of Massachusetts, School of Physical Education, RG 18, series 2, "Matthew Bullock Folder," University of Massachusetts, Special Collections.

19. David K. Wiggins and Chris Elzey, "Creating Order in Black College Sport: The Lasting Legacy of the Colored Intercollegiate Athletic Association," in *Separate Games: African American Sport Behind the Walls of Segregation*, ed. David Wiggins (Fayetteville: University of Arkansas Press, 2016), 145–64; James E. Hawkins, *History of the Southern Intercollegiate Athletic Conference, 1913–1990* (Butler, GA: Benns Printing, 1994); Thomas Aiello, *Bayou Classic: The Grambling–Southern Football Rivalry* (Baton Rouge: Louisiana State University Press, 2010), 16–17; Dennis C. Dickerson, *Militant Mediator: Whitney M. Young Jr.* (Lexington: University of Kentucky Press, 1998), 27.

20. Michael Oriard, *Reading Football: How the Popular Press Created an American Spectacle* (Chapel Hill: University of North Carolina Press, 1993); Julie Des Jardins, *Walter Camp: Football and the Modern Man* (New York: Oxford University Press, 2015).

21. Ethan Michaeli, *The Defender: How the Legendary Black Newspaper Changed America* (Boston: Houghton Mifflin Harcourt, 2016), 22, 54–56; *Chicago Defender*, April 24, 1915.

22. R. Pierre Rodgers, "'It's HBCU Classic Time!': Origins and the Perseverance of Historically Black College and University Football Classic Games," in *The Athletic Experience at Historically Black Colleges and Universities: Past, Present, and Persistence*, ed. Billy Hawkins et al. (Lanham, MD: Rowman and Littlefield, 2015), 149.

23. Rodgers, "'It's HBCU Classic Time!'" 145–65.

24. *Philadelphia Tribune*, November 20, 1933.

25. *St. Petersburg Times*, November 16, 1955.

26. Martin, *Benching Jim Crow*, 70–71; Katz, *Breaking Through*, 65–77.

27. *Ebony*, November 1960.

28. Shaun R. Harper, *Black Male Student-Athletes and Racial Inequities in NCAA Division I College Sports: 2016 edition* (Philadelphia: University Pennsylvania, Center for the Study of Race and Equity in Education, 2016).

29. *Milwaukee Journal*, February 1, 1963.

30. *USA Today*, April 28, 2004, http://usatoday30.usatoday.com/news /nation/2004-04-28-brown-side2_x.htm (accessed November 6, 2014); Carol F. Karpinski, "Bearing the Burden of Desegregation: Black Principals and *Brown*," *Urban Education* 41 (May 2006): 237–76.

31. The use of counternarratives stems from the use of critical race theory in sports. See Billy J. Hawkins, Akilah R. Carter-Francique, and Joseph Cooper, eds., *Black Athletic Sporting Experiences in the United States* (New York: Palgrave Macmillan, 2017).

32. Vanessa Siddle Walker, *Their Highest Potential: An African American School Community in the Segregated South* (Chapel Hill: University of North Carolina Press, 1996); James D. Anderson, *The Education of Blacks in the South, 1860–1935* (Chapel Hill: University of North Carolina Press, 1988); Henry N. Drewry and Humphrey Doermann, *Stand and Prosper: Private Black Colleges and Their Students* (Princeton, NJ: Princeton University Press, 2001); Adam Fairclough, *A Class of Their Own: Black Teachers in the Segregated South* (Cambridge, MA: Belknap Press, 2007); Lovett, *America's Historically Black Colleges and Universities.*

33. Walker, *Their Highest Potential*, 4.

34. Two other documentaries are worth mentioning. The first is on Morgan State University's lacrosse team in the 1970s, and the other is on Howard University's national title winning soccer team in 1974. "MSU Lacrosse Featured on ESPN," Morgan State Athletics, http://www.morganstatebears.com /news/2005/2/23/espn.aspx (accessed September 4, 2017). A copy of the segment may be found on youtube.com; *New York Times*, February 27, 1990; Kenan Holley, "Redemption Song," *ESPN-The Undefeated*, June 7, 2016, http://theun defeated.com/videos/redemption-song/ (accessed September 4, 2017).

35. Derrick A. Bell Jr., "*Brown v. Board of Education* and the Interest-Convergence Dilemma," *Harvard Law Review* 93 (1980): 524.

36. *Florida Today*, February 8, 1969.

37. HBCU Library Alliance, http://www.hbculibraries.org; Marlene D. Allen and Shanesha R. F. Brooks-Tatum, "A Decade of Achievement, a Call to Excellence: The History and Contributions of the HBCU Library Alliance," *International Journal of Academic Library and Information Science* 2 (2014): 14–21.

38. Florida A&M Digital Resource Center, http://famu.digital.flvc.org/is landora/object/famu%3Aroot; Tennessee State University Digital Resources, http://www.tnstate.edu/library/digitalresources/index.aspx; Lincoln University Digital Collections, http://www.lincoln.edu/node/1340/special -collections-and-archives/digital-collections. For yearbooks from many North Carolina colleges, see http://www.digitalnc.org/collections/yearbooks/.

39. http://www.proquest.com/products-services/histnews-bn.html.

40. *New Yorker*, September 11, 2015.

41. Wiggins and Miller, *Unlevel Playing Field.*

42. For example, see Leedell W. Neyland, *Florida Agricultural and Mechanical University: A Centennial History* (Tallahassee: Florida A&M Press, 1987).

43. Evan J. Albright, "Three Lives of an African American Pioneer: William Henry Lewis (1868–1949)," *Massachusetts Historical Society* 13 (2011): 127–63.

44. For background on women's sports at historically black institutions, see Susan Cahn, *Coming on Strong: Gender and Sexuality in Twentieth-Century Women's Sport* (New York: Free Press, 1994), 117–25; Rita Liberti, "'We Were Ladies, We Just Played Like Boys': African-American Womanhood and Competitive Basketball at Bennett College, 1928–42," in *Sport and the Color Line: Black Athletes and Race Relations in Twentieth-Century America*, ed. David K. Miller and Patrick B. Wiggins (New York: Routledge, 2004), 83–99; Pamela Grundy and Susan Shackelford, *Shattering the Glass: The Remarkable History of Women's Basketball* (New York: New Press, 2006), 69–76; Jennifer Lansbury, *A Spectacular Leap: Black Women Athletes in Twentieth-Century America* (Fayetteville: University of Arkansas Press, 2014), 43–74.

45. Patrick Hruby, "The Plot to Disrupt the NCAA with a Pay-for-Play HBCU Basketball League," *Vice Sports*, June 20, 2017, https://sports.vice.com/en_us/article/59zejz/the-plot-to-disrupt-the-ncaa-with-a-pay-for-play-hbcu-basketball-league (accessed December 8, 2017); "The HBCU League Business Plan," https://drive.google.com/file/d/0BxM4wdtZ5uI-Q2FIWkZhRkx2d1E/view (accessed December 8, 2017).

Sports, Civil Rights, and Black Power

Lauren Morimoto

The revolt of the black athlete in America as a phase of the overall black liberation movement is as legitimate as the sit-ins, the freedom rides, or any other manifestation of Afro-American efforts to gain freedom.

Harry Edwards

On the first day of my course, History and Philosophy of Human Movement, students enter the classroom and look at an image projected onto three walls—Tommie Smith, Peter Norman, and John Carlos standing on the podium at the 1968 Mexico City Olympic Games. Straightaway, I ask them if they recognize this iconic image: two black men with their heads bowed and fists raised; one white man standing at attention. Some of them know this image because ESPN bestowed the Arthur Ashe Courage Award on Smith and Carlos in 2008. Others recall seeing it in the assigned sport history textbook or on the cover of a magazine. Most of those familiar with the image see these raised fists as expressions of the Black Power movement and African American pride.[1]

Still, most of my students see only the broad outlines of Smith and Carlos's protest, a perspective that mirrors their broad-brush understanding of the American civil rights movement as a whole. Many conflate the civil rights movement and the Black Power movement and identify Dr. Martin Luther King Jr. as the leader of both. While most of my students have read *The Autobiography of Malcolm X*, few of them link him with the battle for equal rights for black Americans. For them, the lunch-counter protest in Greensboro, North Carolina, the 1963 March on Washington for Jobs and Freedom, and Smith's and Carlos's raised fists form part of a seamless whole, in which all African Americans adopted similar strategies and worked to achieve a single set of goals.

Sports history allows me to deepen this understanding. It explores the ways athletes such as Smith, Carlos, and Muhammad Ali used sports as a realm to develop and project black identity and masculinity, and how the black athletic revolts informed the larger movements for equal rights. It also exposes tensions. Athletes often disagreed over strategies—the raised-fist gesture emerged only because of the failure of an extensive effort to convince black athletes to boycott the 1968 Games. The focus on male sporting accomplishment obscured the activities of black women, intensifying the distorting impression that civil rights was primarily an endeavor of black men.

Making the Battle for Civil Rights Real When We've Had a Black President

My first step is to make the civil rights battle salient for my students. Students frequently argue that because we elected a black president racism must be dead—or at least "not as big of a deal." They generally acknowledge that "race stuff" was bad in the past. Those with some knowledge of the civil rights movement understand that blacks had to sit at the back of the bus and drink out of separate water fountains. But most do not grasp how embedded racial discrimination was in American social structures and institutions. They have limited understanding of the violence perpetrated against black Americans such as the terroristic aspect of public lynching.

Although the California State University (CSU) system serves citizens of an ethnically and racially diverse state, Sonoma State University (SSU) is currently the fifth "whitest" of the twenty-three campuses in the CSU. Since I joined the SSU faculty in August 2009, the kinesiology department's undergraduate population has become more diverse, primarily through increased enrollment of people of Latin American descent. Still, I rarely have black students. In addition, despite SSU's rhetoric prioritizing diversity and inclusion, and the recent hiring of the first female Japanese American president of an American four-year institution, traditionally underrepresented students (ethnic minority, first generation, low socioeconomic status) speak of feeling tolerated rather than accepted.

I use primary sources to make the struggles of black Americans real and to illustrate the type of oppression and repression that civil rights activists confronted. Though most students recognize, "I have a dream," they rarely recall any other content from King's speech or words from any other black activist of the time. I play audio recordings of King's speech from the first "I have a dream" to the last line, "Free at last, free at last; thank God Almighty we are free at last." The students and I briefly discuss King's speech as a text informed by black, southern preaching traditions.[2]

Students then listen to audio of Fanny Lou Hamer's speech to the Democratic National Committee (DNC) on August 22, 1964.[3] Her testimony not only gives students a picture of how the police disenfranchised blacks but offers an appreciation of the violence blacks faced for simply exercising their right to vote. When I disclose that President Lyndon Johnson felt so threatened by Hamer's account of her experiences that he scheduled a live, impromptu press conference to prevent her speech from being televised, students gain even more understanding of the structural racism and white anxiety of the late 1960s.

As we close the discussion about how black Americans were denied their rights, I note that while whites engaged in terrorist violence in order to oppress blacks, incidents such as the high-profile lynching of fourteen-year-old Emmett Till in fact helped galvanize civil rights activists. When Till's mother insisted upon an open-casket funeral for her brutally murdered son, I explain, photographs of Till's mutilated body outraged Americans across the country.

I attempt to bring the emotional piece of civil rights, the sadness, fear, and hope, to my students through music relevant to the movement. I also add a touch of theatricality. Since I often teach in a windowless, basement classroom, I create a "black box" by covering the small window on the door to the hallway and dimming the lights. I dress in all black with a hoodie pulled over my head. With all of us sitting in the dark, I play Billie Holiday's "Strange Fruit"; after a few lines, I light a candle. During the last verse, I project a PowerPoint of images depicting the violence at the Selma march, dogs set on children in Birmingham, and abuse at the Greensboro lunch counter. After a few moments of silence, we process the song, images, and experience of the activity— making space for whatever students need to share.

Finally, students engage with/take in black cultural forms or products that emerged as the civil rights and Black Power movements continued to grow, and the ways black activists began voicing different aspects of black identity and experience. For instance, in music, we have listened to verses of James Brown's "Say It Loud, I'm Black and I'm Proud" and Nina Simone's "Mississippi Goddamn." Students have volunteered to perform the activist Nikki Giovanni's "Rosa Parks" and student leader Julian Bond's "I Too, Hear America Singing." I have shown a video of Alvin Ailey's "Revelations," which speaks of black Americans' faith, sorrow, and joy as they survive slavery and gain freedom.

Sports History Is Civil Rights History

In the late 1960s, black athletes, like black Americans in general, began to question the system of white supremacy that relegated blacks to the back of the bus, dining in the kitchens of restaurants, exercising limited political power, and often living in fear. The heavyweight boxing champion Muhammad Ali emerged as one of the early and most critical athlete-activists. Through his deeds and words, the highly charismatic champion forced Americans to see the inequities facing black Americans—not only in the Jim Crow South but across the entire country. He also asserted an alternative black identity, through his conversion to Islam and his unabashed celebration of black masculine beauty, verbal expressiveness, and physical power and skill.

In 1967, when Ali refused induction into the U.S. Army on religious grounds, he became the first black civil rights figure to speak out against the Vietnam War. (Dr. Martin Luther King, Jr. did so later that same year.) At this point in the war, Ali's refusal to be inducted garnered criticism from many Americans, black and white, who largely supported American efforts in Vietnam. Further illuminating civil rights issues, Ali drew parallels between black Americans and the Vietnamese, both of whom Ali saw as being oppressed by whites with power and wealth. In response to Ali's protest, the U.S. government convicted him of refusing induction, stripped him of his boxing title, and denied him opportunities to earn a living through boxing for the next three years. During these years, Ali earned income by touring college campuses, frequently engaging white students in debates. During one of his campus talks, Ali reiterated his refusal to drop bombs on other "brown" people and reminded the audience that white Americans, not the Vietnamese, were his enemy. Ali emphatically stated, "You my enemy. White people is my enemy. . . . You my opposer when I want freedom. You my opposer when I want justice."[4]

As opposition to the Vietnam War grew, Ali increasingly appealed to other activists, including young black athletes who were pushing back against the war and racial discrimination in the United States. When reading about Ali, my students find it difficult to grasp the radicalness of his politics as well as what made him such a popular global figure from the late 1960s through the 1970s. To help them understand Ali's place in American history—as well as the ways he challenged mainstream conceptions of black masculinity—I employ a range of videos. For instance, I start with a clip of Ali and an upcoming opponent, Ernie Terrel, who refers to Ali as Cassius Clay. Ali, in turn, calls Terrel an "Uncle Tom."[5] We discuss why opponents and sportscasters persisted in calling Ali by his given name, Cassius Clay. In addition, I raise questions about Ali's deploying of the "Uncle Tom" label and the racial politics of that term.

This discussion often leads to what some people consider problematic about Ali's racial politics. I move from the Terrel clip to a videoed exchange of Ali with a primarily white college audience where he speaks out against race mixing, claiming that no white woman or white man wants little black boys coming around their white girls and having to introduce their children as "half brown, kinky headed Negro children."[6] After viewing these snippets, students often wonder how Ali could be considered a civil rights icon when he articulates these positions.

From these videos, I shift to Ali speaking on the Vietnam War as a way to tie him back to the larger social movements of the time, particularly the growing antiwar sentiment. I use a news report that follows Ali into an army office as he refuses induction. Speaking to the media, Ali articulates his religious objection to the Vietnam War and demonstrates his understanding that as a black man, he has more in common with other brown people around the world rather than white Americans.[7] After viewing, I usually ask students to pair up and discuss certain points of Ali's statements. For example, what is Ali protesting when he asks why he should shoot poor or "darker" people for "big, powerful America," or when he declares, "They never called me nigger."

After viewing the videos, students usually understand how Ali provoked uneasiness, distrust, or anger in many Americans. However, I also want students to understand Ali's greatness as a boxer and a public figure, particularly since he inspired other black athletes like Tommie Smith and John Carlos to use their platforms to bring attention to racial and economic inequity in the Unites States. Utilizing the English talk-show host Michael Parkinson's "Great Entertainers" presentation on Ali, which features clips from all four of Parkinson's interviews in the 1970s, I expose students to the witty, playful, and charismatic Ali.[8]

Three moments in the compilation seem to resonate with students and convey Ali's greatness. When Parkinson points at Ali in a 1971 interview, Ali jokes that black people don't like to be pointed at, intimating that what whites see as innocuous, blacks might view as problematic. When discussing Ali as a fighter, Parkinson describes Ali as a psychological warrior. We then see Ali talk about his "rope-a-dope" strategy and how he taunted George Foreman into tiring himself out in the middle of their match. Finally, Parkinson shares a moment from a talk show he cohosted with Dick Cavett; here, Ali appeared with Joe Frazier, his opponent in three of his most memorable fights. Ali and Frazier appear ready to battle on the stage when Ali suddenly shuffles his feet in place. The speed of his footwork amazes the students, who often want me to replay the section. The video then leads to actual Ali–Frazier fight footage, including an Ali knockdown of Frazier, repeated in slow motion. Students see Ali's grace and power in that moment and also recognize the type of physical punishment Ali must have absorbed during his career.

After Parkinson shares his dismay at Ali's final return to the ring, at a time when the ailing fighter had become a "caricature" of his former greatness, I usually show news footage of Ali lighting the Olympic torch at the 1996 Atlanta Games. Ali's speech and movement were altered due to Parkinson's disease, causing him to shake perceptibly as he lit the torch. At the close of the Games, many commentators, reflecting on the entire two weeks of competition, stated that Ali presented the most emotional moment of the Games (which also including a bombing in Olympic Park). I ask students to think about the Ali of the late 1960s and the Ali of 1996—and to complete an informal "quick write" where they assess how Ali moved from public enemy #1 to beloved American figure.

Black College Athletes

A growing focus on the civil rights movement, and on the inequalities embedded in American society, created a rising sense of discontent among many black college athletes as well. Black college athletes symbolized the disconnect between image and reality during the civil rights era. While universities recruited black athletes to strengthen their programs, black student-athletes often received second-class treatment—they lived in segregated housing, were rarely encouraged to excel at their studies, and were instructed not to date white women. Harry Edwards, a former student athlete and sociology professor at San Jose State College helped the black athletes at his school give focus to their dissatisfaction.

Based in part on his experiences as a student athlete, Edwards analyzed sports through the dual lenses of race and ethnicity. His analysis debunked the concept of sport as a racially neutral, meritocratic social world and, instead, highlighted how sports actively contributed to the reinforcement of racial hierarchies and therefore could potentially serve a site to challenge those hierarchies. Under his leadership, San Jose State College's black football players began to analyze their situation and to recognize that despite their race, they held some power within the university's unequal power structure. In the spring of 1968, San Jose State College's black football players refused to play a game against Brigham Young University, citing the racism embedded within the Mormon Church as well as their own mistreatment by the university. Although the San Jose–BYU game took place, protesters surrounded the stadium and the stands remained largely empty.

The black collegiate athletic revolt spread to other universities where black athletes actively participated in and, in some cases, galvanized black student revolts.[9] But as the historian David Wiggins points out, these athletes were in a difficult position. Their protests centered largely on conflicts with white coaches over such issues as dress codes, hair length requirements, lack of black coaches, and coaches' attempts to squash athletes' political voice or protests. Many of these athletic concerns did not readily transfer to the larger battle for civil rights. Athletes also had a great deal to lose: they risked lost scholarships, reduction of playing time, and alienating their coaches. Some schools saw tensions grow between black athletes and other black students who felt that athletes should use their prominent positions to do more to increase civil rights awareness. While 1968 brought organized black student athlete protests at thirty-seven universities (per Harry Edwards), the number diminished sharply during the following years.[10]

Although the majority of my students view athlete activism as a remnant of the past, the University of Missouri football team's 2015 boycott of football-related activities demonstrated how current athletes use their position to demand change. After multiple racist incidents on the Missouri campus—and the administration's failure to adequately address them—students organized, protested, and submitted a list of demands, which included the resignation of the UM president Tim Wolfe. Students argued that Wolfe failed to commit to a plan to address the students' demands. In response to the university's lack of commitment, on November 2, 2015, a graduate student by the name of Jonathan Butler announced the start of a hunger strike that would end in his death or Wolfe's removal from office.[11] By November 7, 2015, the Missouri football players announced they were boycotting all football-related activities in solidarity with Butler, and UM's head coach Gary Finkel tweeted his support of the players. Within two days Wolfe resigned, prompting Butler to discontinue his hunger strike and the football team to resume its activities. The activism of the football players at Missouri recalled the boycott by San Jose College football players undertaken twenty years earlier to call for changes in campus policy and culture.

When my students discuss the Missouri football team's success in forcing the administration to act, they recognize how the business of big-time football rather than a commitment to civil rights sparked the university's response. They note that when a student starved himself, the university did not act. Only when the lucrative football games were threated did Wolfe agree to step down. Perhaps my students reflect my cynicism back at me as they focus on the economic power wielded by the student athletes and the place of football in university culture rather than linking the Missouri students/student-athlete protests to larger issues of racial discrimination and hate speech/acts on college campuses.

Harry Edwards (with microphone) speaking to students at San Jose State College, 1967. (Spartan Daily Negatives Collection, MSS-2010-11-16, San Jose State University Library, Special Collections & Archives)

The Olympic Project for Human Rights

The Olympic Project for Human Rights (OPHR), which Harry Edwards started in 1967, contributed to the development of black athletic consciousness. Project organizers planned to take advantage of the Olympics Games' global spotlight to expose the disconnect between the rhetoric of equality in the United States and the country's actual treatment of its black citizens. They also worked to highlight how this country used its black athletes to project an image of a fair and equitable society to the rest of the world, while actively enacting policies and procedures that subjugated blacks.

Edwards reached out to established civil rights leaders like Louis Lomax, Dr. Martin Luther King Jr., and Floyd McKissick, who helped him draft the OPHR demands.[12] He also attracted prominent black amateur track athletes like Tommie Smith and Lee Evans as well as the college basketball star Lew Alcindor, who later took the name Kareem Abdul-Jabbar. The OPHR's demands included the reinstatement of

Muhammad Ali's boxing title, removal of Avery Brundage as the head of the International Olympic Committee (IOC), disinviting South Africa and Rhodesia from the 1968 Olympic Games, and the hiring of black coaches.

The project helped participating athletes develop a sophisticated understanding of the political dynamics of black athletic success. Like Rosa Parks, whose dramatic decision to remain in her Montgomery bus seat had been preceded by years of civil rights work, Smith and Carlos were seasoned activists by the time they climbed onto the Olympic podium. The OPHR got off to a strong start in February 1968 with a well-publicized boycott of the national track competition held by the New York Athletic Club (NYAC). The NYAC refused to allow blacks and Jews as members, a position that garnered opposition from a variety of organizations, including the NAACP and the American Jewish Council, who supported the OPCR's call for a boycott.

But while Edwards claimed that the successful NYAC boycott demonstrated growing support for the OPHR's proposed Olympic boycott, black athletes were unable to reach consensus on that issue. According to a poll conducted by *Ebony* magazine, only 1 percent of black athletes nationwide supported a potential Olympic boycott. Top black sprinters like Jim Hines and Charlie Greene were determined to run in Mexico City. Similarly, boxer George Foreman intended to take part (and ended up waving an American flag in the ring after his gold medal victory). At the Track and Field Olympic trials held in California, the OPHR hoped to achieve the two-thirds-majority vote required to make the boycott official. In the end, however, they could not muster the votes.[13] Fearing the continued splintering of the black athletic movement, the OPHR elected to release those committed to the boycott "to hold unity."[14] The basketball great Lew Alcindor was the only prominent athlete who decided to stay at home.

When an OPHR member, Lee Evans, announced that black athletes would compete at the 1968 Mexico City Olympic Games, he also declared that they would protest in some way. Because Evans offered no details, the press and spectators wondered which athletes would step up and what they would do. The answer came after the 200-meter sprint, where Smith and Carlos earned the gold and bronze medals. After accepting their medals, both athletes raised their single, black gloved fist and bowed their heads as the American national anthem played. The silver medalist Peter Norman, a white Australian, allied

1968 Olympic boycott leaders Tommie Smith (*left*) and Lee Evans confer after a race. (San Jose State University Student Publications Collection, MSS-2009-08-02, San Jose State University Library Special Collections & Archives)

himself with Smith and Carlos, displaying an OPHR patch on his jacket. Members of the United States Olympic Committee (USOC) were split on what action to take. Eventually, however, they caved to the IOC, which demanded that both Smith and Carlos be removed from the U.S. Olympic squad.[15] The IOC and USOC stripped both men of their credentials, forcing them to depart Mexico within forty-eight hours.

Smith and Carlos were not the only athletes to take a symbolic stand. Bob Beamon, who had boycotted a Brigham Young University track meet in college and who won Olympic gold by obliterating the world long-jump record, climbed the podium with his black socks exposed. Ralph Boston, who took bronze in the event, stood barefoot. The gold-medal 1,600-meter relay team raised their fists. The female track phenomenon Wyomia Tyus publicly dedicated one of her two gold medals to Smith and Carlos. But none of these other athletes were punished by the IOC or the USOC.

While Smith and Carlos's protest elicited mixed responses from the public and media, the critical views often sounded the loudest. The *Los Angeles Times* sportswriters Jim Murray and Jim Hall were, respectively, dismissive and hostile. Reflecting on the 1968 Games thirty years later, Murray lamented that Smith and Carlos ushered in the politicizing of the Games:

> Historians later sadly concluded that the experiences of Mexico brought home to the world what a perfect political forum it was for causes of all sorts. With catastrophic results. The horrors of Munich four years later could have been incubated in the Mexican experience. The boycotts in Moscow and Los Angeles, the bombing in Atlanta were to follow.[16]

The sportscaster Brent Musburger articulated perhaps the harshest critique of the two sprinters, saying of Smith and Carlos that "they looked like a couple of black-skinned storm troopers."[17] Smith and Carlos experienced hostility and racism for years after their protest, along with difficulty finding meaningful employment and opportunities. Despite Smith's good standing in the ROTC, for example, the military declared him unfit for duty in Vietnam.[18]

Both Smith and Carlos had hopes of playing in the NFL. Smith had been drafted by the Los Angeles Rams in 1967 and had borrowed $2000 against his signing.[19] But after his silent gesture on the podium, the Rams quickly dropped him, and the rest of the NFL ignored him until Bill Walsh called to offer a chance to be on the Cincinnati Bengals' taxi squad for $300 a week. Similarly, after finding no shoe sponsorships awaiting him, Carlos entered the 1970 NFL draft, where the Philadelphia Eagles waited until the fifteenth round to select him.[20] When an injury derailed his career with the Eagles, Carlos migrated north to play in the Canadian Football League for one year, before returning to the United States. Despite their success at the 1968 Games, both Smith's and Carlos's athletic careers were over.

Recent events, of course, have given this story from the 1960s new relevance. One can draw parallels between the experience of Smith and Carlos and the way the NFL has seemingly colluded to marginalize the former San Francisco 49er quarterback Colin Kaepernick, who knelt during the playing of the national anthem during the 2016–17 NFL season to protest police brutality against blacks. Mirroring the press's and public's misreading/misinterpretation of Smith and Carlos's gesture in 1968, President Trump and many NFL owners have framed Kaepernick's action as a unpatriotic attack on the military, obscuring Kaepernick's calling out of systemic racism. Although other black football players have overtly supported Black Lives Matter on the field, Kaepernick's protest remains the most visible point of contention.

Both Smith and Carlos have backed Kaepernick, recognizing how many Americans negatively view black athletes who take a stand, and how large sport conglomerates like the NFL and the USOC stifle athletes that challenge the status quo. In a 2016 *USA Today* interview, Smith positioned Kaepernick's protest as an extension of the black athletic activism in the 1960s. "He's being vilified in how he brings the truth out," he said. "I support him because he's bringing the truth out."[21] Carlos described Kaepernick's protest as "shock treatment" for Americans on racial injustice and police brutality, and asserted that "This is a movement. This is not a moment."[22]

But making these connections in a classroom setting has proved challenging. While my students express respect and admiration for Smith, Carlos, and Norman, the majority see Kaepernick's protest as problematic and hypocritical, and many believe that it disrespects country, flag, and military. When I point out that many commentators interpreted Smith and Carlos bowing their heads during the playing of the anthem in the same way, students dismiss that response as over-reactive. They accept that both men sought to draw attention to racial inequality in America and that the Olympic podium served as an appropriate—and far-reaching—platform for conveying their message. A willingness to believe Smith and Carlos stems in large part from students' understanding that racial discrimination was a "real" problem in the late 1960s. They have more trouble believing that racism remains a problem today and thus have trouble seeing Kaepernick's protest as an extension of the battle for civil rights.

Sports and the Erasure of Women

Finally, the story of the OPHR allows us to examine a pattern that proved typical of the civil rights movement in general—the erasure of black women. With the OPHR, this erasure occurred through two main processes: Harry Edwards and his black male supporters failed to recognize female athletes as potential allies in the OPHR, and reporters paid almost no attention to black female athletes, regardless of their actions or achievements.[23]

When Harry Edwards began organizing the OPHR, he recruited black male athletes only, despite the presence of black female track stars like Wyomia Tyus, Edie McGuire, and Barbara Ferrell on the U.S. Olympic team. In *Revolt of the Black Athlete*, Edwards offers a conceptualization of the civil rights effort that casts it in part as an assertion of black masculinity, a stance that appears to exclude female Olympians. In a 1991 look back at the 1968 Mexico City Olympics, Wyomia Tyus expressed disappointment at how the OPHR organizers and athletes treated their female colleagues, stating "It appalled me that the men simply took us for granted. They assumed we had no minds of our own and that we'd do whatever we were told."[24]

Along with exclusion by their male teammates, black female athletes were erased through a lack of media coverage. For instance, Tyus became the first sprinter, male or female, to successfully defend her Olympic gold in the 100-meter dash and ran with the 4×100-meter relay team, which won the gold medal in world-record time. Still, she received minimal media coverage. She was the only female track athlete mentioned in a lengthy Olympic recap article written by *Sports Illustrated*'s John Underwood, and even there, she was described in relation to Smith and Carlos.[25] Although she explicitly supported Smith and Carlos, dedicating her 4×100-meter relay gold medal to them, the media paid little attention. While reporters continually approached black male athletes like Lee Evans and Bob Beamon to explain their protest or non-protest on the podium, Tyus's statement failed to make the news.[26]

This imbalance has changed little with time. Black female athletes remain largely absent from the multiple online media stories revisiting the Smith and Carlos protest and the larger context of the civil rights movement. Recent accounts of the 1968 Games have recently recognized the support displayed by Peter Norman as he stood with Smith and Carlos—for which Norman was denigrated by the Australian Olympic Committee and excluded from the 1972 Munich Olympic squad despite posting qualifying times.[27] But while these accounts critique Norman's erasure from the 1968 Olympic story (until now), no such flood of critiques have arisen in regard the erasure of black women or the exclusion practiced by the black male athletes.

This raises the question of how we "do" history. During the first week of the course, I introduce students to this concept through an article by Murray Phillips, M. E. O'Neill, and Gary Osmond, which argues that cultural products like photographs, film, and monuments can tell us the values or norms of a particular historical time and place.[28] Specifically, the authors look at the iconic image of Smith and Carlos on the Olympic podium, arguing that the history of how that photograph has been deployed by different groups to different ends is as compelling as the protest itself. After we cover the civil rights movement, I circle back to this article and the photo of Smith and Carlos. I project the original photo, and then present the cover of *The Revolt of the Black Athlete*, which crops out Norman. Looking at the photos side by side, we discuss why Harry Edwards (or his editors) chose to use an edited photo rather than a fuller representation of that historical moment. What narrative gets presented in the edited photograph? Why would that narrative be perceived as better than one depicting two black athletes standing side by side with a white ally?

After this discussion, I add a smaller inset photo to Edwards's cover—one of Wyomia Tyus and Barbara Ferrell (gold and silver medalists in the 100-meter sprint) standing on the podium in the rain. I note that the photograph appears in Edwards's book with a caption acknowledging that Tyus dedicated her medals to Smith and Carlos. I ask students to respond to questions like "How does this change what we think of the revolt of the black athlete?" "Would it be historically accurate to juxtapose these two photographs?" and "What positives and negatives could you see—as a publisher, as an author, or as a historian for using the cover I just created?"

Finally, we discuss the consequences of black female athletes' erasure from the "revolt of the black athlete." What gets lost when we fail to include female athletes' achievements, voices, and activism in the story of the 1968 Olympic Games? I note that some might downplay the effect of women's erasure as it is "only" sport history. However, the erasure of black female athletes in the history of the 1968 Olympic protests parallels the partial erasure of black women from the civil rights movement. The students consider why they all know about Martin Luther King Jr. but not Fannie Lou Hamer (they usually say because we have a holiday for MLK). Some interject that they know about Rosa Parks. When I ask them what they know of Parks, however, they usually say she sparked the bus boycott by refusing to give up her seat to a white passenger. They are surprised to learn that Parks was an active member of the National Association for the Advancement of Colored People (NAACP), investigated the gang rape of a black woman by white men, and eventually started the Alabama Committee for Equal Justice for Mrs. Recy Taylor (CEJRT). I add that the Montgomery bus boycott, sparked by Parks's action, was organized by a black educator, Jo Ann Gibson Robinson. I ask them to imagine the civil rights movement differently: for instance, picture black women at the center of the movement, as leaders and organizers. This helps students to understand that social change, while often galvanized behind charismatic individuals, requires action from many and multiple forms of leadership.

Examining the history of the "revolt of the black athlete" from multiple perspectives introduces students to a richer understanding of the American civil rights movement. Students often see that movement as a struggle against institutional racism, embodied in restrictions on bus seating, water fountains, restaurant service, and voting. The emphasis on legal barriers obscures the ways that gender, class, and culture intersected with race, and the challenges these intersections produced for the movement and for the historians who chronicle it. By viewing black athletics from an intersectional perspective, students can widen their understanding. They can learn about the movement's internal arguments over goals and strategies. In addition to examining the actions of Muhammed Ali, John Carlos, and Kareem Abdul-Jabbar, they can consider how combining race and gender might oppress black women while also providing opportunities. (The protests of black female athletes were largely written out of history, but organizers of the Montgomery bus boycott relied on women because they believed black women would be less likely to encounter police violence than black men.) They can learn that part of Smith and Carlos's protest—their shoeless feet on the Olympic podium—explicitly called attention to their childhood poverty, which can lead to an exploration of the reasons behind Martin Luther King Jr.'s support for a living wage and his campaign against poverty.

In the end, teaching about black athletic protests showcases not only the courage of African Americans but also helps students see how parts of history get erased, highlighting how what is not "there" is as significant a part of history as what is "there." I challenge students—through their research projects—to craft a different kind of "there," to provide a messier, more inclusive history of sport and physical activity in the United States. I urge you to do the same.

Notes

1. For the Edwards quote, see Saqib Rahim, "The Agitator: Harry Edwards and the Revolt of Today's Black Athlete," *Vice Sports*, https://sports.vice.com/en_us/article/8qyqxv/harry-edwards-revolt-of-todays-black-athlete (accessed September 3, 2018).

2. Henry H. Mitchell, *Black Preaching: The Recovery of a Powerful Art* (Nashville: Abingdon Press, 1990), 24–30. For Martin Luther King's entire "I Have a Dream" speech, see http://www.npr.org/2010/01/18/122701268/i-have-a-dream-speech-in-its-entirety.

3. For Fanny Lou Hamer's speech to the Credentials Committee, DNC, August 22, 1964, see http://www.americanrhetoric.com/speeches/fannielou hamercredentialscommittee.htm.

4. *Muhammad Ali When They Told Him to Participate on the Vietnam War*, video, 0:38, November 24, 2013, https://www.youtube.com/watch?v=ID3-vqADnRY.

5. *Muhammad Ali: What's My Name?*, video, 2:05, June 8, 2016, https://www.youtube.com/watch?v=_odhmvta_7o.

6. *Muhammad Ali Speech About Race Mixing*, video, 1:08, May 9, 2017, https://www.youtube.com/watch?v=Vo4uywcOiZc.

7. *Muhammad Ali on the Vietnam War-Draft*, video, 2:37, February 20, 2011, https://www.youtube.com/watch?v=HeFMyrWlZ68.

8. *Muhammad Ali—Parkinson's Greatest Entertainers*, video, 7:02, May 12, 2007, https://www.youtube.com/watch?v=Bnz77QSu2HA.

9. David Wiggins, "'The Future of College Athletics Is at Stake': Black Athletes and Racial Turmoil on Three Predominantly White University Campuses," *Journal of Sport History* 15, no. 3 (1988): 304–5.

10. Wiggins, "Future of College Athletics," 332–33.

11. Rohan Nadkarni and Alex Nieves, "Why Missouri's Football Team Joined a Protest against School Administration," *Sports Illustrated*, November 9, 2015, https://www.si.com/college-football/2015/11/09/missouri-football -protest-racism-tim-wolfe.

12. Harry Edwards, *The Revolt of the Black Athlete* (New York: Free Press, 1969), 58.

13. Amy Bass, *Not the Triumph but the Struggle: The 1968 Olympics and the Making of the Black Athlete* (Minneapolis: University of Minnesota Press, 2002), 24, 186–87; Douglas Hartmann, *Race, Culture, and the Revolt of the Black Athlete: The 1968 Olympic Protests and Their Aftermath* (Chicago: University of Chicago Press, 2004), 109–11. The sprinter Lee Evans told the press that the athletes voted unanimously to participate in the Games, but according to Harry Edwards, the vote was evenly split for and against the boycott. Hartmann, *Race, Culture, and Revolt*, 227.

203

14. Kenny Moore, "The Eye of the Storm," *Sports Illustrated*, August 12, 1991, https://www.si.com/vault/1991/08/12/124682/the-1968-olympians-the-eye-of-the-storm-the-lives-of-the-us-olympians-who-protested-racism-in-1968-were-changed-forever#.

15. Joseph M. Sheehan, "2 Black Power Advocates Ousted from Olympics," *New York Times*, October 16, 1968, http://archive.nytimes.com/www.nytimes.com/packages/html/sports/year_in_sports/10.16a.html?scp=2&sq=smith%252520international&st=cse.

16. Jim Murray, "The 1968 Olympics Were Epic for Torchbearers," *Los Angeles Times*, June 14, 1998, http://articles.latimes.com/1998/jun/14/sports/sp-59927.

17. Brent Musburger, "Bizarre Protest by Smith, Carlos Tarnishes Medals," *Chicago American*, reprinted at https://www.thenation.com/article/after-forty-four-years-its-time-brent-musburger-apologized-john-carlos-and-tommie-smith/. For some examples of other editorials, see Will Grimsley, "Opinions Are Wide Ranging," *Kentucky New Era*, October 16, 1968; Louis Duino, "Americans Boo Smith, Carlos," *San Jose Mercury News*, October 18, 1968; Jim Murray, "Excuse My Glove," *Los Angeles Times*, October 18, 1968.

18. Bob Padecky, "Olympian Tommie Smith Knows the Price of an Athlete's Protest," *Press Democrat* (Santa Rosa, CA), April 12, 2017, http://www.pressdemocrat.com/sports/6884004-181/padecky-olympian-tommie-smith-knows; Tommie Smith, *Silent Gesture: The Autobiography of Tommie Smith* (Philadelphia: Temple University Press, 2008); John Carlos and Dave Zirin, *The John Carlos Story: The Sports Moment That Changed the World* (Chicago: Haymarket Books, 2011).

19. Moore, "Eye of the Storm."

20. Ray Didinger and Robert S. Lyons, *The Eagles Encyclopedia* (Philadelphia: Temple University Press, 2005), 244.

21. Nancy Armour, "Tommie Smith, Iconic 1968 Olympics Activist Defends Colin Kaepernick's Protest," *USA Today*, August 31, 2016, https://www.usatoday.com/story/sports/columnist/nancy-armour/2016/08/30/nancy-armour-iconic-activist-defends-colin-kaepernick/89604050/.

22. Curtis Skinner, "Olympian John Carlos on NFL Protests: This Is a Movement, Not a Moment," *Huffington Post*, September 13, 2016, https://www.huffingtonpost.com/entry/olympian-john-carlos-on-nfl-protests-this-is-a-movement-not-a-moment_us_57d81f27e4b0aa4b722c8059.

23. Bass, *Not the Triumph*, 189, 204.

24. Moore, "Eye of the Storm."

25. John Underwood, "The Long Long Jump," *Sports Illustrated*, October 28, 1968, https://www.si.com/vault/1968/10/28/550932/the-long-long-jump.

26. Sheehan, "2 Black Power Advocates," 1; Bob Green, "Black, Not Gold, the Dominant Color of Olympics Today," *Ironweed Daily Globe*, October 17,

1968, 6; "World Mark Set by Tom Smith," *Baltimore Afro-American*, October 19, 1968, 19.

27. James Montague, "The Third Man: The Forgotten Black Power Here," *CNN*, April 25, 2012, https://www.cnn.com/2012/04/24/sport/olympics-norman-black-power/index.html; Dave Zirin, "Australian Government Will Issue Overdue Apology to 1968 Olympic Hero Peter Norman," *Nation*, August 19, 2012, https://www.thenation.com/article/australian-government-will-issue-overdue-apology-1968-olympic-hero-peter-norman/.

28. Murray Phillips, M. E. O'Neill, and Gary Osmond, "Broadening Horizons in Sport History: Films, Photographs, and Monuments," *Journal of Sport History* 34, no. 2 (2007): 401–21.

Diverse Experiences of Latino/a Athletes and Their Role in U.S. Sport History

Jorge Iber

The sporting experiences of U.S. Latinos form an integral part of American sports history. For nearly two centuries, ever since athletic competition became a central component of American culture, U.S. Latinos/as have developed vibrant sporting cultures and have "used" sports in many ways—to break down barriers, challenge stereotypical assumptions, create community networks, and hold on to ethnic and cultural traditions. But although Latinos/as are the largest minority population in the nation, students would be hard pressed to make this connection if they study the "typical" history of American sport. In additions, summaries of Latino history, such as Felipe Fernandez-Armesto's *Our America: A Hispanic History of the United States*, rarely mention sports.[1]

Rectifying these omissions is an enormous task. Latinos/as in the United States come from dozens of different countries and live in communities throughout the nation. The experiences of Mexican Americans in Texas and California, Cubans in Tampa and Miami, Puerto Ricans in Chicago and New York, and Guatemalans in North and South Carolina can be dramatically different. Researchers have also identified many interbarrio differences in political beliefs, religious affiliation, educational attainment, levels of acculturation, and economic status.[2]

For too long, the history of Latinos/as in the United States has focused almost exclusively on matters such as labor organizing, religious entities, and politics. I am by no means arguing that these are not critical aspects of this history. However, there are other ways to approach the study of such topics, and sports provide an effective vein of research to add into this mix. I would argue that sport, in general, provides access to matters of labor, religion, politics, class, gender, and many other topics in a more palatable way for undergraduate and high school students. As historians of sport have clearly demonstrated for other groups, what we do is much more than merely detail the action that takes place on the diamond, pitch, court, or on the gridiron. Why not introduce students to key topics in Latino/a history by focusing on the accomplishments of Spanish-surnamed athletes and coaches?

Fortunately, in the past two decades scholars and researchers have begun to document many aspects of Latino sporting experiences, and to show the ways that sports have figured into past and present efforts by these varied communities to utilize homegrown civic, spiritual, and ethnic pride organizations to counter oppressive practices and discriminatory conventions and to claim "place" for themselves in American society.[3] Space limitations make it impossible to cover all of the materials that have been produced on this broad topic. Rather, I have chosen to detail some of the most prominent works, organized around the key sports of baseball, football, soccer, boxing, and basketball, while tying the stories they tell to the broader framework of Latino/a history. I hope this account will help readers will find multiple ways to incorporate the experiences of Latinos/as into both sports and general history classes.

Baseball

Baseball takes precedent in any historical study of Latinos in the United States. Not only was this the first game in which Latino athletes made it to the highest professional ranks, it was also a key aspect of the daily lives of barrio-dwellers. The two principal studies on this subject, which examine the ways that Latinos have "complicated" the black/white dichotomy in baseball are *Viva Baseball! Latin Major Leaguers and Their Special Hunger* by Samuel O. Regalado and *Playing America's Game: Baseball, Latinos and the Color Line* by Adrian Burgos, Jr.[4]

Both delve into how Latino athletes of varied background—Mexican American, Cuban, Puerto Rican, Dominican, and more—muddied the waters in regard to race in professional baseball. For example, many Cubans, such as Armando Marsans and Adolfo Luque (the first Latino to pitch in a World Series), were light-skinned enough to be considered "Spanish," and thus were able to play in the majors. Others, such as the legendary pitchers Martin Dihigo and Jose Mendez and the slugger Cristobal Torriente were black, and thus were not allowed to play. The trials and tribulations faced by these men are ably described by both authors and demonstrate for students how "race" is often "constructed" in a sports setting.

Both writers also provide a sense of how such athletes faired in minor leagues. Regalado, in particular, includes extensive detail about the difficulties that players such as the three Alou brothers confronted, mostly when they played in the South during the later days of Jim Crow. An overview of some of these players' careers in the lower rungs of the sport also documents how life was different in various sections of the country. For example, Regalado's work argues that Latino ballplayers, frequently abused in the South, were often heartedly welcomed in southwestern minor-league cities, such as Phoenix.

As these players moved into the major leagues, they confronted still other forms of discriminatory practices, such as being asked by managers (Herman Franks of the San Francisco Giants in particular) not to speak Spanish to other Latinos as well as not to play "their" music in the clubhouse. Again, as in the minor leagues, there were distinct situations in different clubhouses. Whereas Latinos in the Franks-led Giants faced intransigence, the opposite occurred among the well-integrated St. Louis Cardinals of the late 1960s, which featured an all-time Latino great, Orlando Cepeda (who had more than one run-in with Franks while with the Giants). John Ingham has written an excellent study of the problems encountered by the Pittsburgh Pirates in 1967 as they sought to blend together a team that included Latinos, African Americans, and whites. His outstanding article presents a nuanced overview of life among a diverse group of ballplayers, managed by a southerner (Harry "The Hat" Walker), in a time of great upheaval in American life.[5]

At the community level, baseball and softball have both played an integral part in Latino life, an aspect of history documented in in a variety of highly accessible sources. With the aid of numerous coauthors

208

and contributors, Richard Santillan has crafted a dozen books focused on the role baseball has played in building community and sustaining ethnic identity and pride in California and Texas and elsewhere.[6] These photo books provide insight into how communities "used" baseball as a key component of daily life, as resistance to injustices by the majority population, and as a way to claim their own "space" in American society. Recent studies by Jose Alamillo and John Fraire further expand on this work in varied locales. The Alamillo study focuses on Southern California and baseball while Fraire's is on Mexican American industrial workers in Indiana Harbor, Indiana.[7]

Biographies such as my own account of the life of former Major League pitcher Mike Torrez bring together all these themes. Through Torrez's life we see the role played by Mexican American sport throughout the Midwest and how it helped to shape the life of this future World Series winner. The story also conveys a sense of what an athlete who competed successfully at the highest levels meant to his barrio and to the general ethnic community. I also use this work in my class as a tool to discuss the notion of using sport to maintain ethnic identity. One of the most important stories I tell about the Torrez family deals with Mike and his brother John (also known as "Johnny Boy") and their time on the basketball courts of the Midwest. By the 1970s, Mexican American basketball tournaments were of long standing in this region. One key element was that the participants had to be "Mexican." By the 1970s, however, that classification had become a bit more "dicey." With rates of intermarriage increasing, there were players with non-Spanish surnames who were "Mexicans." One of Mike Torrez's sisters, for example, married a non-Latino. Would her son qualify as "Mexican?" Cases such as this offer students further opportunities to use sport to consider issues such as how ethnic identity is operationalized.[8]

The Society for American Baseball Research (SABR) has also developed books on baseball greats from various backgrounds, including Cubans and Puerto Ricans, that contain first-rate summaries of players' lives and careers, and can stimulate students to pursue research that will contextualize these athletes into the broader sweep of sports history in the United States.[9] A perspective on Latinos as owners/managers of baseball teams can be found in Adrian Burgos Jr.'s account of the life and career of the entrepreneur and esteemed recruiter of talent, Alex Pompez: *Cuban Star: How One Negro-League Owner Changed the Face of Baseball*.[10]

Football

The single best work for scrutinizing Latino participation on the gridiron is Mario Longoria's *Athletes Remembered*. Delving through records of the National Football League, the Canadian Football League, and numerous colleges, Longoria compiled the stories of more than one hundred athletes to play at the highest levels of the sport from 1929 through 1970 (the year of the NFL/AFL merger). Not only does Longoria present the action on the field, he also proffers a sense of the challenges that these athletes overcame in order to achieve gridiron glory as well as college educations.[11] In *Latinos in the End Zone: Conversations on the Brown Color Line in the NFL*, Frederick Luis Aldama and Christopher Gonzalez present a critical analysis of past racial issues and current roadblocks to participation in football (for example, if Latinos are about 20 percent of the national population, why are they so underrepresented on the football fields of major colleges?).[12]

While much more remains to be learned about Latinos playing football at the high school level, some work has been done on that level as well. My chapter "On-Field Foes and Racial Misperceptions: The 1961 Donna Redskins and Their Drive to the Texas State Football Championship" documents the history of the only Mexican American majority team to win a state title in the history of football-mad Texas. Not only does this essay cover the championship season, it also explains how and why this Donna, Texas, team meant so much to a population that was often greatly mistreated by white Texans in this region and at that time.[13] An incident that occurred as the team made its way through the state playoffs that season illustrates how they challenged stereotypes. Before a game with Sweeny High, the Sweeny coach approached Redskins head coach Earl Scott and asked, "Can these pepper bellies play? I mean, you never hear of any of them playing in the Southwest Conference." That question was answered loud and clear when the Donna players trounced Sweeny, 32–14. This issue, I explain to students, is not that Mexican Americans lacked the ability to play, but rather that the economic, social, and educational circumstances extant at that time in southern Texas made it extremely difficult for families to keep their sons in school (much less on the football field) all the way to graduation.

Jose Angel Gutierrez's *We Won't Back Down: Severita Lara's Rise from Student Leader to Mayor* ties high school football to the Chicano political movement. It recounts how Mexican American students in Crystal City, Texas, inspired by the fervor, rose up and took control of the trappings associated with their school's football team in order to claim their space as members of the band (choosing which songs to play, for example), as well as cheerleaders and members of the homecoming court.[14]

Another work that demonstrates the connection between Mexican Americans, music, and high school football is Lynn Brezosky's article "Tex Mex Songs Part of Pigskin Pride," which regales readers with the story of how different high school teams in the Rio Grande Valley have connected the *corrido* (a Mexican song about heroes and heroic deeds) with their local football teams. Since the early 1970s, a local radio station has been running a scoreboard show that does more than simply inform listeners about final scores: it reinforces cultural pride through performing *corridos* to celebrate victories by individual teams. College and high school students readily connect with these issues of identity maintenance and claiming "space" on the airwaves and in schools.[15]

Other works that shed light on Latino football participation can be found in the areas of marketing as well as in the documentation of new pockets of Latino concentration in the Midwest. A 2017 story by Cecilia Balli in *Texas Monthly* provided an overview of the passionate connection between the Brownsville area (deep South Texas), which is more than 90 percent Latino, and the Dallas Cowboys.[16] This is an excellent example of the type of work that can and should be done with regard to the meaning of the connection between, for example, the Miami Dolphins and their many Cuban American (and other Latino/a) fans. Likewise, now that the Rams have returned to Los Angeles, the team finds itself having to appeal to a city that is more Latino/a than when the franchise relocated to St. Louis.[17] Finally, as Spanish speakers have moved into "new" areas of concentration, Latino athletes have found football to be an effective way to enter into the broader society. Wayne Dreh's "Cultures are Teammates at Iowa High School" can help students think about ways that athletic competition can be utilized to create cross-cultural relationships and camaraderie both on and off the field.[18]

Soccer/*Futbol*

Not surprisingly, there has been a substantial amount of research done on the role of soccer in the lives of Spanish-speakers in the United States. Many of these works argue that this success on the pitch provides Latinos/as with a modicum of acceptance and even support, helping them to counter many stereotypical assumptions. An excellent historical overview of the sport and its significance to barrio-dwellers can be bound in Juan Javier Pescador's essay, "Los Heroes del Domingo: Soccer, Borders, and Social Spaces in Great Lakes Mexican Communities, 1940–1970."[19]

Information on contemporary trends can be found in the works of Paul Cuadros, especially *A Home on the Field: How One Championship Team Inspires Hope for the Revival of Small Town America*, which focused on the success of an overwhelmingly Latino side in Siler City, North Carolina. This work argues that sport has helped to give many of these student athletes a sense of purpose (to remain in school), as well as helped to reshape the view of such youths (often considered to be "troublemakers") in the eyes of the majority population.[20] Similar stories can be found in studies by Steve Wilson, whose *Boys from Little Mexico* covers a team from Oregon, and by Sam Quinones, who examined the development of a title-contending team at Garden City High School in Kansas as part of his *Antonio's Gun and Delfino's Dream*.[21]

Though less valuable than these other studies, since there is no con-textualization or analysis, a picture book by Matt Ziegler, *Total Football: Latin American Soccer in Alabama*, is also worth examining due to the "surprising" location of these teams and leagues.[22] A more instructive (better contextualized and argued) story along these lines can be found in Marie Price and Courtney Whitworth's chapter in Arreola's *Hispanic Spaces*, "Soccer and Latino Cultural Space: Metropolitan Washington Futbol Leagues."[23] Cuadros covers Latina soccer participation in an insightful article titled "'We Play Too': Latina Integration through Soccer in the 'New South,'" which demonstrates how playing soccer helps improve the lives of Latinas in their places of work. All of these works can be utilized to bring up discussions of "others" claiming space for themselves through the use of sport; of the actions of newly arrived immigrants in a "new" regional concentration; and of the ways that women seek to alter/challenge the way that their fathers, brothers, boyfriends, and husbands perceive female athletic capabilities.[24]

Latino/as participate in soccer as fans as well and thus impact "space" in metropolitan sporting arenas as well as by team marketing. Natalia Suarez Montero's "The Expression of Latinidad at Soccer Games in Kansas City" examines how *fanaticos* are using Major League

Soccer matches to claim space in this region.[25] Ric Jensen and Jason Sosa's article, "Major League Soccer Scores an Own Goal in Houston: How Branding a Team Alienated Hispanic and Latino Fans," concerns the "miscue" by the owners of the Houston MLS franchise when they tried to christen the squad the "1836s," not taking into consideration how (mostly Mexican and Mexican American) fans would react to having this team named after the year that Texas battled with, and left, the Mexican nation.[26]

Boxing

Many of the studies that have been done on Latinos and Latinas in regard to pugilism deal with notions of masculinity and femininity, as well as the value of the sport for cultural retention. Gregory S. Rodriguez's thesis, "'Palaces of Pain'—Arenas of Mexican American Dreams: Boxing and the Foundation of Ethnic Mexican Identities in Twentieth-Century Los Angeles," is a wonderful overview of Mexican American boxing in this region and notes how the sport served as a tool for the development and maintenance of cultural identity as well as a mechanism for skirmishes among national and ethnic groups (whites versus Mexicans, Mexicans versus Mexican Americans and so forth).[27] Benita Heiskanen's essay, "The *Latinization* of Boxing: A Texas Case Study," discusses more recent history and focuses on the Austin, Texas, area.[28] Fernando Delgado's "Golden but Not Brown: Oscar de la Hoya and the Complications of Culture, Manhood, and Boxing" is yet another fabulous work, which discusses how de la Hoya's "acceptance" by the majority population complicates his relationship with other Latinos.[29] Finally, there are works that deal with Latinos of other stripes in the ring: Enrique Encinosa's, *Azucar y Chocolate: Historia del Boxeo Cubano* provides a detailed history of the participation of Cubanos in the ring.[30] Christian Giudice's study, *Hands of Stone: The Life and Legend of Roberto Duran*, examines how this fighter used the sport to gain worldwide fame and acceptance, as well as the ramifications for his masculine image after the infamous "no más" incident.[31]

Regarding women, Christy Halbert's essay "Tough Enough and Woman Enough: Stereotypes, Discrimination, and Impression Management among Women Professional Boxers" features interviews with a dozen female boxers concerning, among other topics, how they strategically fashion their identities.[32]

Basketball

Basketball has been a long-standing aspect of daily life among Latinos/as in various parts of the United States. Three recent contributions have added much to the discussion of the role of basketball in Latino life. Ignacio Garcia's excellent *When Mexicans Could Play Ball* sheds light on the role of the sport in the barrio of San Antonio during the 1920s and 1930s. If there is one book that students should be exposed to on the topic of Latinos and sport, this is it.[33] A dissertation by Bernardo Ramirez-Rios, "Culture, Migration and Sport" examines basketball and the community building rituals surrounding the court among immigrants from Oaxaca in various parts of the United States.[34] Finally, a recently published work by Greg Selber, *Bronc Ball*, examines the history of the sport at what is now the University of Texas–Rio Grande Valley (formerly, UT Pan American). Among the legendary players covered is Jesus "Chuy" Guerra, whose career and exploits on the court made him an important figure in the Chicano era in this portion of the state of Texas.[35]

New Directions Concerning Latinos/as and Sport

Almost everywhere one looks today, it is possible to find individuals of Latino background making their mark in athletic competition at all levels. In late 2016, for example, a website compilation by Juan Tornoe, the marketing expert, documented anecdotes that included the decisions of Texas A&M University (TAMU) and Louisiana State University (LSU) to broadcast their Southeastern Conference football games in Spanish; the launching of a new ESPN show specifically targeting Hispanic/Latino fans; the first game broadcast in Spanish by the St. Louis Cardinals; and the establishment of an all-Hispanic basketball league in Richmond, California. It does seem that many are finally noticing that Latinos have been, and are, part of the United States' sporting history.[36]

Lest we present too upbeat of a perspective, however, Torneo also draws attention to less positive stories. For example, an essay by Michael Sayonara points to a troubling trend: If the number of Latinos/as in high school sports is growing rapidly, then why are there not many more Latinos/as on the gridiron, courts, and diamonds of large American universities?[37] A story by Juan Vidal in *Rolling Stone* builds upon this issue by noting that "It's no secret that Latinos consistently dominate in sports like boxing and MMA (mixed martial arts), where college participation is not a requirement. Generally . . . and especially in immigrant households . . . sports are not viewed as something to seriously pursue." Vidal's work also features accounts of the way Latino/a athletes are sometimes harassed for not being "American enough" as happened recently in high school basketball games in Maryland and Iowa.[38]

Men and women of skill and courage have broken down barriers in the past, and their descendants continue to do so in the early twenty-first century. It is imperative to know their stories in order to get a fuller picture of American sports history. A final quote from the Juan Vidal essay summarizes why studying this topic is of substance:

> The fact is, in a time of so much concentrated anti-immigrant and anti-Hispanic rhetoric, young Latinos need to see more relatable heroes that can model a path for them in the world of competitive sports. Ultimately, we need a more pronounced multicultural presence across the board so that our rosters can better reflect what America actually looks like now. Come to my neighborhood, or any neighborhood like it on any given Saturday, and you will see future superstars holding their own. And maybe one of them, if provided with the proper support from parents, coaches and mentors, could even be the first Latino NBA MVP in history. Nothing would be more American.

May this essay help spur even more discussion among students and teachers of the functions and implications of athletic competition regarding the lives of the Spanish-surnamed populace in the United States.

Notes

1. Felipe Fernandez-Armesto, *Our America: A Hispanic History of the United States* (New York: W. W. Norton, 2015).

2. For California and Texas, for example, see Rodolfo Acuna, *Occupied America: The Chicano Struggle toward Liberation* (San Francisco: Canfield Press, 1972); Albert Camarillo, *Chicanos in a Changing Society: From Mexican Pueblos to American Barrios in Santa Barbara and Southern California, 1848–1930* (Cambridge, MA: Harvard University Press, 1979); Arnoldo De Leon, *They Called Them Greasers: Anglo Attitudes toward Mexicans in Texas, 1821–1900* (Austin: University of Texas Press, 1983); and George J. Sanchez, *Becoming Mexican American:*

Ethnicity, Culture, and Identity in Chicano Los Angeles, 1900–1945 (New York: Oxford University Press, 1993). For other communities, see Gary Mormino and George E. Pozzetta, *The Immigrant World of Ybor City: Italians and Their Latin Neighbors in Tampa, 1885–1985* (Urbana: University of Illinois Press, 1990); Maria Cristina Garcia, *Havana USA: Cuban Exiles and Cuban Americans in South Florida, 1959–1994* (Berkeley: University of California Press, 1994); Thomas D. Boswell and James R. Curtis, *The Cuban American Experience: Culture, Images and Perspectives* (Totowa, NJ: Rowan and Allanheld, 1984); Clara E. Rodriguez, *Puerto Ricans: Born in the U.S.A.* (Boulder, CO: Westview Press, 1991); Felix M. Padilla, *Latino Ethnic Consciousness: The Case of Mexican Americans and Puerto Ricans in Chicago* (Notre Dame, IN: Notre Dame University Press, 1985); and Leon Fink, *The Maya of Morganton: Work and Community in the Nuevo New South* (Chapel Hill: University of North Carolina Press, 2003).

3. For one of the first efforts at an overview of Latino sports, see Jorge Iber, Samuel O. Regalado, Jose M. Alamillo, and Arnoldo De Leon, *Latinos in U.S. Sport: A History of Isolation, Cultural Identity, and Acceptance* (Champaign, IL: Human Kinetics, 2011).

4. Samuel O. Regalado, *Viva Baseball! Latin Major Leagues and Their Special Hunger* (Urbana: University of Illinois Press, 1998), and Adrian Burgos Jr., *Playing America's Game: Baseball, Latinos and the Color Line* (Berkeley: University of California Press, 2007).

5. John N. Ingham, "Managing Integration: Clemente, Wills, 'Harry the Hat,' and the Pittsburgh Pirates' 1967 Season of Discontent," *Nine: A Journal of Baseball History and Culture* 21 (Fall 2012): 69–102.

6. Two of the most recent works in this series are Richard Santillan and Joseph Thompson, *Mexican American Baseball in Houston and Southeast Texas* (Charleston: Arcadia Publishing, 2017), and Richard Santillan and Richard Pena, *Mexican Americans and Baseball in East Los Angeles* (Charleston, SC: Arcadia Publishing, 2016).

7. Jose M. Alamillo, "*Peloteros* in Paradise: Mexican American Baseball and Oppositional Politics in Southern California, 1930–1950," *Western Historical Quarterly* 34 (Summer 2003): 191–211; John Fraire, "Mexicans Playing Baseball in Indiana Harbor, 1925–1942," *Indiana Magazine of History* 110 (June 2014): 120–45.

8. Jorge Iber, *Mike Torrrez: A Baseball Biography* (Jefferson, NC: McFarland, 2016).

9. Bill Nowlin and Edwin Fernandez, eds., *Puerto Rico and Baseball: 60 Biographies* (Society for American Baseball Research, 2017), and Peter Bjarkman and Bill Nowlin, *Cuban Baseball Legends: Baseball's Alternative Universe* (Society for American Baseball Research, 2016).

10. Adrian Burgos Jr., *Cuban Star: How One Negro-League Owner Changed the Face of Baseball* (New York: Hill and Wang, 2011).

11. Mario Longoria, *Athletes Remembered: Mexicano/Latino Professional Football Players, 1929–1970* (Tempe, AZ: Bilingual Press, 1997). I am currently working with Longoria to bring this story up to the present time, as well as to include more research materials dealing with Spanish-surnamed football players competing at the local scholastic level.

12. Frederick Luis Aldama and Christopher Gonzalez, *Latinos in the End Zone: Conversations on the Brown Color Line in the NFL* (New York: Palgrave Pivot, 2013).

13. Jorge Iber, "On-Field Foes and Racial Misperceptions: The 1961 Donna Redskins and Their Drive to the Texas State Football Championship," in *Mexican Americans and Sport: A Reader on Athletics and Barrio Life*, ed. Jorge Iber and Samuel O. Regalado (College Station: Texas A&M University Press, 2007), 121–44.

14. Jose Angel Gutierrez, *We Won't Back Down: Severita Lara's Rise from Student Leader to Mayor* (Houston, TX: Pinata Books, 2006).

15. Lynn Brezosky, "Tex Mex Songs Part of Pigskin Pride," *Laredo Morning Times*, November 2, 2005.

16. Cecilia Balli, "How 'America's Team' Became South Texas's Team," *Texas Monthly*, January 15, 2017, https://www.texasmonthly.com/the-culture/americas-team-became-south-texass-team/ (accessed September 3, 2018).

17. See Andrea Canales, "The Rams Are Back, but Los Angeles Has Changed," espn.com, September 15, 2016, http://www.espn.com/blog/onenacion/post/_/id/5222/the-rams-are-back-but-los-angeles-has-changed (accessed September 3, 2018).

18. Wayne Drehs, "Cultures Are Teammates at Iowa High School," espn.com, October 11, 2006, http://www.espn.com/espn/hispanichistory/news/story?id=2618295 (accessed September 3 2018).

19. Juan Javier Pescador, "Los Heroes del Domingo: Soccer, Borders, and Social Spaces in Great Lakes Mexican Communities, 1940–1970," in Iber and Regalado, *Mexican Americans and Sport*, 73–88.

20. Paul Cuadros, *A Home on the Field: How One Championship Team Inspires Hope for the Revival of Small Town America* (New York: Rayo, 2006).

21. Steve Wilson, *The Boys from Little Mexico: A Season Chasing the American Dream* (Boston: Beacon Press, 2010), and Sam Quinones, *Antonio's Gun and Delfino's Dream: True Tales of Mexican Migration* (Albuquerque: University of New Mexico Press, 2007).

22. Matt Ziegler, *Total Football: Latin American Soccer in Alabama* (Amazon Digital Services, 2012).

23. Marie Price and Courtney Whitworth, "Soccer and Latino Cultural Space: Metropolitan Washington Fútbol Leagues," in *Hispanic Spaces, Latino Places: Community and Cultural Diversity in Contemporary America*, ed. Daniel D. Arreola (Austin: University of Texas Press, 2004), 167–86.

24. Paul Cuadros, "'We Play Too': Latina Integration through Soccer in the 'New South,'" *Southeastern Geographer* 51 (Fall 2011): 227–41.

25. Natalia Suarez Montero, "The Expression of Latinidad at Soccer Games in Kansas City" (MA thesis, University of Kansas, 2010).

26. Ric Jensen and Jason Sosa. "The Importance of Building Positive Relationships between Hispanic Audiences and Major League Soccer Franchises: A Case Study of the Public Relations Challenges Facing Houston 1836," *Soccer and Society* 9 (2008): 477–90.

27. Gregory S. Rodríguez, "'Palaces of Pain'–Arenas of Mexican-American Dreams; Boxing and the Formation of Ethnic Mexican Identities in Twentieth-Century Los Angeles" (MA thesis, University of California, San Diego, 1999).

28. Benita Heiskanen, "The *Latinization* of Boxing: A Texas Case-Study," *Journal of Sport History* 32 (2005): 45–66.

29. Fernando Delgado, "Golden but Not Brown: Oscar de la Hoya and the Complications of Culture, Manhood, and Boxing," in *Sporting Cultures: Hispanic Perspectives on Sport, Text and the Body, International Journal of the History of Sport* 22 (2005): 196–211.

30. Enrique Encinosa, *Azúcar y Chocolate: Historia del Boxeo Cubano* (Miami, FL: Ediciones Universal, 2004).

31. Christian Giudice, *Hands of Stone: The Life and Legend of Roberto Duran* (Wrea Green, UK: Milo, 2006).

32. Christy Halbert, "Tough Enough and Woman Enough: Stereotypes, Discrimination, and Impression Management among Women Professional Boxers," *Journal of Sport and Social Issues* 21 (1997): 7–36.

33. Ignacio Garcia, *When Mexicans Could Play Ball: Basketball, Race and Identity in San Antonio, 1928–1945* (Austin: University of Texas Press, 2013).

34. Bernardo Ramirez-Rios, "Culture, Migration and Sport: A Bi-National Investigation of Southern Mexican Migrant Communities in Oaxaca, Mexican and Los Angeles, California" (PhD diss., Ohio State University, 2012).

35. Greg Selber, *Bronc Ball: The History of College Basketball at Texas Pan American* (Edinburg, TX: University of Texas–Pan American Press, 2013).

36. Juan Torneo, "Hispanic Trending: Documenting Latinos' Imprint in America," http://www.hispanictrending.net/sports/ (accessed December 29, 2016).

37. Michael Sayonara, "No Access to Higher Ed Barring Latinos from Professional Sports?," http://juantornoe.blogs.com/hispanictrending/2016/09/no-access-to-higher-ed-barring-latinos-from-professional-sports.html (accessed September 3, 2018).

38. Juan Vidal, "Why Does American Sport Have a Latino Problem?," http://www.rollingstone.com/sports/news/why-does-american-sports-have-a-latino-problem-w440069 (accessed September 3, 2018).

What's in a Name?

Teaching the History
of American Indian Mascots

Andrew Frank

In 2013, President Barack Obama spoke out on an un-usual subject for a president: the name of a profes-sional football team. "If I were the owner of the team and I knew that there was a name of my team—even if it had a storied history—that was offending a sizeable group of people, I'd think about changing it," he said.[1] The president's decision to criticize the NFL's Washington "Redskins" marked a shift in a long-standing national discussion about the use of Indigenous mascots and iconography. Rooted in public con-troversies that started in the 1960s, the debate has moved beyond uni-versity campuses and stadium parking lots. The NCAA has banned most Indigenous mascots, some news organizations have refused to use names deemed offensive, the Smithsonian Institution has hosted a con-ference on the issue, and many teams have abandoned or altered their iconography.[2]

On the other hand, many Americans, including some team owners, remain unconvinced. Donald Trump, when still a private citizen, tweeted that the president should refrain from interfering with the de-cisions of business owners. The owner of the Redskins maintained the position he had held since the team name was first challenged in the 1960s: "We'll never change the name. It's that simple. NEVER—you can use caps."[3]

Students often mistakenly imagine that the mascot controversy recently burst onto the scene and that the protests have largely failed. They tend to see the world through their own experiences, and the persistence of team names like the Washington Redskins and Florida State University Seminoles reinforces the belief that Native American mascots have rarely been dropped. Examining the history of Native American mascots thus allows the students to think beyond their personal experiences, discover the historical successes of protest, and learn how to think historically about this and other hot-button issues.

This approach contrasts with most public and academic discussions of Native American mascots. Those discussions favor psychological and legal debates and also issues of private property and free speech. They frequently get reduced to a rather simple debate: Should owners of teams and university administrations continue to use these mascots and the associated imagery in spite of protests by Native (and some non-Native) people who find them insulting? Defenders of the mascots often point to questionable surveys that suggest most Americans and Native Americans do not care about the issue. They also call upon specific Native American individuals or communities to sanction their use. Opponents counter with surveys of their own, with studies that point to the detrimental impact team names and mascots have on Indigenous communities, and with expressions of personal indignation.[4]

In my classes, I begin this discussion by brainstorming with my students about which schools and teams have or have had Native American mascots and imagery in the United States. Armed with some readings and a few internet clicks, we start collecting as many team names as we can find. Students are typically shocked at their omnipresence.[5] Along with prominent teams such as the Florida State University Seminoles, the University of North Dakota Fighting Sioux, the Atlanta Braves, the Cleveland Indians, and the Kansas City Chiefs, they discover plenty of teams that are off the national radar. They also recognize some of the iconography associated with the team names. For decades, Major League Baseball's Milwaukee and then Atlanta Braves employed "Chief Noc-A-Homa" to lead cheers from the field, and fans of the University of Illinois cheered Chief Illiniwek's "war dance" at various sporting events. In many instances, fans have been encouraged to engage in playing Indian—the act of performing tropes and wearing costumes that are stereotypically Indian without regard for cultural and historical context from which they derived. The "Tomahawk

Activists protest the use of Native American mascots at the University of Illinois, 2004.
(Courtesy of Illini Media Company/Illio Yearbook and University of Illinois Archives,
Chief Protest, image 0002350)

Chop" cheer and arm motion began at Florida State University before
being adopted by the Atlanta Braves, Kansas City Chiefs, and several
other Native-named teams.

When we map these names on a timeline, we begin to see chronological clusters. The first group emerged during the Progressive Era,
when various sporting teams first embraced Indian mascots. The second
took shape after World War II, during the postwar boom in professional
and collegiate athletics. In the third era, which began in the late 1960s,
many teams abandoned Native American mascots or refined their
iconography in response to the Red Power movement. The latest push
against their use began in the 1990s, and continues into the present.

After establishing this general timeline, we explore the historic phenomenon of "playing Indian" and the other ways that non-Native
Americans have appropriated Indigenous clothing, appearances, or
identities outside of athletics. White Americans have a long history of
playing Indian that has rarely demonstrated respect for Indigenous

peoples. I help my students list as many as they can. We begin with the use of Indian disguises at the Boston Tea Party and then discuss the omnipresence of Indian costumes at various Halloween shops in the present. Students are also aware of Hollywood Westerns, Boy Scout traditions, clothing designs, and various other forms of popular culture where non-Indians play Indian characters or roles. In this discussion, I make sure that we explore the widespread lack of Indigenous sanction of their actions.[6]

We then return to the history of athletic mascots. In the late nineteenth century, a few local baseball teams like the Osceolas of Brooklyn, the Redjackets of Calumet, Michigan, and the Tecumseh Baseball Club in Michigan employed Indian names but did not use mascots or iconography that referenced their Native American roots.[7] These teams appropriated their town names, famous Native Americans who once lived in the region, or the organizations that sponsored the teams, but they did not do so in consultation with Native peoples. The semipro Brooklyn Osceolas baseball team, for example, took its name from the exclusive (and racially mixed) Rotary club that ran it.[8] Other teams were euphemistically called "Indians," "Red Indians" (to distinguish them from individuals from India) or even "Blue Indians" (in reference to jersey colors). The association with Indians extended to ballplayers being occasionally called "savages" to indicate the stereotypical lack of civilization associated with baseball players who had reputations for "rowdy misbehavior, spitting tobacco, rank body odor, drunkenness, yellow-toothed smokers, and womanizing."[9]

America's sporting culture—especially baseball—more fully embraced Indigenous costumes and mascots in the early twentieth century. Major League Baseball's Boston (later Milwaukee and then Atlanta) Braves took on the name in 1912, and hundreds of other professional, amateur, and local teams followed suit over the next generation. Along with Native American names, teams also began to incorporate stereotypically Indigenous iconography (feathered headdresses, tomahawks, warpaint) on their uniforms. Off the playing field, dugout assistants (known as mascots) donned costumes and became sideshows of their own. Within two decades, all of the major sporting leagues as well as colleges and universities across the country had embraced names such as Braves, Chiefs, Apaches, Hurons, Indians, Mohawks, Redmen, Savages, and Warriors, and they increasingly used Indigenous costumes. A few teams chose to name themselves after local Indigenous communities, but most teams opted for more generic terms. Early adopters included baseball's Cleveland Indians (1914) and the William and Mary College's Indians (1916). Notable choices made near the end of the era include Stanford University's Indians (1930), Miami University's Redskins (1931), and the NFL's Washington Redskins (1932).[10]

Tracking the emergence of Native American team names and mascots is relatively easy; figuring out why teams chose them is more difficult. My students expect a public relations campaign and a press release to announce the change and explain the action. They are disappointed by what they find. Historical research, they discover, rarely results in proverbial smoking guns. Most teams left no contemporaneous explanation for why they named their teams Braves, Indians, Redmen, or Seminoles. (Nor, for that matter, did many teams explain their choices of Ducks, Bears, or Lions.) My students discover that most teams did not explain their choices until many decades later when they were forced to defend their actions. Indeed, the choice of mascots often occurred without fanfare or public discussion.

When decisions were explained publicly, they often involved such institutions as Dartmouth College and the University of North Carolina at Pembroke, both of which historically served as Indian schools or had specific historic relationships to, and ongoing conversations with, local Native communities.[11] An especially intriguing discussion emerges from the National Hockey League's Chicago Blackhawks. In 1926, the expansion team's owner. Frederic McLaughlin, reused the nickname of the U.S. Army battalion he commanded in World War I—the "Blackhawks Division." For some students, this decision seems innocuous. I push them, however, to recognize some complications. Naming the team after his battalion reflected the owner's personal experience, but it also replicated a decision by the U.S. military to deploy Indian names as a way of espousing an ancient martial spirit, one that also casts Indians as the nation's first enemy. The military has used Indian names for Tomahawk cruise missiles, dozens of ships (there have been several ships named the USS *Osceola*), missions (Osama Bin Laden was killed in Operation Geronimo), squadrons (the Air Force's 93rd "Scalp Hunters" Bomb Squadron), and helicopters (Apache, Black Hawk, and others). The military also uses the euphemism "Indian county" for enemy territory.[12] In this context, the NHL owner repeated the military's act of appropriation.

Most team decisions, however, can be understood only by situating the choice in the history of the era. I encourage my students to consider the use of Indian mascots as one of the many attempts by white Americans to demonstrate their mastery over a rapidly changing world. At the turn of the twentieth century, middle- and upper-class white American men faced new threats to the privileges afforded to them by their race, class, and sex. Waves of immigrants from Eastern Europe, the continued restructuring of the postbellum racial order, women's suffrage, and urbanization and industrialization at a new scale led many men to experience "a crisis of masculinity." This crisis was augmented when many World War I conscripts were deemed unfit for military service. Various reformers sought to bring order to this chaos and confirm the authority of the white middle class. Their "fixes" included expanding public schooling, overhauling labor laws, consolidating Jim Crow segregation, and prohibiting alcohol.[13]

Naming athletic teams after Native Americans reaffirmed a form of masculinity that seemed lost in the modern age. As such, Indians themselves were deemed relics of the past rather than active agents in contemporary affairs. The federal government designed various policies to make this idea a reality. It funded boarding schools that were designed to eradicate Indigenous culture. Congress passed the Dawes Act that converted collectively governed Native lands into privately owned property. The motto at the Carlisle Boarding School in Pennsylvania—"Kill the Indian; Save the Man"—explicitly stated the hostility to Indian culture. During this era, some Native Americans also began to "play Indian" for tourists and other audiences who were willing to pay to look at what they believed to be vanishing remnants of the nation's past.[14] The decision to use Native American names and mascots occurred in this context, a context where Native Americans were routinely disregarded rather than honored.

Native American names and iconography proliferated once again with the post–World War II boom in professional and, especially, collegiate athletics. By paying the tuition for nearly half of the country's male college students in the decade after the war, the GI Bill increased enrollments. My students often know (at least part of) Florida State University's version of events. The Florida State College for Women went coeducational in 1947, changed its name to Florida State University, and after an allegedly crooked student vote chose to become the "Seminoles." FSU's story paralleled that of many other schools who revamped their iconography after World War II. Several collegiate and professional athletic teams named or renamed themselves after Native

Americans, and the growing spectacle associated with college and professional sports led to more exaggerated and stereotypical portrayals. The Cleveland Indians created "Chief Wahoo" in the late 1940s, and the Atlanta Braves concocted "Chief Noc-a-Homa" in the 1950s. The University of Oklahoma Sooners began to use their "Little Red" mascot in 1953. Teams with Native American names also created elaborate public rituals in which white fans donned costumes and "played Indian" with drums, headdresses, and other performances.[15]

As in earlier decades, few teams left explicit rationales for their postwar decisions to claim Indian names and use Indigenous iconography. They did so, however, in a historic era that increasingly celebrated Indians as "noble savages." In the 1950s, Hollywood Westerns dominated popular culture, as did comparable radio and television shows and traveling "Wild West" performances. The nation's preoccupation with American exceptionalism during the early years of the Cold War also supported the use of Indian mascots. Nothing epitomized the unique American story better than the nation's roots in the "nobility" of the continent's first inhabitants and the ultimate victory over the "savage Indians" in the years that followed. In an intriguingly contradictory set of mental gymnastics, "noble savages" could be embraced for their warrior spirit as well as for the story of American progress that led them to "disappear."[16]

In the 1960s, however, this history changed course, and mascots and iconography slowly went into retreat. Led by organizations like the National Congress of the American Indian and the American Indian Movement, Native American activists argued that using Native American mascots and team names was offensive and inflicted harm on modern Indigenous people. These claims, supported by civil rights activists and some academics, were made as part of a larger Red Power movement that sought to return self-determination to Indian communities. The effective expression of discontent led many teams and universities to abandon the use of Native American mascots and alter their iconography.[17]

Starting in 1968, the National Congress of American Indians (NCAI) coordinated its efforts nationally and locally, pushing for changes at various colleges and universities, and finding allies in the American Indian Movement (AIM) and Red Power more generally. The NCAI enjoyed some regional and local successes, especially in the Midwest where Red Power had particular resonance. Connected to civil rights protests across the nation, the efforts to change Indian mascots typically relied on local activists more than national leaders. In 1970, for example, members of the local chapter of the National Indian Youth Council convinced the University of Oklahoma—located in the state with the largest number of Native American nations—to rid itself of the "Little Red" mascot.[18] Other universities made similar decisions. The University of Nebraska at Omaha, for example, had called its athletic teams the Indians since 1939. Native American students, who had been recently recruited to attend the university, protested the use of the "Owumpie the Omaha Indian" mascot, an "angry, dark-red cartoon character with a hooked nose swinging a club and doing a war dance."[19] Boosters and university officials initially insisted, as elsewhere, that the name was an honor. The conversation changed when Native people were consulted. The university president reached out to the Omaha Nation in 1970 and quickly learned the term was deemed offensive. In 1971, the school teams became the Mavericks.[20]

Despite the ongoing resistance, Native American voices prevailed at some schools. Stanford University, for example, changed its name in 1972. After choosing to become the Indians in 1930, and having a mascot called Prince Lightfoot cheer for them for several decades, the university's student senate voted to stop using the name and instead be known for the school's distinctive cardinal red uniforms.[21] The university held off creating a new mascot, until a 1975 vote in which the student body overwhelmingly rejected Indians and chose Robber Barons instead. School officials rejected that choice, leaving the Cardinal (the color rather than the bird) as the team name.[22]

Dozens of universities and a handful of professional teams followed suit, decisions that were encouraged and cheered by NCAI, AIM, and other Native American organizations. My students quickly cobble together lists of teams that voluntarily walked away from their mascots. Dartmouth College, which had the goal of educating Native Americans in its original charter, stopped calling its teams Indians (now Big Green) in 1974. The NHL's Kansas City Scouts changed its name in 1976, when it moved and became the Colorado Rockies. The NBA's Buffalo Braves moved to San Diego and became the Clippers in 1978, and FSU replaced Sammy Seminole and Chief Fullabull, both generic Indian caricatures, with Osceola, a real Indian leader from the nineteenth century. They replaced a Siouan-style headdress with a turban designed by members of the Seminole Tribe of Florida. These moves won them approval from some Seminoles, although others continued to condemn the use of the name and mascot.[23]

In the 1990s, Native American activists capitalized on a series of events to bring their cause back to the national stage. One stellar moment was during the 1991 World Series. With the national media looking on, AIM targeted the use of Native iconography and the tomahawk chop by the Atlanta Braves and their fans. Clyde Bettencourt and other AIM leaders called upon the actress Jane Fonda, who had protested alongside AIM members for Indian rights and whose husband Ted Turner owned the Braves, to help with their crusade. "It's not so much the name," Bettencourt said. "It's the chanting and the chopping." They displayed a banner that stated "Indians Are a People, Not a Mascot for America's Fun and Games" and otherwise pressured fans to "stop the chop."[24] AIM and others followed up with protests at the 1992 Super Bowl, which featured the Washington Redskins, and at the 1997 MLB All-Star Game in Cleveland. As one newspaper explained, the moment allowed it "to come to a head—namely Chief Wahoo's." The game's celebration of the fiftieth anniversary of Jackie Robinson's crossing the color barrier in baseball contrasted with the omnipresence of the "Red Sambo" in the stands. Atlanta (and Washington, DC) dug in and dismissed the complaints, and defenders of the mascot dismissed the protests as "political correctness gone too far."[25] Atlanta may have billed itself as "The City too Busy to Hate," but it joined most of the American South in resisting the push to eliminate Indian mascots.

Consciousness raising on the national level was combined with renewed efforts at the local level, and dozens of colleges began to abandon their mascots and alter their iconography as a result. St. John's University in New York dropped the name Redmen (now Red Storm) and its Indian mascot in 1994. Seattle University, which became known as the Chieftains in 1938, became the Redhawks in 2000. "The whole purpose of a mascot was to unite people." explained the president of the Jesuit institution. "If it offends people, what's the purpose?" Miami University in Ohio abandoned the name Redskins in 1997 (now RedHawks) after conversations with leaders from the neighboring Miami Indian Tribe.[26]

Even as Native American activists made headway, however, dissent within the Native and non-Native American community remained. In some instances, team owners and universities found Native Americans who supported the use of Indian names; other teams conducted various polls to support their claims that Native Americans supported the issue.

A 1992 debate between John Ketcher (chief of the Cherokee Nation) and Vernon Bettencourt (a member of the White Earth Anishinabe People of the Chippewa People, also known as Wabun-Inini) typified the arguments among many Native Americans. Neither man proclaimed the term harmless. The debate was over the utility of the fight. Ketcher argued that the struggle to end the use of Native American mascots took attention away from more important issues. Bettencourt reserved most of his ire for the names "Redskins" and "Savages," and for the associated iconography, contending that "The use of our names, spiritual and cultural symbols, coupled with mascots, pseudo-Indian attire and cheap Hollywood chants" created "a hostile environment for Indian people by perpetuating racist stereotypes," and were "demeaning and degrading depictions of our true culture."[27]

The debate and controversy over American Indian mascots continued into the twenty-first century. In 2005, for example, the NCAA announced a postseason ban on schools that continued to use Indian mascots on the grounds that they were "hostile or abusive." Only those institutions that received sanction from an appropriate Indian government could maintain their use. The University of Illinois retired Chief Illiniwek in 2007, although the mascot remains an unofficial presence at many university athletic events. Others made similar decisions. Still, a divide formed between institutions such as Central Michigan (Chippewas), Florida State (Seminoles), and Utah (Utes), who obtained sanction for their names, and those such as the North Dakota Fighting Sioux, who retained their names without sanction and ignored or deflected criticism.[28]

Since 2005, most teams that still have Native American names and mascots have dug in and declared, as in the past, that their actions are not offensive. Although supporters of the Washington Redskins are the most visible, even local secondary schools have engaged in similar acts of defense. Such was the case in New Hampshire when the New England Anti-Mascot Coalition called upon the Wilton-Lyndeborough Cooperative High School Warriors and the Merrimack High Twin Tomahawks to change their respective names. One athletic director insisted that the Warriors was a "regal" name rather than racist one. The editorial page of a local newspaper repeated this claim and insisted that local New

Hampshire teams had done nothing wrong—unlike the Washington Redskins and "perhaps" the Cleveland Indians (due to Chief Wahoo). Instead, the editorial stated that the author had "never seen nor heard anything that would indicate disrespect for Native Americans" even as it advocated for an airing of grievances that could determine "ground rules for behavior" to ensure that Indians would not be offended. Yet the editorial board used "On the Warpath" for its headline, followed by the line "Well, we knew we shouldn't have said that."[29]

Incorporating the history of mascots into my U.S. history course allows students to historicize an event that they rarely imagine has a history. They learn not only why professional, collegiate, and other athletic teams employed Indian names, mascots, and iconography for most of the twentieth century, but also about the important role that protest has played in the nation's history and about the marginal position that Native Americans have held for most of the century. They also discover that their understanding of the history had been mistaken all along. The Cleveland Indian's decision to retire "Chief Wahoo" in 2018 was part of a historical trend that began fifty years ago. Rather than seeing the Washington Redskins as the normative experience, they discover that it is the exception.

Notes

1. *Washington Post*, October 5, 2103.

2. "Racist Stereotypes and Cultural Appropriation in American Sports," conference held at the National Museum of the American Indian, February 7, 2013.

3. Doug Chriss, "A President Shouldn't Tell an NFL Team What to Do, Trump Tweeted . . . in 2013," http://www.cnn.com/2017/09/25/politics/trump-nfl-tweet-four-years-ago-trnd/index.html (accessed September 3, 2018).

4. For a good overview of these issues, see C. Richard King, "Introduction," in *The Native American Mascot Controversy: A Handbook*, ed. C. Richard King (Lanham, MD: Scarecrow Press, 2010). See also Adrienne Keene, "Native Appropriations," http://nativeappropriations.com/.

5. There are many online lists of Native American mascots. The list at Wikipedia is among the most comprehensive. See "List of Sports Team Names and Mascots Derived from Indigenous Peoples," https://en.wikipedia.org/wiki/List_of_sports_team_names_and_mascots_derived_from_indigenous_peoples (accessed September 3, 2018).

6. Philip J. Deloria, *Playing Indian* (New Haven, CT: Yale University Press, 1999); Elizabeth Bird, ed., *Dressing in Feathers: The Construction of the Indian in American Popular Culture* (Boulder, CO: Westview Press, 1996).

7. David Arcidiacono, *Major League Baseball in Gilded Age Connecticut: The Rise and Fall of Middletown, New Haven, and Hartford Clubs* (Jefferson, NC: McFarland, 2010), 51–54, 58, 60, 64; Richard Worth, *Baseball Team Names: A Worldwide Dictionary, 1869–2011* (Jefferson, NC: McFarland, 2013), 52.

8. William B. Gatewood, *Aristocrats of Color: The Black Elite, 1880–1920* (Fayetteville: University of Arkansas Press, 1990), 128.

9. Worth, *Baseball Team Names*, 78, 251.

10. King, *Native American Mascot Controversy*; Jennifer Guiliano, *Indian Spectacle: College Mascots and the Anxiety of Modern America* (New Brunswick, NJ: Rutgers University Press, 2015).

11. Colin G. Calloway, *The Indian History of an American Institution: Native Americans and Dartmouth* (Hanover, NH: Dartmouth College Press, 2010).

12. Vincent Shilling, "From Geronimo to 'The Scalp Hunters': 10 Military Uses of Native Imagery," *Indian Country Today*, July 31, 2014, https://indian countrymedianetwork.com/news/veterans/from-geronimo-to-the-scalp -hunters-10-military-uses-of-native-imagery/ (accessed September 3, 2018).

13. Nell Irvin Painter, *Standing at Armageddon: A Grassroots History of the Progressive Era* (New York: W. W. Norton, 2008).

14. Donald Fixico, *The Invasion of Indian Country in the Twentieth Century* (Boulder: University of Colorado Press, 2011); Laura Peers, *Playing Ourselves: Interpreting Native Histories at Historic Restorations* (Lanham, MD: AltaMira Press, 2007). In these tourist ventures Native peoples conformed their behavior to meet the expectations of their audiences, largely middle-class white tourists who expected stereotypical Indians devoid of modern technology or evidence of their continued presence into the future.

15. Thomas Bender, "Politics, Intellect, and the American University, 1945– 1955," in *American Academic Culture in Transformation: Fifty Years, Four Disciplines*, ed. Thomas Bender and Carl E. Schorske (Princeton, NJ: Princeton University Press, 1997), 25; Murray Sperber, *Onward to Victory: The Creation of Modern College Sports* (New York: Henry Holt, 1998), 168–69; Kurt Edward Kemper, *College Football and American Culture in the Cold War Era* (Urbana: University of Illinois Press, 2009), 13–15.

16. Jacquelyn Kilpatrick, *Celluloid Indians: Native Americans and Film* (Lincoln: University of Nebraska Press, 1999); Peter Rollins, ed., *Hollywood's Indian: The Portrayal of the American Indian in Film* (Lexington: University of Kentucky Press, 1998).

17. King, *Team Spirits*, 289.

18. Barry Tramel, "Little Red Sparked Indian Symbolism Debate," *Oklahoman*, July 14, 2002.

19. John F. Else, "Indian Mascot Ban Needn't be Difficult," (Omaha) *World-Herald*, December 18, 2005.

20. Bruce E. Johanson, *Encyclopedia of the American Indian Movement* (Santa Barbara, CA: ABC-CLIO, 2013), 229.

21. Guiliano, *Indian Spectacle*.

22. "Stanford Vote Favors 'Robber Barons,'" Associated Press, December 5, 1975.

23. Bruce E. Johansen, "Putting the Moccasin on the Other Foot: A Media History of the 'Fighting Whites,'" in King, *Native American Mascot Controversy*, 163; Dave Zirin, "The Florida State Seminoles: The Champions of Racist Mascots," January 7, 2014, http://www.thenation.com/blog/177800/florida-state-seminoles-champions-racist-mascots (accessed September 3, 2018).

24. "Jane Fonda to Give Up Tomahawk Chop," Associated Press, October 20, 1991.

25. *Kingman (AZ) Daily Miner*, July 6, 1997.

26. "Seattle U Switches Nickname from Chieftains to Redhawks," Associated Press, January 6, 2000.

27. *Glenville Democrat*, May 7, 1992.

28. *New York Times*, August 6, 2005 and July 13, 2011.

29. *Cabinet* (Milford, NH), June 14, 2007.

Part Four

Case Studies

Colonial Sporting Cultures

Brad Austin

W hat were the most important differences between British colonial settlements in Massachusetts and the Chesapeake Bay in the seventeenth and early eighteenth centuries?"

Teachers have asked questions similar to this one for generations. It's a standard approach to encouraging students to reflect on the commonalities and complexities of American colonial history. During my doctoral exams, I composed about twenty pages in response to a similar prompt: my middle-school-aged daughter was recently tasked with creating a Venn diagram that noted the similarities and differences between those two settlements. At Salem State University, I ask my American History survey students to compare and contrast Massachusetts and Virginia, and my "methods of teaching history" students inform me that they have faced this question on the Massachusetts Test for Educator Licensure. Clearly, we've reached a professional consensus that this is an important question (or we've accepted that we're simply too lazy to come up with something new).

If we can safely dismiss the accusation of generational, disciplinary laziness, then another obvious question presents itself: Why do so many instructors, at levels ranging from elementary schools through graduate programs, think this is an important topic for students to consider? Why do these two British colonies, among eleven other British mainland North American colonies and thirteen other British Caribbean colonies, attract so much attention? Why haven't we settled on a standard question that juxtaposes Georgia and New Hampshire? Jamaica and Delaware?

I suspect that teachers focus on Massachusetts and Virginia because we believe that the circumstances of those colonies' founding and the course of their development can provide our students with important insights into more than the vagaries of colonial life. Whether explicitly or implicitly, we use these case studies to reveal something about the origins of a nation's culture and identity.

Classroom investigations of Massachusetts and Virginia often focus on several key themes. One is demographics. As students study the Massachusetts Bay Colony, they learn about how large, occupationally diverse but theologically similar groups, usually from the same areas of East Anglia (and, increasingly, from swaths of West Africa) displaced the preexisting Native American occupants. These English migrants established churches and settled in towns, often recycling place names from the home country, trying to re-create through the formation of covenanted communities the best elements of Olde England in New England.

In contrast, the Virginia Bay Company's English transplants were mainly young men, often unbound by family structures and constrained less by the legal requirement to settle in towns. In Virginia, English colonists also seized land from the indigenous occupants as they sought the best farmland and dispersed themselves along rivers, especially when it became clear in the 1630s that tobacco would become the region's much-desired cash crop. Teachers also certainly point out that while the first laws establishing slavery appeared in Massachusetts (1641) a generation before they did in Virginia, Virginia transitioned much more completely into "a slave society." Massachusetts remained "a society with slaves," even as it depended on slavery elsewhere to provide markets for its fish and agricultural products.[1]

Historians and teachers can thus locate in Massachusetts and Virginia the foundations of at least four important elements of early American history: the establishment of racialized hierarchies; the importance of religious freedom (for some, not all); the creation of different economic models with associated differences in organizing labor and societies; and the often competing impulses of individualism and prioritizing the common good. It's no accident that Massachusetts and Virginia are both "Commonwealths" now, not mere "states."

For teachers who are constantly aware of the constraints imposed by the school calendar and the need to "cover" almost everything, it makes sense that focusing on Massachusetts and Virginia has become a common approach for providing an overview of American colonial development. These are important topics, and the Massachusetts and Virginia examples do reveal something significant about the colonies and the country they would later become. That said, this traditional approach can also produce significant boredom among our students, especially those in secondary or university classes who are convinced that they've "learned all of this before" and that there's nothing new or interesting for them to discover.

This is where asking students to consider the colonists' attitudes toward sports and games can be enormously beneficial. Not only can we tap into many of our students' latent interest in games, pastimes, rules, and rule-breakers, we can also get them to craft their own interpretations by presenting them with primary sources to consider. If we inaugurate our courses by asking students to think about topics they haven't encountered before (or at least to consider previously studied subjects from different perspectives), and if we encourage them to create their own interpretations based on engaging primary sources, then we can demonstrate to them that history is a discipline of inquiry and evidence, of questions and answers. We might also, just maybe, be able to convince them that studying the daily lives of ordinary people can be both valuable and rewarding.

I've come to rely on several key primary sources to engage students and to connect the sporting lives of British colonists with the earlier-identified "big" themes that dominate curriculum standards and remain important to understand. I've chosen them because they've proven effective in sparking classroom discussions, because they are easily accessible, and—not incidentally—because they are all fairly short.

The first source—one of the most important seventeenth-century British documents relating to sports—establishes an English baseline and reminds students that in the 1600s most of the voluntary immigrants to North America came from a common homeland. The colonists' attitudes toward sport and recreation were not created from scratch in the New World. As the historians Elliott Gorn and Warren Goldstein explain:

[For] over two hundred years, England's colonies remained, for the most part, outposts of English culture. Cockfighting, horse racing, and animal baiting; hunting, angling, and fowling; throwing quoits (similar to horse-shoes), cudgeling, and rounders (an antecedent to baseball); contests in which we would recognize the outlines of modern wrestling, football, and cricket—indeed a hundred games of chance and skill, played according to a thousand unwritten rules, were brought to the colonies.[2]

When English colonists brought their games and pastimes to the colonies, they also brought debates about how Christian societies should view leisure activities. Throughout the late 1500s and the early 1600s, the growing number of Puritans in England found fault with the traditional manner of celebrating feast days—events that involved drinking, dancing, and many forms of popular games and recreation. In 1583, the Puritan Philip Stubbs's *Anatomie of Abuses* (available online) attacked all manners of problems he saw in society, addressing men's and women's dress, the performance of plays, and the influence of "Popish" norms in Anglican practice that he claimed had no basis in scripture. His list of deplorable customs included "all sorts of traditional recreations, from feast days to bearbaiting, from Christmas celebrations to cockfighting." Like many of his time, Stubbs was not against all forms of recreation, but he wanted to protect the sanctity of the Sabbath and believed that small temptations would lead to an avalanche of sinful thoughts and deeds.

Over the next several decades, as English Puritans became a more significant bloc of society (and as the separatist Pilgrims experimented with life in the Netherlands), debates over proper forms of recreation escalated. This conversation culminated in 1618, when King James I (of King James Bible fame) issued his "Kings Majesties Declaration to His Subjects concerning Lawfull Sports to bee used." Most scholars refer to this publication by its less cumbersome title, *The Book of Sports*, but I prefer to introduce it to students by using the original title, asking them to consider both the authority being claimed ("Kings Majesties Declaration") and the purpose of the document (to divide sports into "lawfull" and "unlawfull" categories). In my classes, we look at sections of the document, trying to learn what we can about English life a decade after the founding of Jamestown and just before the Mayflower sailed.

Some context is in order. James commissioned the book because he was tired of Puritan carping about excesses and improprieties, and wanted to rally the non-Puritan majorities to his side by making a firm statement about what was proper and improper, lawful and unlawful. In 1633, James's son, Charles I, reissued the *Book of Sports* and explained his father's original motivation this way:

> Our dear father of blessed memory, in his return from Scotland, coming through Lancashire, found that his subjects were debarred [by Puritan ministers] from lawful recreations upon Sundays after evening prayers ended, and upon Holy-days; and he prudently considered that, if these times were taken from them, the meaner sort who labor hard all the week should have no recreations at all to refresh their spirits: and after his return, he further saw that his loyal subjects in all other parts of his kingdom did suffer in the same kind, though perhaps not in the same degree: and did therefore in his princely wisdom publish a Declaration to all his loving subjects concerning lawful sports.[3]

There's a lot for students to unpack in this preamble, from how James I unified the crowns of Scotland and England, to the regional power bases of Puritanism, to the clear frustration James felt toward these dissidents, to the realities of work (breaks were possible only on Sundays after worship and on holy days), to the perceived purpose and value of sports ("to refresh their spirits"). Using this passage alone helps to connect sports history to more traditional subjects.

If time allows, additional excerpts offer many other opportunities to identify and discuss key topics. Students can explore how James (and later Charles) explained the origins of the document, looking for the reasons that the monarchs give for supporting "lawful" sports. These justifications include responding to the will of the people; encouraging people to join the church; preparing future soldiers for war; and preventing people from sliding into drunken idleness. A class discussion of similarities and differences between this and present-day justifications of sports can make this seventeenth-century document seem surprisingly relevant to students' lives.

> With our own ears we heard the general complaint of our people, that they were barred from all lawful recreations and exercises upon the Sunday's afternoon, after the ending of all divine service, which cannot but produce two evils: the one the hindering of the conversion of many, whom their [Puritan] priests will take occasion hereby to

vex, persuading them that no honest mirth or recreation is lawful or tolerable in our religion, which cannot but breed a great discontentment in our people's hearts, especially of such as are peradventure on the point of turning: the other inconvenience is, that this prohibition barreth the common and meaner sort of people from using such exercises as may make their bodies more able for war, when His Majesty or his successors shall have occasion to use them; and in place thereof sets up filthy tippling and drunkenness, and breeds a number of idle and discontented speeches in their ale-houses. For when shall the common people have leave to exercise, if not upon the Sundays and Holy-days, seeing they must apply their labor and win their living in all working days?[4]

The section of the document that lists the allowed and prohibited sports and activities lends itself well to short research assignments (what is bearbaiting?) and also to questions about why, given the purposes of sports identified earlier in the text, the government would support these particular activities. Questions about the continued centrality of religion (activities are permitted "after the end of divine service"), the seasonal natural and rhythms of agricultural work ("May-poles"), the significance of class ("meaner people" are prohibited from bowling), and the importance of gender roles also emerge from a close reading. This is the most relevant section:

[A]s for our good people's lawful recreation, our pleasure likewise is, that after the end of divine service our good people be not disturbed, letted or discouraged from any lawful recreation, such as dancing, either men or women; archery for men, leaping, vaulting, or any other such harmless recreation, nor from having of May-games, Whitsun-ales, and Morris-dances; and the setting up of May-poles and other sports therewith used: so as the same be had in due and convenient time, without impediment or neglect of divine service . . . but withal we do here account still as prohibited all unlawful games to be used upon Sundays only, as bear and bull-baitings, interludes, and at all times in the meaner sort of people by law prohibited, bowling.[5]

Documents related to colonial sports offer many of the same opportunities to spark interest and promote inquiry. I generally focus on the laws of Puritan New England and the importance of horse racing in colonial Virginia. When I think and teach about the recreational lives of these English colonists, I rely heavily on the work of two groundbreaking scholars, Nancy Struna and Timothy Breen. I was in graduate school when I first encountered their work, and, from the very beginning of my teaching career as a nervous discussion-section leader, I have drawn from both Struna and Breen to teach important themes in early American history. Anyone who wants to dive more deeply into these topics should begin with Struna's *People of Prowess: Sport, Leisure, and Labor in Early Anglo-America*, and Breen's "Horses and Gentlemen: The Cultural Significance of Gambling Among the Gentry of Virginia."[6]

Although they are looking at vastly different cultures, both Struna and Breen convincingly argue that one can learn a great deal about a society by examining what its members do with their nonworking time. Breen highlights how the culture of high-stakes gambling among the planter class mirrored the risks inherent in the eighteenth-century boom-or-bust tobacco economy and how the races themselves, in which clear class-based lines divided the elite participants from the commoner spectators, both reinforced and reflected the society's social stratification. Struna underscores the tremendous effort that Massachusetts religious and civic leaders put into trying to control and direct what others did with *their* time. Using primary sources to explore both these dynamics can be both fun and productive, allowing us to approach important, traditional topics through nontraditional approaches.

Massachusetts

An easy way to teach this is to have students examine the texts of relevant colonial laws. The Massachusetts state government website is the best (and most stable) place to find a manageable roster of the Massachusetts statutes. By looking at the laws, students can see how religious belief profoundly shaped civil law, particularly in the criminal sections where the lawmakers cite specific Bible verses to explain the punishment attached to many laws (e.g., "If any person shall slay another through guile, either by POYSONING, or other such develish practice, he shall be put to death. Exod. 21.14.").[7]

Students are often especially interested in the text of the 1659 law that established clear penalties for "keeping Christmas" and also in the 1648 statute specifically targeting shuffleboard. Yes, shuffleboard. The 1648 statue reads:

UPON complaint of great disorder by the use of the game called Shuffle-board, in houses of common entertainment, wherby much pretious time is spent unfruitfully and much wast of wine and beer occasioned, it is therefore ordered and enacted by the Authoritie of this Court; That no person shall henceforth use the said game of Shuffle-board in any such house, nor in any other house used as common for such purpose, upon payn for every Keeper of such house to forfeit for every such offence twenty shillings; and for every person playing at the said game in any such house, to forfeit for everie such offence five shillings; Nor shall any person at any time play or game for any monie, or mony-worth upon penalty of forfeiting treble the value thereof: one half to the partie informing, the other half to the Treasurie. And any Magistrate may hear and determin any offence against this law.

There's a lot going on in this—to modern eyes—peculiar law, and it's well worth discussing with students. First, it is based on the assump-tion that private individuals wasting time, wine, and beer is a matter of public concern. Second, the law introduces students to "houses of common entertainment" and helps raise questions about who might frequent such places in 1640s Massachusetts. Besides the obvious answer of, well, shuffleboard enthusiasts, other categories of people include travelers and single people without permanent homes, just the types of people who might be immune from social pressures exerted by closely knit communities of Calvinists. These were the very folks who seem-ingly demanded scrutiny in colonial Massachusetts.

Third, it's also worth noting that such specific laws usually arise in response to perceived problems. (I didn't always have a cell phone policy in my syllabus, but I certainly do now.) The fact that less than two decades after the founding of Boston, colonial leaders were passing legislation regarding gaming activities and other forms of gambling can serve as evidence that the "city upon a hille" experiment wasn't going as well as the founders had originally hoped. Asking students to consider the broader implications of the last provision of the law, the part that specifies that the fine will be triple the wager made and that the informer gets half of the increased amount, can also lead the class discussion in productive directions about the perceived need for resi-dents to monitor, to seemingly police, each other in order to produce a cohesive, godly society. My students recognize why the leaders might want society to function this way, but they can also see why many might resist the expectation that they "snitch" on their friends and colleagues, especially if subsequent generations are not quite as devout as the generation that was willing to cross an ocean to plant a new society on the rocky shores of New England.

This is precisely the argument that Struna offers in her book: that Massachusetts's laws regarding sports correspond broadly with larger trends in the colony's religious and social history. As I teach about the half-way covenant and the wider issues of Puritan declension in the later seventeenth century (including our discussions of King Philip's War and the Salem Witch Trials), deploying examples related to sports and games help highlight the ongoing tension between Puritan visions of a cohesive covenanted community and the actual realities of life.

Virginia

As I noted earlier, colonial Virginia developed very differently than its northern Puritan counterpart. One of the many ways the cultures differed was captured in a fascinating 1895 essay in the *Historical Journal of Virginia* titled, "Racing in Colonial Virginia." Any teacher with access to JSTOR can easily find this essay and mine it for key quotes and information to use with students. In many ways, that essay serves as a perfect complement to Breen's later work "Horses and Gentlemen" and is an ideal resource for teachers wanting to use primary sources to spark a conversation, as it strings together long quotes from court cases and contemporary commentary to establish the particular details and the significance of horse racing to the colony. One 1724 quote is particularly telling: "The common Planters leading easy lives don't much admire Labour, or any manly Exercise except Horse racing."[8] In seventeen words, this sentence introduces class (Planters), elite disdain for physical labor (class divisions and racial slavery), notions of masculinity, and a significant sporting and social pastime (horse racing).

A quick review by students of the essay's quoted court records and descriptions makes several points clear. By the mid-1600s, horse racing had become an important status-building and status-confirming activity for colonial Virginians, a system with an emerging infrastructure of established race courses, standard distances, and standard weights. It is also obvious that gambling played an important role in establishing the race days' drama and, as numerous court records attest, that the legal system was committed to principles of fair competition (among gentle-man) and to having bettors pay their often quite large gambling debts.

The author of this 1895 essay begins by explaining the role of horse racing in the hierarchy of Chesapeake game options and by implicitly contrasting colonial Virginians with their Massachusetts cousins. He writes, "Our Colonists liked cards and dancing, could not see that damnation was incurred by the celebration of Christmas or lurked in a mince pie, and entertained a strong partiality for fox-hunting, and above all, racing. Horses increased in number rapidly after their introduction, and the settlers became a race of unsurpassed riders, the ownership of a good horse being not only a necessity, but a matter of pleasure and pride. All of the early writers in Virginia speak of the quality of the horses, and of the fondness of the people for riding."[9]

One of the most classroom-friendly primary source descriptions of colonial Virginia horse races comes from the journal of Philip Vickers Fithian, a native of New Jersey and a Princeton-educated tutor to one of Virginia's "first families." In 1773, Fithian described a day at the races in Richmond:

> Rode this morning to Richmond Court-house, where two Horses run for a purse of 500 Pounds: besides small Betts almost enumerable.
>
> One of the Horses belonged to Colonel John Tayloe, and is called *Yorick*—The other to Dr Flood, and is called *Gift*—The Assembly was remarkably numerous; beyond my expectation and exceeding polite in general.
>
> The horses started precisely at five minutes after three; the Course was one Mile in Circumference, they performed the first Round in two minutes, third in two minutes and a half. *Yorick* came out the fifth time round about 40 Rod before *Gift* they were both, when the Riders dismounted very lame; they run five Miles, and Carried 180 lb.[10]

Asking students what they can learn from this brief account of a day at the races will lead them toward conclusions made by Breen and others. Horse racing was a serious business, with high stakes (500 pounds!) for the gentlemen involved and plenty of public interest expressed via side bets among the more common folk. The event must have been well planned, based on the precise distance of the race and the requirement that both horses carry 180 pounds on their backs. The large size of the crowd speaks to the publicity the event must have received and to the social significance of the day's events. I always have fun working with students to see how a single source can lead to a wide variety of questions and information. We usually conclude that we need more information and more perspectives to feel confident in our interpretations.

For that, I often turn to two other primary source quotes. These come from the account of a traveler who passed through Virginia a year earlier, in 1772. This reading allows teachers to discuss the stratification of white Virginian society, the considerable travel between houses and towns that settlement patterns required, and the way that owning horses (especially well-bred) ones served as a form of conspicuous consumption in a status-driven society.

> There are races at Williamsburg twice a year; that is, every spring and fall, or autumn. Adjoining to the town is a very excellent course, for either two, three or four mile heats. Their purses are generally raised by subscription, and are gained by the horse that wins two four mile heats out of three; they amount to an hundred pounds each for the first days runing, and fifty pounds each every day after; the races commonly continueing for a week. There are also matches and sweep stakes very often, for considerable sums. Besides these at Williams burg, there are races established annually, almost at every town and considerable place in Virginia; and frequent matches, on which large sums of money depend; the inhabitants, almost to a man, being quite devoted to the division of horse-racing. . . .
>
> The Virginians, of all ranks and denominations, are excessively fond of horses, and especially those of the race breed. The gentlemen of fortune expend great sums on their studs, generally keeping hand some carriages, and several elegant sets of horses, as well as others for the race and road; even the most indigent person has his saddle horse. which he rides to every place, and on every occasion; for in this country nobody walks on foot the smallest distance, except when hunting; indeed a man will frequently go five miles to catch a horse to ride only one mile upon afterwards. In short, their horses are their pleasure and their pride.[11]

When combined with the earlier accounts, the first paragraph in this excerpt allows students to identify many indicators of the importance Virginians placed on horse racing. The second paragraph provides other opportunities for us to think about how people used possessions—in this case, horses—to demonstrate their social standing in the 1770s Virginia of Jefferson and Washington. Many of our students (and perhaps some of our colleagues and maybe more of our administrators) will relate to colonial Virginians' belief that one's "ride" communicates a great deal about that person's wealth, status, and style. This link to an emerging consumer culture is yet one more way that discussing the British North American colonists' attitudes toward games, sports, and gambling can make the pre-Revolutionary past seem both more relatable and more interesting to our classes.[12]

In our efforts to teach our students both content and skills, it's worth returning a final time to the earlier cited 1724 quote, "The common Planters leading easy lives don't much admire Labour, or any manly Exercise except Horse racing." As discussed before, focusing our attention on the ways that "Horse racing" is defined as "manly exercise" and something worthy of admiration opens a lot of doors to classroom discussions. This part of the quote leads to questions about how masculinity was valued and performed, and it's easy to see how students can see links between the social value, and gendered messages, of certain sports in the eighteenth and twenty-first centuries.

The first part of the quote is noteworthy as well, though, and not just because it will remind some students of Alexander Hamilton's jab at Thomas Jefferson in Lin-Manuel Miranda's *Hamilton*. In the song "Cabinet Battle #1" Jefferson taunts Hamilton by singing "In Virginia, we plant seeds in the ground. We create. You just want to move our money around." Hamilton's response brings the thunder, "A civics lesson from a slaver. Hey Neighbor. Your debts are paid cuz you don't pay for labor. 'We plant seeds in the South. We create.' Yeah, keep ranting. We know who's really doing the planting." If students pay attention to the initial part of the 1724 quote ("The common Planters leading easy lives don't much admire Labour"), then they will almost certainly ask the logical question of "just who *was* doing the planting (and the horse training)?"

This question allows teachers to take the conversation in two worthwhile directions. First, we can introduce the idea of historiography and point out that Breen's work, while formative and still influential more than four decades after its publication, was a product of its time and focused on what white Virginians did and thought. More recently, Katherine Mooney's book *Race Horse Men* has examined the lives of people and experiences that were not as well documented and has directed scholarly attention to the African Americans who trained and cared for the region's race horses. It's a fascinating and award-winning book, and anyone who wants to use sports to teach about the complexities of slavery and freedom would be well served by reading it.

Mooney argues in her prologue that, "for many Americans of earlier times, horse racing was not merely a leisure pastime but a practice to which they owed a powerful and tenacious allegiance; the racetrack was an institution that determined who they were or who they wished to become."[13] This was true for both white and black colonists and, later, Americans. Mooney describes the long history of excellent horsemen in the Middle East and North Africa and highlights how the enthusiasm for horse racing extended across most of the Atlantic colonies. Intriguingly, African equestrian expertise was especially important in the French Caribbean colonies, as most of the veterinarians who cared for the horses on the region's lucrative sugar plantations were highly skilled enslaved people of African descent. These experts were enormously valuable, both through their financial value in a market that treated them as commodities and through the tangible value they added to the operation of eighteenth-century plantations across the Atlantic world.

In the American South, Mooney explains, "the racetrack was not just a stage on which white men acted out the world they wanted to make. It was a place run on the labor and skill of black men." In the eighteenth and nineteenth centuries, African Americans ran the stables of most large plantations. These men's knowledge and expertise often earned them the esteem of their white enslavers, and the requirements of their work provided them more latitude than most other enslaved people experienced.

It's worth discussing with students how this special status—within the destructive constraints of enslavement—might have made these men feel. As Mooney explains, while they might have had more autonomy than most, the horsemen, "were also subject to more subtle pressures than many of their contemporaries—the knowledge of their own difference, the fear of their privilege's fragility, and the tension of constantly calculating self-interest that often divided them sharply from loved ones and colleagues." While horsemen "enjoyed many of the conventional signifiers of freedom—the ability to move without impediment, to exercise some control over their employment, to offer opinions that might well be heeded," she concludes that "the story of the slaves who worked American Thoroughbreds illuminates just how complex and insidious human bondage could be, how deeply and how differently it marked the disparate people who lived in it."[14]

No essay can capture and convey all of the insights that a field of historical study can provide to nonspecialists, and this brief essay has only scratched the surface of the ways that teachers can bring some of the information, questions, and insights from sports history into their more traditional American history classrooms. Nonetheless, I hope that I have accomplished two things. First, I hope this essay provides some ideas and strategies for teachers who want to diversify and enliven their discussions of how English colonists brought particular ideas and cultural practices to the New World, and how sports can help us understand aspects of colonial life as varied and as important as religion, class, and slavery. Second, I hope that by introducing readers to a handful of resources and scholars, this essay will inspire them to continue the interesting and rewarding work of finding other primary and secondary sources that help us understand our sporting past.

Notes

1. For more on the distinctions between these types of societies, see Ira Berlin's *Many Thousands Gone: The First Two Centuries of Slavery in North America* (Cambridge, MA: Harvard University Press, 2000).

2. Elliott J. Gorn and Warren Goldstein, *A Brief History of American Sports*, 2nd ed. (Chicago: University of Illinois Press, 2013), 6.

3. The 1633 document is available online through *The Norton Anthology of English Literature*. See https://www.wwnorton.com/college/english/nael/17century/topic_3/sports.htm.

4. Ibid.

5. Ibid.

6. Nancy Struna *People of Prowess: Sport, Leisure, and Labor in Early Anglo-America* (Urbana: University of Illinois Press, 1996); Timothy Breen, "Horses and Gentlemen: The Cultural Significance of Gambling Among the Gentry of Virginia," *William and Mary Quarterly* 34 (April 1977): 239–57. Teachers can find additional articles by searching the *Journal of Sport History*'s comprehensive and free database. It's a fantastic scholarly resource for teacher or student research projects and incredibly convenient for those who want to get up to speed on a topic relatively quickly. The best, and most relevant, recent scholarship on

colonial sports include Kenneth Cohen, *They Will Have Their Game: Sporting Culture and the Making of The Early American Republic* (Ithaca, NY: Cornell University Press, 2017), and Katherine Mooney, *Race Horse Men: How Slavery and Freedom Were Made at the Racetrack* (Cambridge, MA: Harvard University Press, 2014).

7. All of the links to Massachusetts laws originate at http://www.mass.gov/anf/research-and-tech/legal-and-legislative-resources/body-of-liberties.html.

8. W. G. S., "Racing in Colonial Virginia," *Virginia Magazine of History and Biography*, vol. 2 (January 1895), 298.

9. Ibid., 293.

10. See Gorn and Goldstein, *Brief History of American Sports*, 17, for an introduction to Fithian and a discussion of some of the "fist battles" he also describes. To see the journal itself, including its seemingly countless references to riding and horses, visit the Library of Congress website: http://cdn.loc.gov/service/gdc/lhbtn/30673/30673.pdf.

11. W. G. S., "Racing in Colonial Virginia," 299–300.

12. For more information on colonial Virginia's racing cultures, teachers can have students read this nice overview from Colonial Williamsburg's education website, which includes primary sources, http://www.history.org/history/teaching/enewsletter/volume4/march06/sport.cfm (accessed September 3, 2018), or this *Smithsonian* essay from 2004, https://www.smithsonianmag.com/history/off-to-the-races-2266179/ (accessed September 3, 2018).

13. Mooney, *Race Horse Men*, 3.

14. Ibid., 9.

Baseball and American Exceptionalism

Leslie Heaphy

Well—it's our game: that's the chief fact in connection with it.

Walt Whitman

Where did baseball come from?[1] For decades, that question seemed to have had a simple answer. In 1907, a commission charged with investigating the matter proclaimed that a young man named Abner Doubleday, who organized the first contest on June 12, 1839, in a field outside of Cooperstown, New York, had invented baseball. A hundred years after that day, on June 12, 1939, the Baseball Hall of Fame opened in Cooperstown to great fanfare; the U.S. Postal Service even issued a commemorative stamp. In 2007, a century after the commission's report, nearly three hundred thousand visitors made the "pilgrimage" to Cooperstown to pay homage to the sport's greats.

Recently, however, more thorough investigations have shown this story to be a carefully constructed myth. Even the Hall of Fame itself now acknowledges the fiction, although in 2010 one of its officials made the intriguingly phrased claim that the Doubleday myth had "grown so strong that the facts will never deter the spirit of Cooperstown."[2]

That leaves two questions: "Where did baseball really come from?" and "What made the Doubleday myth so strong?" Having students investigate these questions is an effective way to spark interest in the past and to teach research and analytical skills. Students can see first-hand how historians interpret the same documents in different ways. They can trace the developments that helped baseball surpass other popular pastimes, such as horse racing and boxing, and earn the distinction of being a uniquely "American" sport. In the process, they will learn larger lessons about the emergence and endurance of historical narratives and misperceptions. Since baseball's origins are highly debated and difficult to pin down, this is a perfect topic to spark student interest and to help them to think like historians.

You might start by asking your students when and where they think baseball began. There will likely be a spectrum of opinion. Some students will tag baseball as a modern game. Others will think it is older but will not be sure exactly how old. Baseball fans may actually bring up Abner Doubleday and Cooperstown. The varying responses should set the stage for a lively debate over the game's origins as well as a discussion of how the Doubleday myth arose, why it matters, and why it endures.

After the initial discussion, you can send students out to do research. The Protoball website created by the "Origins Committee" of the Society for American Baseball Research (SABR) includes hundreds of primary sources relevant to the game's origins.[3] Having students work with these primary documents allows them to develop their own ideas about where baseball came from. Presenting their findings in class helps them to see how historians make choices about the documents they use, and how scholars sometimes interpret the same documents in different ways. Examining the sources can also lead to greater understanding of the differences among different parts of the United States: they can, for example, contrast the town ball and rounders games played in the New England colonies with the bare-knuckle fighting and hunting that were more widespread in the southern colonies. By the end of the exercise, it should also be abundantly clear that Abner Doubleday had nothing to do with baseball's creation.

This brings up the questions: Who is Abner Doubleday, and why is baseball associated with him? More important, why has the story persisted even when we can prove it is not true? These questions allow students to talk about how history is created and interpreted. It can also lead to conversations about why certain, usually flattering, national narratives persevere, even when abundant counterevidence exists. Major League baseball's official historian, John Thorn, provides an excellent framework for this conversation. He writes, "If baseball is played everywhere today, and bat-and-ball games have been played everywhere for centuries, why do visitors to Cooperstown have such a sense of reverence, even a belief that baseball started here?" Thorn claims, "There are several answers, and they tell a wonderful American tale, equal parts history and myth, which begins with Abner Doubleday and ends with him. Along the way, his legend was created, enlarged, punctured and enriched. He is not baseball's inventor, but has become, oddly, its Father Christmas, offering bounteous gifts with a wink and a nod."[4]

One way to generate classroom discussions of narrative creation is to focus on the central personality of the story—not Abner Doubleday, who never claimed to have invented baseball, but rather Albert Spalding. Spalding, a star baseball player who used fierce determination and entrepreneurial creativity to become a team owner, league founder, and creator of a sporting goods empire, was one of baseball's most influential ambassadors and mythmakers. You can either lecture about him or, even better, send students off to do some research and report back to the class on Spalding, as well as some other great salesmen of the game: Henry Chadwick, Abner Graves, John Montgomery Ward, and Abraham Mills. Among other things, students should come back with the story of the Mills Commission, created in 1905 by the presidents of the National and American Leagues to settle the question of the origins of baseball once and for all.

As students will come to realize, unlike serious historians who look for credible evidence regardless of whether it supports the theories they would like to prove, the men on the Mills Commission set out to gather evidence that proved the point they wanted to make. They located a Colorado businessman named Abner Graves, who gave them just what they needed. Graves wrote a pair of letters in which he described a group of young boys playing a game of bat and ball outside the village of Cooperstown, New York, in 1839. According to Graves, the boys had been playing a folk game called "town ball" that had no fixed rules. Then Abner Doubleday drew a diamond in the dirt, assigned the players to positions, and drafted the rules that changed the game. (Doubleday, a respected Civil War general, had passed away in 1893 so could not be consulted on the matter.) The Graves letters are widely available online, along with numerous analytical rebuttals that can introduce students to various strategies for investigating the truth of historical claims.[5]

At the end of 1907, when the commission members issued their final report, baseball was officially America's game. The league presidents eagerly accepted the commission's findings and set the stage for the eventual establishment of the Hall of Fame in Cooperstown. (The effort was aided by a Cooperstown resident, Stephen Clark, who later "discovered" a trunk that contained things that Graves had supposedly left behind when he moved from New York to Colorado. In the trunk was a tattered and torn baseball, which has since come to be known as the Doubleday ball and is currently displayed at the Hall of Fame.)[6]

Why would baseball executives—most prominently Albert Spalding—want to prove that baseball was American and American only? Was it just a way to finally win a long-standing debate with Henry Chadwick, who always claimed the game of baseball came from the British game of rounders? The evidence suggests that the stakes were in fact far higher, especially if students consider that the debate over baseball's origins took place at the end of the nineteenth century, following the Industrial Revolution and during the era of the Spanish-American War, which sent American troops to Cuba and the Philippines. The Spanish-American War brought the United States onto the world stage, where it joined its European counterparts as an imperial power. American leaders justified their overseas actions with a theory known as "American Exceptionalism," frequently defined as "the belief that the United States is an extraordinary nation with a special role to play in human history; a nation that is not only unique but also superior."[7]

This justification had profound consequences. For example, although American leaders initially said they were sending troops to the Philippines to help the Filipinos win independence from Spain, American troops occupy military bases there to this day, as they do in Cuba's Guantanamo Bay. Maintaining a military presence in the Philippines helped facilitate U.S. trade in Asia. But American leaders justified their decision to remain not in terms of economics but by claiming that the Filipinos were not ready to govern on their own. Less "civilized" nations, they argued, needed to be shown how to govern themselves, to absorb American ideals and the American way of life.

253

Albert Spalding had already linked baseball to the concept of American exceptionalism, when he launched a six-month-long "goodwill" world baseball tour that sought to "establish baseball as the centerpiece of a uniquely 'American' way of life characterized by the distinctive promises of hope, renewal, and infinite opportunity."[8] Spalding described the game in grand terms, writing at one point, "I claim that baseball owes its prestige as our National Game to the fact that as no other form of sport it is the exponent of American Courage, Confidence, Combativeness; American Dash, Discipline, Determination; American Energy, Eagerness, Enthusiasm; American Pluck, Persistency, Performance; American Spirit, Sagacity, Success; American Vim, Vigor, Vitality."[9]

For Spalding, the connection between baseball and American exceptionalism offered economic as well as psychological advantages. Labeling baseball a uniquely American game increased its attractions among proud American citizens, among immigrants seeking to become an integral part of their new country, and in nations that aspired to match American achievements. And if baseball was an American game, who would turn to anything but an American company such as Spalding's to purchase equipment, uniforms, and rule books?

The sense of American exceptionalism has not, of course, been limited to the late nineteenth century—the idea was articulated by Alexis de Tocqueville in 1835 and is frequently invoked today. Students can find plenty of examples—the Monroe Doctrine and the Roosevelt Corollary, declaring American interests to be supreme in the Western Hemisphere; or the idea of the United States as the policeman of the world, as in Woodrow Wilson's famous World War I promise to "make the world safe for democracy," and regular references by presidents and politicians to the Puritan idea of a "city on a hill." Spalding himself used similar language, writing about baseball as a "transcendent 'beacon,' lighting us all 'to a future of perpetual peace,'"[10] as did Herbert Hoover, who once stated "Next to religion, baseball has furnished a greater impact on American life than any other institution."[11] With these as examples, students could search out other statements that link baseball to American identity and greatness to share with the class. Each of the quotes can be used as a springboard to contextualize the statement by discussing about the individual and the time period. Teachers looking for examples of additional quotes can screen the first twenty minutes of Ken Burns's *Baseball* documentary or visit the website associated with the film.

What's in a National Pastime?

Another way to approach the historic role of baseball in American culture is through the frequent description of baseball as the "national pastime." A national pastime by definition is tied directly to the values that a nation holds dear. As Mark Dyreson notes: "The very concept of a national pastime implies a firm idea of a nation as well as a clear notion of a popular 'habit' that allegedly betrays key characteristics of its citizens. National pastimes frequently generate massive audiences who manifest deep attachments to these cultural forms. National pastimes can also generate massive corps of participants who spend their leisure time engaged in these activities."[12] It is a powerful concept: the *International Journal of the History of Sport* devoted a recent issue to the question of American national pastimes, bringing together a collection of articles that covers not only baseball, basketball, and football but also horse racing, prizefighting, hunting, and miniature golf.[13]

The details of baseball's origin story, which connected with a cherished set of "American" values, helped cement baseball's status as a national pastime. Abner Doubleday's status as a respected general made him a perfect, if fictitious, founder. Cooperstown was also an ideal location. The site had originally been made famous in the Leatherstocking books of James Fenimore Cooper, a connection that offers an opportunity to have students read some of Cooper's writings and consider why this romantically rendered village might have seemed the perfect spot to support the birth of an American game.

This exercise can in fact help puncture another myth—one that portrays baseball as primarily a rural game. While baseball was played all over the country, it achieved its greatest popularity in the city streets of New York and New Jersey rather than the cornfields of Iowa or the grassy expanses of Cooperstown. The national version of the game was in large part the product of the Civil War, whose soldiers spread the game, and of the Industrial Revolution, which brought more people into cities, where they joined teams and paid to see professional games (see Horger, "Organized, Team, Sport").[14]

While the concept of national pastime is generally portrayed as positive, it can also point to some harsh realities. If baseball's status as a national pastime embodied what it meant to be American, then being American must also have involved the long-standing exclusion of African Americans and women. As Mitchell Nathanson noted in 2012, baseball "has been used to inform us as to our national values and beliefs, to promote and reaffirm what it means to be an American, to define the essence of our country (if there is one), practically from the time it first gained popularity in the mid-nineteenth century. Even in its shortcomings it has, in a way, defined us, represented us, and told us who we are."[15]

Students are generally fascinated to learn that in the early history of the game, baseball was much more inclusive than it was during its "golden era." Early on, baseball was an amateur game, and contests involved neither money nor a city's reputation attached to the contests. But as the sport developed a wider national association, team owners seized on the opportunity to control both who played and who watched. The National Association of Baseball Players, formed in 1857, required member clubs to pay a fee to join. Right after the Civil War, African American teams such as the Philadelphia Pythians were playing white teams and winning regularly (Octavius V. Catto, one of the Pythian owners/players, was a longtime civil rights activist with a long and fascinating career well worth exploring.)[16] But in 1867, when the Pythians applied to join the National Association of Baseball Players, their application was overwhelmingly turned down. By the end of the nineteenth century, the "Gentleman's Agreement"—an unwritten rule that barred African Americans from major league baseball—was fully in force and remained so until Jackie Robinson was signed by the Brooklyn Dodgers in 1945 (more details on the exclusion of African Americans from major American sporting organizations at the end of the nineteenth century can be found in Grundy, "Jim Crow at Play").

Gender can be also brought into the same discussion. Initially, women were avid baseball players. Vassar College was one of the first colleges to give women the chance to play baseball at school. Other women's schools followed suit, while "Bloomer" teams and other independent women's clubs popped up all over the country. But these teams faced significant criticism, and many were eventually eliminated (for similar changes in women's basketball, see Grundy, "The Shaping of 'Women's Sport'").

Newspaper coverage in particular offers fascinating insights into larger concerns about "acceptable" women's activities. For example, an 1895 article in the *Brooklyn Daily Eagle* declared, "Not even the circus created such a stir in Freeport as the coming of the women base ball players," who were "attired in uniforms which some of the members of the town board declared objectionable." The members of the town board had actually spent three hours arguing over whether to allow the team to come to town, worrying that it would "not elevate the moral tone of the village" if the game took place.[17] Students can link discussions of how female ball players were viewed to an examination of the fight for women's suffrage, in which similar concerns were raised. Having students consider news articles about both experiences allows them to see for themselves the similarities in the rationales deployed to prevent women's full participation in both sports and politics.

As these examples and teaching exercises demonstrate, the debate over baseball's status as a national pastime is a great one for a sports or American history survey class to take on as it raises questions of American values and how they are represented in different sports and at various times. In the 1970s, for example, the historian Robert F. Wheeler focused on the values represented by what he called "traditional" sports such as baseball versus "modern" sports like basketball and American football. "In every case part of the attraction of the newer sport appears related to its connection with more modern values as opposed to the more traditional attitudes associated with the older sport," he stated.[18] By using a variety of primary and secondary sources from the 1830s to the more recent past, students can engage in a debate about baseball's founding, development, and continuing status in American society.[19] Students can also engage in a larger debate over the question of "traditional" versus "modern" values and whether those ideals are found in sports. Why is baseball the national pastime? What does that mean in terms of values for America? In questioning these ideas, teachers could lead a discussion regarding which characteristics are traditional and modern and how different sports might or might not embody those characteristics. This is often a great debate to lead off or end a sports history class.[20]

Notes

1. The epigraph is from John Thorn, "Whitman, Melville and Baseball," https://ourgame.mlblogs.com/whitman-melville-and-baseball-662f5ef3583d (accessed September 3, 2018).

2. *New York Times*, November 12, 2010.

3. http://protoball.org/Welcome_to_Protoball.

4. John Thorn, "How It Came to Be in Cooperstown," https://amp.mlb.com /79079370-how-cooperstown-became-home-to-baseball.amp.html (accessed September 3, 2018). Thorn's *Baseball in the Garden of Eden: The Secret History of the Early Game* (New York: Simon & Schuster, 2011) puts forth his own theories in detail.

5. Christopher Klein, "Baseball's Cooperstown Myth," June 11, 2014, http:// www.history.com/news/baseballs-cooperstown-myth (accessed September 3, 2018); *Chicago Daily Herald*, November 1, 1975.

6. "The Abner Doubleday Myth," http://www.19cbaseball.com/game-2 .html (accessed September 3, 2018).

7. Steven W. Pope, "Rethinking Sport, Empire and American Exceptionalism," *Sport History Review* 38 (2007): 93.

8. Kenneth Robert White, "Baseball and the American Character: Exploring the Influence of the National Pastime on the Origins of the Contemporary American Identity," http://www.ncurproceedings.org/ojs/index.php/NCUR 2015/article/view/1515 (accessed September 3, 2018).

9. Lowell Edwin Folsum, "America's 'Hurrah Game': Baseball and Walt Whitman," *Iowa Review* 11 (Spring–Summer 1980): 68.

10. Ibid., 73.

11. Dan Cohen, *Play Ball, Mr. President: A Century of Baseballs Signed by U.S. Presidents* (Charleston, SC: Elevate, 2008), 18.

12. Mark Dyreson, "American National Pastimes: The Genealogy of an Idea," *International Journal of the History of Sport* 31 (2014): 8.

13. *The International Journal of the History of Sport* 31 (2014).

14. Michael Aubrecht, "Battlefield Baseball," http://www.pinstripepress .net/CWHBaseball.pdf (accessed September 3, 2018); "Baseball: Across a Divided Society," http://www.loc.gov/teachers/classroommaterials/primary sourcesets/baseball/pdf/teacher_guide.pdf (accessed September 3, 2018); "Conservation, Preservation and the National Parks," http://www.crf-usa .org/images/pdf/gates/conservation-preservation-nationalparks.pdf (accessed September 3, 2018); The section 1:20 to 1:36 of "Inning One" in Ken Burns's *Baseball* series offers a succinct summary. Ken Burns, "Inning One: Our Game (1840–1900)," https://www.thetvdb.com/series/ken-burns-films/episodes /5338044.

15. Mitchell Nathanson, quoted in Daniel Nathan's fascinating article "Baseball as the National Pastime: A Fiction Whose Time Is Past," *International Journal of the History of Sport* 31 (2014): 91–108. See also Susan Berkson, "Baseball Plays America's Other Game—Sexism," *Minneapolis Star-Tribune*, October 2, 1994.

16. The following link provides a listing of primary sources that could be used in a classroom: https://hsp.org/sites/default/files/octaviuscattopythians

baseballclub.pdf (accessed September 3, 2018). See also Daniel Biddle and Murray Dubin, *Tasting Freedom: Octavius Catto and the Battle for Equality in Civil War America* (Philadelphia: Temple University Press, 2010).

17. *Brooklyn Daily Eagle*, August 11, 1895. Many more such stories can be found in Debra Shattuck, *Bloomer Girls: Women Baseball Pioneers* (Urbana: University of Illinois Press, 2017).

18. Robert Wheeler, "Teaching Sport as History, History as Sport," *History Teacher* 11 (May 1978): 314.

19. The journalist Russell Baker, for example, has written a number of articles over the years that explore this question and the debate with others over which sport is the national pastime and why it matters. Russell Baker, "Our National Pastime," *Honolulu-Star Bulletin*, November 20, 1965; Baker, "The Real National Pastime," *Cincinnati Enquirer*, July 24, 1985. See also, Larry Gallup, "Meet the New National Pastime," *Wisconsin Post-Crescent*, April 4, 1993; Howard Holt, "Is Golf Eclipsing Baseball as American National Sport?" *Jackson Clarion-Ledger*, September 13, 1931.

20. Allen Guttman, *From Ritual to Record: The Nature of Modern Sports* (New York: Columbia University Press, 1978).

NASCAR 101

Moonshine, Fast Cars, and Southern Working-Class Agency

Daniel Pierce

In 1965 the journalist Tom Wolfe penned a legendary *Esquire* magazine article: "The Last American Hero Is Junior Johnson. Yes!" Bravery, ingenuity, and intelligence suffuse the portrait of the NASCAR star, perhaps most dramatically when Wolfe, in his inimitable way, describes a night when federal revenue agents thought they had the moonshine-running Junior trapped by a roadblock:

> There's no way out of there, they had the barricades up and they could hear his souped-up car roaring around the bend, and here it comes—but suddenly they can hear a siren and see a red light flashing in the grille, so they think it's another agent, and boy, they run out like ants and pull those barrels and boards and sawhorses out of the way, and then—Ggghhzzzzzzzzhhhhhggggggzzzzzzeeeeong!—gawdam! There he goes again, it was him, Junior Johnson!, with a gawdam agent's si-reen and a red light in his grille![1]

Whether this story was the product of Wolfe's vivid imagination, the stuff of local lore, or an actual event we'll never know (Johnson has never shared this particular story in his many interviews over the years). But it illuminates both the origins of NASCAR and its growth into a mainstream American sport. That larger story not only spotlights the audacious driving talents of southern drivers who hauled liquor one night and raced the same car at a dirt track the next, it also represents the agency, creativity, and genius of individuals who grew up "dirt poor" but used what they had at hand to become master auto mechanics, creative engineers, successful racetrack owners, and entrepreneurial marketers of their sport. Individuals like Johnson took the sport from poor, rural places like Wilkes County, North Carolina, to the boardrooms of Madison Avenue and television screens in the living rooms of every American family.

Stock car racing was largely created by the southern white working class, especially its mountain farmers and Piedmont region mill workers. The historian Pete Daniel places southern stock car racing alongside the blues and country music as examples of important American cultural manifestations that emerged from "low down" roots.[2] And perhaps no figure in NASCAR history better exemplifies the working-class agency that created the sport and attracted so many fans than Robert Glenn Johnson Jr. Johnson's life can be used to examine multiple aspects of the lives of working-class white southern men, including their economic opportunities and limits, the forms of self-expression they fashioned and celebrated, and the ways that southern stereotypes were shaped and used.[3]

Limited Options

Junior Johnson was born on a Wilkes County family farm in 1931. It was the heart of the Great Depression, but as in much of the South, Wilkes County residents hardly noticed—they had been in the midst of agricultural decline for generations. Population growth combined with the equal division of property among male heirs created a cycle of smaller and smaller farm size, while the cultivation of steep slopes, rapid soil exhaustion, and deeply eroded and denuded hillsides reduced yields. As early as 1913, Horace Kephart wrote of one mountain farmer who complained that only a few crops of corn rendered the soil "so poor hit wouldn't raise a cuss fight."[4]

Farmers like Junior's daddy, Robert Glenn Johnson Sr., faced few viable options. Some of Johnson's neighbors migrated out of the mountains and foothills of Wilkes County to work in the Piedmont's burgeoning number of textile mills, furniture plants, or tobacco factories. A move to such places meant relatively steady wages and, in the case of textiles, employment for the whole family, including children. Textile mill villages offered low-cost housing as well as access to health care, churches, educational facilities, more varied entertainment options, and the consumer goods found in company commissaries. Those benefits, however, came at a cost. Mill owners kept their workers under intense supervision, even outside the factory, and made them increasingly dependent on mill work to survive. As W. J. Cash observed, "Even more definitely than the tenant and the [share] cropper, the cotton mill worker of the South would be stripped of the ancient autonomy and placed in every department of his life under the control of his employer."[5] This oppressive environment produced intense conflict. A series of textile mill strikes took place not far from Wilkes County in the late 1920s and early 1930s, and the violence used to suppress them curtailed the growth of labor unions throughout the region.[6]

For independent-minded individuals like Robert Sr., intent on holding onto the family farm and loath to work long hours indoors under close supervision, factory work was not a viable alternative. Johnson turned instead to his other option: supplementing his farm income by following the craft he learned from his daddy, who learned it from his daddy, who learned it from his daddy, on back to the original Johnsons who migrated from the British Isles. That craft was manufacturing unaged corn liquor, better known as moonshine.[7] "Trust me. There was nothing to do in the mountains of North Carolina back in the thirties, forties, and fifties," noted Benny Parsons, a Wilkes County native, NASCAR champion, and racing broadcaster. "You either worked in a hosiery mill, a furniture factory or you made whiskey."[8]

Generations of mountaineers had found in moonshine an ideal way to increase a corn crop's value while reducing transportation costs, and the Wilkes County that produced Junior Johnson had long been a hotbed for the business. Not long after the Civil War, the press dubbed it the "Kingdom of Wilkes" for its independence and lawlessness, and in his book *Mountain Spirits*, the author Joseph Dabney included Wilkes County among his list of four "Moonshine Capitals of the World."[9] Making moonshine was an important part of providing for many families' basic needs, part of what Crandall Shifflett has called a "patchwork quilt" existence where people found ways to supplement their meager farm income in order to pay property taxes and mortgages.[10] Unlike the stereotype of the mountaineer as ignorant, lazy, and unambitious—a stereotype often used to justify exploiting mountaineers and their land—Robert Sr. worked hard on his farm and supplemented that income by running a small sawmill as well as making moonshine.[11]

Robert Sr. also showed his entrepreneurial streak when he expanded his moonshine business during the years of national prohibition and then under continuing local prohibition, a time when profits were at their highest. By the mid-1930s he had become one of the largest operators in Wilkes County. In 1935 he was the target of the nation's largest single inland illegal liquor bust to date—the agents who raided his Ingle Hollow home seized 7,100 gallons of moonshine and five stills capable of producing 2,000 gallons of liquor per week. Like many boys (and girls) in such families, Junior started helping out at the still at an early age, carrying sacks of corn meal and sugar, stirring the mash, stoking the fires, and helping bottle the liquor.[12]

Junior also grew up in an area increasingly obsessed with the automobile. Like moonshining, the automobile represented independence. Alex Mull and Gordon Boger, who grew up in neighboring Catawba County, recalled that an old Model T could be acquired for $50, and "a kid with just a little mechanical ability could keep one running with a couple of tin cans, some bailing wire, a pair of pliers and a screwdriver."[13] Johnson himself had fond memories of learning the basics of auto mechanics with a Model T: "Most of the time us kids, if somebody had a old T-Model or A-Model that they had kindly junked, we would pool our money and buy it and fix it up and ride and mess around on the farm with it."[14]

"Hell of a Fellow"

While Johnson grew up in a Wilkes County that was rapidly modernizing, it was also a place still steeped in the cultural attitudes of the Old South. In particular, he grew up in an area that still prized the male attributes characterized by W. J. Cash in his classic work *The Mind of the South* as the "hell of a fellow." Cash described this cultural archetype as "a hot, stout fellow, full of blood and reared to outdoor activity" who was "full of chip-on-the-shoulder swagger," and who would "knock hell out of whoever dared to cross him," run "spontaneous and unpremeditated footraces," and "let off wild yells" for no apparent reason."[15]

Moonshining, the automobile, and the "hell of a fellow" ethos converged as the illegal liquor business became increasingly dependent on cars and young, daring drivers. Indeed, by age fourteen Junior Johnson had dropped out of school and begun hauling liquor in the dead of night to customers in nearby towns like Elkin and Yadkinville. He soon became a skilled driver who could outrun pursuers even when his car was loaded to the windowsills with cases of liquor. Such a feat required more than driving skill. The young moonshiner also developed a talent for modifying cars, using techniques such as boring out the engines and adding high-performance cylinder heads and carburetors imported from California.

Junior's help in the family business became especially important as Robert Sr. and older brothers L. P. and Fred spent increasing amounts of time in federal penitentiaries.[16] By his late teens, Junior was making three or four runs per night with his car loaded with twenty-two cases of moonshine. Depending on the going rate, he could make more than $100 per run and up to $400 per night. That money meant food for the family. It was also poured back into the business in the form of new stills, supplies such as sugar, yeast, and containers, better cars, and imported performance parts.[17]

Rural Appalachian counties like Wilkes had few entertainment options, and young people had to use their own creativity to come up with diversions. A natural one for the young men of Wilkes, given their competitive nature, a surfeit of testosterone, and their "hell of a fellow" ethos, was to take their cars out on the roads and race one another to see who was most daring and had the most mechanical skill. Junior Johnson quickly proved himself as a superior mechanic and driver.[18]

In the immediate post–World War II era, Wilkes County became caught up in the growing popularity of the new sport of stock car racing. In 1946, a group of what local newspapers characterized as "sportsmen" began constructing a dirt racetrack on the edge of North Wilkesboro. The two principal builders, Charlie Combs and Enoch Staley, were locals with deep roots in the community. Their biographies reveal that Combs and Staley also had deep roots in the local moonshine business and had made good money in the business during World War II. Many of the early owners of NASCAR tracks were heavily involved in the illegal liquor business, primarily as financiers. Building race-tracks gave them a legal, potentially lucrative investment in a booming sport that they already loved. It also provided an opportunity to funnel large amounts of illegally gained cash through racetracks and into local banks.[19]

Combs, Staley, and other entrepreneurial and stock-car loving boot-leggers found a willing and able partner in William Henry Getty "Big Bill" France, a Daytona Beach, Florida, mechanic and race car driver turned stock car racing impresario and promoter who was looking for new tracks to host his new NASCAR series of races. The ensuing partner-ship between France, who had deep connections in the racing commu-nity as well as the trust of top drivers, and men like Combs and Staley, who had the cash to build race tracks and provide attractive race purses, fueled the stock car racing boom in the late 1940s.[20]

Junior's experience at evading the law and racing fellow moon-shiners eased his transition to the racetrack As Junior himself explained, "It was a kind of a help to me that I had been in the moonshine business, cause I had a head start on my career. I was as good a driver as I was ever going to be."[21] His "career" as a stock car racer began somewhat accidentally in 1949 when his brother L. P. pulled the seventeen-year-old away from plowing a cornfield with a mule and took him down to North Wilkesboro Speedway to drive L. P.'s liquor car in a special pre-liminary race for local amateurs. Junior jumped at the chance to race in front of a crowd of people and against fifteen or twenty locals (mostly other bootleggers). Junior finished second in the race to his liquor-hauling compatriot Gwyn Staley, brother of the speedway's owner/promoter and soon-to-be NASCAR star in his own right. That contest gave Junior the racing bug. While hauling liquor remained his primary source of income into the late 1950s, he increasingly focused his atten-tion and energies on racing.[22]

In 1953 Junior made his debut in NASCAR's top-ranked Grand Na-tional Series at its biggest race, the Southern 500 at Darlington Raceway in South Carolina. In 1955 he went racing full-time in a car funded by local businessmen. Their confidence in his driving abilities was rewarded when he won the twelfth race of the season at Hickory Speedway in Newton, North Carolina. Junior would go on to win four more that season, making him the most successful rookie in NASCAR history. His racing style also made him a fan favorite. Like many of his liquor-running compatriots, Junior knew only one speed: "flat out." On one memorable occasion at North Wilkesboro, he entered a curve too fast, went over the bank, kept his foot to the pedal, sped through the weeds, then catapulted back over the bank and onto the track without losing his lead. The fans went crazy.[23] The sports reporter Dick Thompson asserted that the two-hundred-plus pound Johnson "looks like a wrestler and drives like a maniac."[24] After a brief stint in prison, following a 1956 raid on the family still, Johnson returned to the top ranks of NASCAR, with a driving career that lasted into the mid-1960s.[25]

Limits to Agency

For the growing number of NASCAR fans in the 1950s and 1960s, drivers like Junior Johnson often represented the ultimate example of agency, of controlling one's own life and destiny. But as NASCAR grew in popularity, and as it drew Detroit automakers into the sport, its owner, Bill France, became increasingly dictatorial, acting much like the all-controlling southern textile mill owners. NASCAR drivers were the textile workers of American professional sports—the lowest paid athletes by almost any measure. The *Charlotte Observer* reporter George Cunningham observed in 1961 that while a race at Bristol Speedway drew twenty-five thousand fans paying $8 a head (a $200,000 gross), NASCAR paid out only $15,000 in prize money, $4,000 of which came from the auto manufacturers.[26] "We weren't making no money," asserted Tim Flock, the star driver and two-time NASCAR champion. "We were only getting a thousand dollars for first place in most races. They were probably paying about 7 percent of the gross."[27]

France also used the vague, catchall charge of "actions detrimental to auto racing" to cover any penalty he chose to assess on drivers, enhancing his reputation as a ruthless and sometimes capricious leader. In 1959, when the newly deposed Cuban strongman Fulgencio Batista settled near NASCAR's Daytona Beach headquarters, a *Charlotte News* reporter named Max Muhlman quipped that "now there are two dictators in Daytona Beach." True to form, France flew to Charlotte in an unsuccessful effort to get Muhlman fired.[28]

In August 1961, these and other factors spurred the race-car drivers Curtis Turner and Tim Flock to lead a drive to join the Federation of Professional Athletes, a Teamster's Union affiliate. (The 1960s were a strong period for U.S. labor unions, and professional athletes in several sports were exploring unionization.) Almost all of the top drivers paid their dues and signed union cards, including Junior Johnson. Another driver, Glenn Wood, explained his reasons for joining. "I have been at races before when drivers would want to strike because of a low purse and a large crowd," he observed, reasoning that it would "only cost me $10" to find out if the FPA would help improve conditions.[29]

Drivers soon learned, however, that efforts to unionize stood to cost them much more. France marshaled his forces to combat the drive, got promoters and track owners to back him, and employed every tried-and-true union-busting tactic used against southern textile workers over the years. He called a meeting at the next NASCAR race, held at Bowman-Gray Stadium in Winston-Salem, North Carolina, and told the drivers that before he would allow a union in the sport he would shut down all the tracks in which he had a direct interest, plow them up, and plant corn. He laid down a decree that no known union member would be allowed to race in a NASCAR contest and asserted that if needed he would "use a pistol to enforce it. I have a pistol, and I know

Junior Johnson with his smashed windshield after the Grand National race at Asheville-Weaverville Speedway, August 1961. (Don Hunter/Smyle Media)

how to use it, I've used it before." He then promised to allow drivers back into his good graces if they signed affidavits nullifying their union memberships. He banned Turner and Flock from driving in NASCAR "for life," although he did reinstate them some years later.[30]

Junior, like all the other top drivers, knew when he was licked. He resigned from the union. He won the next race, an event at the Asheville-Weaverville Speedway in which the track came up in chunks, the race was shortened, and angry fans refused to let the drivers leave. Junior finished the race with a hole the size of a softball in the windshield.[31] He and other drivers would have to find more subtle ways to exercise their independence.

Racial Constraints

Another limitation to agency in NASCAR involved race. For most of its history, the sport has been a "whites only" enterprise in terms of both drivers and fans. NASCAR had no formal Jim Crow rules during the 1940s, 1950s, and 1960s. But as in the cotton mills where many fans worked, it was understood that African Americans were not welcome. The sport's officials also allowed tracks to set their own policies regarding entry eligibility, and many tracks—including the prominent Darlington Raceway—refused entries from black drivers well into the 1960s. Even tracks that allowed black drivers often enforced Jim Crow along the sidelines—in 1955, for example, a track in Atlanta allowed the African American driver Wendell Scott to enter a race but refused to let him take the track until a "colored" ambulance arrived to carry him to the hospital if he crashed.[32]

Scott, who hailed from Danville, Virginia, went on to become the one notable exception to the NASCAR color line, racing in NASCAR's top division from 1961 to 1973. Like many drivers of his era, Scott gained driving experience hauling moonshine in southern Virginia. He was also a skilled mechanic who owned his own garage and made a living contracting with funeral homes and taxi companies. In the 1950s, a local short-track owner recruited Scott to race as a gimmick. He shocked everyone by going on to win more than two hundred races on Virginia's Dixie Circuit and to capture the Virginia State Championship in 1959.[33]

In 1961, Scott made his debut in NASCAR's top Grand National Division as an "independent" driver without factory support. He ran his operation on a shoestring—his crew consisted largely of his sons,

Frank and Wendell Jr., and his daughter, Deborah. He famously painted "Mechanic—Me" on the side of his racecars. Scott proved a master at navigating the racial animosity his presence often created, making friends (including Junior Johnson) where he could and confronting intimidation when he had to. Despite his underfunded operation, he averaged forty-six races a year during his Grand National career and finished in the top ten in points four times. He won his only race on December 1, 1963, at the Jacksonville (Florida) Speedway.[34]

That victory underscored Scott's marginal status in the sport. Although it was obvious that Scott was leading the race, when he crossed the finish line he was not shown the checkered flag. Two laps later the flagman waved the checkers for Buck Baker. Official scorers credited Scott with third place. Baker proceeded to the victory stand to accept the trophy, check, and traditional kiss from the beauty queen. Scott spent four hours protesting the results. Finally, long after the crowd and beauty queen had gone home, NASCAR scorers declared him the winner. He did collect a winner's check for $1,000 but never received the trophy (promoters later gave him a cheap substitute). When Scott recalled the experience later in life, he had his own ideas about why he was not given the victory on the spot. "They had Miss Florida there that day to kiss the winner," he said. "While all the pictures were being taken, they said Buck Baker won. Then, after they got her away from there, they saw where they had made a mistake in scoring. I think that was how it happened."[35]

Scott retired from racing after a violent crash at Alabama's Talladega Speedway in 1973. No African American drivers were there to take his place. Since then few African Americans have raced in NASCAR in any division. Indeed, it was not until 2018 that Darrell "Bubba" Wallace became the next black driver to race full-time in NASCAR's top Cup division.[36]

More than a "Lead-footed Chicken Farmer"

Junior Johnson retired as a driver in 1966, the year after Tom Wolfe dubbed him: "a coon hunter, an ex-whiskey runner, a good old boy who hard-charges stock cars 175 m.p.h. Mother dog! He is the lead-footed chicken farmer, the true vision of the New South."[37] But Johnson's career was far from over. He had always provided significant input into the building and prerace preparation on his cars. By the mid-1960s, unlike most other drivers, he owned his own cars and essentially served as chief mechanic. He also knew how to exploit the sport's rules. One of the important components of success in NASCAR, up to the present day, is the ability to read the rulebook creatively, exploit the gray areas, and stretch the rules a bit to find an edge over your competitors. Some folks call this cheating, but it is standard practice in stock car racing. As Richard Petty once put it, "If you aren't cheating then you aren't trying."[38]

One of the most famous incidents of a "creative" reading of the rule book came in 1966 when Junior brought a yellow Ford Galaxie to Atlanta for a big race. The Ford bore little resemblance to Galaxies sold on the car lot: it had a raised rear end, a severely sloped front end, and a cut-down roof line. Indeed, mechanics had to lower driver Fred Lorenzen's seat so he would fit in the car. Hank Schoolfield wrote, "The car looked weird enough to be put together by committee," and wags around the track dubbed it the "Yellow Banana." Weird maybe, but the car was an aerodynamic gem, and fellow competitors complained vociferously. Bill France, however, needed Johnson's car and Lorenzen in the race at a time when fan interest was waning (which Junior knew). He let the car run. Although engine troubles took it out of the race early, fans still talk about the legendary "Banana."[39]

The "Yellow Banana" demonstrates both Johnson's creative mind and his grasp of physics. I've often said that while Junior Johnson probably never read a physics book, he could probably write one. He somehow intuitively understood the physical interaction between car and track and the influence of environmental forces on the way a car handled. This grasp of physics came in especially handy in the 1960 Daytona 500. Johnson got a last-minute ride in master mechanic Ray Fox's Chevrolet. When he arrived at the track for practice, he realized that the car was grossly underpowered, especially compared to the dominant Pontiacs that were turning in laps up to 30 miles per hour faster than he could manage. But then he noticed something strange. If he got right up to the rear bumper of Cotton Owens's Pontiac, he could stay with the much faster car. He had discovered the "aerodynamic draft," sometimes referred to in racing circles as the "slipstream." While competitors thought Johnson and Fox had discovered some extra power in their engine, Junior used this secret knowledge, aided by mechanical difficulties in some of the top Pontiacs, to win the race and go down in racing lore. This grasp of physics, combined with his mechanical abilities, helped make him one of the most successful car owners in NASCAR history, with 139 wins and six series championships to his credit.[40]

Junior Johnson also understood marketing and human psychology, and he pioneered their application in NASCAR. He had an uncanny ability to motivate his drivers and find the thing that would get them to drive their cars to the very limit. After winning three Winston Cup championships with Cale Yarborough, who shared Johnson's "hell of a fellow" roots, Johnson hired the talented but mercurial Darrell Waltrip as his top driver. When Waltrip's results fell short of expectations, Johnson decided to try some psychology. When Waltrip was not pushing the car as far as Junior thought he could, Johnson would get on the radio and call him "Cale." This infuriated Waltrip and caused him to push the car to the very limit. In the end, Waltrip would go on to match Yarborough's record, winning Junior three more championships.[41]

Johnson also had a sharply honed sense of business. He hated to lose money, and was a pioneer of the use of corporate sponsorships, particularly non-automotive ones. One of the first major connections he made was with Holly Farms Chicken, a Wilkes County company that helped transform the county from a moonshine capital to a chicken capital. In fact, Junior is fond of saying that the chicken farms that came to the county in the 1960s were what killed (or at least greatly diminished) moonshining there. In 1964, Holly Farms became one of the first major non-automaker sponsors in NASCAR history.[42]

Johnson's most important sponsorship deal boosted the entire sport. In 1970, Congress banned cigarette advertising on television. Johnson knew that the nearby tobacco giant R. J. Reynolds had spent a lot of money on television advertising, and he made the short trip to Winston-Salem to talk to the RJR marketing folks. He needed $50,000 to $75,000 to operate his team successfully. When RJR officials informed him they had $10 million in their advertising budget, Johnson told them to talk to Bill France: RJR ended up sponsoring the entire series for thirty-three years, forming one of the longest-lasting and most effective marketing partnerships in sports history.[43] Johnson's last major marketing move came in 2007 when he partnered with the "legal moonshine"–maker Piedmont Distillers, located in Madison, North Carolina, to produce "Junior Johnson's Midnight Moon." Supposedly made using an old Johnson family recipe, the product is now available in all fifty states and several foreign countries, ensuring Junior's legacy, and his family's prosperity, well into the future.[44]

To be sure, in the words of Richard Petty, Junior Johnson is an "unusual cat" and is unique in the variety of areas where he excelled. At the same time, he represents hundreds, if not thousands of NASCAR participants who transcended their roots and used their intelligence, courage, creativity, and work ethic to produce one of the most popular and important professional sporting enterprises in American history.

Teaching and Sources

The story of the rise of NASCAR and of Junior Johnson is rich in historical lessons for any classroom. For me, lessons about historical agency—about the many ways that humans have creatively sought to overcome disadvantages, barriers, and discrimination—are some of the most important we can teach. The story of NASCAR is replete with stories of individuals who had few material resources and little education, and who were often denigrated and stereotyped by polite society but used their intelligence and drive to not only make it in life but to create one of the most important sporting enterprises in American history. I especially like teaching about the ways that Junior Johnson and other NASCAR figures turned the low expectations of people who believed they were ignorant rednecks to their own advantage.

That said, the story of NASCAR also demonstrates the limits of human agency. Like the cotton-mill workers who formed the core of NASCAR's fan base in its early days, even NASCAR's stars faced a dictatorial management structure that limited their freedom. In the 1960s, NASCAR drivers twice tried to unionize. Both efforts were crushed by NASCAR's owner Bill France Sr. And while Junior Johnson walked away from his career as a very wealthy man, many early pioneers retired with no money, no retirement fund, no insurance, and little but their names in the record books to live out their final days.

In addition, race still remains a limiting factor in NASCAR. While the sport has a highly publicized "diversity" program to recruit minority and female drivers, crew members, team owners, and even fans, success has been limited. The burden of history weighs heavy on NASCAR with an environment that makes some African Americans feel unwelcome, an impression reinforced by its fans' longtime affection for the Confederate battle flag and the public support of NASCAR's owners, the France family, and for politicians like George Wallace and Donald Trump.[45]

One of the advantages of teaching NASCAR through the lens of Junior Johnson is that there is a wealth of excellent source material readily available to teachers and students, including books such as my own *Real NASCAR*, Neal Thompson's *Driving with the Devil*, Peter Golenbock's *American Zoom*, Sylvia Wilkinson's *Dirt Tracks to Glory* (the latter two primarily contain transcripts of interviews with NASCAR pioneers), and Steve Waid and Tom Higgins's excellent biography, *Junior Johnson: Brave in Life*.[46]

I would also recommend tapping into the treasure trove of available primary sources. Junior Johnson has generously made himself available to journalists and historians over the years and, unlike many people in NASCAR, he is incredibly candid, especially in dealing with the sensitive issues around the moonshine business. I spent a particularly memorable morning in 2005 at the Johnson farm shop listening to Junior and his friends tell stories about their days in the moonshine business and in NASCAR. A transcript of that conversation can be found at the UNC Asheville Special Collections website along with transcripts of interviews with other NASCAR pioneers, including Richard Petty.[47] The best interview with Johnson available was conducted by Pete Daniel in 1988. Transcripts of that interview are available on the UNC Chapel Hill DocSouth website.[48] The account of Peter Golenbock's interview with Johnson is in his book *American Zoom*.[49]

A fun way to teach NASCAR history through Junior Johnson's story would be to use Junior's own words juxtaposed against the over-the-top prose of Tom Wolfe in "The Last American Hero Is Junior Johnson. Yes!" Wolfe's article is accessible and entertaining; using it with the transcripts of Johnson interviews is a great way to engage students in exploring NASCAR's origins and examining the stereotypes surrounding the sport, its origins, and the South and the Southern Appalachian region in general. In conjunction with this, teachers can consider playing some segments of Hollywood's treatment of Johnson in *The Last American Hero*, a 1973 Jeff Bridges vehicle based on the Wolfe article.[50]

Questions that students might ask include: How does NASCAR's history illustrate the concept of working-class agency? How does it compare to other areas of working-class life? How does the story of NASCAR illustrate the limitations of working-class life, especially in regard to labor issues and race? What does the real story of NASCAR, and of Junior Johnson, say about stereotypes of moonshiners, NASCAR, the South, and the Southern Appalachian region? How have such stereotypes been both detrimental and helpful in promoting NASCAR? Why is NASCAR hesitant to embrace its roots in the illegal liquor business? Was Junior Johnson in fact "the true vision of the New South" as Tom Wolfe contended? Searching for the answers should prove entertaining, informative, and thought-provoking.

Notes

1. Tom Wolfe, "The Last American Hero Is Junior Johnson. Yes!" *Esquire*, March 1965, 73–74.

2. Pete Daniel, *Lost Revolutions: The South in the 1950s* (Chapel Hill: University of North Carolina Press, 2000).

3. The best source on Junior Johnson is Tom Higgins and Steve Waid, *Junior Johnson: Brave in Life* (Phoenix, AZ: David Bull, 1999).

4. Horace Kephart, *Our Southern Highlanders: A Narrative of Adventure in the Southern Appalachians and a Study of Life among the Mountaineers* (New York: Outing Publishing Company, 1913), 36.

5. W. J. Cash, *Mind of the South* (New York: Vintage Books, 1969), 201.

6. The classic account of life in Southern textile mills, including the strikes and their outcomes, is Jacquelyn Hall et al., *Like a Family: The Making of a Cotton Mill World* (Chapel Hill: University of North Carolina Press, 1987).

7. Higgins and Waid, *Junior Johnson*, 19.

8. *The Fifty: Sincerely Bill France*, video (Indianapolis: Ligner Group Productions for ESPN Video, 1998).

9. Joseph Earl Dabney, *Mountain Spirits: A Chronicle of Corn Whiskey from King James' Ulster Plantations to America's Appalachians and the Moonshine Life* (New York: Scribner, 1974).

10. Crandall Shifflett, *Coaltowns: Life, Work, and Culture in Company Towns of Southern Appalachia, 1880–1960* (Knoxville: University of Tennessee Press, 1995).

11. Higgins and Waid, *Junior Johnson*, 14–20.

12. Ibid., 19–20.

13. J. Alexander Mull and Gordon Boger, *Recollections of the Catawba Valley* (Boone, NC: Appalachian Consortium Press, 1983), 116.

14. Daniel S. Pierce, *Real NASCAR: White Lightning, Red Clay, and Big Bill France* (Chapel Hill: University of North Carolina Press, 2010), 24–25.

15. Cash, *Mind of the South*, 50.

16. Junior Johnson interviewed by Pete Daniel, June 4, 1988, transcript at http://docsouth.unc.edu/sohp/C-0053/menu.html (accessed September 3, 2018).

17. Ibid.

18. Pierce, *Real NASCAR*, 30.

19. Ibid., 81–88.

20. Ibid.

21. Johnson interview by Daniel.

22. Higgins and Waid, *Junior Johnson*, 13–14.

23. Ibid., 40.

24. *National Speed Sport News*, October 6, 1965.

25. Higgins and Waid, *Junior Johnson*, 31–37.

26. *Charlotte Observer*, August 10, 1961.

27. Peter Golenbock, *The Last Lap: The Life and Times of NASCAR's Legendary Heroes* (New York: Macmillan, 1993), 220.

28. Ibid., 139.

29. *Charlotte Observer*, August 10, 1961.

30. Greg Fielden, *Forty Years of Stock Car Racing*, vol. 2 (Surfside Beach, SC: Galfield Press, 1992), 93–100.

31. *Asheville Citizen-Times*, August 14, 1961.

32. The track's policy proved lucky for a white driver who was injured seriously in a crash that day, and who was taken to the hospital in the black ambulance when the white ambulance failed to start. Wendell Scott never forgot that incident. "I often wondered, if I had a wreck and the black ambulance wouldn't start, would they have taken me in the white ambulance?" he later explained. "They probably would've let me lay there and die, back in them days." Sylvia Wilkinson, *Dirt Tracks to Glory: The Early Days of Stock Car Racing as Told by the Participants* (Chapel Hill, NC: Algonquin Press, 1983), 118–19.

33. The best sources on Scott are Brian Donovan, *Hard Driving: The Wendell Scott Story: The American Odyssey of NASCAR's First Black Driver* (Hanover, NH: Steerfort Press, 2008); and Wilkinson, *Dirt Tracks to Glory*. See also Derek H. Alderman and Joshua Inwood, "Mobility as Antiracism Work: The 'Hard Driving' of NASCAR's Wendell Scott," *Annals of the American Association of Geographers* 106 (2016): 597–611.

34. Donovan, *Hard Driving*.

35. Wilkinson, *Dirt Tracks to Glory*, 119.

36. *USA Today*, January 16, 2018.

37. Wolfe, "The Last American Hero," 73.

38. Tom Jensen, *Cheating: An Inside Look at the Bad Things Good NASCAR Winston Cup Racers Do in Pursuit of Speed* (Phoenix, AZ: David Bull, 2002).

39. Pierce, *Real NASCAR*, 251–52.

40. Higgins and Waid, *Junior Johnson*, 47–51.

41. Ibid., 143.

42. Pierce, *Real NASCAR*, 225.

43. Ibid., 287–90.

44. See http://www.juniorsmidnightmoon.com/ (accessed September 3, 2018).

45. *Washington Post*, June 6, 2017.

46. Neal Thompson, *Driving with the Devil: Southern Moonshine, Detroit Wheels, and the Birth of NASCAR* (New York: Crown, 2006); Peter Golenbock, *American Zoom: Stock Car Racing: From the Dirt Tracks to Daytona* (New York: Macmillan, 1993); Wilkinson, *Dirt Tracks to Glory*.

47. Junior Johnson interview by Daniel Pierce, October 17, 2005, transcript at Special Collections, D. Hiden Ramsey Library, UNC Asheville, http://toto.lib.unca.edu/findingaids/oralhistory/NASCAR/johnson_junior.pdf (accessed September 3, 2018).

48. Ibid.

49. Golenbock, *American Zoom*, 15–23.

50. *The Last American Hero* (Rojo Productions, 1973).

The Political Olympics

Derek Charles Catsam

"Stick to sports!" That is the catchall demand from any sports fan who believes that sports and politics can exist in separate, hermetically sealed ecosystems. There is a combination of naïveté and hostility contained in the demand. It reveals naïveté because "stick to sports" misunderstands the history of sports, which have always been intertwined with issues that can be called "political" in the broadest conception. It is hostile because the demand tends to be selective, aimed at those who see the links between sports, racism, sexism, and homophobia, who see how professional sports owners have managed to privatize profits and socialize risk, and who see many of the issues in society at large playing out on the fields and courts and tracks and other facilities where athletes ply their trades. Thus those athletes who protest, say, police brutality and systemic racism by sitting for the National Anthem are told to "stick to sports" and are accused of disrespecting the flag, the military, or the country, even though the very playing of the National Anthem at sporting events is an overtly political manifestation. "Stick to sports" is an assertion of privilege. It also reveals a woeful, and perhaps willful, ignorance of the history of sports.[1]

Those of us who teach sports history classes have to deal with the misguided belief that sports are or even ought to be apolitical. Indeed, it is hard to imagine any sports history class being anything but deeply committed to addressing questions about such wide-ranging topics as race and gender, sexuality and masculinity, power and powerlessness, imperialism and nationalism, socioeconomics and ideology. A sports history class that simply recounts who won what when, who was better than whom, who deserved this award or that? Even for those of us who are sports fans, that is not the stuff of history classes. It is a bar argument or an afternoon show on ESPN where everybody yells at one another.

The Olympic Games

Perhaps no sporting spectacle offers richer terrain for examining the intersections between sports and larger questions than the Olympic Games. The Olympics have been infused with politics from the moment of their revival in 1896. The earliest Games, as conceptualized by Baron de Coubertin, represented an internationalist ideal of peace and harmony and sportsmanship. De Coubertin and many of his colleagues were especially wary about nationalism taking over the Games. Yet the participating nations quickly came to see the Olympics as a testing ground. Medal counts, the waving of flags, national pride—all took hold. In 1936, Adolf Hitler used the Berlin Games to glorify Nazism.[2] In 1972, the Black September group used the Munich Games to slaughter Israeli athletes. Nations have used the Olympics to show national greatness, to enter the ranks of premier nations, or to humiliate their global rivals. In short, the Olympics have never existed separate from their political contexts. It would be naïve to expect anything else.

As a result, the Olympics represent fertile fields for those who teach sports, politics, history, and international relations, and other subjects where the Games can be used to elucidate broad trends and explore major questions. Myriad themes await a teacher wanting to explore the intersection of sports and politics, whether from a predominantly American or a global perspective. This essay emphasizes global politics, albeit through the American lens.

International Prestige

For many countries, simply sending a team to the Olympics could make a political point and build national pride. The Olympics had begun as a white, European affair. But starting in the 1920s the Games began to see challenges to the foundational ideas of white and imperial supremacy, as China, the Philippines, Egypt, Japan, and India all fielded teams. In 1900 India had sent a single athlete to the Paris Games—Norman Pritchard, of British descent, who won silver medals in the 200-meter dash and 200-meter hurdles. In the 1928 Amsterdam Games, however, the Indian field hockey team won the gold medal. They would win every gold medal in the sport through 1956, would take silver in 1960, and would return to the podium as gold medalists in 1964.

In the years after World War II, as colonies throughout Asia, Africa, and the Middle East became independent nations, fielding Olympic teams became a point of pride. Many traditionalists, who believed the Olympics ought to be the domain of "civilized" nations—including U.S. Olympic impresario Avery Brundage—were initially reluctant to allow newly independent nations a place at the table. Eventually, though, they relented. Students interested in this facet of postwar politics might research when particular nations gained independence and how long it took them to become part of the Olympic movement.

Nationalism took on a new intensity during the Cold War, when global jockeying for power focused on the deeply ideological conflict between the United States and the Soviet Union. The global politics of the Cold War era, far from being a distraction or an afterthought, heightened the meaning of the Olympics. Medal counts were cast as assessments of national, cultural, political, and economic superiority. Clashes between the United States, the Soviets, and increasingly the East Germans, became proxy wars even in events to which most people otherwise never paid attention.

The nations embroiled in the Cold War (which is to say most nations) saw sports, and especially Olympic sports, as a way to reveal national character.[3] In the 1920s, when the Soviet Union was founded, its leaders saw sports as frivolous, decadent and—as a consequence—western and capitalist. The Soviets did not compete in the Olympics until 1952. By then, their ideological compass had shifted, and they saw the Olympics and other sporting endeavors as a way to demonstrate the superiority of the Soviet system.[4]

If the Olympics were the proxy wars, the specific events were the battlefields, with victory determined by medal counts. The Summer Olympics were the prime event. The Soviets finished first in the medal counts in 1956, 1960, 1964, 1972, 1976, 1980 (when the United States

279

boycotted), and 1988. The United States claimed the medal counts in 1952, 1968, and 1984 (when the Soviets boycotted). In 1988 the Americans only managed third, behind both the Soviets and East Germany. By 1992 the Cold War had effectively come to an end, but the "Unified Team" of the former Soviet Union won the most medals, with the United States second, and a unified German team finishing a relatively distant third. The Soviets and East Germans were even more dominant in the Winter Olympics, with one or the other topping the medal counts in every Cold War Games with the exception of 1968, when Norway came away with the most medals.

Medal counts can reveal the competitiveness of the nations relative to one another and indicate the general level of commitment to the Olympic project of the Cold War nations. But the intensity of Cold War rivalries also manifested in the drama of the Games themselves. While space limitations leave room for only a couple of examples, a great student project would be to use magazine and newspaper databases, along with other sources, to develop narratives of the Cold War rivalry as it played out in the Games.

The Melbourne Olympics of 1956 offers one such opportunity. Because of the differences in seasons between the Southern and Northern Hemispheres, the Melbourne Games were held from November 22 to December 8. That October a student protest movement in Hungary had expanded to a full-on uprising against Communist rule and overarching Soviet control of Hungary. Initially, the Hungarian security forces were responsible for maintaining order. In early November, however, the Soviets sent in their military, which crushed the uprising and imposed a ruthless control that would eventually result in a Soviet-controlled government that would make the mere mention of the uprising a dangerous act.

It was within this context that the so-called "Friendly Games" took place in Melbourne. On December 6, Dezso Gyarmati, arguably history's greatest water polo player, led Hungary's water polo team against the Soviet Union. Hungary was the defending Olympic champion and the winner of three of the previous four gold medals (they had earned silver in 1948.) The brutal game that resulted came to be known as the "Blood in the Water" match. Police presence grew over the course of the contest, as punching, gouging, and other violence filled the pool with blood, and the tensions extended to the capacity crowd of five thousand.

The game was ended early because of the violence, with Hungary declared the winner. Hungary would go on to win another gold medal, while the Soviets took bronze. While this match did not involve the United States, it served as a prime example of the ways that Cold War politics infused the Olympics.

For Americans the high-water mark of the Cold War Olympics surely came in the form of a ragtag bunch of amateur hockey players who shocked the world, and more importantly the mighty Soviet team, at Lake Placid in 1980. The victory came at a time when American confidence had been shaken by years of economic stagnation and by political setbacks in the crucial oil-producing region of the Middle East. In addition, the December 1979 Soviet invasion of Afghanistan had ratcheted up tensions after several years of détente between the antagonists. The Americans played with a group of college players and graduates who remained amateurs. The Soviets, who had won the last four Olympic hockey gold medals and five of the previous six, were amateurs in name only, putatively "employed" by various military, police, and industrial organizations but in reality compensated handsomely to play hockey. The contest highlighted a facet of American ideology that had infused the Games for decades—the idea that American athletes embodied the passion and spirit of American democracy, while the Soviets were mechanical products of an all-controlling state.[5]

When the Soviets and Americans faced off in the semifinals, the United States held their own but trailed going into the third and final period. They scored two goals in that final stanza and held off a furious Soviet onslaught to pull off what came to be known as "The Miracle on Ice." (The Americans still had to defeat Finland, 4–2, to win the gold.)

The Miracle on Ice represents a plucky underdog story, the kind that Americans, perpetual overdogs, love to tell about themselves. And the epic upset makes for a great story. Of course, it is also worth noting that the contest was not broadcast live. While more than 32 million Americans watched the game on tape delay that night, word of the upset victory had already spread. The Miracle on Ice has taken pride of place in American sports lore, and rightfully so. But Americans only embraced the team after it upset the Soviets.

In those Olympics as a whole the Soviets emerged with the most golds (10 to the 6 of the United States). The East Germans took the most overall medals (23 compared to 22 for the Soviets and 12 for the United

States). Only a selective reading of history allows the Americans to emerge as winners from the 1980 Olympics, when in reality the Soviets came into enemy territory and walked away as conquerors across myriad sports. Furthermore, the Soviets would recover, winning the 1984 and 1988 hockey gold medals. Nonetheless, the 1980 hockey triumph can provide rich territory for students, especially if they work to come to grips with the larger contexts of the Miracle on Ice.

Apart from the dramatic victories, the Cold War emphasis on the Olympics had more subtle effects as well. At the same time that Cold War politics were pressing postwar American presidents into addressing civil rights, U.S. leaders used the accomplishments of black athletes to counter accusations of American racism—presenting the world with a public face of racial equality that masked the genuine failings at home (for a more detailed account of race, sports, and the Cold War, see Liberti, "Sports and the Cold Warriors").

Similarly, Cold War politics pressed U.S. officials to pay more attention to women's sports, especially in track ánd field. In addition to championing imperialism and white supremacy, the original Olympics had been heavily masculine: women were barred from the inaugural 1896 Games and were not allowed to compete in track and field until 1928, after a group of European women had protested their exclusion by organizing a competing Women's Olympic Games. The U.S. Olympic Committee had been less than encouraging—when women's swimming was introduced in 1912, for example, American women were unable to participate because U.S. Olympic rules allowed them to compete only in events where they could wear long skirts. Track and field was considered particularly unwomanly, and for many years the nation's only serious women's track teams competed for underfunded historically black colleges.

The Soviets, in contrast, encouraged women's competition, and the Olympic successes of Soviet women boosted their medal totals. After unsuccessful efforts to denigrate Soviet female athletes and to convince Olympic officials to report men's and women's medals separately, the U.S. officials realized that to keep up they would need to change national attitudes toward women's sports. Newly formed organizations, such as the U.S. Olympic Development Committee and the President's Council on Youth Fitness, launched extensive programs to convince young women that competing in sports such as track and field was not only patriotic but could also make them more physically attractive.[6]

Boycotts

The global prominence of the Olympic Games meant that nations also used them to highlight other conflicts. The 1908 London Games, for example, revealed tensions within the United Kingdom when Irish athletes who advocated Home Rule for Ireland refused to be part of a United Kingdom team. The boycott threat led to the creation of a Great Britain/Ireland team, a semantic change that placated most Irish athletes, even though Irish field hockey and polo players refused that gesture and competed independently for Ireland.

Perhaps not surprisingly, the 1936 "Nazi Games" were the most deeply political of Olympics (and thus one of the richest to teach). The Games had been awarded to Germany before Adolf Hitler rose to power. Once the Nazis launched their takeover of the German government and began their persecution of Jewish Germans, the question of boycotting the games arose in many nations, including the United States. In the end, however, only Spain, on the cusp of its dreadful civil war, and the Soviet Union, which had yet to compete in the Games, chose to avoid Berlin. Some Spanish sports officials tried to work with socialist and labor groups around the world to establish the "People's Olympiad," but the outbreak of the Spanish Civil War in July of 1936 scuttled those plans. (Indeed there is a fascinating history of proposed and attempted alternatives to the Olympics to be written, which would make for a fantastic student project.)

Despite strong calls for a boycott in the United States, Avery Brundage, the head of the powerful American Olympics Committee, derided the idea, at times in terms that bordered on anti-Semitism. Brundage would be one of the loudest voices against what he perceived as the mingling of politics and the Olympics for well more than a generation, even as he routinely made explicitly political decisions. This is a good spot to make the point that there are occasions, such as the American involvement in the Berlin Games, where no matter what decision is made, there will be political implications. It then comes down not to whether to make political choices but rather which political choice to make.

Boycott efforts proliferated in the years after World War II, amid the tensions of the Cold War and the breakup of the European colonial order. Virtually every Summer Olympics from 1956 to 1988 saw boycott efforts, with varying degrees of success. A simple annotated listing of boycotts, their causes, and their occasional consequences will reveal the myriad topics that Olympic boycotts present for those who want to teach or write about the Olympics within the context of global politics or vice versa:

1956, Melbourne

In the wake of the Soviet invasion of Hungary, the countries of Spain, Sweden, Lichtenstein, and the Netherlands boycotted the Melbourne Games. The Suez Crisis prompted a boycott by Egypt, Iraq, and Lebanon. After the IOC gave Taiwan permission to compete as the Republic of China, the People's Republic of China, which claimed (and continues to claim) Taiwan as its own territory, refused to participate. China would not compete in another Olympics until the 1980 Lake Placid Winter Games.

1964, Tokyo

The politics that infused the 1960 Games in Rome did not involve boycotts.[7] But the next few years saw a flurry of activity. Part of this involved the role of apartheid South Africa.[8] Even prior to the rise of the National Party and its apartheid policies in 1948, South Africa was a deeply segregated country by law and custom. The implementation of apartheid created the most rigidly racially stratified nation on earth, exacerbated by the fact that whites represented a small minority of South Africa's population and showed a willingness to engage in the most brutal means to maintain white supremacy. After the 1960 Games, the IOC violated its own no-politics policy by suspending and then expelling South Africa from the Olympics. South Africa would not compete in an Olympics again until 1992 (and even then many critics argued that the inclusion of the country was premature given that despite tentative negotiations, apartheid had not ended).

Rising tensions over the spread of socialism in the Third World sparked other actions. In 1963, for example, Indonesia had been the leading force behind the Games of the Newly Emerging Forces (GANEFO), consisting of newly emerging, largely socialist nations, as an explicitly political counterbalance to the Olympics. The country also had barred Israel and Taiwan from the fourth Asian Games, which it hosted in 1962, prompting the IOC to suspend Indonesia from the IOC. For their part, Indonesians pointed out that the allegedly apolitical IOC itself refused to recognize North Vietnam and the People's Republic of China. Indonesia and North Korea eventually boycotted the 1964 Games.

1968, Mexico City

Arguably the most politicized Olympics since Berlin, the 1968 Games first saw controversy flare when the IOC issued a tentative invitation to South Africa, even though the nation had done nothing to reform and a great deal to exacerbate apartheid in the years since its expulsion. The invitation prompted threats of boycotts from African nations, the Eastern Bloc, and African American athletes, and was eventually rescinded.

The threatened boycott by African American athletes as part of the Olympic Project for Human Rights offers an intriguing example of using an Olympic boycott to highlight a nation's internal struggles— black athletes threatened to boycott in order to protest unequal treatment of African Americans in the United States (for more detail on the Olympic Project for Human Rights in the context of the U.S. civil rights and Black Power movements, see Morimoto, "Sports, Civil Rights and Black Power"). There are multiple interesting examples of similar efforts, such as those made by Australian Aboriginal activists at the 2000 Sydney Games.[9]

1972, Munich

West Germany wanted the 1972 Games to represent a friendly return of Germany to the global stage after the swastika-festooned 1936 Games and the subsequent horrors of World War II and the Holocaust. The host's motto for the 1972 Olympics was "Die heiteren Spiele," or "The Cheerful Games." They would prove to be anything but.

The main political issue leading up to the 1972 Games was the inclusion of a Rhodesian Olympic team, which led to threats of boycotts from the Ethiopian and Kenyan delegations and established the real possibility of a flood of followers from newly independent African countries who condemned Rhodesia's racist white government and its extreme segregationist politics.[10] Rhodesia had been excluded from the 1968 Mexico City Games but received an invitation to the 1972 Munich Olympics. Rhodesia agreed to send forty-four athletes under some restrictions (using essentially a British identity), but furor over the compromise led to the IOC withdrawing the invitation after the Games had commenced, thus allowing the Rhodesian athletes to remain in the Olympic Village and to attend but not participate in their events.

This controversy would disappear from memory after the tragic events of the 1972 Games in which eight members of the Black September faction of the Palestinian Liberation Organization (PLO) entered the Israeli team quarters in the Olympic Village on September 5, killing two of the athletes in the process of taking the rest of the delegation hostage.[11] Eventually, after a prolonged standoff witnessed on international television, the hostages were granted passage to the nearby NATO airbase where they were to get access to a plane that would fly them to Cairo. A poorly planned rescue mission took place in which snipers engaged in crossfire. In the end, all nine of the Israeli athletes and coaches were killed in the gunfire and a grenade explosion. Five of the eight kidnappers died, but three were able to escape to safety suspiciously easily.

Because the West Germans had wanted to reveal a friendly face to the world, the Olympic Village where the athletes stayed was largely free of onerous security and the reaction to the Black September attack was haphazard. There is little ground to blame the West Germans for malice in their response to the events at Munich when simple incompetence stands as a sufficient explanation.

1976, Montreal

The 1976 Games in Montreal were a legendary boondoggle, a costly yoke on the city for more than a generation, and a precursor to the absurd lengths cities would go to justify the Olympic Games as a moneymaker when they were in fact increasingly a drain on local and national economies. Those Games also saw the first widespread boycott, albeit one that has been largely overlooked because it involved African nations that the Western world in particular felt free to ignore. In 1976 New Zealand's All Blacks national rugby team had toured South Africa against the explicit opposition of not only African nations but also an increasingly vocal global antiapartheid movement. In the face of the New Zealand engagement with the pariah apartheid state and the IOC's unwillingness to censure or exclude New Zealand from the Montreal

Games, twenty-six African countries boycotted. Egypt competed for the first three days of the Games and then withdrew. The sticky situation of the Taiwanese team continued as well. Initially, Canada refused to allow the Taiwanese team into the country. They then offered to relent if the team agreed not to compete as "The Republic of China." The Taiwanese withdrew, considering such a compromise humiliating and intolerable.

1980, Moscow

In the wake of the Soviet invasion of Afghanistan, President Jimmy Carter pushed the U.S. Olympic Committee to withdraw from the Moscow Games, which would have provided a propaganda stage for the USSR. More than sixty countries followed the Americans' lead, some because they believed in the cause, most to protect their own self-interest as allies of the United States who wanted to remain in good standing. A number of nations refused to participate in the opening and/or closing ceremonies. Still others allowed individuals to compete under the Olympic rather than their national flag. In the end, only eighty countries attended the Moscow Games, down from 122 in Munich in 1972.

1984, Los Angeles

The Soviets and fourteen of their allies got their revenge in the next Games, held in Los Angeles. The Soviets claimed that their concerns regarded security, not politics, though the transparency of that assertion was plain. Albania, Iran, and Libya had their own conflicts with the United States and independently boycotted the Games. While a record 140 nations competed in LA, the American dominance of the medal count was clearly the result of watered-down competition. There had also been threats to boycott the 1984 Olympics in the wake of a 1981 South African Springbok rugby tour of the United States and New Zealand (which turned out to be one of the most controversial and political sporting events in history). While nothing came of the threats, the clash between two runners—the American Mary Decker and the South African-turned-British citizen Zola Budd—highlighted the tensions. That rivalry was portrayed as a deeply gendered conflict in which two world-class athletes and tough competitors were cast in the infantilized, feminized roles of "princess" and "pixie," as well as a proxy battle between supposed western superiority and the evils of apartheid (despite the fact that Americans had few claims to superiority on racial issues in sports or beyond).[12]

1988, Seoul

For the first time since the 1972 Games, there were no widespread boycotts. North Korea boycotted the Games after being refused recognition as co-hosts with South Korea (the two countries were still technically at war). Cuba and Ethiopia, both countries that punched above their weight at the Olympic level, joined the North Koreans in a show of sympathy and solidarity. Still, the era of boycotts had come to an end. There have been intermittent threats since the 1980s but no substantial, widespread boycotts, especially when compared to the 1976–84 era. Boycotts and the politics surrounding them remain fertile ground for allowing students to understand the intersection of global politics and sports. Various role-playing exercises and paper assignments can provide them with the opportunity to dig into these topics and their global meanings.

One assignment that can prove effective in addressing most any of the political questions surrounding the Olympics, but is especially useful when it comes to the debate over boycotts, is to have students role play, taking on the roles (and thus having to articulate the perspectives) of various protagonists—political and sporting officials from both host nations and those weighing whether to boycott, athletes from all sides, and other relevant figures. One of the questions that students will almost certainly come up with on their own, but that they can be steered to in case they do not, is whether it makes a better statement to boycott to draw attention to a political question or to go to the games and to get the platform the Olympics provide, especially for those athletes with a real chance to succeed at the Games.

On certain questions, it might be more effective to go to the Games and triumph. At both the Berlin and Mexico City Olympics, the actions of African Americans—Jesse Owens in Berlin and Tommie Smith and John Carlos in Mexico City—gained attention in a far more dramatic way than was possible with a boycott. Does that mean it was better *not* to boycott? Was showing up Adolf Hitler's racism on the playing field more effective than refusing to compete on moral grounds? People of course remember Smith and Carlos (who suffered tremendously after the Games as a result of their courageous stand). Virtually no one knows that Kareem Abdul Jabbar chose not to go. On the other hand, for African nations in 1976 there were likely to be no Jesse Owens triumphs, no chances to make political statements on the medal podium. Obviously the specific context matters.

Other Topics for Consideration

The Olympics provide an incalculable range of possible ways to explore the intersections of sport, politics, and social issues. The terrorist attacks on the Munich Games and the Atlanta Olympic bombing can provide a backdrop for explorations of the Olympics, terrorism, violence, and security. These security concerns often provide the justification for ruthless treatment of locals—usually the most poor and most vulnerable—in host cities and countries.

The seemingly geometrically rising costs of hosting Olympics have also led to fewer cities bidding because, increasingly, many cities and countries recognize that the costs usually outweigh the benefits of hosting. These economic realities have been confirmed for Olympics, for hosting the FIFA World Cup, and for the alleged (and almost always illusory) benefits of public funding for professional sports stadia. Virtually all academic studies reveal that providing public funds is a losing proposition; even loyal fans are coming to recognize that such investments in infrastructure, which will end up in the hands of billionaires, results in allowing the rich yet again to suckle from the public teat while promising much but guaranteeing little in return. Corruption within the IOC and other global sports bodies exacerbates these economic realities. Forced removals of locals for the purpose of building Olympic and other sports facilities reveals further socioeconomic realities of global sports events—the most vulnerable often pay an especially high cost for the upper-middle-class playground that is the Olympics.[13]

In short, the Olympics provide a constantly renewing resource for studying a broad range of social and political issues, whatever those demanding we just "stick to sports" might prefer.

289

Notes

1. Most great books about sports are about more than merely the outcome of games. A small sampling of recent overviews of the intersection of sport and politics includes Jan Stradling, *More Than a Game: When Sport and History Collide* (Millers Point, NSW: Pier 9, 2009); David W. Zang, *Sports Wars: Athletes in the Age of Aquarius* (Fayetteville: University of Arkansas Press, 2001); and two books by Dave Zirin, *What's My Name Fool? Sports and Resistance in the United States* (Chicago: Haymarket Books, 2005) and *Welcome to the Terrordome: The Pain, Politics, and Promise of Sports* (Chicago: Haymarket Books, 2007). There are several important books on the Olympics. The single best among these, one rife with explications of the myriad political issues that have always infused the Games, is David Goldblatt, *The Games: A Global History of the Olympics* (New York: W. W. Norton, 2016). An invaluable resource for sheer data on the outcome of every Summer Olympics event, along with lots of background, is David Wallechinsky (the longtime chronicler of Olympic history) and Jaime Loucky, *The Complete Book of the Olympics*, 2012 ed. (London: Aurum Press, 2012). Other valuable books include Jules Boykoff, *Power Games: A Political History of the Olympics* (London: Verso, 2016); David Goldblatt and Johnny Acton, *How to Watch the Olympics: The Essential Guide to the Rules, Statistics, Heroes, and Zeroes of Every Sport* (New York: Penguin Books, 2011); Allen Guttmann, *The Olympics: A History of the Modern Games*, 2nd ed. (Urbana: University of Illinois Press, 2002); and Marc Perelman, translated by John Howe, *Barbaric Sport: A Global Plague* (London: Verso, 2012).

2. On the 1936 Olympics, see Richard D. Mandell, *The Nazi Olympics* (New York: Ballantine, 1971); Guy Walters, *Berlin Games: How the Nazis Stole the Olympic Dream* (New York: William Morrow, 2006).

3. On the Cold War and the Olympics, see Gerald R. Gems, *The Athletic Crusade: Sport and American Cultural Imperialism* (Lincoln: University of Nebraska Press, 2006); Erin Elizabeth Redihan, *The Olympics and the Cold War: Sport as Battleground in the U.S.–Soviet Rivalry* (Jefferson, NC: McFarland, 2017); Toby C. Rider, *Cold War Games: Propaganda, the Olympics, and U.S. Foreign Policy* (Urbana: University of Illinois Press, 2016); Damion L. Thomas, *Globetrotting: African American Athletes and Cold War Politics* (Urbana: University of Illinois Press, 2012); and Molly M. Wood, "'Spanning the World to Bring You the Constant Variety of Sports': Teaching the United States and the World in the Cold War," *Journal of American History* 103 (March 2017): 1004–11.

4. In a stellar example of the tension between unity and nationalism, the starkly divided Federal Republic of Germany (West Germany) and German Democratic Republic (East Germany) did not compete as separate entities until the 1968 Mexico City Games. From 1956 to 1964 the two countries competed

uneasily as Germany and were sometimes referred to in Olympic circles as the "United Team of Germany."

5. This ideology can be strikingly illustrated with a clip from the Sylvester Stallone vehicle *Rocky IV* (United Artists, 1985), which juxtaposes scenes of Rocky Balboa working out by himself in an isolated mountain cabin with scenes of his Soviet opponent, Ivan Drago, training in a high-tech facility under the guidance of multiple coaches and doctors.

6. Mary Jo Festle, *Playing Nice: Politics and Apologies in Women's Sports* (New York: Columbia University Press, 1996), 86–97.

7. On the various politics surrounding the 1960 Rome Games, see David Maraniss, *Rome 1960: The Olympics That Changed the World* (New York: Simon & Schuster, 2008).

8. Among the many words on South African sports and politics, see Robert Archer and Antoine Bouillon, *The South African Game: Sport and Racism* (London: Zed Press, 1982); Douglass Booth, *The Race Game: Sport and Politics in South Africa* (London: Frank Cass, 1998); John Nauright, *Long Run to Freedom: Sport, Cultures, and Identities in South Africa* (Morgantown, WV: Fitness Information Technology, 2010).

9. On the 1968 Games, see Amy Bass, *Not the Triumph But the Struggle: The 1968 Olympics and the Making of the Black Athlete* (Minneapolis: University of Minnesota Press, 2002); Harry Edwards, *The Revolt of the Black Athlete*, 50th anniversary edition (Urbana: University of Illinois Press, 2017); Douglass Hartmann, *Race, Culture, and the Revolt of the Black Athlete: The 1968 Olympic Protests and Their Aftermath* (Chicago: University of Chicago Press, 2003); Richard Hoffer, *Something in the Air: American Passion and Defiance in the 1968 Mexico City Olympics* (New York: Free Press, 2009); and Kevin Witherspoon, *Before the Eyes of the World: Mexico and the 1968 Olympic Games* (DeKalb: Northern Illinois University Press, 2008).

10. See, for example, *New York Times*, August 17, 1972. Newspapers, which increasingly are archived on databases and oftentimes are readily available online, provide a rich resource for students.

11. On the 1972 Games see David Clay Large, *Munich 1972: Tragedy, Terror, and Triumph at the Olympic Games* (Lanham: Rowman and Littlefield, 2012), and Simon Reeve, *One Day in September: The Full Story of the 1972 Olympics Massacre and the Israeli Revenge Operation "Wrath of God"* (New York: Arcade, 2011). Students especially appreciate seeing the outstanding documentary *One Day in September* (Sony Picture Classics, 1999) directed by Kevin Macdonald.

12. See Jason Henderson, *Collision Course: The Olympic Tragedy of Mary Decker and Zola Budd* (Edinburgh: Arena Sport, 2016); Kyle Kiederling, *Olympic Collision: The Story of Mary Decker and Zola Budd* (Lincoln: University of Nebraska Press, 2016); *IX for IX: Runner* (ESPN Films, 2014), directed by Shola Lynch.

13. Just one example of the folly of hosting mega-events such as the Olympics can be seen in Dave Zirin, *Brazil's Dance with the Devil: The World Cup, the Olympics, and the Struggle for Democracy* (Chicago: Haymarket Books, 2014).

Lights, Camera, Action

Teaching American Sport through Film

Ron Briley

"Rudy, Rudy, Rudy" roars the crowd as the Notre Dame football coach Dan Devine (Chelcie Ross) inserts the diminutive Daniel "Rudy" Ruettiger (Sean Astin) into the last home game of his senior season. On the final play of the game, Rudy tackles the Georgia Tech quarterback for a loss; he is carried off the field on the shoulders of his teammates as the crowd goes wild. In the fulfillment of his American dream, Rudy overcomes his working-class background and learning disabilities to achieve admission to Notre Dame, where he joins the legendary football program as a nonscholarship player. The 1993 film *Rudy* is based on a true story, although the filmmakers take some liberties with the facts.

Rudy is an excellent example of the Hollywood sport film in which hard work and effort allow athletes to surmount obstacles and the individual or team achieves the American dream. In this traditional sport film scenario, athletic participation is celebrated for building character and contributing to American democracy by endorsing such principles as perseverance and equality of opportunity. The reality of American sport and history is, of course, far more complex. History teachers could well serve their students by fostering a more critical analysis of how American sport itself is treated by filmmakers, introducing the complexities that questions of race, gender, and class bring to the notion that

Actor Sean Astin (#45) portraying Notre Dame's Daniel "Rudy" Ruettiger in the 1993 Sony Pictures film *Rudy*.

athletic competition promotes the formation of a democratic national character.[1]

Both film and sport occupy important roles in the lives of young people. But all too often the approach to these staples of adolescent culture is uncritical. As it is unfortunately true that many students today learn their history through cinema, it is imperative that history teachers provide their students with critical viewing skills. But while media literacy should equip students to use detailed examination of facts to detect fake news and propaganda, in the analysis of feature films teachers and students need to be wary of getting bogged down in detail. Rather, as the film historian Robert Rosenstone suggests, they should concentrate instead on the larger historical truths that the film-makers are attempting to convey.[2]

Hard Work and Character

A good way to begin a discussion of possible film texts, which one might incorporate into an American history or sport history course, is to return to the traditional values of hard work and the

American dream celebrated in *Rudy*. In mainstream Hollywood feature films, the athletic field almost always helps to shape character by emphasizing the discipline and teamwork necessary to achieve success in sport and in the larger society. It is a democratic ethos in which achievement is valued above race, gender, or one's station in life, fulfilling the promise of the American dream and American exceptionalism.

Even before their work on *Rudy*, the director David Anspaugh and the screenwriter Angelo Pizzo created one of the most beloved sport films in American cinema: *Hoosiers* (1986). Named by *Sports Illustrated* as the sixth-best sports movie of all time, *Hoosiers* attempts to reconstruct the "Milan Miracle" of 1954 in which the Milan Indians, a school of only 161 students, defeated Muncie Central, with an enrollment of more than two thousand students, for the Indiana boys' state basketball championship.[3] Milan's victory was a classic David-and-Goliath story in which the underdog, through hard work, virtue, and initiative, defeats the seemingly invincible adversary. After ESPN Classic rebroadcast the Milan game in 2004, the National Public Radio commentator Bob Cook noted that Milan represented the "triumph of the small-town way of life and perhaps the pull-up-your bootstraps ideal, that no matter where you are from, and what disadvantage you may have, if you work hard, you'll succeed." While most students will undoubtedly enjoy viewing the popular film, teachers should encourage students to take a closer look at its historical and cultural contexts.[4]

Classroom discussion and research might begin by considering why the film resonated so well with audiences during the 1980s. This might involve an exploration of the imagery that Ronald Reagan used in asserting that the United States must be restored to a "city upon a hill" where all things are possible. The same concept, rendered in less oratorical splendor, animated the 2016 slogan of Donald Trump "to make America great again." Teachers should encourage students to examine whether such rhetoric reflects the realities of the 1950s, 1980s, or today, including why such a message would resonate with certain populations in certain historical moments.

Examining Race

In examining *Hoosiers* as a historical film text, instructors should also encourage students to take a closer look at the subtext of race—a subject essentially ignored by most critics when the film premiered. When the all-white team from Milan (Hickory in the film) meets mixed-race South Bend Central in the finals, the confrontation is dominated by an extremely percussive music track, while the crowd noise is distorted to create a menacing sound. A long shot of the South Bend Central team entering the court introduces a sense of apprehension and foreboding. (In the movie, the team confronts no black competition until meeting South Bend Central in the finals; in reality Milan defeated the storied all-black Crispus Attucks High School and its star player, Oscar Robertson, in the semifinals, and then beat a mixed-race team from Muncie Central High in the finals. Attucks would go on to win the state championship in 1955, becoming the first team from an African American school to do so. That achievement has yet to be immortalized in film.)[5]

Initially, the boys from Hickory are intimidated by the athleticism of South Bend Central's black players. One shot especially makes this point. A jumper from a Hickory player bounces off the front rim, which is framed in the shot. Then two black hands enter the frame and aggressively pull down the rebound. The boys from Hickory rally, and with their ingenuity and work ethic they are able to defeat their opponents.[6]

The historian David Zang argues that the popularity of *Hoosiers* can be attributed to the nexus of the film that transported viewers back to a pre-Vietnam period and place of lost innocence. Zang concludes that the boys from rural Indiana "appeared to stress all the aspects of character and value the modern sport seemed to have ceded in the name of dollars, image, and media hype in post-sixties culture."[7] In prompting students to carefully interrogate *Hoosiers* through the lens of cinematic techniques that include music, editing, and shot framing, history instructors may suggest to students the centrality of race to reading a film text such as *Hoosiers*, while also sparking discussions about the racial realities of life in the Midwest and elsewhere during the 1950s.

Race is an essential element in another of Hollywood's most popular sport films, Sylvester Stallone's *Rocky* (1976).[8] The racial symbols employed in *Rocky*, however, are subtler, and students sometimes need prompting to decode the racial arguments at the core of the film text. Rocky Balboa (Sylvester Stallone) garners the sympathy of viewers as a poor, young, Italian fighter with little education and few economic prospects. Although he is only a journeyman boxer, Balboa is given a chance to fight for the heavyweight championship against Apollo Creed (Carl Weathers), clearly based upon Muhammad Ali. Creed needs an opponent after the number-one contender has to pull out of a scheduled bout, and he picks Balboa, known as the "Italian Stallion," from the ranks of unknown fighters and decides to give him a shot at the title. Creed believes that providing a white ethnic boxer an opportunity to fight the flamboyant black champion will be good for the box office and fits well into the theme of the American dream during the nation's bicentennial celebration. Thus, the film becomes an insightful representation of America during the mid-to-late 1970s and provides a useful teaching tool.[9]

The late 1960s and early 1970s were a turbulent period in American history during which the nation was bitterly divided over such issues as the Vietnam War and the legacy of the civil rights movement. These conflicts, along with the abuses of power revealed in the Watergate scandal, fostered considerable pessimism in American culture, which is reflected in such films as Roman Polanski's *Chinatown* (1974). After these difficult years, the bicentennial offered an opportunity to rearticulate the American dream, although the reality of life for American workers in the decade did not quite measure up to the promise. But Rocky is an optimist whose dreams are somewhat limited. After a brutal battle, Rocky loses the fight but achieves his dream of going fifteen rounds and, with his arms around his girlfriend while the stirring *Rocky* theme plays in the background, the "Italian Stallion" becomes the latest embodiment of a version of the American dream that we may all attain through hard work and perseverance.[10]

Teachers, however, should encourage students to take a closer look. Most notably, *Rocky* perpetuates racial stereotypes. Apollo Creed is a gifted athlete, but he refuses to train for the fight. Instead of working hard, Creed devotes his energy to hyping the fight. In contrast, the underdog Rocky demonstrates a strong work ethic highlighted by the famous training-scene segment of the film. In the final analysis, Rocky's determination allows him to achieve his dream of going the distance with a better fighter whose lack of a work ethic almost leads to his demise as champion.

Racial issues also surface in the portrait of Rocky's future brother-in-law Paulie (Burt Young). Paulie struggles economically, sees Rocky as a potential meal ticket, and blames his economic woes not on the larger forces of globalization and automation that are endangering the livelihood of the white ethnic working class, but rather on affirmative action programs that give preference to minorities. Paulie's anger provides a link to what the journalist Peter Schrag called the "forgotten American." Writing in 1969 for *Harper's*, Schrag argued that hardworking white men were frustrated that the rules that governed civil society were changing to favor black Americans. He concluded that the forgotten American "cannot imagine any major change for the better; but he can imagine change for the worse. And yet for a decade he is the one who has been asked to carry the burden of social reform, to integrate his schools and his neighborhood, has been asked by comfortable people to pay the social debts due to the poor and the black."[11]

Rocky has his own encounter with changing racial times when he goes to his gym locker only to discover that a rising young black fighter has been given his space. These "forgotten Americans" would become the so-called Reagan Democrats of the 1980s; they were also the voters that Donald Trump attracted in 2016 with his calls for economic nationalism. Screening *Rocky* along with reading Schrag's article provides an avenue for history classes to examine trends in American political discourse from the 1970s to the present day.

The latest installment in the *Rocky* series, however, provides a more optimistic take on race relations. In *Creed* (2015), the African American director Ryan Coogler, whose credits include *Fruitvale Station* (2013) and *Black Panther* (2018), focuses upon the grit and determination exhibited by Apollo's son Adonis Creed (Michael B. Jordan) now managed by Rocky Balboa. Teachers might encourage students to compare and contrast the film texts of *Rocky* and *Creed* and reflect on what the differences may or may not suggest about broader changes in American politics and society.

Athletics, Academics, and Exploitation

Despite the negative racial images perpetuated in films such as *Rocky*, sport has often been celebrated as a means through which minority youth may escape poverty. This version of the American dream for young black men is explored in the documentary *Hoop Dreams* (1994), whose makers spent years documenting the lives of two black Chicago players. The renowned film critic Roger Ebert described *Hoop Dreams* as "one of the best films about American life that I have ever seen," while Hal Hinson of the *Washington Post* credits the documentary with challenging the positive sport stereotypes perpetuated by films such as *Rudy*. Hinson wrote, "*Hoop Dreams* isn't about the triumph of the human spirit or any of the other top 10 favorite sport clichés. It's about something far rarer in the movies and of vastly greater significance—it's about real life."[12]

Hoop Dreams tells the story of William Gates and Arthur Agee, both of whom are recruited to play basketball at the affluent and predominantly white St. Joseph High School in Westchester, Illinois. At first the young men cope with the academic, social, and basketball demands of their new environment. St. Joseph's coach Gene Pingatore becomes disappointed with Agee's development as a basketball player. The sponsorship for Agee's tuition is dropped, and he transfers to a Chicago public school. Gates completes his degree at St. Joseph's, but a serious knee injury limits his college basketball prospects. Agee ended up playing basketball with Arkansas State, and Gates gained a scholarship to Marquette, but neither of the young men achieved their hoop dream of playing professional basketball with lucrative multimillion-dollar contracts. Agee evaluated the film project as both "a blessing and a curse," although he credited the film with providing an opportunity to move his family out of the Chicago projects.[13]

Bringing the acclaimed film into the history classroom provides an excellent venue to address issues of race and class: the filmmakers Steve James, Peter Gilbert, and Frederick Marx document the exploitation of Agee and Gates who, similar to all too many athletes, were sidelined eventually by injury and did not gain the educational foundation that a focus on academics might have provided. It also documents how a professionalization of youth sport leads to considerable burnout as sport ceases to become fun. As the historian Richard O. Davies laments, "It is ironic that one of the results of organized youth sports has been that by the time youth athletes reach high school many have already reached a state of burnout."[14]

The imbalance between academics and athletics—and the way that Hollywood often obscures such issues—can also be explored by comparing H. G. Bissinger's 1990 book, *Friday Night Lights*, with the 2004 film.[15] Residents of Odessa, Texas, felt betrayed by Bissinger, who lived in Odessa during the 1988 school year, receiving the hospitality of townspeople along with the cooperation of the coaching staff and players from the Odessa Permian Panthers. While the people of Odessa saw themselves as hardworking, decent, caring, and patriotic, Bissinger also encountered widespread sexism, racism, anti-intellectualism, and poverty. Those who found their economic dreams crushed by collapsing oil prices in the 1980s attempted to find solace in the accomplishments of the Permian Panthers in football-crazed West Texas, placing an incredible amount of pressure on the high school athletes. Bissinger also argues that players were given preferential treatment in the classroom, and they were usually poorly prepared for life beyond the football field.

The film adaptation, by Bissinger's cousin Peter Berg, paints a more positive portrait of Odessa's football obsession. Coach Gary Grimes (Billy Bob Thornton) is a compassionate man dedicated to his players and the pursuit of excellence. The film's villains are local businessmen boosters who place undue pressure upon the coach and his athletes. Although Permian falls a yard short of winning the state championship, Berg's film shows the positive effects of youthful competition outweighing the negative aspects of boosterism and a cultural obsession with winning. The film embraces the idea that football does, indeed, build character. The racism and sexism described in Bissinger's book is downplayed, and the film does not address the imbalance between academics and athletics. Bringing *Friday Night Lights* into the curriculum—and teachers might also consider the excellent television series *Friday Night Lights* (2006–11)—should foster a much-needed dialogue regarding the proper balance between academics and athletics in both high schools and universities. Its legacy remains more troubling than Peter Berg's film suggests.

The perseverance of black athletes against racism is exhibited in numerous biographical pictures such as *42* (2013), directed by Brian Helgeland and starring Chadwick Boseman. The film concentrates on the courage and integrity of Jackie Robinson as he integrates Major League Baseball during his 1947 rookie season. These heroic films, however, may be somewhat misleading, and students should be encouraged to investigate Robinson's life beyond the 1947 campaign. Robinson enjoyed an outstanding career and was elected to the Baseball Hall of Fame in Cooperstown in 1962. Yet, his managerial ambitions were never realized; when he died from a heart attack on October 24, 1972, Robinson was only fifty-three years old and nearly blind, suffering from hypertension and diabetes. One can only surmise how the strain of the 1947 season contributed to the athlete's premature aging.[16]

Women's Sport Films

While Hollywood also often perpetuates negative stereotypes of women and sport, an excellent film focusing on female athletes
is *A League of Their Own* (1992) directed by Penny Marshall. The film
tells the story of the All-American Girls Professional Baseball League
(AAGPBL) during World War II; it features a piece of history forgotten
by most Americans until the release of Marshall's film. Similar to the
iconic Rosie the Riveter and other women who took factory jobs to re-
place men who were drafted into military service, the AAGPBL sought
to fill a gap in professional baseball as the many top players serving in
the military reduced the quality of play at the Major League level. Although forced to play in dresses and adhere to traditional female roles
off the playing field, the women of the AAGPBL were outstanding athletes who relished the opportunity to display their skills. While drawing
good crowds during the war years, they were forced off the playing
field when men returned from military service, and the league was
eventually disbanded.

Even though Marshall documents the accomplishments of the
AAGPBL, instructors might want to encourage students to ponder
whether the film privileges traditional female roles over athleticism.
For example, Dottie Henson (Geena Davis) is the best player in the
league, yet exhibiting stereotypical female virtues of sacrifice, she gives
up her career for marriage and a family. In addition, Dottie appears to
intentionally drop the ball at home plate so that her younger sister Kit
(Lori Petty) may score the winning run in the championship game. The
film also fails to acknowledge the lesbian players who were key components of many AAGPBL teams.[17]

There are a growing number of films that move beyond gender
stereotypes. *Girlfight* (2000) tells the story of Diana Guzman (Michelle
Rodriguez) who finds her identity in the world of boxing. Monica
Wright (Sanoa Latham) of *Love and Basketball* (2000) is able to enjoy a
family and a career in professional basketball. The film critic Viridiana
Lieberman believes in the transformative power of cinema for forming
more positive attitudes toward women in sport. She wrote, "If we can
cinematically imagine that a female athlete can have equal access to explore her skills in a predominantly male sport, without having to fit
into a patriarchal definition, we can then apply this mentality to our

everyday lives."[18] The ESPN documentary series, *Nine for IX*, features accounts of female athletes told by female filmmakers, with subjects that range from Venus Williams and her campaign for equal prize money for female players to the challenges faced by female sports reporters covering male teams to the life of Sheryl Swoopes, the phenomenal basketball player who is also openly gay.[19]

30 for 30

Another documentary ESPN series, *30 for 30*, also deserves a place in the sport history curriculum. The approximately hour-long length of each film makes them especially valuable for classroom use. Although the contemporary technological environment offers the opportunity for most students to access longer film texts on various mobile devices as well as personal and school computers, there is often a great deal to be gained from a class screening a film or clip together, as this communal experience allows the instructor to emphasize essential points as well as observe student reactions to the film text. The *30 for 30* series was the brainchild of then-ESPN sportswriter Bill Simmons who pitched the idea of producing sport documentaries to celebrate the thirtieth anniversary of the network in 2007.

Simmons and his colleagues approached filmmakers about making a series of thirty sports documentaries of approximately sixty minutes each, placing sport within historical and cultural context. The success of this initial project resulted in the sports network producing two more episodes of *30 for 30*, in addition to the "mini-series event" *O. J.: Made in America*, which premiered on ESPN in June 2016 before enjoying a theatrical release and receiving the Academy Award for Best Documentary at the Eighty-Ninth Academy Awards. Although the documentary's length makes it problematic to screen the entire film for the classroom, clips from it can be used to raise essential questions about the roles of race, sport, and celebrity in modern America. Teachers wanting to incorporate the *30 for 30* series into the history curriculum should consult the network's archives to see which documentaries best meet the needs of their students. There are many excellent choices.[20]

In *King's Ransom* (2009), Peter Berg examines the cultural impact of Wayne Gretzky's 1988 trade from the Edmonton Oilers to the Los Angeles Kings. (This film would complement Brad Austin's earlier suggestions about how to teach about demographic and economic changes by using sports franchise locations.) Similarly, the cultural relationship between the Raiders of the NFL and a black fan base in Los Angeles, during the team's thirteen seasons in the city (1982–94), is explored by the rapper Ice Cube in *Straight Outta L.A.* (2010). When teaching about the civil rights movement, teachers will appreciate the connection between an undefeated all-white football team and the violent response to James Meredith and integration at the University of Mississippi, the subject of *Ghosts of Ole Miss* (2012).

While these film documentaries primarily present sport as a male enclave, several focus on issues of gender and sexuality. In *Marion Jones: Press Pause* (2010), the filmmaker John Singleton investigates the superlative track-and-field career of Marion Jones, which was marred by her 2007 admission of using performance-enhancing drugs. *Renée* (2011) depicts the life of a transgender athlete, Renée Richards, providing instructors and students an opportunity to address issues of transgender rights in American sport, politics, and society. In *The Price of Gold* (2014), Nanette Burstein examines the 1994 assault on the Olympic figure skater Nancy Kerrigan, which was orchestrated by her rival Tanya Harding—a topic students may be familiar with due to the 2017 film *I, Tonya* that also does a good job of exploring class issues. With *Fantastic Lies* (2016), Marina Zenovich provides a ten-year retrospective on allegations of rape against the Duke University lacrosse team, which were later acknowledged as false.[21]

Clearly, sporting cinema is a rich field for historians to cultivate, and an excellent way to engender discussion of how sport as a genre reflects as well as influences the larger society. Classroom debate and discussion—and follow-up essay assignments exploring the major themes of a film—will help students get the most out of the experience. As some students are a little more reticent to comment in class, having students maintain a classroom journal in which they react to the issues raised by the films is also a useful strategy. Broader participation may also be enhanced through more digital forms of communication such as classroom chat rooms monitored by the instructor. In addition, the scope of the class may be broadened by having students share and write commentaries or reviews of older films or recent releases, which are not included in the class syllabus.

This extended level of analysis might encourage students to explore making their own films. This could be fostered in a number of ways. History teachers unfamiliar with filmmaking might team with a colleague more experienced in media arts to aid students with the preparation of short films, either documentaries or dramatic features, expanding upon the issues of sport and society raised in the class. Sharing these works would provide a stimulating conclusion to the course. When such filmmaking resources are unavailable, teachers might simply have students share proposed film scripts. Students who do not wish to try their hand at filmmaking might instead submit a research paper or do a presentation on how a particular sport film or genre sheds light upon American history and culture.

Sport films are often considered rather simplistic exercises in cheerleading and clichés, and the association of sport and film in the classroom may provoke suspicion regarding academic integrity.[22] This is especially true in high school, where history teachers often serve as coaches, and frequently operate under the suspicion that they prioritize athletic over academic achievement. But as this brief survey suggests, a carefully selected group of films and clips can deepen students' understanding of American history, while emphasizing that the reality of history and culture as mirrored in the nation's sporting life is far more complex than the refrain of "Rudy, Rudy, Rudy" might imply.

Notes

1. *Rudy*, directed by David Anspaugh (Sony Home Pictures Entertainment, 2000), DVD.

2. For discussions regarding the challenges and opportunities offered by introducing film into the history classroom, teachers should consult Robert Brent Toplin, *Reel History: In Defense of Hollywood* (Lawrence: University Press of Kansas, 2002); Robert Toplin, *History by Hollywood: The Use and Abuse of the American Past* (Urbana: University of Illinois Press, 1996); Robert A. Rosenstone, *History on Film/Film on History* (New York: Pearson, 2006); Mark C. Carnes, ed., *Past Imperfect: History According to the Movies* (New York: Henry Holt, 1995); James J. Lorence, *Screening America: United States History through Film since 1900* (New York: Pearson, 2000); and Ron Briley and Robert Toplin, eds., "Teaching Film and History," *OAH Magazine of History Special Issue* 16 (Summer 2002). For an excellent introduction to film terms and analysis, see David Bordwell and Kristin Thompson, *Film Art: An Introduction* (Boston: McGraw Hill, 2004; originally published 1979).

3. *Hoosiers*, dir. David Anspaugh (Orion Pictures, 1996), DVD; and "The 50 Greatest Sports Movies of All Time," *Sports Illustrated*, August 4, 2003, 62–71.

4. Bob Cook, "Commentary: Enduring Memory of Milan High's Winning of the 1954 Indiana State Basketball Championship," National Public Radio, February 18, 2004. For a more detailed discussion of *Hoosiers,* see Ron Briley, "Basketball's Great White Hope and Ronald Reagan's America," in *All-Stars and Movie Stars: Sports in Film and History,* ed. Ron Briley, Michael K. Schoenecke, and Deborah A. Carmichael (Lexington: University Press of Kentucky, 2008), 155–71.

5. For a different reading of black Americans and basketball, sport history classes should examine the significance of how an all-black starting lineup from Texas Western University (now the University of Texas at El Paso) defeated the all-white University of Kentucky team for the 1966 NCAA national men's college basketball championship. Hollywood has documented the UTEP championship in the 2006 film *Glory Road,* although the film's emphasis tends to be on Don Haskins (Josh Lucas), the white coach who recruited the black players, reflecting a Hollywood tendency to concentrate upon white characters when treating black themes. For an account of the Crispus Attucks championships in 1955 and 1956, see Randy Roberts, *"But They Can't Beat Us": Oscar Robertson and the Crispus Attucks Tigers* (Urbana, IL: Sagamore Publishing, 1999).

6. Deborah V. Tudor, *Hollywood's Vision of Team Sports: Heroes, Race, and Gender* (New York: Garland Publishing, 1997), 152–56.

7. David W. Zang, *Sports Wars: Athletes in the Age of Aquarius* (Fayetteville: University of Arkansas Press, 2001), 153.

8. The boxing genre is a staple of Hollywood, often with a somewhat leftist political orientation in which a working-class protagonist is exploited by forces of greed and corruption. Films that fit this category include *Golden Boy* (1937), *Body and Soul* (1947), *Champion* (1949), and *On the Waterfront* (1954). For the boxing film genre, see Frederick V. Romano, *The Boxing Filmography: American Features, 1920–2003* (Jefferson, NC: McFarland, 2004); and Leger Grindon, *Knockout: The Boxer and Boxing in American Cinema* (Jackson: University Press of Mississippi, 2013).

9. For *Rocky,* see Larry Powell and Tom Garrett, *The Films of John Avildsen: Rocky, The Karate Kid and Other Underdogs* (Jefferson, NC: McFarland, 2015); Frank Sonello, *Stallone: A Rocky Life* (New York: Mainstream Publishing, 1998); Tom O'Brien, *The Screening of America: Movies and Values from Rocky to Rain Man* (New York: Bloomsbury Academic, 2016); and Victoria A. Elmwood, "'Just Some Bum from the Neighborhood': The Resolution of Post–Civil Rights Tension and Heavyweight Public Sphere Discourse in *Rocky,*" in Briley, Schoenecke, and Carmichael, *All-Stars and Movie Stars,* 172–98.

10. *Rocky,* dir. John Avildsen (Twentieth Century Fox Home Entertainment, 2006), DVD.

11. Peter Schrag, "The Forgotten American," *Harper's,* August 1969.

12. Roger Ebert, *"Hoop Dreams," Chicago Sun Times*, October 21, 1994; and Hal Hinson, *"Hoop Dreams," Washington Post*, November 4, 1994.

13. *Guardian*, February 18, 2015; and *Hoop Dreams*, dir. Steve James (Criterion Collection, 2015), DVD.

14. Richard O. Davies, *America's Obsession: Sports and Society since 1945* (New York: Harcourt Brace College Publishers, 1994), 126. In 1996, *Jump Cut* published two sharply contrasting assessments of the film's message, which provide material for provocative class discussions. See Murray Sperber, "Hoop Dreams: Hollywood Dreams," and Lee Jones, "Hoop Dreams: Hoop Realities," *Jump Cut: A Review of Contemporary Media* 40 (March 1996): 8–14.

15. H. G. Bissinger, *Friday Night Lights: A Town, a Team, and a Dream* (New York: Addison-Wesley Publishing Company, 1990); and *Friday Night Lights*, dir. Peter Berg (Universal Studio Home Entertainment, 2005), DVD.

16. *42*, dir. Brian Helgeland (Warner Brothers Entertainment, 2013), DVD; Arnold Rampersad, *Jackie Robinson: A Biography* (New York: Alfred A. Knopf, 1997); Jules Tygiel, *Baseball's Great Experiment: Jackie Robinson and His Legacy* (New York: Oxford University Press, 1983); and Jackie Robinson, as told to Alfred Dockett, *I Never Had It Made* (New York: Harper Collins, 1995; originally published 1972).

17. *A League of Their Own*, dir. Penny Marshall (Sony Pictures Home Entertainment, 1997), DVD. For the AAGPBL see Merrie A. Fidler, *The Origins and History of the All-American Girls Professional Baseball League* (Jefferson, NC: McFarland, 2010); Lois Browne, *Girls of Summer: The Real Story of the All-American Girls Professional Baseball League* (New York: Harper Collins, 1993); and Barbara Gregorich, *Women at Play: The Story of Women in Baseball* (New York: Harcourt, 1993).

18. Viridiana Lieberman, *Sports Heroines on Film: A Critical Study of Cinematic Women Athletes, Coaches, and Owners* (Jefferson, NC: McFarland, 2015), 173; *Girlfight*, dir. Karyn Kusama (Sony Pictures Home Entertainment, 2001), DVD; and *Love and Basketball*, dir. Gina Prince-Bythewood (New Line Cinema, 2000), DVD.

19. Jennifer Cingari Christie, "ESPN Films and espnW Announce Nine for IX," February 19, 2013, https://espnmediazone.com/us/press-releases/2013/02/espn-films-and-espnw-announce-nine-for-ix/, and "ESPN Films and espnW Announce Nine for IX Shorts Documentary Series," June 4, 2014, https://espnmediazone.com/us/press-releases/2014/06/espn-films-and-espnw-announce-nine-for-ix-shorts-documentary-series/ (both accessed September 3, 2018).

20. "Bill Simmons on *30 for 30*," September 8, 2009, espn.com https://we.archive.org/web.archive.org/web/20090908075845/https://30for30.espn.com/bill-simmons-essay (accessed June 13, 2017).

21. *30 for 30*, espn.com http://www.espn.com/30for30 (accessed June 1, 2017).

22. John F. O'Conner, "Reading, Writing, and Critical Viewing: Coordinating Skill Development in History Learning," *History Teacher* 34 (February 2001): 180–83.

Resources and Suggestions

Brad Austin and Pamela Grundy

Teachers seeking to add sports history to their repertoire have access to a wealth of information. While the essays in this book examine many potential subjects, they leave out many others. Here, we offer some guidance for exploring beyond this book's parameters: textbooks, archival resources, and snapshot summaries of a few subjects we especially enjoy teaching.

Textbooks and References

Although many teachers have wisely stepped away from relying on textbooks to provide the bulk of student reading material or to structure classes, they still play an important role in classrooms. Put simply, it's useful to have a single resource on the shelf that can provide the "big picture" narrative while also supplying anecdotes and examples that can spice up a conversation and spark student interest.

Benjamin Rader of the University of Nebraska pioneered this field in 1983, with *American Sports: From the Age of Folk Games to the Age of Spectators*. An enormously important and successful book, *American Sports* has undergone multiple revisions. Pamela Grundy has recently taken over as lead author for this text, which entered its eighth edition in 2018. Unsurprisingly, the structure of the most recent edition, subtitled *From the Age of Folk Games to the Age of the Internet*, meshes particularly well with the material we have presented here. Other wide-ranging treatments include Richard Davies's *Sports in American Life: A History*, which provides a highly readable narrative perfect for mining lecture examples; Warren Goldstein and Elliott Gorn's *A Brief History of American Sports,* which offers an excellent introduction to the field's key themes and topics; and Dave Zirin's *People's History of Sports in the United States,* which charts the long history of using sports to promote social change.[1]

For background and classroom material, we recommend Steven Riess's *Major Problems in American Sports History.* Teachers familiar with the *Major Problems* formula will immediately see how Riess's text can help them expand their own knowledge while also providing abundant primary sources to use as centerpieces of activities or lessons. Each of the chronologically arranged chapters includes excerpts of key passages from some of the field's most significant books, organized into easily digestible sections that can help teachers (or advanced students) grapple with key scholarly arguments. Each chapter also includes primary sources selected specifically for their relevance to central themes and their utility in classrooms. Those wishing to delve further into sports historiography can consult S. W. Pope's prizewinning essay collection, *The New American Sport History: Recent Approaches and Perspectives,* and Riess's fine collection *A Companion to American Sport History.*[2]

Archives

The Journal of Sport History database

The Journal of Sport History is the journal of record for the field. Published by the University of Illinois Press, this is the official organ of the North American Society for Sport History (NASSH), and for more than four decades it has shared the leading scholarship of the field via original articles and reviews of major sports history books and films.

Fortunately for teachers and scholars, the entire archive of the *Journal of Sport History* is available for free searching and browsing. It is frankly incredible that this wealth of scholarship is not hidden behind a paywall or open only to NASSH members. Having access to this resource means that teachers are only a quick search away from more information about almost any topic in American (or global) sports history. Every teacher looking to incorporate sports history into their classes, or interested in designing a sports history class, should have this site bookmarked.

That statement would be true if the database provided access only to *Journal of Sport History* resources. It provides, however, much more than that. The database allows visitors to search the partial or complete archives of more than twenty sports history publications, including the *Journal of Olympic History, Sport in History, International Sport Studies,* and the *Journal of the Philosophy of Sport.* It also offers a wealth of Olympics-specific material, ranging from the United States Olympic Committee Reports (1920–88) to the Official Olympic reports (1896–2010, winter and summer) to dozens of oral histories from past Olympians. If teachers want students to read the words of Louis Zamperini, the subject of Laura Hillenbrand's best-selling book *Unbroken: A World War II Story of Survival, Resilience, and Redemption,* they can access them here. The same goes for readers who were captivated by Daniel James Brown's *The Boys in the Boat: Nine Americans and Their Epic Quest for Gold at the 1936 Olympics*—the site includes an oral history conducted with Gordan Adams, a member of that team.

Sports Illustrated Archive

Another free, searchable, and useful database is the *Sports Illustrated* archive, available at https://www.si.com/vault. Imaginative teachers will find in its pages a wealth of opportunities for creative assignments.

For example, when discussing the 1968 "Revolt of the Black Athlete," Brad once asked students to look at all the *Sports Illustrated* covers from one year in the 1960s. They chose 1966, and soon realized that the weekly magazine published only five covers with African American athletes that year. Even the landmark 1968 *Sports Illustrated* series "The Black Athlete—A Shameful Story" (worth discussing in class) had a black athlete on the cover of only one of five issues, with Mark Spitz and Ted Williams each getting equal cover space during that span. Having students read that series, along with contemporary essays on Ali, Tommie Smith, Billie Jean King, and other significant athletes has enriched classroom discussions throughout his courses. Teachers can have students look at media representations of different groups, track the prominence of coverage/general popularity of particular sports, and read "real time" reactions to events such as baseball's performance-enhancing drug crisis, Olympic boycotts, or the 1980 U.S. hockey "Miracle on Ice."

Indigenous Sports

Native American Ball Games

The stickball games played by North American natives from the snowy regions of the North to the hot and humid South offer a great opportunity for examining Native American cultures and demonstrating the different roles that sports can play in societies. Most Native American groups embrace a sacred worldview that does not draw hard-and-fast divisions between physical and spiritual, and which stresses the importance of maintaining balance in the world. Examining the religious and social rituals that surround stickball (which Europeans later dubbed lacrosse) helps highlight some of the components of this worldview.[3]

This approach can be also expanded to the ball game played throughout the region that became known as Latin America. Examining the level of social organization and complexity necessary to construct the hundreds of ball courts created throughout the region makes it possible to highlight the sophistication of many indigenous societies.[4] Asking students to read about the organization, planning, religious significance, and gender dynamics in these various matches will also help them recognize the different ways that native peoples used sports in their societies.

Native American Boarding Schools

Modern team sports held both attractions and perils for Native Americans, particularly those who attended the federally run boarding schools that were engaged in the culturally and psychologically destructive process of "civilizing" Native American youth. While students resisted efforts to destroy their traditional cultures, sports became a popular activity at many schools, and both students and school leaders saw them as a way to demonstrate Native Americans' ability to excel in the "modern" world. Native American school teams ranged from the renowned Carlisle Indians, who played for Pennsylvania's Carlisle Indian Industrial School against the nation's top college football teams, to the girls' basketball team from Montana's Ft. Shaw Indian School, which represented the school at the 1904 World's Fair in St. Louis.[5]

312

Nineteenth-Century Sports

Harness Racing

Although one would never know it from the contemporary sporting landscape, harness racing was a national obsession in the early nineteenth century. The sport's development, which involved jaunts up and down Manhattan's major thoroughfares as well as the establishment of associations, fan groups, official rules, and clubs, makes an ideal case study of how athletic pastimes were transformed into fully functional, modern sports. The early national era is also an excellent period for examining how theater, games, and sports played active roles in shaping American democracy and provided opportunities for Americans to debate and contest the ways that power and rights would be exercised in the new nation.[6]

Prizefighting

Prizefighting, the nation's most popular spectator sport throughout much of the nineteenth century, provides insights into multiple facets of American history. Prizefighting's close association with masculinity makes it an especially valuable focus for tracing discussions about, shifts in and conflicts over changing masculine norms. The sport's move from a disreputable, generally illegal pursuit to a form of "respectable" entertainment provides a classic example of the ways sports and society influence each other.[7]

Because of the way prizefighting pits one individual against another, fights also provide multiple insights into social tensions. Early in the nineteenth century, for example, prizefighting publicity often highlighted contests between native-born fighters and Irish immigrants, reflecting the widespread social tensions that accompanied the decline of artisan independence, the rise of factory labor, and the advent of mass immigration. As the U.S. population expanded and diversified, so did prizefighting's meanings—points of conflict could include race, ethnicity, level of education, military records, and countless other distinctions. Because investing a fight with larger issues increases interest, crowds, and profits, fight promoters have regularly played up these divisions, creating a wide range of sources that can be mined for insights.[8]

Bicycling

In the 1890s, when a series of inventions and the growth of the sporting goods industry made bicycles more available and easier to ride, the United States was swept by what became known as "the bicycle craze." The many technical developments required to create "modern" bicycles make a fascinating discussion (and help explain why the first successful powered airplane was built by a pair of bicycle mechanics). Bicycles are also a marvelous way to examine the aspirations of the era's middle-class women, who quickly embraced the independence and mobility the new vehicles offered. A treasure trove of visual material—drawings, advertisements, cartoons—can be used to vividly convey the excitement and anxiety created by this new female endeavor, as well as by the controversial "bloomer costumes" that became standard bicycling attire.[9]

Early Twentieth Century Sports

The Era of Sports Heroes

The decade of the 1920s offers teachers a wide range of options when they are structuring their classes. There are countless themes and topics that attract student interest and thus allow teachers to challenge, or at least complicate, preexisting stereotypes about the era. Teaching about the 1920s as an "era of sports heroes" is an effective way to weave many of these threads into one conversation.

Almost every discussion of the Roaring Twenties would normally include conversations about the importance of cities and the perceived rise of "modern morality," flappers and women's suffrage, the political power of the new Klan, the wide-ranging effects of the Great Migration, and the consumerism associated with a flood of new products and the growing availability of credit. Subjects such as Babe Ruth, Gertrude Ederle, Red Grange, Knute Rockne, the Negro Leagues, the introduction of women's sports to the Olympics (along with the significant backlash), the attendance figures for baseball and college football games (seven new college football stadia seating more than seventy thousand were built during this decade), and the rise of the athlete as product endorser all offer ways to discuss issues of gender, race, commerce, and urbanization during this period.[10]

Baseball and Japanese Internment

After the Japanese attack on Pearl Harbor, President Franklin Roosevelt wrote what has become known as the "green light" letter to baseball's commissioner, Kennesaw Mountain Landis, endorsing the continuation of professional baseball since the games offered "a chance for recreation and for taking their minds off their work." Shortly thereafter, Roosevelt signed another document, one that paved the way for the relocation of more than one hundred thousand Japanese Americans to internment camps across the American West and South.

Despite losing their families' possessions and their personal freedom, many camp residents sought to prove their loyalty to the nation that had forcibly relocated them. Internees volunteered to fight in Europe as part of the predominantly Japanese American 442nd Regimental Combat Team, a unit that became the most highly decorated in American military history. Playing baseball became another way to display American identity. In the Manzanar camp, located in Central California, internees formed more than one hundred baseball teams, including a dozen or more women's teams. As Takeo Suo, a prisoner at Manzanar phrased it, "Putting on a baseball uniform was like wearing the American flag." There is a wealth of resources available for teachers who want their students to consider the multiple meanings of the creation of federal internment camps for those citizens who sought to prove their loyalty by playing "the national game."[11]

Post–World War II Sports

Jackie Robinson and Larry Doby

If a U.S. history class includes only one athlete in its curriculum, that person is usually Jackie Robinson, the former U.C.L.A. multisport star. He served in the army during World War II, then played in the Negro Leagues before he signed with the Brooklyn Dodgers and became the first black player in modern-day Major League Baseball in April 1947. A superficial telling of Robinson's story lends itself nicely to a narrative of post–World War II racial progress. But the messy reality of the integration of professional baseball is more interesting for classroom discussions and much more useful for teasing out larger themes in American history.

When teaching about Jackie Robinson, it is easy to connect his family's background as Georgia sharecroppers, who left the South for California, to the history of Jim Crow and the Great Migration. Discussing his experiences in the segregated military can include the way he was court-martialed for refusing to give up his seat on a military bus to a white soldier, more than a decade before Rosa Parks came to the public's attention for a similar act. His interview with the Dodgers' Branch Rickey, in which he famously promised not to retaliate to the inevitable barrage of verbal and physical assaults that would come his way, previews the nonviolent protests of the civil rights movement. Examining both white and African American newspapers can help students get a sense of the magnitude of the challenges Robinson faced during his first season with the Dodgers and the grace with which he faced them.[12]

The story of baseball's integration is also valuable if we want our students to question the accuracy and completeness of dominant narratives; many might forget that Jackie Robinson desegregated only one of the two Major Leagues. What Robinson faced in National League ballparks, Larry Doby confronted in American League stadiums when he integrated the Cleveland Indians in July 1947. While Doby is also a Hall of Fame baseball player and the first black ballplayer to hit a home run in the World Series, he has been largely ignored in the national recognition of Robinson and the hope for racial progress that he personified. Discussing his experiences, alongside those of Robinson, allows for a richer, more complete conversation about the past and the ways we tell and remember it.

The Decline of Women's Sports and the Rise of Cheerleading

After World War II, even as male African Americans gained new sports opportunities, arenas for both black and white women's sports began to shrink—a response to the reconfiguration of gender roles in the culturally conservative Cold War era. This shift can be effectively underscored by examining the changes that took place in high school and college sports rituals during the era. In the 1920s, 1930s, and 1940s, grassroots women's basketball teams flourished around the country, and the departure of Major League Baseball stars for World War II created an opening for the All-American Girls' Baseball League. Cheerleading, originally the preserve of male college students, was a mixed-gender endeavor. But after the war, many women's sports teams were disbanded, and cheerleading became a highly sexualized, predominantly female endeavor. Examining the process by which this happened helps students explore the formation of institutions that most of them take for granted and also emphasizes that history does not always move in a "progressive" direction.[13]

Television and Football

In the 1940s, the National Football League was a relatively marginal endeavor, with limited fan base and geographic reach. Two decades later, it had shot past baseball to become the dominant American spectator sport. The reason: television. Football televised more effectively than baseball, and the NFL's scrappy owners were far savvier about dealing with television networks than baseball's ensconced elite. They reconfigured the sport to suit the television networks' needs and took steps to maintain parity among teams, which ensured that the majority of games would be worth watching. Cleveland Browns owner Art Modell once happily quipped, "We're twenty-eight Republicans who vote socialist."[14]

Television also had a huge effect on college football. It infused unprecedented amounts of money into the college game, heightening the stakes for success. As a result, it magnified the power of the NCAA and intensified debates over the relationship between sports programs and colleges' broader educational missions. Examining these transformations offers another way to explore the factors that drive the creation of American cultural institutions.[15]

Figure Skating

In the eighteenth century, figure skating was a gentlemanly pastime. At the end of the nineteenth century, it had developed into a fledgling sport where men and women competed against each other and were judged relatively equally according to similar standards of grace, beauty, and power. By the end of World War II, however, skating had become a "girls' sport"—an increasingly glamorous arena where female stars reigned and male competitors struggled to define their performances as satisfactorily masculine. In the process, the sport became an especially rich site for examining a range of issues regarding gender, sexuality, race, and class, including how and why those categories shifted over time. Sources for examining contemporary skating multiplied in 1994, when supporters of Tonya Harding ambushed and attacked her rival, Nancy Kerrigan, during the Olympic trials, prompting an outpouring of popular-culture commentary, including the recent movie *I, Tonya*. This history of feminization and the struggles it created for both the men who loved the sport and for the women who did not fit the feminine mold offers an especially intriguing contrast to the definition of most other sports as masculine and the resulting challenges that female athletes faced.[16]

Sports and Gambling

Although gambling has always been an integral part of sports, betting on sports events has been illegal throughout most of U.S. history. This has made the history of sports and gambling in the United States a fascinating subject, one that includes developments as disparate as the connections between urban numbers runners and professional sports teams; the rise of Las Vegas as a center for sports betting; the development of the point spread and subsequent point-shaving scandals; and the recent legal struggle over whether the federal government has the power to ban gambling on sports.[17]

African American Female Athletes in the Twenty-first Century

As exemplified by the reaction to the argument between Serena Williams and the umpire Carlos Ramos in the finals of the 2018 U.S. Women's Open, African American female athletes continue to spark particularly intense cultural conflicts, with as much attention focused on their actions and appearance as on their athletic achievements. The 1980s, for example, saw the dramatic ascent of the stylish track champion Florence Griffith-Joyner, whose long, streaming hair, elaborately painted nails, and form-fitting bodysuits projected a striking, confident version of womanhood and sparked both admiration and critique. Similarly, the long journey of Venus and Serena Williams from their youthful entrance into professional tennis to their dominance of the sport has made them some of the world's most visible and admired African American women, even as they have faced an almost unending stream of criticism and controversy. The many layers of these experiences, from the historical meanings ascribed to black women's bodies to the varying strategies black female athletes have used to make space for themselves in different sports, provides an abundance of material for lectures, class discussions, and student projects.[18]

Final Words

Sports have become such an integral part of American society and culture that they can help illuminate almost every aspect of American history. Excellent resources can be found for countless stories not covered here: the transformation of golf from a country club pursuit into a spectator sport; the rise of the highly expressive realm of "extreme" sports; the contrasting fortunes of U.S. men's and women's soccer; and the question of whether college athletes should be paid, to name only a few. In coming years, the efforts of a growing range of topflight sports scholars will no doubt shed light on many other subjects. Using sports to help our students explore this nation's history has given us some of the most enjoyable and insightful experiences of our careers. We highly recommend it. We hope this book will help.

Notes

1. Pamela Grundy and Benjamin Rader, *American Sports: From the Age of Folk Games to the Age of the Internet*, 8th ed. (New York: Routledge, 2018); Richard Davies, *Sports in American Life: A History*, 3rd ed. (Oxford: Wiley-Blackwell, 2016); Elliott Gorn and Warren Goldstein, *A Brief History of American Sports*, 2nd ed. (Urbana: University of Illinois Press, 2013); Dave Zirin, *People's History of Sports in the United States: 250 Years of Politics, Protest, People, and Play* (New York: New Press, 2008).

2. Steven Riess, *Major Problems in American Sports History*, 2nd ed. (Stamford, CT: Cengage Learning, 2014); S. W. Pope, ed., *The New American Sport History: Recent Approaches and Perspectives* (Urbana: University of Illinois Press, 1996); Steven Riess, ed., *A Companion to American Sport History* (Oxford: Wiley-Blackwell, 2014).

3. See Thomas Vennum Jr., *American Indian Lacrosse: Little Brother of War* (Washington, DC: Smithsonian Institution, 1994); Joseph B. Oxendine, *American Indian Sports Heritage* (Lincoln: University of Nebraska Press, 1995); Michael J. Zogry, *Anetso, the Cherokee Ball Game: At the Center of Ceremony and Identity*

(Chapel Hill: University of North Carolina Press, 2010). For a detailed anthropological description of stickball rituals, see James Mooney, "The Cherokee Ball Play," *American Anthropologist* 3 (April 1890): 130–31.

4. E. Michael Whittington, ed., *The Sport of Life and Death: The Mesoamerican Ballgame* (Charlotte, NC: Mint Museum of Art, 2001).

5. Material on boarding-school sports can be found in John Bloom, *To Show What an Indian Can Do: Sports at Native American Boarding Schools* (Minneapolis: University of Minnesota Press, 2000), David Wallace Adams, *Education for Extinction: American Indians and the Boarding School Experience, 1875–1928* (Lawrence: University Press of Kansas, 1995), and Kate Buford, *Native American Son: The Life and Sporting Legend of Jim Thorpe* (New York: Knopf, 2010). For a comprehensive account of the lives and activities of the Fort Shaw basketball team, see Linda Peavy and Ursula Smith, *Full-Court Quest: The Girls from Fort Shaw Indian School, Basketball Champions of the World* (Norman: University of Oklahoma Press, 2008). Material on the Carlisle Indians can also be found in Michael Oriard, *Reading Football: How the Popular Press Created an American Spectacle* (Chapel Hill: University of North Carolina Press, 1993), 233–47.

6. Melvin Adelman's *A Sporting Time: New York City and the Rise of Modern Athletics, 1820–1870* (Urbana: University of Illinois Press, 1985) remains one of the best books on how "modern" sports, including harness racing, developed. More recently, Kenneth Cohen has examined the emergence of a recognizably American sports world in his award-winning *They Will Have Their Game: Sporting Culture and the Making of the Early American Republic* (Ithaca, NY: Cornell University Press, 2017).

7. Elliott Gorn's *The Manly Art: Bare-Knuckle Prizefighting in America* (Ithaca, NY: Cornell University Press, 1986, 2010) was one of the first books to weave sports into a rich historical account of changes and conflicts in the realms of economy, society, and culture, and remains a classic example of sports history at its best.

8. The history of prizefighting has a rich store of sources. Randy Roberts, one of sports history's finest practitioners, and Andrew Smith have put together an excellent account of the field's top works. Randy Roberts and Andrew R. M. Smith, "Boxing: The Manly Art," in Riess, *A Companion to American Sport History*, 271–91.

9. For a firsthand account of a woman's bicycling adventures, penned by the renowned temperance advocate Frances Willard, see *Wheel within a Wheel: A Woman's Quest for Freedom* (New York: Fleming H. Revel, 1895). For an African American critique of bicycling, see W. F. Foneville, "Taint of the Bicycle," in *A Hammer in Their Hands: A Documentary History of Technology and the African American Experience*, ed. Carroll W. Pursell (Cambridge, MA: MIT Press, 2005). Sue Macy's *Wheels of Change: How Women Rode the Bicycle to Freedom (With a Few Flat Tires Along the Way)* (Washington, DC: National Geographic, 2011)

contains a wealth of useful bicycle-related material, including advertisements and cartoons.

10. The previously mentioned textbooks provide a wide range of examples that teachers can use, and there are abundant excellent biographies of sports stars from the period, many targeted for lower grade levels, for additional teacher or student research. If teachers want to give students a visceral sense of the writing style of the era, as well as a journalist's engaging account of the 1920s and the "ballyhoo" it included, Frederick Lewis Allen's *Only Yesterday: An Informal History of the 1920s* (New York: Harper's Perennial Modern Classics, 2010) remains an essential resource.

11. One starting point for a discussion could be Ansel Adams's photograph of a Manzanar baseball game, which highlights a competitive game and an engaged crowd while keeping guard towers and restraining fences out of the frame. Adams's Manzanar photographs are available at the Library of Congress website, www.loc.gov/pictures/collection/manz/highlights.html (accessed September 13, 2018). An illustrated children's book, *Baseball Saved Us* (New York: Lee & Low Books, 1993), authored by an internee's son, Ken Mochizuki, offers another perspective. See also Michael Bechloss, "For Incarcerated Japanese-Americans, Baseball Was 'Wearing the American Flag,'" *New York Times*, June 20, 2014.

12. Ken Burns's *Baseball* documentary has an especially good segment on Robinson's debut campaign, and Jules Tygiel's *Baseball's Great Experiment: Jackie Robinson and His Legacy* (New York: Oxford University Press, 1997) remains the standard analysis of Robinson's experiences. Another classic text, Robert Peterson's *Only the Ball Was White: A History of Legendary Black Players and All-Black Professional Teams* (New York: Oxford University Press, 1992), offers a detailed celebration of the Negro Leagues and a sobering chapter on their demise once the best black players migrated to the Major Leagues. If teachers are looking for primary sources to use, they might prefer to use Robinson's own account of this period. His *I Never Had It Made* recounts not only his childhood and baseball experiences but also discusses his relationships with a number of notable figures, including Malcolm X and Martin Luther King Jr. Jackie Robinson with Alfred Duckett, *I Never Had It Made: An Autobiography* (New York: G. P. Putnam's Sons, 1972).

13. The most succinct account of this change can be found in Pamela Grundy, "'From Amazons to Glamazons': The Rise and Fall of North Carolina Women's Basketball," *Journal of American History* 87 (June 2000): 134–55. See also Pamela Grundy and Susan Shackelford, *Shattering the Glass: The Remarkable History of Women's Basketball* (New York: New Press, 2005), 109–23. For more about the development of cheerleading, see Natalie Guice Adams and Pamela J. Bettis, *Cheerleader! An American Icon* (London: Palgrave-MacMillan, 2003). For the background on Cold War gender relations, see Elaine Tyler May, *Homeward*

Bound: American Families in the Cold War Era, twentieth-anniversary ed. (New York: Basic Books, 2008).

14. *Sports Illustrated*, October 15, 1979, 24.

15. The classic early account is Benjamin Rader, *In Its Own Image: How Television Transformed Sports* (New York: Free Press, 1984). NFL player-turned-English-professor Michael Oriard has written a trilogy of fine works that offer provocative insights into the media portrayals and cultural ramifications of several phases of American football history: *Reading Football* (Chapel Hill: University of North Carolina Press, 1993), *King Football: Sport and Spectacle in the Golden Age of Radios and Newsreels, Movies and Magazines, the Weekly and the Daily Press* (Chapel Hill: University of North Carolina Press, 2007), and *Brand NFL: Making and Selling America's Favorite Sport* (Chapel Hill: University of North Carolina Press, 2007).

16. For a brilliant assessment of figure skating's changing gender dynamics, see Mary Louise Adams, *Artistic Impressions: Figure Skating, Masculinity, and the Limits of Sport* (Toronto: University of Toronto Press, 2011). For scholarly reactions to the Harding-Kerrigan events, see Cynthia Baughman, ed., *Women on Ice: Feminist Essays on the Tonya Harding/Nancy Kerrigan Spectacle* (New York: Routledge, 1995).

17. For a comprehensive history of American sports betting, see Richard O. Davies and Richard G. Abram, *Betting the Line: Sports Wagering in American Life* (Columbus: Ohio State University Press, 2001). For a detailed account of the role played by Gus Greenlee, an athlete, businessman, numbers runner, and philanthropist in the segregated Pittsburgh sports scene, see Rob Ruck, *Sandlot Seasons: Sport in Black Pittsburgh* (Urbana: University of Illinois Press, 1986).

18. For an analysis of Griffith-Joyner's career, as well as the contrasting image and experience of her sister-in-law, Jackie Joyner-Kersee, see Jennifer H. Landsbury, *A Spectacular Leap: Black Women Athletes in Twentieth-Century America* (Fayetteville: University of Arkansas Press, 2014), 191–245. For Venus and Serena Williams, see Nicole Fleetwood, *On Racial Icons* (New Brunswick, NJ: Rutgers University Press), 97–110. See also Susan Cahn, *Coming on Strong: Gender and Sexuality in Women's Sport*, 2nd ed. (Urbana: University of Illinois Press, 2015), and David J. Leonard and C. Richard King, eds., *Commodified and Criminalized: New Racism and African Americans in Contemporary Sports* (Lanham, MD: Rowman and Littlefield, 2011). In the wake of the 2018 U.S. Open controversy, researchers began a #SerenaWilliamsSyllabus endeavor that has gathered many other resources.

Contributors

Matthew Andrews is a teaching associate professor of history at the University of North Carolina at Chapel Hill. His research and teaching explores the links between sport, politics, and political protest in the United States. Among the courses he teaches are Sport and American History, Baseball and American History, The Olympic Games—A Global History, and Race, Basketball, and the American Dream.

Brad Austin is a professor of history at Salem State University, where he teaches courses on modern U.S. history, sport history, the Vietnam War, and slavery in New England, in addition to a variety of methodological courses. He coordinates a nationally accredited teacher education program and has served as the chairperson of the American Historical Association's Teaching Prize Committee. He is the author of *Democratic Sports: Men's and Women's College Sports during the Great Depression* (2015) and the coeditor of *Understanding and Teaching the Vietnam War* (2013). In 2012 the Northeast Association of Graduate Schools recognized him as the outstanding Master's-Level Graduate Professor for that year.

Ron Briley taught history and film studies for thirty-eight years at Sandia Prep School in Albuquerque, New Mexico, where he also served as assistant head of school and is now faculty emeritus. In addition, Briley was an adjunct professor of history at the University of New Mexico, Valencia campus, for twenty years. He is the recipient of the New Mexico Golden Apple Award for excellence in teaching as well as national teaching awards from the Organization of American Historians, American Historical Association, National Council for History Education, and the Society for History Education. The recipient of Fulbright awards to the Netherlands, Yugoslavia, and Japan, Briley has also served on numerous committees for the Organization of American Historians and American Historical Association. A Distinguished Lecturer for the Organization of American Historians, he is the author of six books and numerous scholarly articles and encyclopedia entries on the history of sport, music, and film.

Derek Charles Catsam is a professor of history and the Kathlyn Cosper Dunagan Professor in the Humanities at the University of Texas of the Permian Basin and is a senior research associate at Rhodes University in Grahamstown, South Africa, where he spent 2016 as the Hugh Le May Fellow in the Humanities. He is the author of *Freedom's Main Line: The Journey of Reconciliation and the Freedom Rides* (2009), *Beyond the Pitch: The Spirit, Culture, and Politics of Brazil's 2014 World Cup* (2014), and *Bleeding Red: A Red Sox Fan's Diary of the 2004 Season* (2005). He is currently working on books about bus boycotts in the United States and South Africa in the 1940s and 1950s, and on the 1981 South African national rugby team's tour to the United States.

Susan E. Cayleff is a professor in the Department of Women's Studies at San Diego State University. She has authored three books in the history of medicine, *Wash and Be Healed: The Water-Cure Movement and Women's Health, Wings of Gauze: Women of Color and the Experience of Health and Illness,* and *Nature's Path: A History of Naturopathic Healing in America*; she coedited *Women in Culture: An Intersectional Anthology for Gender and Women's Studies.* She has written two biographies of Babe Didrikson Zaharias. *Babe: The Life and Legend of Babe Didrikson Zaharias* was nominated for a Pulitzer Prize and a Lambda Literary Award in 1995. She teaches American women's history, women and sports, and autobiographical writings. She is a committed activist working for race-aware, feminist, and LGBTQ social change.

Lars Dzikus is an associate professor in sport studies at the University of Tennessee, Knoxville. He received his master's and doctoral degrees with a specialization in cultural studies in sport from the Ohio State University. Dzikus's primary research interests lie in sport and globalization (e.g., diffusion of American football to Europe), sport and religion (e.g., collegiate sport chaplains), and sport and violence (e.g., sexual abuse in youth sport). He has published in *Sportwissenschaft, Journal of Sport and Social Issues,* and *Sport Psychologist,* among others, and he teaches graduate and undergraduate courses in sport studies.

Chris Elzey is a faculty member in the History and Art History Department at George Mason University and director of the Sport and American Culture minor at George Mason. He has written on global politics and sport, basketball history, and the Olympics. He is coeditor of *DC Sports: The Nation's Capital at Play* (2015), which won the North American Society for Sport History's best anthology award for 2016.

Sarah K. Fields is an associate dean in the College of Liberal Arts and Sciences and a professor of communication at the University of Colorado Denver. She received a BA from Yale University, a JD from Washington University in St. Louis, an MA from Washington State University, and a PhD in American studies from the University of Iowa. She is the author of *Game Faces: Sport Celebrity and the Laws of Reputation* (2016) and *Female Gladiators: Gender, Law, and Contact Sport in America* (2005); she also coedited *Sport and the Law: Historical and Cultural Intersections* (2014).

Andrew Frank is the Allen Morris Professor of History at Florida State University. He is the author of numerous books and articles on Native American and Southern history. His books include *Before the Pioneers: Indians, Settlers, Slaves, and the Founding of Miami* (2017) and *Creeks and Southerners: Biculturalism on the Early American Frontier* (2005). He is currently writing a book on the history of the Seminoles and other Indigenous Floridians. He received his PhD from the University of Florida.

Pamela Grundy is an independent historian living in Charlotte, North Carolina. Her work on sports includes *Learning to Win: Sports, Education and Social Change in Twentieth-Century North Carolina* (2001), *Shattering the Glass: The Remarkable History of Women's Basketball* (coauthored with Susan Shackelford, 2005), and *American Sports: From the Age of Folk Games to the Age of the Internet* (coauthored with Benjamin Rader, 2018). Her writing has received awards from the American Historical Association, the North American Society for Sport History, the Oral History Association, and the History of Education Society.

Leslie Heaphy is an associate professor of history at Kent State University Stark. She is also the director of the Honors Program for the campus. She is the author and/or editor of six books related to the Negro Leagues, women's baseball, and the New York Mets. In addition, Heaphy serves as editor for *Black ball*, a national peer-reviewed journal on black baseball. In teaching she is a two-time winner of the Stark Campus Distinguished Teaching Award (DTA), as well as a winner of the DTA for the entire Kent State University. She was also the recipient of the annual teaching award from the Honors College and in 2015 was the winner of the Ohio Academy of History Teaching Award.

Marc Horger is a senior lecturer in the Department of Human Sciences at Ohio State University. He specializes in the cultural and intellectual history of the late nineteenth and early twentieth centuries, the history of American sports and recreation, and the early history of basketball. He has been published in *New England Quarterly* and *Journal of Sport History* and is a regular contributor to *Origins: Current Events in Historical Perspective* at origins.osu.edu.

Jorge Iber is a professor of history and an associate dean in the Student Division of the College of Arts and Sciences at Texas Tech University. He was born in Havana, Cuba, and raised in the Little Havana neighborhood of Miami, Florida. He is the author/coauthor/editor/coeditor of thirteen books and numerous scholarly and encyclopedic articles. Recent projects include *Mike Torrez: A Baseball Biography*, a full-length biography of the former Major League Baseball pitcher, the Mexican American Mike Torrez, and *Moments of Joy and Heartbreak*, an edited collection of essays on the history of the Pittsburgh Pirates. In 2019 he will have three more books published: *Latinos in American Football*, an anthology on Latino/as in sport, and a youth-targeted biography on Mariano Rivera.

Bobbi A. Knapp is a sports sociologist at Southern Illinois University whose research, teaching, and service focus on the critical examination of intersectional gender within physical spheres such as sports and the military. An award-winning educator, Knapp was also awarded the Jane Addams Outstanding Service Award from the Midwest Sociological Society in recognition of her efforts to elevate the status of girls and women in society.

Rita Liberti is a professor in the Department of Kinesiology and director of the Center for Sport and Social Justice at California State University, East Bay. She has written extensively on sport, race, and gender, and her coauthored book *(Re)Presenting Wilma Rudolph* (with Maureen Smith, 2015) won the 2016 Best Monograph award from the North American Society for Sport History.

Adam Love is an assistant professor in sport studies at the University of Tennessee, Knoxville, where he also received his master's and doctoral degrees. Prominent themes in his research include gender and racial ideology, public sociology, and motivations and experiences in sport participation. These themes are united by imagining how sports can be done in such a way that they produce more positive outcomes, more often, for more people. He has published in *Sociology of Sport Journal*, *Journal of Issues in Intercollegiate Athletics*, and *Ethnic and Racial Studies*, among others, and he teaches graduate courses in sport studies.

Lauren Morimoto is a professor of kinesiology and the former Director of Diversity and Inclusive Excellence at Sonoma State University. She founded the Sport and Social Justice Lecture Series in August 2016 to provide students the opportunity to engage with sport activists and scholars. Her teaching and research center on race, ethnicity, and sport; Japanese American sport during Hawai'i's plantation era; critical perspectives of the body; intersections of race, gender, and disability; and experiential education in kinesiology. She was one of two recipients of the 2016–17 Sonoma State University Excellence in Teaching Award.

Daniel Pierce is the Interdisciplinary Distinguished Professor of the Mountain South at the University of North Carolina at Asheville. He is widely recognized as one of the nation's experts on the culture and history of stock car racing and has consulted on films and museum exhibits in addition to writing and teaching. He is the author of *Real NASCAR: White Lightning, Red Clay and Big Bill France* (2010) and is currently completing books about the Great Smoky Mountains National Park and the history of moonshine in North Carolina.

Derrick E. White is a visiting associate professor of African and African American studies at Dartmouth College. He is a scholar of modern black history, sports history, and intellectual history. He is the author of *The Challenge of Blackness: The Institute of the Black World and Political Activism in the 1970s* (2011). His forthcoming book is titled *Blood, Sweat, and Tears: Jake Gaither, Florida A&M University, and the Golden Age of Black College Football* (2019).

327

Index

AAU (Amateur Athletic Association), 30–31, 101–3, 116

Abbott, Cleveland, 116

Abdul-Jabbar, Kareem, 195–96, 202, 289

Addams, Jane, 13

African American Newspapers (database), 164

African Americans: cultural hegemony and, 142; discrimination in sports and, 146–49; emancipation and, 144–46; female athletes and, 110–21, 122n3, 124n24, 318–19; horse racing and, 141, *142*, 243, 246–48; Jack Johnson and, 155, 157, 164; Kaepernick protest and, 3; lynchings and, 155–57, *156–57*, 162, 189; NASCAR and, 268–69, 272, 275n32; Olympic Project for Human Rights and, 195–202; race riots and, 163–64; slavery and, 143–44, *144*; white supremacy and, 150–53, 159, *162*, 224, 278–79. *See also* civil rights movement; Historically Black Colleges and Universities (HBCUs); Jim Crow; Johnson, Jack; race and racism

Agee, Arthur, 299

Ailey, Alvin, 190

Alabama Committee for Equal Justice for Mrs. Recy Taylor (CEJRT), 202

Alamillo, Jose, 209

Alcindor, Lew. *See* Abdul-Jabbar, Kareem

Aldama, Frederick Luis, 210

Ali, Muhammad, 190–93, 196, 202, 296

All-American Girls Prófessional Baseball League (AAGPBL), 301

"All Coons Look Alike to Me" (song), 162

Alou brothers, 208

Althea (documentary), 120

Althea Gibson: Tennis Champion (film), 47–48

Amateur Athletic Association (AAU), 30–31, 101–3, 116

amateurism: eligibility scandals and, 28–31; Gulick and, 11, 22–23; roots of, 28

American Expeditionary Force, 22

American Football League (AFL), 61

American Forces Network (AFN), 72

American Indian Movement (AIM), 225–27

American Jewish Council, 196

American Mercury, 47

American Tennis Association (ATA), 118, 171

American Zoom (Golenbock), 273

A.M.E. Zion Quarterly Review, 149

Amherst College, 145

amphetamines. *See* drugs and doping

Anatomie of Abuses (Stubbs), 238

Andrews, Matthew, 323

Anglo-Saxonism, 14–15

Anspaugh, David, 295

Antonio's Gun and Delfino's Dream (Quinones), 212

apartheid, 284

archive.org, 19

Associated Press Female Athlete of the Year, 108

329

Association of Intercollegiate Athletics for Women (AIAW), 130–31, 135

Astaphan, Jaime, 33

Athletes Remembered (Longoria), 210

Atlanta Braves, 59, 220–22, 225, 227

Atlanta Daily World, 50, 180

Atlanta University, 93

Atlantic Monthly, 31

Austin, Brad, 323

Australian Olympic Committee, 200

Autobiography of Malcolm X, The, 188

Azucar y Chocalate: Historia del Boxeo Cubano (Encinosa), 213

Babe Didrikson. *See* Didrikson, Mildred "Babe"

Baby Boom, 55

Baer, Clara, 95

Baker, Buck, 269

Baldwin, Tammy, 85

Balli, Cecilia, 211

Ballplayer: Pelotero (documentary), 66

Baltimore Afro-American, 50, 115

baseball: "Babe" Didrikson and, 104; congressional hearings on steroids in, 33; creation of, 250–54; discrimination against African Americans and, 145–48, 151, 255–56, 315–16; Doby and, 316; Dominican players and, 66; Doubleday and, 250–53, 255; Hall of Fame, 250–53, 255, 300; Jackie Robinson and, 176, 256, 300, 315–16; Japanese internment and, 315; Latino/a athletes and, 207–9; masculinity and, 81; as the national pastime, 255–57; Negro Leagues and, 141, 171, 176; post-emancipation era and, 145; regional concentration of MLB teams, 56–59; scandals in, 35–36; traditional versus modern values and, 257; western expansion of, 57–59; women and, 256–57, 301. *See also* Native American mascots

Baseball (documentary), 58, 254

Baseball Magazine, 30

basketball: "Babe" Didrikson and, 101;

barnstorming and, 171; Bennett College and, 110–12, 114–15; development of, 15–18, *16–17*, 95–96; first women's intercollegiate game, 92; gender and, 80, 93–97; interracial competition and, 169–70; Latino/a athletes and, 214; Senda Berenson and, 95–96; spread of, 21; teaminess of, 17; women and, 18–20, *19*, 88–98, *91*, *94*, 99nn12–13

Batista, Fulgencio, 266

Battle of the Sexes, 83

Bauman, Zygmut, 66

Bayh, Birch, 129

Bayh, Marvella, 129

Beamon, Bob, 197, 200

Bell, Derrick, 178

Bennett College, 110–12, 114–15

Berenson, Senda, 18, 95–96

Berg, Peter, 300, 302

Bettencourt, Clyde, 227–28

bicycling. *See* cycling

Bissinger, H. G., 299

Black Lives Matter, 199

Black Magic (documentary), 178

Black Power movement, 187–88, 190

Black September, 278, 286

Black Sox, 36

"Blood in the Water" match, 280–81

Boger, Gordon, 263

Bond, Julian, 190

Book of Sports, The (King James I), 238–39

Boston, Ralph, 197

Boston Braves, 57, 59

Bowen, Bertha, 105

boxing, 313; bareknuckle, 67; color line and, 158–59; Johnson v. Burns, 159; Johnson v. Jeffries, 160–64; Johnson v. Ketchel, 160; Johnson v. Moran, *162*; Latino/a athletes and, 213; racism and, 27, 145, 148, 150–52. *See also* African Americans; Johnson, Jack; race and racism

Boys from Little Mexico (Wilson), 212

Branch, Taylor, 31

Breen, Timothy, 241, 243–44, 246

See also Didrikson, Mildred "Babe"; Title IX
Women's Tennis Association (WTA), 83
Wood, Glenn, 266
"Word to the Black Man, A," 164–65
World Anti-Doping Agency (WADA), 33
World Hockey Association, 62
World League of American Football, 72
World Series, 227
World War I, 21, 224
World War II: American demographics and, 55; boom in professional and college athletics and, 224; globalization of football and, 72; Lavender Scare and, 107; stock car racing and, 264; suspension of the Olympics and, 116; women and, 105–6, 301

Yarborough, Cale, 271
YMCA Training School, 14–15, 22
Young, Frank "Fay," 175

Zaharias, George, 105–7
Zaharias, Mildred "Babe" Didrikson. *See* Didrikson, Mildred "Babe"
Zang, David, 296
Zenovich, Marina, 303
Ziegler, Matt, 212